Research
Methods in
Social Work

Nelson-Hall Series in Social Work

Consulting Editor: Charles Zastrow
University of Wisconsin—Whitewater

Research Methods in Social Work

SECOND EDITION

David Royse
University of Kentucky

Nelson-Hall Publishers
Chicago

Project Editor: Rachel Schick
Typesetter: Precision Typographers
Printer: Capital City Press
Cover Painting: Grace Cole, "Requiem of Frozen Tears," oil on linen.
From the collection of Bristol Meyers, Inc., Evansville, IN.

Library of Congress Cataloging-in-Publication Data

Royse, David D. (David Daniel)
   Research methods in social work / David Royse. — 2nd ed.
     p.   cm.
   Includes bibliographical references and index.
   ISBN 0-8304-1409-6
   1. Social service—Research—Methodology.   I. Title.
HV11.R69   1995
361.3'2'072—dc20   94-16190
                                    CIP

Manufactured in the United States of America

10 9 8 7 6 5 4 3 2

∞ ™ The paper used in this book meets the
minimum requirements of American
National Standard for Information
Sciences—Permanence of Paper for
Printed Library Materials, ANSI
Z39.48-1984.

Contents

Preface   xi

CHAPTER 1
Introduction   1

Where Does Research Start?
Why Study Research?
Social Work Students and Research
Why Research Is Required
How Research Benefits Social
    Workers
Desired Outcome
Questions for Class Discussion
Mini-Projects for Experiencing
    Research Firsthand
Resources and References

CHAPTER 2
The Way Research
Proceeds   17

The Research Process
    Step 1: Posing a Question or Stating a
    Hypothesis

Step 2: Reviewing the Literature
Step 3: Developing a Research Design
Step 4: Operationalizing
Step 5: Collecting Data
Step 6: Analyzing and Interpreting the
    Data
Step 7: Writing the Report
Social Work Research and Practice
Questions for Class Discussion
Mini-Projects for Experiencing
    Research Firsthand
Resources and References

CHAPTER 3
Single System Designs   49

The Origin of Single System
    Designs
Single System Designs and Practice
A Closer Look at the Single System
    Design
Starting a Single System Study
    The Case Study or **B** Design
    The **AB** Design
    The **ABA** and **ABAB** Designs
    The **ABC** and **ABCD** Designs
    Multiple Baseline Designs
Statistical Analysis

Contents

Advantages and Disadvantages of
Single System Designs
The Choice and Use of Single
System Designs
Questions for Class Discussion
Mini-Projects for Experiencing
Research Firsthand
Resources and References

CHAPTER 4
Research Designs for Group Comparisons   79

Choosing the Right Design
Experimental Research
The Classic Experimental Research
Design
The Posttest Only Control Group
Design
The Solomon Four-Group Design
Internal and External Validity
Pre-Experimental Designs
Quasi-Experimental Designs
Design and Validity Considerations
Questions for Class Discussion
Mini-Projects for Experiencing
Research Firsthand
Resources and References

CHAPTER 5
Understanding and Using Research Instruments   105

Reliability
Validity
Locating Research Instruments
When You Can't Find the
Instrument You Want
A Sampling of Instruments

The Community Living Skills Scale
(CLSS)
Description
Psychometric Data
Availability
Scoring
The Social Work Empowerment
Scale (SWES)
Description
Psychometric Data
Availability
Scoring
Prosocial Tendencies Scale for
Children (PTS-C)
Description
Psychometric Data
Availability
Scoring
Attitude Toward the Provision of
Long-Term Care (ATPLTC)
Description
Psychometric Data
Availability
Scoring
The Maternal Characteristics Scale
(MCS)
Description
Psychometric Data
Availability
Scoring
Helping Behavior Checklist
Description
Psychometric Data
Availability
Scoring
Role Strain Index
Description
Psychometric Data
Availability
Scoring
Job Satisfaction Scale (JSS)
Description
Psychometric Data
Availability
Scoring
Questions for Class Discussion
Mini-Projects for Experiencing
Research Firsthand
References and Resources

Contents

CHAPTER 6
Survey Research   145

The Mail Questionnaire
Getting the Most Out of Mail
    Questionnaires
The Telephone Survey
Getting the Most Out of Telephone
    Surveys
Personal Interviews
Getting the Most from Personal
    Interviews
Comparison of the Three
    Approaches
Sampling Theory
The Accuracy of Probability
    Samples
Determining Sample Size
Nonprobability Sampling Designs
Additional Survey Designs
Mistakes to Avoid
A Final Note about Surveys
Questions for Class Discussion
Mini-Projects for Experiencing
    Research Firsthand
Resources and References

CHAPTER 7
Designing Questionnaires for
Surveys and Agency Use   181

Beginning the Development of a
    Questionnaire
Closed-Ended Questions
Open-Ended Questions
Pitfalls in Writing Good Questions
Double-Barreled Questions
Leading Questions
Unavailable Information
Use of Jargon and Technical Terms
Insensitive Language

Inflammatory or "Loaded" Terms
Mutually Exclusive Response
    Choices
Vague and Ambiguous Terms
All-Inclusive Terms
Negatively Constructed Items
Sequence of Questions
Thinking about Guidelines
Self-Anchored Scales
The Role of Questionnaires in
    Generalizing Results
Questions for Class Discussion
Mini-Projects for Experiencing
    Research Firsthand
Resources and References

CHAPTER 8
Unobtrusive Approaches
to Data Collection:
Secondary Data and
Content Analysis   205

Advantages and Disadvantages of
    Unobtrusive Approaches
State-Maintained Data Sets
Applications of Secondary Data
    Analysis
Secondary Analysis of Survey Data
Secondary Survey and Additional
    Secondary Data Sources
Content Analysis
Advantages and Disadvantages of
    Content Analysis
Essentials of Content Analysis
A Practical Application of Content
    Analysis
Using Unobtrusive Approaches
Questions for Class Discussion
Mini-Projects for Experiencing
    Research Firsthand
Resources and References

CHAPTER 9
Preparing and Analyzing Data 233

The Use of Computers for Data Processing
Coding Data for the Computer
Univariate Analysis of Data
Bivariate Analysis of Data
Practical Application of Statistics
Multivariate Analysis of Data
Final Thoughts
Questions for Class Discussion
Mini-Projects for Experiencing Research Firsthand
Resources and References

CHAPTER 10
Program Evaluation 259

Starting to Think about Conducting a Program Evaluation
Beginning a Program Evaluation
Types of Program Evaluation
Experimental and Quasi-Experimental Designs
The Discrepancy Model
The Hammond Model
The Judicial Model
Client Satisfaction Approaches
Other Models
Practical Considerations
Reading Program Evaluation Reports
Final Comments
Questions for Class Discussion
Mini-Projects for Experiencing Research Firsthand
Resources and References

CHAPTER 11
Qualitative Research 283

Methods of Qualitative Research
Steps in Doing Qualitative Research
The Great Debate
Final Thoughts on the Quantitative-Qualitative Controversy
Questions for Class Discussion
Mini-Projects for Experiencing Research Firsthand
Resources and References

CHAPTER 12
Ethical Thinking and Research 301

Historical Context
Institutional Review Boards
General Guidelines for Ethical Research
Guideline 1: Research Subjects Must Be Volunteers
Guideline 2: Potential Research Subjects Should Be Given Sufficient Information about the Study to Determine Any Possible Risks or Discomfort as Well as Benefits
Guideline 3: No Harm Shall Result as a Consequence of Participation in the Research
Guideline 4: Sensitive Information Shall Be Protected
Potential Ethical Problems in Research
Deception
Denial of Treatment
Should Some Research Questions Not Be Investigated?
Compensation
Research Without Clients' Consent

Contents

Final Thoughts
Questions for Class Discussion
Mini-Projects for Experiencing
    Research Firsthand
Resources and References

Writing for Professional Journals
Reading and Critiquing Research
    Manuscripts
Questions for Class Discussion
Mini-Projects for Experiencing
    Research Firsthand
Resources and References

No Covering in class

CHAPTER 13
Writing Research Reports and
Journal Articles   323

Publication as a Practice Goal
Components of a Research Report
    Introduction
    Review of the Literature
    The Method
    The Results
    The Discussion
    References, Appendices, and
        Abstracts

Appendices   341

A. Attitudes about Research
    Courses
B. How to Use a Table of Random
    Numbers
    Table of Random Numbers
C. Drug Attitude Questionnaire

Index   353

Preface

Not wanting to risk receiving an unacceptable grade, I bailed out of my first statistics course before midterm, even though it was required for graduation. Although I wasn't sure I could do any better in any other statistics course, I knew when I wasn't comprehending the material—none of it made any sense to me.

The next semester I found a new statistics course in another department that required a two-hour lab each week. I swallowed hard a couple of times, took a deep breath, and slumped into my seat in the lecture hall. However, much to my surprise, that instructor used real, concrete examples that made sense. I understood, for the first time, how statistics could be used to solve actual problems. As I look back now, the most important difference in the two courses was that the first instructor seemed unable to illustrate his points with realistic examples. The second instructor succeeded in communicating because of his examples.

Although I did not go on to become a statistician, I've never forgotten that lesson I learned as an undergraduate. In my teaching and writing, I strive to engage students' interest by using as many illustrations as possible. Accordingly, you will find that this text draws heavily upon examples of research conducted by actual social workers. Also, you'll find that I've tried to present essential information with a minimum amount of dry prose. You won't get lost in too much technical detail. Perhaps with a little luck, you'll be able to say at the end of the book, "Hey, research isn't too bad! I understand this stuff!"

I have designed this text for both undergraduate and graduate audiences. Those students who desire more information on a given topic are encouraged to make use of the extensive references at the end of each chapter. By reading those books and journal articles, students can vastly expand upon their knowledge and the coverage provided in this introductory text.

Whether you are an undergraduate or a graduate student, I hope that this text will help you develop critical thinking skills. Although you will probably want to memorize some vocabulary items (these are indicated in **boldface type**), it is much more important that you learn how to question assumptions about "facts" and "good" research. I've never known a fact that couldn't be challenged or a piece of research that couldn't be improved upon!

While I don't hope to make researchers out of all of you, I do at least aspire to help you comprehend and critique the research you will encounter as you continue in your professional career. As you develop a greater understanding of the research process, you'll be able to discern the difference between "good" research and worthless drivel. By sharpening your research perspective, you'll find yourself able to make suggestions for improving the research that may be going on in your practicum agency, where you are employed, or where you volunteer. And even if no research is going on there, maybe you'll recognize the need to evaluate your own practice or the performance of a key program. Who knows? As you become empowered with these research tools, you may become an advocate for research and evaluation!

Thanks to all the students whose questions, life experiences, and involvement with research (even if only through wrestling with my assignments) have provided examples that will benefit other students. I'm indebted to you, even though you are too numerous to mention by name.

I would appreciate any comments or suggestions about how to improve this book. My mail address is 641 Patterson Office Tower, College of Social Work, University of Kentucky, Lexington, KY 40506-0027; my BITNET computer address is SPR103@ukcc.uky.edu.

1
Introduction

Where Does Research Start?

Have you ever noticed that unanswered questions, riddles, and mysteries surround us? If we were face-to-face in a classroom, I'd ask you to take a minute or two to think about some of the questions percolating in the back of your mind that have never been satisfactorily answered. I'm not talking about questions like "I wonder what's for supper?" or "Who on earth did Jimmy go out with last night?" but larger questions like "Is heredity or environment the more powerful influence in alcoholism?" or "To what extent do most victims of child abuse recover from their trauma?"

For some of you, life's mysteries involve specific individuals and their behavior. You may wonder why a favorite cousin committed suicide in the prime of his life, or why Aunt Martha can't seem to quit drinking. Maybe you have grown up with a schizophrenic parent or sibling and wonder if you somehow unintentionally contributed to their illness.

Research seeks to provide answers to life's enigmas by exploring questions that originate from people just like yourself. You see, ideas for suitable research projects often stem from our own life experiences or observations. Allow me to give you a brief illustration of this.

Close to the end of a spring semester several years ago, I was concluding a lecture on qualitative research methods. (Qualitative research methods seek to help the investigator understand the experi-

1

ence or viewpoint of another person or group of persons.) As I typically do during that lecture, I introduced material from Clifford Beers's book, *A Mind That Found Itself* (1910). Beers was a college student around the turn of the century who, after breaking up with his fiancé, began losing his mind. He kept a diary of the events that occurred during this period of his life—he talks, for instance, of feeling a compulsion to jump out of a third-floor window, at the same time knowing that it was a crazy thought.

"What would it be like," I asked the class, "to feel torn between wanting to injure yourself and knowing that those thoughts were crazy? To be unable to stop obsessing about something?" I had the class's attention, but paused for a moment to switch examples.

In a recent series of articles on child abuse our local newspaper had portrayed a number of officials (judges, lawyers, and, yes, social workers) who had not done enough to protect vulnerable children. Most students probably were familiar with the newspaper accounts, but I wanted to impress upon them that knowledge of the statistics and facts about child abuse is quite different from the experience of abuse.

"What would it be like," I asked the class, "to be chained in a dark, damp basement as a child? To have your cries of hunger ignored by your parents—or worse, to be sexually abused on a filthy mattress on the cold concrete floor? Would you understand child abuse any differently than you do now? How might living in a different culture or taking on a different lifestyle provide you with knowledge that you wouldn't get just by reading a book or journal article?"

A student raised her hand and when I acknowledged her, she simply pointed to the student beside her. Even from the front of the classroom, I could see that something was unusual about Frank. As the whole class turned to look at him, he sat rigid, eyes glazed over. I walked closer and called his name several times. There was no response. Gently I reached over and tugged on his sleeve. Again, there was no indication that Frank recognized he was the focus of the class's attention. I shook Frank harder. Nothing. I checked for blink and startle reflexes . . . he had none.

Never had I encountered such a problem in the classroom! My first thought was that he was having some sort of seizure, although I had never seen one like it. Someone suggested that we look in his wallet to see if it contained any emergency medical information. It did. We found the number of a clinical social worker whose office wasn't too far from campus.

With the card in my hand, I sprinted to the nearest pay phone on the next floor and dialed the number. I insisted that the receptionist who answered call the social worker to the phone immediately. Frank's social worker confirmed that he became temporarily catatonic from time to time; not all of his triggers had been identified. However, she assured me, Frank usually recovered on his own within twenty minutes to an hour.

I went back to the classroom and found my students anxiously gathered around Frank, watching for some blink or sigh, some indication that he was in the land of the living. The bell rang, signaling the end of class. Anticipating that another class would be coming into our classroom, I asked a student to help me lift Frank to see if we could assist him in walking out of the classroom. However, Frank was not aware of our efforts and was unable to help. It was like lifting a 150-pound bag of potatoes. Rather than risk dropping him, we decided to leave Frank in his seat.

Several students volunteered to stay with Frank, but I encouraged them to go on to their own classes, assuring them that I would remain behind. About this time, I looked back at Frank and noticed a single tear slipping down his cheek. He blinked his eyes and turned his head as if to acquaint himself with his surroundings. "Are you okay?" I asked. Frank responded by nodding his head affirmatively. It took a few more minutes for Frank to compose himself enough to walk to my car so that I could take him to his therapist.

I saw Frank again about a week later when he took his final exam for my class. He did well, and finished in the top third of the class.

Frank had been a victim of nightmarish child abuse. Something I had said, some image I evoked, summoned a flood of memories so painful that Frank's catatonia had resulted. But Frank's experience also had an effect upon me. Maybe not that afternoon, but shortly thereafter, I began wondering about the extent to which other students of social work might have been impaired by early childhood or dysfunctional family experiences. That thought spun off others— could early childhood experiences affect the choice of social work as a career? Could unfortunate childhood experiences affect our satisfaction with life as adults? (Two colleagues and I have reported on this last question. See Royse, Rompf, and Dhooper, 1991. A manuscript examining the first question will be published in 1994.) That remarkable experience with Frank fueled my curiosity about a whole set of questions I had never seriously contemplated before and was the catalyst for several research projects.

Like the clinical social worker looking for clues to aid in understanding the client by observing his language, speech (was it slurred, full of hesitations, grammatically precise?), and manner of dress (was

he wearing worn-out jeans or a three-piece business suit?) to supple-
ment the information drawn from agency files, intake information,
or questions asked, the researcher is also in the business of collecting
and interpreting clues to unravel some mystery.

Different experiences raise different questions. A paraplegic
MSW student once remarked in class that few professionals know
how to talk to persons with handicaps. He speculated that because
their training had taught them not to ask questions for which they do
not need answers, professionals often did not inquire as to how he
lost the use of his legs. As a result, they often made erroneous
assumptions—and in doing so, failed to get to know him as a person.
"I would much rather," he said, "have them ask, 'What happened to
you?' so that I can explain something about me as a person. As I tell
them about my former career as an electronics engineer and the air-
plane crash, they begin to know me as a human being. I'm no longer
some vegetable in a wheelchair."

As he talked, I realized that other persons with handicaps may
feel as he did. And, you guessed it, a number of questions about disability and preferences for disclosure began forming in my mind.
Later, the two of us combined our knowledge and conducted a study
(Royse and Edwards, 1989). While our investigation was not definitive by any means, it did provide some beginning evidence suggesting
that persons with disabilities are frequently open to disclosing. As a
small study, it is only one piece of evidence, a starting place for other
researchers interested in this issue, possibly persons like yourself, to
build upon.

Unanswered questions, riddles, and mysteries surround us and
provide the stimulus for research. Over the years, I've lost track of the
number of students who've come to me to explore some particular
research interest. Those able to conceptualize their projects clearly
and those with lots of perseverance (willingness to revise and rewrite)
have been rewarded by seeing their efforts published in professional
journals. Who creates knowledge for social workers? Individuals like
yourself. The research process can (and should) start with you.

Why Study Research?

Social work is an exciting career choice. Students select this profession because they like people and want to help families where there
has been abuse, mental illness, or alcoholism and to assist such special populations as the aged and the homeless. As a consequence, social work students are often eager to soak up instruction that will assist them in becoming better counselors or practitioners. They

4

approach practice-oriented courses with enthusiasm and vigor. All goes well until they learn that they must take a research course (sometimes two courses) as part of the requirements for a degree. Immediately some students are resentful. "Research!" they say. "Why do I have to take research?" "I don't want to do research. I want to work with the severely mentally ill." Variations of this are: "I want to work with children" and "I want to work with adolescents who have eating disorders."

Why, then, must social work students study research? Consider a few examples that will demonstrate its usefulness to practitioners of social work.

1. You are asked to direct an adolescent AIDS prevention program. The goal of the program is to supply adolescents with information about how to avoid contracting the AIDS virus. After several months you are convinced that the adolescents in your program are more knowledgeable after participation in the program. How would you convince others of the success of your intervention?

2. You are hired by an agency that provides counseling to families in which children have been sexually assaulted by a family member. You are assigned to work with the offenders. Counseling seems to go well with your first several clients and it is now time for the perpetrators to return to their families. How would you go about providing evidence that your intervention was effective—that it was safe to reunite the family members?

3. You are a case manager for a program that has matched severely mentally ill clients with volunteers. At the end of two years, the clients are telling you that they have benefited greatly from the involvement of the volunteers. They tell you that they have gained a better understanding of mental illness and learned how to self-monitor their illnesses. Some have begun living independently. A few have started college or begun new jobs. Overall, though, on a psychological battery of tests, most clients appear to have about the same symptoms that they had prior to the beginning of this program. How would you determine whether this program should be continued or not?

In each of these three examples, some research skills are required—skills that can be used with other problems and concerns. However, before these skills can be taught, oftentimes it is necessary to address and "neutralize" negative attitudes about research so that there is the greatest opportunity for learning to occur.

Social Work Students and Research

Few students come into their first research methods class under-standing the necessity for the course. In fact, Epstein (1987) has ob-served that "no other part of the social work curriculum has been so consistently received by students with as much groaning, moaning, eye-rolling, bad-mouthing, hyperventilation, and waiver-strategizing as the research course" (p.71). Epstein has cited other studies that document social work students' disinterest in research—what he calls the "resistance phenomenon" (Rosenblatt, 1968; Kirk and Fisher, 1976; Dane and Epstein, 1985).

We can understand why students may not want to study re-search. Oftentimes students misunderstand both the value of re-search and the research process. Briar (1980) has noted that there is a widespread belief among social workers that the same person cannot be both a good researcher and a good practitioner. He continues:

> The personal qualities believed to make a good researcher are seen as handicaps for a practitioner, and the reverse also has been said to be true. The stereotypes are familiar. Researchers are supposedly intellec-tual, rational, unfeeling creatures who lack the sensitivity to under-stand the subtle nuances that are of primary concern to practitioners. Practitioners are purported to be intuitive, sensitive, creative persons more akin to artists than scientists; they emphasize the importance of seeing clients as whole persons who should not be subjected to the cate-gorization and atomization that research allegedly requires. It is easy, of course, to show that these stereotypes are invalid, but such beliefs, although less prevalent than they once were, continue to influence the relationship between practice and research in social work. (P. 31).

As research instructors soon learn, many social work students do not want to take a research methods course. How would you ex-plain this? Do some students choose social work as a major because it is perceived to have less of a quantitative emphasis than such dis-ciplines as sociology, psychology, and medicine? Other disciplines are better known for their research emphasis. The research tradi-tion in clinical psychology, for instance, dates back to its roots in experimental psychology; precise methods and procedures were de-veloped for studying such phenomena as sensation and perception. Later, Alfred Binet's work with intelligence tests led to psycholo-gists becoming interested in the quantitative problems associated with testing and test construction. This interest in the quantifica-tion of phenomena generalized to other areas. Shortly after World War II clinical psychology programs adopted an integrated

Scientist-Professional Training Model that has become their preeminent approach (Hersen and Bellack, 1984).

The dual emphasis on research and practice has been absent in social work programs. As a result, social workers seem to have little identity as researchers and may be ill prepared or uncomfortable in conducting it. Some evidence of this can be seen in Glisson's study (1983), which reviewed all articles published over a six-year period in five major social work journals. He found that less than half of the articles in these journals reported or summarized the results of empirical research. Other studies have reported even lower percentages of articles with empirical research (Jayaratne, 1979; Simpson, 1978; Weinberger and Tripodi, 1969). This compares with a research content of over 90 percent in the articles published during 1986 in five American Psychological Association journals and 90 percent of the articles published in four American Sociological Association journals (Glisson and Fischer, 1987).

While social workers' identity as researchers may not be quite as strong as psychologists' and sociologists', this is not to say that it is nonexistent. Howe (1974) proposed use of the term "caseworker-researcher" for the clinician engaged in research. A few years later Briar (1979, 1980) began writing about a *Practitioner-Scientist Training Model.* What do you think are the implications for our profession when the "scientist" aspect of our training model comes first or last?

One of the unanswered mysteries, as far as I'm concerned, is why students choose social work as a career. Wouldn't you think there would be a lot of information on this topic? One of the very few studies in this area (Gockel, 1966) concluded that students are attracted to social work mostly because it offers an opportunity to work with people. Wouldn't it be interesting to know if most social work students choose this career precisely because research is emphasized less than practice?

Some social work students may believe that research is less interesting than "people work" because they do not immediately see how research can have a practical application for them or their clients. These students may have an image of researchers as academics who contemplate social problems from a distance. They may not understand that social work research also involves interviewing and talking with clients, and that it aims to improve their lives by a better understanding of their problems and the effectiveness of our interventions.

As long as we are speculating, we might consider the possibility that social work students *fear* research. And perhaps this fear is grounded in reality. Maybe they have always done poorly in math—

7

even in elementary school. It is not uncommon for students, given a choice, to avoid those courses that they perceive to be too difficult for them to master. Students may not be interested in taking a research course because they perceive it to be laden with statistics and mathematical computations for which they see absolutely no utility. They anticipate that the course will be boring and a waste of their time, so they don't attend class or apply themselves. At the end of the term they find themselves in a position where they have not understood what was going on and are even more angry because they were *required* to take a research course for which they did not get a good grade. However, learning research methodology does not require performing mathematical computations. If you skim quickly through these pages, you'll find no statistical formulas of any kind!

Human nature is complex. It is likely that no one explanation but rather several interrelated factors together best explain why social work students don't always look forward to their research courses. For instance, a multivariable explanation could be as follows: (1) a student has a beginning attitude that research has no practical application, (2) as a consequence, not enough time is spent in mastering the subject, (3) which leads to poor performance, and (4) all of this results in a self-perception that the subject is too difficult or that the student doesn't have an aptitude for research. What other variables do you think might be involved?

Why Research Is Required

There are several reasons why you, as a social work student, should take at least one research course. First of all, both as a student and as a social worker you will be reading journal articles and technical articles in which research results are presented. You need to have a basic knowledge of how research is conducted, or could be conducted, to help you evaluate the strengths and weaknesses of the published research. As an informed consumer of information you ought to be able to know if too few subjects were interviewed, if the methodology was flawed, or if the author generalized well beyond his or her findings. Research studies can be biased or flawed for a lot of different reasons, and you might not be able to detect these reasons without a basic understanding of research methodology. To make effective use of research that you encounter, whether in journals or unpublished reports produced in your agency, you need to know something about how proper research is conducted.

Second, social workers are accountable for their interventions. As a professional, you must be able to determine whether the intervention you are using with a client is making any difference. Could you demonstrate that the client is improving? Or, at the very least, could you show that your intervention has not harmed the client? Even if you are not interested in conducting research on a large scale, you owe it to your clients and yourself to be able to evaluate your practice with them. A research approach discussed in this book, the single system design, will help you evaluate your practice with individual clients.

Accountability is important on another level. Social service agencies vary enormously in size and may employ several to many hundreds of social workers (e.g., in large state departments of human resources). Taxpayers, governmental agencies, and funding sources, such as United Way organizations, often expect social service agencies to conduct or provide evaluation research on such issues as client utilization of the agency's services and the effects or outcomes of the services provided. Agencies must show that they are meeting the needs of their target populations, that their clientele feel satisfied with services, and that the agency's operation is productive and efficient. Even as a new social worker, fresh from the university, you might be asked to conduct research to meet some reporting or accreditation requirement. Occasionally, students tell me how surprised they were on their first jobs when they were assigned a research project—especially when it was not even discussed during the job interview. Would you be more interested in learning how to conduct research if you knew you would be responsible for conducting research sometime in the near future?

Suppose you become a program director or manager in a social service organization, and the executive director wants you to begin a new program. The director insists that the program have a good evaluation system built into it. Would you know how to go about evaluating a social service program? Would you know a poor evaluation if you saw one? Programs are sometimes funded with the provision that they can demonstrate some impact on the problem. This usually means that research in some form or fashion is required. Faced as we are with major social problems and fairly limited amounts of monies that can be applied to these problems, it is incumbent upon us social workers to strive for implementation of programs that have the best success rates. Frequently, it is not an outside consultant who is brought in to plan or conduct the research, but someone within the agency. A little knowledge of research could provide you with a stepping stone to involvement in administrative or policy issues. Graduates of social work programs are often surprised by how rapidly they become involved in middle management even though they always thought of themselves as caseworkers.

As a profession, social work must have individuals who can conduct research on social policies at the state and national levels. While it may seem unlikely that you would ever be involved in such research, consider for a moment the extent to which most social workers are affected by state and national policies. Some of these policies are good, and some could use modification. Consider, for example, how you might go about convincing legislators and government officials that cutting funds to social services will have an adverse effect upon your client population. Can you see the value of having "hard data" to show skeptics how many people depend upon a certain social service and how their lives might be affected if funds were cut? The profession needs researchers who can show that cuts in social service programs ultimately result in greater tax burdens. I am convinced that greater funding for social services will come as social workers are better able to demonstrate that adequate levels of social services are cost-effective for reducing or eliminating some of the major social problems facing us today.

Another reason for studying research as an undergraduate is that it will provide the necessary foundation for other research courses in graduate school. It's very likely you will be required to take at least one research course (and probably more) in a master's program in social work. Should you work on a doctorate, you will be required to complete more research courses and may conduct original research for a dissertation. By that time you may be taking elective courses in research and statistics because you see their usefulness!

One more good reason for studying research methods is that this is required by the Council on Social Work Education (CSWE). CSWE is a national, nongovernmental organization, recognized by the U.S. Department of Education, that has the responsibility for accreditation and other standard-setting activities. The council sets curriculum policy for baccalaureate and master's degree social work programs. Research is one of the five professional foundation content areas required by CSWE. Each institution that grants degrees in social work must periodically submit documentation that it conforms with curriculum policy in order for the institution's program to be accredited by CSWE.

The Council on Social Work Education's curriculum policy would have social work students (at both the BSW and MSW levels) understand that a "spirit of inquiry" and "informed criticism" are the bases of scientific thinking and lead to the acquisition of knowledge and the application of that knowledge in practice. Research content is expected to help students learn the critical appreciation and use of research and program evaluation as they learn the methods and designs for evaluating their own practice and service delivery in all areas of practice. The clear expectation is that students will move from a position of only being able to consume research to being able to evaluate practice systematically. (Council on Social Work Education, 1993).

Without basic research competencies, social workers cannot develop and advance practice theories. New practice principles ought to come from practitioners who are able to objectively test and demonstrate their usefulness. To the extent that social workers do not have research skills, new practice theories and principles will come from researchers in other disciplines and not from social workers. Unlike some academic research endeavors, social work research has the goal of advancing theory (Polansky, 1986). However, in social work there has been a tendency for practice to outdistance its knowledge base. Unlike medicine, for example, where practice follows research, social work practice has often been the source of innovation, and research has followed (Reid, 1987).

How Research Benefits Social Workers

Much of our knowledge about the specific problems experienced by our clients comes to us as a result of research. Consider the case of John, a veteran and an alcoholic, who is facing the loss of his job and family because he refuses to admit to himself that he has a drinking problem. We can predict that John is on a downward spiral and that further problems are in store for him, because as an alcoholic John is similar to other alcoholics. If we were interested in doing so, we could find a body of literature on alcoholism, and we might even find some specialized literature on young male alcoholics who are veterans. This body of knowledge exists because practitioners and researchers saw beyond the individual client and conceptualized a group of persons having similar characteristics and problems. Some of these practitioners and researchers gathered data and conducted studies that have become part of our literature. All alcoholics might not look like John; their age and marital status may vary. But they will have some identifiable characteristics in common. This body of knowledge will assist us in knowing how best to treat this special population. The more John is like other alcoholics discussed in the professional literature, the more confident we will be with our predictions and interventive approaches. Research can help us know more about our clients and our interventions. (We could use a research instrument to help us assess the extent of John's alcoholism and later to determine if treatment was effective.)

The illustration of John is used here to show not only that research has some benefits to social workers, but also that you can start thinking about research even if you have an individual client focus. Research is composed of individual cases, but often goes beyond a single case. Research is a systematic process that examines problems or questions in an orderly and logical way. Just like good therapy, good research does not proceed without a plan or design. It states its intentions early, defines what will be examined, follows a specific methodology, and examines the results. These findings can expand our knowledge base and are often of direct benefit to practitioners.

Like it or not, we are all consumers of research. We hear the results of studies or polls on the television and radio, and we read about studies that are reported in newspapers, magazines, and journals. Some of this information may be clearly applicable for social workers. However, how do you know if these studies are any good? Could you identify a poorly designed study? What criteria would you use? One recent bestseller that used thousands of questionnaires to support its conclusions has been called the "functional equivalent of malpractice for surveys" (Butterfield, 1987). Just because something finds its way into print does not mean that it is based on good research or scholarship. Learn to be a skeptical reader. Ask questions of what you read. Do the findings seem consistent with what you know about the subject? Even a little knowledge of research will help you become a more informed consumer of the information you routinely encounter.

Being an informed consumer will lead you to evaluate the reported research and enable you to make more substantial contributions when you are called upon to disseminate knowledge in your everyday practice. Social workers are often required to prepare reports, conduct inservice training, or make workshop presentations. Information is shared not only with fellow professionals but also with clients and the community. As you make greater use of professional journals, you will find that you need an understanding of research in order to fully comprehend what is being reported.

As a professional you may wish to report on the effectiveness of some treatment approach or exciting innovation that you have devised. You believe that your approach works; you have demonstrated it repeatedly and convinced a lot of your skeptical colleagues. Do you know enough about research to know what and how to report and whether your research methodology was rigorous enough for a professional journal or conference paper? There may be times when even the most thoroughly convinced "I'll-always-want-to-be-a-clinician" wishes that he or she understood a little more about research.

Finally, social work research is important because, as Fanshel (1980) has noted:

> a sustained and creditable program of research is also essential to a profession's self-respect and to its ability to maintain the positive regard of outsiders whose opinions help support and legitimize the profession's endeavors. No profession can afford any equivocation on the importance of research. (P. 3)

Social science research is exciting because it studies a lively topic—people. As we learn more about people and their problems, we become better practitioners. Research is conducted by social workers in the field and in universities who are adventurers extending the frontiers of their field of knowledge. Much about human nature is yet to be discovered. Our clients supply a seemingly endless list of problems about which we need more information. One of the characteristics of social work research is that it is oriented toward solving problems. Social work research is applied; it seeks knowledge that will be put to use on behalf of those needing our services. Forget your notions that research is so theoretical that it will be of no use to you. The research skills that you can acquire, described in this text, can make you a more competent practitioner!

Desired Outcome

Every social work educator wants his or her students to be skilled, expert practitioners. Research can play an instrumental role in making you the best practitioner possible. Siegel (1984) has described the social worker who engages in empirically based practice as one who can use research as a tool. Her description of such a social worker is one that I hope you embody as a result of using this text to learn research methods. Siegel identifies the characteristics of a social worker who engages in empirically based practice as one who:

1. makes maximum use of research findings;
2. collects data systematically to monitor the intervention;
3. demonstrates empirically whether or not interventions are effective;
4. specifies problems, interventions, and outcomes in terms that are concrete, observable, and measurable;
5. uses research ways of thinking and research methods in defining clients' problems, formulating questions for practice, col-

lecting assessment data, evaluating the effectiveness of interventions, and using evidence;

6. views research and practice as part of the same problem-solving process; and

7. views research as a tool to be used in practice. (P. 329)

The best way to approach research methodology is to think of a question or a problem that you have encountered at work with your clients or that suggests itself from your life experiences or reading. This should be a question that interests you—one that piques your curiosity. Keep this question in the back of your mind as each new chapter is presented. As you review each chapter, think about how that information could be used to assist you in answering your question.

Research begins when people like you develop questions from real-life situations or become concerned about problems that have not been satisfactorily answered. Questions arise from observations of human nature and social problems. We wonder whether an old theory can explain some new phenomenon or whether a new theory can explain a recurrent problem. In some instances, a thorough search of resources in the library will provide answers to these questions, but not always. If the question cannot be adequately answered after a careful search, we may have identified a gap in our field's knowledge base, one that is in desperate need of research. Finding gaps in the literature (or areas where more is unknown than known) is exciting to those with inquiring minds. There is no shortage of problems needing additional investigation; many opportunities exist for social work researchers to make important contributions to our knowledge base. If you had the time and the funding to explore one unanswered question about human behavior, what would it be?

Questions for Class Discussion

1. What are your fears about taking a research class?
2. What do you hope to learn from this research class?
3. What experiences have you had that might help you in this research class? Describe any research-related experiences you may have had.
4. What are the problems that might develop when a profession's knowledge base and research lag behind its forms of practice?
5. As a class, make a list of problems and questions that you think need to be researched.

6. Have you ever come across a piece of research that you thought was worthless? Why did you have this opinion?
7. What stereotypes do you have about researchers?
8. In what ways could research be used to affect a local, state, or national policy that you think needs to be changed?
9. Discuss ways you might go about investigating the problems in the three examples at the beginning of this chapter.
10. Make a list of reasons why it is important for social workers to engage in empirically based practice.

Mini-Projects for Experiencing Research Firsthand

1. As a class, conduct a survey to find out the most popular explanation for why social work students do not want to study research methods.
2. Design a questionnaire that will allow you to investigate whether there are major differences in the opinions of social work, psychology, and nursing majors about the importance of taking research methods and statistics courses.
3. Think of a social problem that you have recently read about (e.g., homelessness). Do we need more research on this problem? What additional research should be conducted? What is it that we don't know about the problem? List what you feel to be gaps in our knowledge of this problem.

Resources and References

Briar, S. (1979). Incorporating research into education for clinical practice in social work: Toward a clinical science in social work. In Allen Rubin and Aaron Rosenblatt (Eds.), *Sourcebook on Research Utilization.* New York: Council on Social Work Education.

Briar, S. (1980). Toward the integration of practice and research. In David Fanshel (Ed.), *Future of Social Work Research.* Washington, DC: National Association of Social Workers.

Butterfield, F. (1987). Hite's new book is under rising attack. *New York Times* (Nov. 13), B4.

Council on Social Work Education. (1993). Curriculum policy for the master's degree and baccalaureate degree programs in social work education. New York.

Dane, E. and Epstein, I. (1985). A dark horse in continued education programming at the post-master's level: Monitoring and evaluation skills for social workers in middle management. *Journal of Continuing Social Work Education,* 3(2), 3–8.

Epstein, I. (1987). Pedagogy of the perturbed: Teaching research to the reluctants. *Journal of Teaching in Social Work*, 1(1), 71–89.

Fanshel, D. (1980). The future of social work research: Strategies for the coming years. In David Fanshel (Ed.), *Future of Social Work Research*. Washington, DC: National Association of Social Workers.

Glisson, C. (1983). Trends in social work research. Presented to the annual meeting of the Group for the Advancement of Doctoral Education at the University of Alabama, Tuscaloosa.

Glisson, C. and Fisher, J. (1987). Statistical training for social workers. *Journal of Social Work Education*, 23(3), 50–58.

Gockel, G.L. (1966). Social work as a career choice. In E.E. Schwartz (Ed.), *Manpower in Social Welfare: Research Perspectives*. Washington, DC: National Association of Social Workers.

Hersen, M. and Bellack, A. (1984). Research in clinical psychology. In A.S. Bellack and M. Hersen (Eds.), *Research Methods in Clinical Psychology*. New York: Pergamon.

Howe, M. (1974). Casework self-evaluation: A single-subject approach. *Social Service Review*, 48, 1–24.

Jayaratne, S. (1979). Analysis of selected social work research journals and productivity rankings among schools of social work. *Journal of Education for Social Work*, 15 (3), 72–80.

Kirk, S. and Fisher, J. (1976). Do social workers understand research? *Journal of Education for Social Work*, 2(1), 63–71.

Polansky, N.A. (1986). There is nothing so practical as a good theory. *Child Welfare*, 65(1), 3–15.

Reid, W.J. (1987). Research in social work. In Anne Minahan (Ed.), *Encyclopedia of Social Work*. Silver Spring, MD: National Association of Social Workers.

Rosenblatt, A. (1968). The practitioners' use and evaluation of research. *Social Work*, 13(1), 53–59.

Royse, D. and Edwards, T. (1989). Communicating about disability: Attitudes and preferences of persons with physical handicaps. *Rehabilitation Counseling Bulletin*, 32(3), 203–209.

Royse, D., Rompf, E.L., and Dhooper, S.S. (1991). Childhood trauma and adult life satisfaction in a random adult sample. *Psychological Reports*, 69, 1227–1231.

Siegel, D.H. (1984). Defining empirically based practice. *Social Work*, 29(4), 325–331.

Simpson, R.L. (1978). Is research utilization for social workers? *Journal of Social Service Research*, 2 (2), 143–158.

Specht, H. (1972) The deprofessionalization of social work. *Social Work*, 17 (March), 3–15.

Weinberger, R. and Tripodi, T. (1969). Trends in types of research reported in selected social work journals. *Social Service Review*, 43(4), 439–447.

2
The Way Research Proceeds

Research in the social sciences usually results from a real problem or a problematic situation. The process is logical and similar to the problem-solving model so familiar to social workers. You may be surprised to find that the research process is not much different from the way that you normally go about solving problems. This chapter will provide an overview of the various steps.

The research process (sometimes called the scientific method) is based on the assumptions that the natural world is essentially orderly and that observed phenomena have some stimulus or cause. If the laws of nature are not haphazard in their operation, then it follows that laws that govern the phenomena can be learned. Our knowledge about the world is obtained through the use of a logical sequence of steps. It is only when we don't know very much about a phenomenon that there seem to be no discernible laws. The more we know about something, the better we can see certain laws or principles in action. Let's take an example of a problematic situation suggested by Leedy (1974) that illustrates a research-like process.

You leave your home to go to class. You are running a little bit late, and you are in a hurry. You put the key in your car's ignition and turn it. Nothing happens. At first you don't believe your bad luck. You turn the key again and again. Nothing happens. You pull the key from the ignition and look at it to make sure that it's the right key. You try again. Nothing. At this point you have a problematic situation and almost immediately you pose questions to yourself. Did I leave the lights on? Is there enough gas? You select a logical explanation and begin the "research" process. Suppose you have a notion (or hypothesis) that you left the car lights on all night. You can test the hypothesis of weak battery by turning on the car's radio or the car's headlights. If they work, then you can assume that the car's battery still has a charge, and you can move on to another hypothesis. You remember telling your brother to put gas in the car, and you wonder whether or not he did. You look at the fuel indicator and see that it registers "Full." Does the gauge work properly? Assuming it does, you move on to the next hypothesis: perhaps your ten-year-old car is in need of spark plugs, or the distributor got wet from last night's rain. Those of you who have had the experience of owning an old car could probably proceed with such hypotheses longer than anyone else would be interested. The point is that a series of questions needing investigation flows from the problematic situation. As this example reveals, research involves an orderly thought process that moves from what is known to what is not known. Numerous and varied hypotheses may be tested. Information gained leads to the consideration of other questions or hypotheses.

The Research Process

As illustrated in the example above, the research process is composed of a few relatively simple steps or stages. For instructional purposes, these steps are presented as being sequential. However, sometimes they are taken out of order. For instance, once a question is formulated, we might start thinking about how to collect the necessary data before we go to the library and begin a literature search.

Step 1: Posing a Question or Stating a Hypothesis

Before you can begin conducting research you must necessarily limit yourself to one question (or at least to a small set of related questions) or one specific topic to investigate. Ideas may emerge from observations of clients, personal experiences, discussions with colleagues, or reading the literature pertinent to a certain problem.

Research questions may come about as a result of **deduction** (where knowledge of a theory or general principle allows you to make a prediction or an application to a single specific case) or from **induction** (where your observations about a case or cases seem to suggest a theory or set of principles). For instance, learning of a two-year-old child in a housing project who has been eating plaster may result in your concluding that this problem is widespread. Induction goes from the specific to the general. Unlike research questions in other disciplines, those in social work generally stem from problems that actually need to be solved. We tend as professionals to be inductive rather than deductive thinkers because our research tends to have more of an applied focus.

Once a question has been roughly posed or drafted, it will often need to be restated as a researchable question. Not all questions can be answered—and the purpose of research is to generate information that can be verified by others. "Why is there suffering?" is an example of a question best left to philosophers or theologians. Social scientists are interested in concrete, tangible, objective evidence.

Sometimes, however, it is possible to give a slightly different emphasis to an expansive question like "Why is there suffering?" and thereby make it a researchable question. "How do children with leukemia explain the origin of their illnesses?" is a question that could be investigated. Often, very broad questions can be narrowed down by considering how you would go about collecting data, and what could be done within a reasonable period of time—say, a semester, or six months.

There is a definite knack to developing a good question. If too few words are used, the question tends to be too large to investigate. "What causes child abuse?" is an example of a research question that needs to be narrowed down. There is nothing wrong with wanting to provide answers to such questions, but practically speaking, the research needed to answer them would be well beyond the resources of most undergraduate or graduate students. As you read about child abuse, you will discover that the role of certain factors has already been demonstrated. It is usually better to ask questions that allow you to examine a specific theory or perhaps a small part of the problem. A better question might be "Were child abusers abused themselves as children?" or "Do perpetrators of child abuse tend to be chemically dependent?"

Questions that are asked in research studies are often very specific. This specificity is reflected in the titles of journal articles. Browse through an issue of *Social Work Abstracts*. Then look up some of the abstracts listed in the Index under "Child abuse." The abstracts will demonstrate how specific research questions are. The research process starts with *either* a question to be answered *or* with a hypothesis to be tested. Most students find it easier to understand the research process in terms of asking questions rather than testing hypotheses. However, a **hypothesis** is simply an assumption expressed as a statement. Hypotheses are formal versions of hunches, expectations, or speculations that make a prediction or express an assumed relationship between variables. Hypotheses and research questions are both legitimate starting points for the research process. Either one can be converted into the other; the following question and hypothesis deal with the same research.

Example of a research question: What is the level of empathy among fathers who have sexually abused their children?

Example of a hypothesis: Fathers who have sexually abused their children will have less empathy than nonabusing fathers.

Elaborate studies may have several major hypotheses as well as a number of minor or subhypotheses. Occasionally hypotheses are stated neutrally (e.g., there is no relationship between high school grade point averages and college grade point averages); these are known as **null hypotheses**. A null hypothesis states that there is no difference between the groups being compared (e.g., adolescent males are no more impulsive than adolescent females). Researchers sometimes hope to find sufficient evidence to allow for rejection of the null hypothesis. The researcher does not have to believe that there is no difference or no relationship in order to state a null hypothesis.

Example of a null hypothesis: There is no difference in the empathy level of fathers who have sexually abused their children and nonabusing fathers.

Hypotheses, like research questions, may be suggested from theories, the literature, or interactions with colleagues or clients. Hypotheses need not always be stated but may be the driving force behind exploratory or descriptive studies. After such studies have been conducted and more data are available, hypotheses can be tested in a more formal manner.

Step 2: Reviewing the Literature

Once you have a question or hypothesis in mind, the second step is to review the professional literature to see what others have already written about the topic. There are many good reasons for learning as much as possible about your subject before beginning to conduct a study. First of all, a careful review of the literature can save you a lot of unnecessary work and prevent you from wasting your time studying a problem that has already been thoroughly investigated. (Just because we don't know the answer to a question doesn't mean that there is a scarcity of research on the topic.) Also, as you discover how others have studied the problem, approaches that you hadn't considered may be suggested. You may find new instruments or ways for measuring your **dependent variable**. (The dependent variable is the topic of your investigation—what you are trying to explain or predict.) And, a solid review of the literature will help you ground your research interest and possible findings within a theoretical framework. Finally, acquainting yourself with the literature can provide you with data to compare with your own findings. Particularly if you are evaluating the success of an intervention, you may want to know how successful other approaches have been.

Why is a theoretical framework so important? Let me give you an example from a practicum seminar that I led one summer. As was our custom, the students each took about ten minutes at the beginning of class to report the progress of their clients or to share something new they had learned in the previous week. When it was Marcie's turn, she reported working with an alcoholic client who was heavily into denial. He maintained that he did not have a drinking problem, although he was beginning to have some liver complications, and that he could quit drinking any time he wanted. Since she didn't feel she was making much headway with him, Marcie, noticing that her client was a chain smoker, asked if he could give up cigarette smoking as a way of showing that he could quit drinking. Since both were addictive habits, she reasoned that he might be more willing to quit drinking once he realized that he could live without cigarettes.

"Marcie," I asked when she had finished her account, "what theory or whose intervention are you following?"

"What do you mean?" she asked.

"Who has suggested that asking clients to give up their cigarettes helps them give up alcohol?"

"Well," she said, looking skyward for inspiration, "no one that I can think of. I thought of this all by myself."

"What happens," I asked, "if your client tries to quit smoking but fails? Could that experience convince him that he couldn't quit drinking even if he wanted to?"

"Oh," she said, her face blushing, "I didn't think of that."

At that point, we began a discussion about the importance of theory and how it can help guide our efforts, whether we are researchers or direct service practitioners. Theories are equally valuable to the practitioner and the researcher. Practitioners employ theories in their interventions, and these theories provide guidelines or suggest techniques as well as offer explanations of observed phenomena.

Theories vary considerably in their complexity, their perspective or orientation, and the amount of evidence that can be mustered to support them. A good example of how various theories from different disciplines might be used to explain a social phenomenon is found in *Incest as Child Abuse: Research and Applications* (Vander Mey and Neff, 1986). Chapter 3 in their book reviews anthropological, psychological, ecological, and feminist theories that attempt to explain incest using somewhat different mechanisms.

The research you do, or at least the way you go about it, is strongly influenced by your theoretical orientation. If you assume that "deviant socialization" or cultural explanations largely explain the occurrence of incest, then the types of questions you ask will be different from questions you would ask if you assume "mental illness" will explain most cases of incest. Your theoretical orientation directs your attention to events that are assumed to be important and allows you to ignore those that are expected to be irrelevant.

A good theory focuses your attention, saves energy, and builds upon existent knowledge. For instance, if you stopped in a city where you had never been before and needed aspirin, where would you find it? Would you start at the stockyards? the bank? the library? (Polansky, 1986, has written a wonderful article on the value of good theory from which I drew this idea of looking for aspirin.) Theories lead to predictions about the world in which we operate and might be likened to mental maps that suggest avenues or directions.

A good theory explains, organizes, and predicts (Munson, 1983). It allows you to go beyond the known facts, suggesting what you might expect in the future and allowing you to integrate the facts you already have. Theories provide clues or suggestions for interventions and help explain things that we don't understand very well. For instance, remember in chapter 1 the discussion about why social work students may not look forward to their research methods class? Here's a theoretical explanation for you that I didn't present at that time—social work students may have more anxiety about math than other college students.

In one small study (Royse and Rompf, 1992), a colleague and I found that undergraduate social work students at our university rated themselves more anxious on a twenty-four-item Mathematics Anxiety Rating Scale than did a cross section of undergraduate students enrolled in a required introductory statistics course. The presence of greater math anxiety might explain why many social work students are reluctant to take quantitative courses and often perform poorly in these classes. Even though we weren't able to account for why social work students registered greater anxiety, our research and the theoretical model we used open the door a little wider for future researchers who want to explore this phenomenon further.

Since we seem to have been the first to examine math anxiety in social work students, there wouldn't be a great deal of research you would have to read on this topic if you wanted to pursue it yourself. However, this is not always the case. Sometimes there is so much literature on a topic that it is almost unmanageable.

There is so much literature on schizophrenia, for instance, that it would take years to read all the relevant journal articles and books. Once again we can see the utility of having a research question that is relatively narrow in its focus. How might this topic be narrowed down? (Hint: by searching for explanations of etiology—genetic evidence, for instance; diagnostic criteria for different types of schizophrenia; use of specific antipsychotic drugs for treatment; psychosocial intervention and management; the history of institutional treatment of schizophrenia; relapse; or by narrowing the topic by looking within particular populations or age groups.)

There are several ways to begin a literature search; you might use only one approach or many, depending upon your success in finding relevant articles of interest. If you love to browse in libraries, a laid-back approach is to check the subject index to find where the books on your topic are located. Then examine the books on those shelves. As you review these books, you may find references to other books or journals. The more you read, the more you have "reviewed the literature."

The approach I sometimes use is to go to specific journals that I know publish articles on the subject of my literature review. For instance, *Child Abuse and Neglect: An International Journal* would be a logical place to start if one wanted to find journal articles on child abuse. You might also look at *Child Welfare* or *Social Work*, and skim the table of contents in issues of the last two years. If you find several articles of interest, they almost always direct you to additional journal articles or studies that you can use to further explore what is known about your question.

A third approach is to use the various abstracting services in the reference section of your library. *Psychological Abstracts* will provide you with a comprehensive subject index that will guide you to articles about your topic in a large number of professional journals. An abstracting service called *Sociological Abstracts* will direct you to articles that have appeared in sociological journals. If your topic borders upon the medical realm (e.g., the treatment of hyperactivity), you could consult *Index Medicus*, one of the more comprehensive abstracting services that includes relevant social work and psychology articles as well as those from the field of medicine. *Social Work Abstracts* is the resource that will be most helpful on issues of interest primarily to social workers.

I usually start probing the literature by searching through the index in the most recent issues of *Social Work Abstracts*. As I'm looking at the various titles listed under the subject I'm trying to find information on, I'm hoping to find an article that has recently surveyed the available literature on that topic. Some examples are: Grief and Hegar (1992), "Impact on Children of Abduction by a Parent: A Review of the Literature"; Solkoff (1992), "Children of Survivors of the Nazi Holocaust: A Critical Review of the Literature"; Berrick and Barth (1992), "Child Sexual Abuse Prevention: Research Review and Recommendations"; and Bergman, et al. (1993), "High-Risk Indicators for Family Involvement in Social Work in Health Care: A Review of the Literature."

Even if you don't discover titles or abstracts clearly suggesting a review of the literature on your topic, most articles in professional journals will contain some survey of the literature. Whether the article contains an extensive or more restricted list of references will depend somewhat upon the journal and the nature of the article. It is likely, however, that the literature review stopped two years or more before the article was published. (It may take an article three to ten months to be examined by a journal's reviewers, and even if no revisions are required of the author, many journals have a backlog of a year or longer before a manuscript is published.) So, even if you find a rather complete review of the literature in an article published in 1994, the author's references may not include any sources published later than 1992. Odds are, however, that you won't be so lucky as to find one article that does all your library work for you. But don't despair. If you don't like to manually search through journals, you can also search by computer.

If you've never used a computer to search information data bases, it's usually helpful to consult with a reference librarian first. Librarians can help you narrow your topic and may suggest key words that the data bases use to index the topic. Let's say you are still interested in locating articles on child abuse. Since there may be hundreds of articles on child abuse, the librarian may ask you what aspect of child abuse interests you. Let's say that you narrow the topic by indicating that the treatment of adults who are child abusers is your primary interest. A search for the key words *treatment* and *child abuse* would likely turn up more references pertinent to the treatment of child victims than to adult perpetrators. By reviewing ten or so of the citations produced from this search, you may find it more profitable to use the key word "offenders" and "treatment."

24

If at all possible, work with a librarian or at least someone familiar with the data base until you learn some of the shortcuts and procedures for producing the best searches. In some instances, you are better off not linking two terms like *older* and *adult* or *child* and *abuse*.
Generally speaking, the more terms you link together for a search
(e.g., *abuse, older, adults*) the fewer articles you may find in the data
base. How do you know how many terms would be too many or too
few? This is why you should consult with a reference librarian.

Computerized data bases abound. For instance, there is at least
one dedicated only to gerontology. If you are searching in this data
base, it wouldn't be necessary to specify *older adult* for articles on the
abuse of older adults. Other excellent computerized data bases include PsycINFO, Social Work Abstracts, ERIC, and Child Abuse and
Neglect. Your reference librarian will know of many others.

Increasingly, data bases can now be accessed from your home if
you have a personal computer and a modem, or if you don't, from
your university's library. Most university libraries have compact
disk (CD-ROM) readers that will allow you to search through *Psychological Abstracts* (PsychLit) and *Social Work Abstracts Plus* and
other data bases without any charge. The advantage of the CD-ROM
readers is that many of the data bases are on compact disk and with
them there are no online costs or hourly fees for usage.

In many libraries you have a choice of using their CD-ROM
readers or, if you want to go back further and do a more comprehensive search, doing an online search using a modem to connect with
information clearinghouses located off-campus. Online searches usually produce a large number of references, cover many more journals
than you could reasonably expect yourself to browse through, and are
flexible in the sense that several terms or related topics can often be
combined in one search. On the other hand, with these searches you
usually have to pay for the time you are connected with the data base.
A simple search could cost under $20, but a more difficult one (arti-
cles on your topic may be hard to find) could easily run over $100.

However, librarians can often provide you with a rough estimate of how many references there are and how much the search will
cost. Since chronological listings of references can be provided to you
(with the most recent ones first), you can pare down expenses when
there are many references by printing only the most recent ones (e.g.,
those published within the last three years).

While some information data bases may contain book titles, do
not be surprised if all of the references produced from a computer
search are found in journals (many of which you may not have known
existed). New knowledge in a field is often first introduced or reported

in that field's journals. Unlike magazines that are written largely for public entertainment, journals report studies and new thinking about old problems for students, professionals, and scholars. Journals usually lack vivid graphics and multicolor advertisements.

An information data base like *Infotrac* may mix some professional journal articles with magazines like *Newsweek, Time, U.S. News & World Report,* and *Reader's Digest.* While these magazines are useful for providing current statistics about social problems and experts' opinions, they are not considered professional literature. Many instructors will not count magazine or newspaper articles when students are given the assignment of preparing a bibliography on a special topic.

A number of social work journals are listed below to help you become familiar with some of the important journals in our profession. This is by no means a comprehensive listing. There are many more journals than could conveniently be listed here, and the number of new journals has increased in recent years. Also, there are many specialized journals (e.g., *Crime and Delinquency, Gerontologist, Evaluation Review*) that are not listed but may be of interest to some students.

SELECTED SOCIAL WORK JOURNALS

Administration in Social Work
Affilia: Journal of Women and Social Work
Arete
Child and Adolescent Social Work Journal
Child Welfare
Clinical Social Work Journal
Families in Society
Health and Social Work
Human Services in the Rural Environment
International Social Work
Journal of Applied Social Sciences
Journal of Gerontological Social Work
Journal of Multicultural Social Work
Journal of Social Service Research

Journal of Social Welfare
Journal of Social Work and Human Sexuality
Journal of Social Work Education
Journal of Sociology and Social Welfare
Journal of Teaching in Social Work
Public Welfare
Research on Social Work Practice
School Social Work Journal
Smith College Studies in Social Work
Social Service Review
Social Work
Social Work Abstracts
Social Work in Education
Social Work with Groups
Social Work in Health Care
Social Work Research

Such journals as these and other very specialized journals allow for in-depth reporting and discussion of a topic because they are written for a specific audience. Typically, a journal article starts with a literature review or a historical overview of the problem and then explains the current study. At the end, the findings are discussed in terms of implications for professionals. An article may also identify areas where future research should be directed. Contrast this with the coverage of a report in a newspaper article or a magazine; often these accounts do not explain the investigator's approach (the methodology), the sample size, and how the data were analyzed, or address implications of the findings. You should get all of this information in a journal article. At the end, you should be able to make a conclusion about the worth of a study.

As you become more familiar with the literature relevant to your research problem, you will be able to refine your question and might even decide to significantly change or modify it. You may delight to discover that researchers have suggested that the study you are planning is desperately needed. Even if it is not so directly stated, you may find gaps in our knowledge about the problem that interests you. These are fertile areas where you as a social worker can make an important contribution with your research.

The necessity for immersing yourself in the literature cannot be emphasized strongly enough. Research builds upon the accumulated efforts of all those laboring to expand our knowledge and correct our misconceptions. But to make a contribution in the social sciences, we first must be familiar with what is known about the problem. This includes theories that have attempted to explain the phenomenon, interventions that have tried to correct it, and instruments that have been designed to assess and evaluate it. As you familiarize yourself with the professional literature, ask yourself: What do the authors of these studies conclude? Are they unanimous in their findings? How could their research efforts have been improved?

If you are unfamiliar with the library and would like to learn more about such things as how to find public documents, federal publications, and other references or handbooks relevant to your interest, *A Guide to Information Sources for Social Work and the Human Services* by Henry Mendelsohn (1987) is strongly recommended. You may also want to examine *Where to Find What: A Handbook to Reference Service* by James Hillard (1991) or *How to Use a Reference Library* by David Beasley (1988).

Step 3: Developing a Research Design

A research design or methodology is something like a blueprint. It outlines the approach to be used to collect the data. It describes the conditions under which the data will be collected, how the subjects or respondents will be selected, what instrument will be used, and generally provides information about the who, what, when, where, and how of the research project.

The research design should be carefully thought out to ensure that the information you obtain will be the information you need to support or reject your hypothesis. In developing a research design, ask yourself, "What do I need to know?" and then "How will I go about getting it?" The answers to these two questions will guide the development of a research design.

Several types of research designs exist and there are variations within these major types. Further information about specific designs and their use is provided later in this text. For now, research designs can be broadly categorized as having one of three prime purposes:

1. Exploration
2. Description
3. Explanation

Exploratory research designs are used with topics about which very little information is available. For example, the first studies on the psychosocial impact of AIDS on the lives of gay men were important even if they involved only a relatively small number of respondents. Because these exploratory studies are responsive to new concerns or to areas that have not been subjected to research, they tend to be more tentative and small-scale. Their value derives from the new insights they provide or the unanswered questions they generate for future research. The data they produce may not be conclusive, and, as a consumer of a report of some exploratory data, you may come away wishing that they had included a larger number of respondents. Exploratory studies generally do not have stated hypotheses. An example of an exploratory study is "The Duration of Homeless Careers: An Exploratory Study" by Piliavin et al. (1993).

Descriptive studies tend to build upon exploratory efforts, but these studies are generally surveys on a large scale that adequately represent the population being studied. Descriptive studies can provide precise information on the characteristics of a group of respondents. For example, the characteristics and service needs of black homeless persons are described in First, Roth, and Arewa's (1988) article, "Homelessness: Understanding the Dimension of the Problem for Minorities." Descriptive studies tend to be concerned with sample size, representativeness, and generalizability.

Explanatory studies test hypotheses and attempt to explain a phenomenon. These studies may involve comparison groups or social experiments. (See, for example, Kohn and Smart's 1984 study, "The Impact of Television Advertising on Alcohol Consumption: An Experiment.") Explanatory studies tend to be elaborate and focus on the way one or more variables affect another (dependent) variable. For instance, Richard Gelles (1989) explored three explanatory hypotheses for explaining increased risk of violence for children in single-parent households using data from a sample of 6,002 households. The findings confirmed that children in single-parent homes are at increased risk of abuse but that age of caretaker did not appear to be a factor. Poverty was associated with increased risk of abuse in mother-only homes but not father-only homes.

Although this is probably an enormous generalization based on the last several students who have come to me with questions about the research they were planning, I suspect the projects that most students have in mind are more exploratory than descriptive or explanatory. They are exploratory because the student has discovered a problem about which very little has been published (e.g., bulimics who don't purge). These are often exciting projects—particularly when they can be completed in the course of a semester or two. (One of the exploratory studies I'm the proudest of investigated the amount of money that trash pickers of aluminum cans earned on an average day. When I did the literature review, I couldn't believe that I was the first to write on the topic. We've all seen trash pickers rooting around in our garbage cans. How many are impaired because of mental illness or alcoholism? For more information on what we learned, see the reference for Royse, 1987.)

Sometimes it is hard to advise a student about how many subjects to include in an exploratory study. The best advice is to plan your study to be roughly comparable to similar studies being reported in the journals that you are reading or hope will favorably receive your manuscript. So, if you find several recent articles on bulimics with sample sizes of about fifty, this is an approximate number to aim for. Having a small number of subjects is not likely to jeopardize the potential of your manuscript being published if your research project is exploring new terrain.

If, however, you are planning a more elaborate study in an area where there is already a good deal of research, sample size is much more critical, and you will want to pay close attention to this topic in chapter 6.

In chapter 4 we'll learn much more about research designs and how those employing random assignment of subjects and control groups can be very powerful (providing solid information in which we can place a fair amount of confidence) or very weak. Choosing the right research design is much more involved than the brief description provided here. I've only introduced the topic at this point so that you can see how choice of a design is part of the research process.

Step 4: Operationalizing

In everyday conversation we easily accept concepts that are somewhat vague because we think we understand what they mean. However, researchers must be precise about the concepts employed in their studies; this is called developing **operational definitions.** For instance, in most conversations we all understand the terms "heavy," "frequent," and "problem drinker" to mean the same thing. However, the way one researcher defines problem drinking for the purposes of a study may be quite different from the way another investigator defines the concept. Robertson's (1989) article on the development of a tool to assess adolescents' involvement with alcohol is a good illustration. From this article we learn that one research team defined a problem drinker as a person who was drunk five or more times in the past year or had experienced two or more negative consequences from drinking. Another research team defined the same concept (only they called it "heavy drinker") as a person who drank several times a week. Obviously, operational definitions have considerable impact on who is included or excluded from studies.

As a researcher, you may use the operational definitions employed by other researchers or you may revise and improve upon them. Whatever the case, it is important to state your operational definitions so that others can understand the characteristics of persons who were a part of (or excluded from) your study. Operational definitions facilitate the **replication** (or reproduction) of your research by giving others enough information to locate persons having the same characteristics as those in your study.

Before you can begin to collect data, an important part of the research process is to define the concepts or phenomena that are to be recognized or counted in your study so precisely that no one would have any problem understanding exactly what was measured or observed. For instance, to conduct research on the topic of child abuse, you must be specific as to what manifestations of child abuse you will be studying. Will the study be concerned only with physical abuse to a child? Will it include or exclude sexual abuse and emotional abuse? Is neglect to be considered? Most important, what will constitute evidence of the abuse or neglect? Since it would be almost impossible to know about every episode of abuse in a community, you might have to settle for counting or measuring the extent of abuse by using substantiated reports from child protection workers. Obviously, this operational definition would be a conservative one, lacking all those incidents of abuse that are never reported or investigated.

The way we operationalize our variables has a direct bearing on what our research can potentially reveal and the use we can make of the data. Imagine that you are working in a mental health center providing services to the chronically mentally ill. The agency director asks you to determine which clients have improved over the last twenty-four months. How will you operationalize improvement? Will you look at the number of hospitalizations? The length of stay in the hospital? Improved functioning in the community as measured by the Denver Community Mental Health Questionnaire? Reduction in psychological distress as measured by the Symptom Checklist-90-Revised? Changes in self-esteem?

Let's say that you want to measure changes in self-esteem. Could you come up with a single indicator of good or poor self-esteem that everyone in your class would agree with? The review of literature assists with this problem; you can learn how others have defined the concept of self-esteem. If they have used a standardized instrument to measure self-esteem, you may want to use the same approach. Self-esteem is then operationalized in terms of the instrument, and individuals would have good self-esteem if their scores are high and poor self-esteem if their scores on the instrument are low.

The importance of operationalizing variables might be better understood with the following example. Suppose a friend is going to fix you up with a date. Your friend knows a lot of people and asks you what you are looking for. You indicate that you appreciate people who have a nice smile. "Well," your friend says, "that's no problem. What else?" You think a bit more and reply that you would prefer someone tall to someone short. Again, your friend knows several individuals who fit into that category. Your friend asks, "Is that all you are looking for?" Now you become concerned, because you realize that you would actually prefer a date who is somewhat athletic and who has values and interests about the same as yours. You end up giving your friend a list of five more essential characteristics. Now you have operationalized what you want in the way of a date. Similarly, researchers must define rather precisely what is to be measured in their studies and who is qualified to be a subject.

Think about the problem of defining the dependent variable, homelessness. Is a person homeless who has no other place to go and sleeps in his car? What if his girlfriend threw him out for just one night and they patch things up the next day? Would he still be homeless if he slept in his backyard? What if his girlfriend threw him out permanently but he slept at a friend's house on the couch? See what I mean?

Independent variables such as age, gender, race, marital status, political affiliation, and religion tend to be easier for us to operationalize than dependent variables. **Independent variables** are variables that are suspected to influence, affect, or cause the event or situation that you are studying. For example, prior hospitalizations for mental illness or alcoholism might be important independent variables to use to help explain or predict the problem of homelessness. Also, you might want to include such independent (or socio-demographic) variables as age, education, and job skills.

In experimental settings, independent variables are those that the researcher can manipulate or control. For example, in studying the effect of positive reinforcement upon the retention of research terminology, the researcher might decide to examine the usefulness of candy as a reinforcement for each new vocabulary term learned. The amount, type, and timing of the receipt of the candy are controlled by the researcher and could be considered independent variables. The number of vocabulary items retained would be the dependent variable.

Dependent variables in one study may be used as independent variables in another study. For instance, you could start off your research career by studying the level of self-esteem in ninth grade boys. In a subsequent study, you may wish to use those self-esteem scores to predict juvenile delinquency (which is now the dependent variable).

Social workers deal with a lot of intangible concepts. We might talk about Susan's self-esteem, and we all tend to know what that means. Similarly, we may have a client who is depressed, one who has school phobia, and still another who is passive-aggressive. We have to deal with differences in intelligence and motivation, power, social status, and pathology. These abstract concepts must become operationalized if we are to employ them as variables in a research project.

One of the keys to understanding social science research is the notion that if a thing can be defined, then it can be measured. If we can precisely define concepts such as depression and anxiety, for example, then we can measure how much less a client is depressed or anxious after intervention. Since problems brought to social workers are sometimes indefinite or ambiguous, it is helpful to collect data in order to determine the intensity or severity of these problems. Just how anxious is the client? How severe is the depression? Social workers sometimes design or use instruments to measure the extent of such problems. These instruments provide quantifiable (numerical) values for problems like depression so that we can discuss relative levels of depression and talk more precisely about those who are very depressed and those who are somewhat less depressed. Simply stated, **measurement** is the process of quantifying states, traits, attitudes, behaviors, and theoretical concepts (e.g., hyperactivity).

The importance of measurement is revealed in two axioms of treatment formulated by Walter Hudson (1978): "The first states: 'If you cannot measure the client's problem, it does not exist.' The second, a corollary of the first, states: 'If you cannot measure the client's problem, you cannot treat it' " (p. 65). While some may feel that these axioms are overstated, they have a direct applicability to research. Clinicians and researchers alike must be able to precisely assess (measure) clients' problems. Without precise measurement, it may be impossible to show that clients have improved as a result of intervention. Researchers attempt to obtain this precision by using scales and instruments when they operationalize their variables.

A **scale** is a cluster or group of statements or questions (items) that are designed to measure a single concept. Social scientists constantly work on and develop new scales to measure more accurately concepts of interest to them. It is not unusual for scales to be revised over time. Also, you will find that different investigators approach the measurement of even the same concept in different ways, so scales measuring the same general concept may vary in length, in the type of item used, and in the response categories available to the subject. For example, it is possible to find a ten-item self-esteem inventory (Rosenberg, 1965) and a twenty-five-item one, which Hudson (1982) calls the Index of Self-Esteem.

Hudson and his associates have developed several scales of interest to social work practitioners. Some of the others are the Index of Marital Satisfaction, the Index of Sexual Satisfaction, the Index of Parental Attitudes, the Child's Attitude toward Father, the Index of Family Relations, and the Index of Peer Relations, (Nurius and Hudson, 1993). Scales can be developed to measure many different kinds of problems or concepts.

Corcoran and Fischer (1987) have collected over 125 brief scales, which they refer to as "rapid assessment instruments," for social workers to use with problems commonly encountered in clinical practice. Complete scales as well as information on the scales' availability, primary reference, scoring, and other essential information are found in their reference book, which contains many interesting and useful scales to use for research projects and for evaluating one's practice.

It is likely that sometime in your life you have been asked to complete a questionnaire that used a *Likert* scale (sometimes referred to as a five-point scale). In this usage of the term, the scale is the standard set of response choices: (1) strongly agree, (2) agree, (3) undecided, (4) disagree, and (5) strongly disagree; these are used to record the degree of agreement or disagreement with the statement. While Likert-type response choices are commonly used, there are variations. Hudson (1982) uses the following five-point response set to measure the variation in frequency or intensity associated with items composing such scales as the Index of Marital Satisfaction: (1) rarely or none of the time; (2) a little of the time; (3) some of the time; (4) a good part of the time; and (5) most or all of the time. Each of the response choices has a certain numeric value attached to it that is used to compute a client's score on that scale. Each of Hudson's scales is designed to have a score ranging from 0 to 100. A low score indicates the absence of the concept or trait being measured, while a high score indicates the presence of the concept. High scores, then, indicate to the practitioner the possibility of a severe problem in this area.

Scales vary enormously in how well they measure the concept they were designed to measure and in how dependable they are. The terms that researchers use to describe the worth or value of scales are **reliability** and **validity.** While these topics will be discussed below, it is worth noting that scales may contain many items (which improves their reliability), or they may be composed of a single item. The reliability of single-item scales cannot be computed.

The following is an example of a single-item scale:

Rate how useful you think your research course will be to you:

Not very useful					*Some use*				*Very useful*
1	2	3	4	5	6	7	8	9	10

Instruments. An **instrument** is a questionnaire or test that is usually completed by the respondents. When completed by a subject, the instrument is often referred to as a self-report or a self-inventory (meaning that persons can complete the instrument on their own with minimal supervision). The instrument provides data for the study. An instrument might, for instance, measure a person's potential for abusing children (Milner, 1986) or could be used to determine the amount of psychopathology present (Derogatis, 1983). Numerical values obtained with instruments allow one to monitor the amount of improvement or change in a client and to make comparisons with other clients.

An instrument is often a scale or, more precisely, composed of several scales, in addition to items that seek socio-demographic information (e.g., age, sex, race). For instance, Milner's Child Abuse Potential Inventory contains an abuse scale as well as scales to measure distress, rigidity, unhappiness, problems with child and self, problems with family, and problems caused by others. Derogatis's Symptom Checklist-90-R contains scales to measure phobic anxiety, paranoid ideation, depression, anxiety, hostility, psychoticism, and interpersonal sensitivity (among others). Attitudes about Research Courses and the Drug Attitude Questionnaire, instruments with several scales, are provided for your review in the appendix.

Instruments should not be understood as having only a clinical application. Social scientists have developed instruments (1) to measure antisemitism and authoritarianism; (2) to study values; and (3) to measure such concepts as faith in people, social responsibility, radicalism-conservatism, and hundreds (if not thousands) more. There are instruments already available and ready for use no matter what your research interest. A good place to begin to review some of these instruments is in collections that have applications for research and program evaluations in a variety of social service settings, such as Corcoran and Fischer (1987), McDowell and Newell (1987), Brodsky and Smitherman (1983), and Robinson and Shaver (1973).

Many social workers first realize that they have to operationalize certain concepts when they begin to develop a questionnaire for use within their agencies. Some early advice for when you have to operationalize such common variables as age, education, and income—try to avoid using broad categories for respondents. For instance, "What is your present age _____ (yrs.)?" provides specific information that allows you to arrive at the average age for the group. (With the information provided to you, age categories could be created later.) However, if for the same question you were to provide the following response choices, then you would be unable to obtain a numerical average for the class and would be limited in the ways you could analyze your data:

WHAT IS YOUR PRESENT AGE?
_____ Adolescent (18 and under)
_____ Young Adult (19 to 30)
_____ Adult (31 to 44)
_____ Middle-aged Adult (45 to 65)

Any operationalization or measurement of a concept should meet the test of clarity. It would do little good to create an age category, for instance, of "pre-middle age," or "old old" if there was confusion as to what ages went into these groupings. A concept has not been operationally well-defined (e.g., emotional exhaustion) if you don't know or can't tell who is and who isn't emotionally exhausted.

Often, behaviors are very indicative of the concepts we want to measure. For instance, a racist might attend white supremacist meetings or tell ethnic jokes, a sexist might use "girls" in speech when referring to women. Some students find it helpful to think of operationalizing concepts in terms of behaviors that you could detect from watching a videotape. A "good" student might be one who studies at his or her desk at least four hours a day; an emotionally neglectful mother might be one who never touches, hugs, or kisses a young child.

You don't have to have a scale to operationally define a concept: it's just that scales tend to allow for more possibilities so that gradations (think of a continuum running from low to high) of the concept can be measured. Does it make sense to try to distinguish persons who are a little sexist from those who are profoundly sexist in their thinking?

Step 5: Collecting Data

This step is sometimes referred to as "implementation of the study." Depending upon your research design, you interview people, mail out questionnaires, or go to the library to obtain data that have already been published (such as suicide rates, marriages, divorces, or births by county and year).

This phase of the research process is obviously important. Without data you will have nothing to analyze or report. If your choice of methodology was well-considered, it will not allow for unconscious influence (bias) upon the responses you hope to obtain. Even though you may hope to find a specific outcome, you don't want to gather your data in such a way that the respondents tell you what they think you want to hear.

Researchers strive to eliminate **bias** from their studies. Bias is an outside influence or prejudice that tends to produce some distortion from what is actually occurring or present. This results in inaccuracy. Bias can be conscious or unconscious, glaring or subtle, and may creep in and affect the research process at various points. For instance, in developing a questionnaire you might inadvertently use all masculine pronouns and offend female readers. Offended respondents, if they are angry, may not respond to the questionnaire as you had intended. Complex instructions (which might be confusing to persons with less than a high school education) can also result in biased data. While we all have values and biases of our own, researchers should strive to keep their studies as free from bias as possible. A biased questionnaire can give information that does not produce a true picture or representation of the attitudes or behaviors you are investigating.

Bias can also result from the way we select interviewees or respondents. This commonly happens when not enough thought has been given to the sampling design. For example, suppose you are interested in getting social work majors to evaluate their undergraduate program. You decide, because it is convenient for you, to go to a nearby men's dormitory and interview all of the social work majors you can find. Obviously, if you base your study on just the interviews from that one dorm, you will have ignored all female social work majors. Your study, then, will be very biased, as female social work students may have different experiences and evaluations of the social work program.

The way, the time of day, and the place you collect your data can have major effects upon the outcome of your study. Suppose you go to a neighborhood supermarket to conduct a survey on attitudes about abortion. You choose to do your interviewing on Mondays, Wednesdays, and Fridays for two weeks during the hours between 9:00 A.M. and 4:00 P.M. However, a friend tells you that a better day to go is Saturday because everyone is more talkative. When should you collect your data?

Had you chosen to interview solely on Mondays, Wednesdays, and Fridays until 4:00 P.M., you may discover that your study underrepresented those persons who generally are at work during those hours. By interviewing persons who buy their groceries only on Saturday, you may collect a group of respondents who are employed Monday through Friday. The older, retired, or unemployed persons could be underrepresented. One approach would give respondents who would likely be older and possibly more conservative, while the other could result in younger, potentially more liberal respondents. If you choose to do your interviewing on Sunday mornings between 10:00 A.M. and 12:00 noon, what segment of the population would be underrepresented?

Some research questions or populations of interest determine how the data will be collected. Because homeless persons do not have telephones and may not have an address to which mail could be sent, it would be ludicrous to attempt a mail or telephone data collection procedure with this population. Pragmatic considerations such as the amount of time available to conduct the study, the amount of money that can be spent, the availability of subjects, and the ease of locating them all have a direct bearing on the way researchers go about collecting their data and the research design chosen.

Bias is generally minimized as survey samples approach **representativeness**—that is, as samples more closely resemble the larger population being studied. Remember that there can be many sources of bias, but in the conduct of research, objectivity is the proper and necessary stance. You want your data to be as free from bias as possible.

Studies that are free from bias generally have much greater generalizability than those with overt bias. **Generalizability** means how well the findings from a specific study fit another situation. Let's say that I think that my spaghetti sauce is the greatest in the world. I invite my aunt Bessie over to try it. She agrees that it is the best she has ever tasted. My wife also agrees. Even the kids like it. I then decide that I am ready to sell it across the country. Is it reasonable to assume from a small sample of family members that enough of the American public would buy my spaghetti sauce to justify spending all my savings to market it? In this instance I would have been guilty of **overgeneralization**. In other words, I assumed too much. I went beyond what my data would support.

Suppose that you are interested in predicting an upcoming presidential election. You ask all the social work majors in your college or university how they will vote. In this instance, a much larger sample is involved, but will your findings indicate which candidate will win the national election? The answer is: probably not. Why? Because social work majors do not adequately represent a cross-sampling of American voters. For one thing, social work majors probably tend to be more liberal and younger than the average voter. Social work majors at any one school may or may not represent the opinions of other students attending the same school. Similarly, you probably could not predict a national election based upon interviews of all the residents of several retirement centers located in South Carolina. However, depending upon the size of your sample and how the retirement centers were selected, you might be able to discover the candidate most preferred by older adults living in retirement centers in South Carolina.

As a rule, you can generalize only to the specific universe of people from whom you selected your subjects. If you draw an unbiased national sample, then you can speak to the attitudes or preferences of the nation. If you draw an unbiased sample from all the adults in a given state, then you can speak about the knowledge or attitudes of

38

adults residing in that particular state. An unbiased sample from a large city will allow you to speak only about the citizens of that city. It would not be responsible, for instance, if you had data from a sample of adults living in Las Vegas, Nevada, concerning their attitudes towards prostitution to assume that the data were representative of attitudes in other American cities.

Studies that are relatively free of bias are the wheels that allow science to move forward. By allowing us to generalize our findings to similar populations, they improve our knowledge and guide our practice. And while the ideal is to have a bias-free study representative of the population being studied from which we can generalize to similar populations, in reality our data collection methods are often compromised.

I recently attended a conference that brought together researchers and chronically mentally ill who had been studied for four years as part of a special project. The principal investigator, armed with charts and transparencies, began explaining that the battery of eight different psychological tests administered before and after the project began showed no significant changes. He was a little perplexed by this, but took the tack of justifying the findings by saying that at least the chronically mentally ill in the study weren't any worse off. There were a couple of snickers from the audience, and after a few minutes, one of the consumers revealed a possible reason why the psychological tests hadn't found any changes. He said that some in his group had been afraid that if they answered honestly they could ultimately lose their disability checks!

So while the investigators had gone to great lengths to protect their study from known sources of bias by using such procedures as random assignment of consumers to the different intervention groups and sensitive instruments, some of the subjects, acting in their own self-interest, appeared to have biased the findings. I suspect the researchers had not prepared for this turn of events. Who would have? The researchers knew that the information they were collecting from individuals in the study would not be shared with any governmental agencies. They may even have explained this to their subjects. However, to individuals who had much less education and were not informed about what researchers actually do with their data, integrity of the research was less important than preserving the few resources available to them.

Keep this story in mind as you plan your research projects. At each stage of the research process, consider how bias might creep into your study and what you could do to minimize it. If you anticipate problems, you may wish to strengthen your design or change the way you operationalize your dependent variable or the way you collect your data.

Step 6: Analyzing and Interpreting the Data

Once you have finished interviewing or have obtained the information that you sought, you are ready to analyze your data. One of the purposes of analysis is to express the data in a way that is "mentally digestible." It may be easy to present detailed responses from three or four individuals, but when you have more than five responses, full descriptions become very cumbersome. Further, it is awkward, if not impossible, to display information from a large number of persons (e.g., fifty or more) without summarizing the data in some fashion.

Why summarize the data? Which of the statements below do you find easier to understand?

1. The ages of respondents in Group A were: 12, 14, 15, 12, 13, 14, 12, 13, and 14.
2. The average age of respondents in Group A was 13 years.

Basically, we summarize in order to comprehend the information that we have at our command. Your research design should suggest ways that you can summarize, categorize, or organize your data. For instance, if your hypothesis is that women voters are more supportive than men of tax levies that directly benefit persons with low income, your data naturally suggest two divisions: male and female voters. In your analysis, you will compare and contrast the voting behavior of males and females on specific social service election issues.

Analysis is a logical process that begins with looking at the raw data. For example, you will first want to determine how many persons of each sex, race, or age grouping completed your questionnaires. More than likely, you will then order or arrange your data in some fashion. If you looked at several elections in different years, you might array the data by year of the election. You may begin to notice a trend, for example, of women being more supportive of social service issues.

As you categorize your data, you may identify patterns or directions that have been suggested in the literature. However, this is not always the case. Sometimes the data are hard to interpret, and the findings are not intuitively obvious.

Interpreting the data is made easier by comparing your findings with those of other studies. Perhaps your respondents are more conservative or less knowledgeable than those in a study that you found during the literature search. Often it is helpful to brainstorm with others as to what could account for the findings that you obtained. Then, look for evidence to support these findings.

Occasionally, research findings can be portrayed in the form of pie or bar charts. Sometimes maps can be shaded to indicate high or low densities of one variable or another. These visual presentations are useful for helping others understand the results of your study. However, statistical methods may also be needed to determine if there is a statistically significant difference between two or more groups. Statistics aid in the interpretation of data. With the advent of computer technology, the computation of statistical tests has become relatively easy.

Chapter 9 presents most of the statistics that you'll need to know to begin to analyze your data. That chapter will present a quick overview of descriptive (e.g., measures of central tendency like mean and median) and inferential statistics (e.g., t-tests and one-way analysis of variance). Descriptive statistics help us understand how much our variables vary (like the range of years between the oldest and youngest participant). Inferential statistics are used to test hypotheses about differences between groups and to aid us in understanding the probabilities of obtaining our results by chance.

There is one statistic, however, that we need to become familiar with prior to chapter 9. A **correlation coefficient** (sometimes expressed as r) is a statistic that helps us understand relationships between two variables. This relationship is summarized as a numerical value that ranges between − 1.00 and + 1.00. For example, test grades in this research course may have a strong positive relationship (.50 or higher) to the amount of time students spend studying. With this correlation coefficient, we would predict that as students' studying time increased, their test grades would improve. If a negative correlation (e.g., − .40) had been obtained, this would indicate the ludicrous situation where test grades deteriorate the more students study.

Just because two variables are correlated, this does not mean that one variable caused the other. Not long ago I read about a study that found that nearsightedness was correlated with high intelligence. This study found that persons who do well on intelligence tests tend to be nearsighted. This does not mean, however, that all nearsighted persons are intelligent or that one could improve one's I.Q. by becoming nearsighted.

Step 7: Writing the Report

Once the data have been collected and analyzed, the final step is preparing your findings in such a way that they can be made available to others. There may be times when a memorandum to your supervisor or director summarizing the results of your study will be adequate. If you received funding for the research, it is very likely that you will be required to write a report of your findings. If what you found was especially interesting, you may want to submit your findings to a professional journal. Journals, even those in different fields, tend to be organized in the same format as research reports.

The first part of a research report, the Introduction, puts the research question or hypothesis in context (a description of the extent or severity of the problem, the length of time it has been a problem, what is generally known or believed about the problem) and reviews the important studies found in the literature.

The next section, Methods, is an explanation of the research methodology—how the data were collected, which variables were included and how they were operationalized, and who the subjects were, their characteristics, and how they were recruited. Enough information should be presented so that others can follow what you did and replicate the study.

The third section of the research report presents what was actually learned from the study. Tables and graphs may be employed to visually demonstrate differences and to help with comparisons. Statistical tests may be used.

Finally, the Discussion section addresses the implications of your findings, speculates why those particular results were obtained, and suggests how future research in this area might be conducted.

It almost goes without saying that many fine research reports are filed away or relegated to dusty shelves because the social work investigators did not exert a little extra effort and prepare the report for publication in a journal or as a paper for a professional symposium. In order to rectify this situation, the last chapter of this text will focus on writing the research report.

Social Work Research and Practice

While it is often convenient to think of social work practice and research as completely separate and sharply contrasting with each other, they both share a logical problem-solving process. A number of social work educators have discussed the similarities between the two (Fischer, 1983; Karger, 1983; Rosen and Proctor, 1978). Both Grinnell (1985) and Powers, Meenaghan, and Toomey (1985) have thoroughly discussed the commonalties in the problem-solving processes used by researchers and practitioners in their research texts. Powers et al. (1985, p. 50) have correctly noted:

Much of what the practitioner does, or ought to do, in the process of solving problems in practice is essentially the same as what the researcher does, or ought to do, in the process of solving problems in science—frame questions for practice, collect and/or access data, posit possible meaning, and test effects of intervention.

We can briefly summarize the similarities between the research process and the task-centered or problem-solving process used by social workers as follows:

RESEARCH PROCESS	TASK-CENTERED PROCESS
Starts with a problem, question, or hypothesis	Starts with a client's problem
Review of the literature	History-taking, identification of resources, strengths, networks
Development of research and operationalization of variables	Negotiate a contract design
Data collection	Begin intervention
Data analysis	Evaluation of intervention
Final report	Termination

Look for the areas of overlap between research and practice, and use these to further your understanding and competencies in both. The similarities in the problem-solving process used in social work research and practice make it one generic process (Fischer, 1981).

The research process is no more complicated than a good problem-solving model that is used every day by most social workers in practice. The research process is not an artificial contrivance to make life difficult for you; it is an orderly and logical process that is familiar to all social workers.

Questions for Class Discussion

1. Practice developing hypotheses and research questions on the following list of topics:
   a. alcoholism
   b. effective psychotherapy
   c. fear of open spaces
   d. depression
   e. good students
   f. social drinkers
   g. racist attitudes
   h. heavy cigarette smokers
2. Take a hypothesis or research question from question 1 and convert it into a null hypothesis.
3. Identify as many theories used by social work practitioners as you can.

4. Identify the dependent variables in the following studies:
   a. Relapse in Alcoholism: New Perspectives
   b. Repeat Pregnancies among Unmarried Teen Parents
   c. Financial Independence Achieved by AFDC Mothers Receiving Intensive Case Management
   d. Do All-Nighters Pay Off? An Examination of Test Scores and Cram-studying Techniques in First Year College Students
   e. Weight Gain in a Sample of Anorexics Receiving Cognitive Therapy
5. Operationally define a "bad marriage" so that a clinical social worker could locate couples who might benefit from a new twelve-week intervention designed to help those with troubled marriages.
6. Operationally define each of the following:
   a. A humorous television program.
   b. An educational television program.
   c. An offensive television program.
7. Examine "Attitudes About Research Courses" in the appendix and discuss how many different scales it contains.
8. Make up examples of how bias could affect a study.
9. Look around the classroom. In how many different ways do your classmates vary? Make a list of as many different independent variables as may be represented by the diversity of characteristics found among your classmates.

Mini-Projects for Experiencing Research Firsthand

1. Select a social problem and state it clearly.
   a. Frame either a research question or a hypothesis suggested by what you know or would like to know about the social problem.
   b. What is the dependent variable?
   c. What data would you need to collect in order to test your hypothesis? Who would be your subjects?
   d. What independent variables would help you analyze and understand your findings? List them.
   e. Operationally define your dependent variable.
2. Select a social problem and locate relevant abstracts on the same subject using *Social Work Abstracts*.
3. Refer to Corcoran and Fischer's (1987) *Measures for Clinical Practice*, Robinson and Shaver's (1973) *Measures of Social Psychological Attitudes*, or McDowell and Newell's (1987) *Measuring Health: A Guide to Rating Scales and Questionnaires*. Try

to find a scale that you could use in planning some future research. As you look at the instrument you have chosen, make a list of the questions that occur to you when you think about employing such an instrument for research or evaluation purposes. Write a brief description of the population that will be the subjects of your study. What hypothesis will you test? What will the instrument tell you?

4. Sue Fictitious is a manager of an intake unit in a state agency responsible for investigating complaints of child abuse and neglect. She also is a part-time MSW student. One day, while in the library, she came across an article in a professional journal describing the Child Abuse Potential Inventory. She began to think of applications—ways in which her office might use the instrument to identify adults who are potential abusers.

   a. What hypotheses would interest you if you were Sue?

   b. Who would be your subjects?

   c. What personal or independent variables would you like to include?

5. Browse through research articles in a professional journal until you find one where the operational definition for the dependent variable is clearly stated. In an accompanying brief paragraph, state the limitations and advantages of defining the dependent variable in this way.

Resources and References

Beasley, D. (1988). *How to Use a Research Library*. New York: Oxford University Press.

Bergman, A. et al. (1993). High-risk indicators for family involvement in social work in health care: A review of the literature. *Social Work*, 38(3), 281–288.

Berrick, J.D. and Barth, R.P. (1992) Child sexual abuse prevention: Research review and recommendations. *Social Work Research and Abstracts*, 28(4), 6–15.

Brodsky, S.L. and Smitherman, H.O. (1983). *Handbook of Scales for Research in Crime and Delinquency*. New York: Plenum Press.

Corcoran, K. and Fischer, J. (1987). *Measures for Clinical Practice*. New York: Free Press.

Derogatis, L.R. (1983). *SCL-90-R: Administration, Scoring and Procedures Manual: II. For the Revised Version*. Towson, MD: Clinical Psychometric Research.

Epstein, L. (1980). *Helping People: The Task-centered Approach*. St. Louis, MO: Mosby.

First, R.J., Roth, D., and Arewa, B.D. (1988). Homelessness: Understanding the dimensions of the problem for minorities. *Social Work*, 33(2), 120–124.

Fischer, J. (1981). New and emerging methods of direct practice: The revolution in social work. In N. Gilbert and H. Specht (Eds.), *Handbook of the Social Services*. Englewood Cliffs, NJ: Prentice-Hall.

Fischer, J. (1983). Evaluations of social work effectiveness: Is positive evidence always good evidence? *Social Work*, 28, 74–77.

Gelles, R.J. (1989). Child abuse and violence in single-parent families: Parent absence and economic deprivation. *American Journal of Orthopsychiatry*, 59(4), 492–501.

Gilgun, J.F. (1992). Hypothesis generation in social work research. *Journal of Social Service Research*, 15(3/4), 113–35.

Grief, G.L. and Hegar, R.L. (1992). Impact on children of abduction by a parent: A review of the literature. *American Journal of Orthopsychiatry*, 62(4) 599–604.

Grinnell, R.M. (1985). *Social Work Research and Evaluation*. Itasca, IL: Peacock.

Hillard, J.M. (1984). *Where to Find What: A Handbook to Reference Service*. Metuchen, NJ: Scarecrow Press.

Hudson, W.W. (1978). Notes for practice: First axioms of treatment. *Social Work*, 23(1), 65–66.

Hudson, W.W. (1982). *The Clinical Measurement Package*. Homewood, IL: Dorsey.

Karger, H.J. (1983). Science, research and social work: Who controls the profession? *Social Work*, 28, 200–205.

Kohn, P.M. and Smart, R.G. (1984). The impact of television advertising on alcohol consumption: An experiment. *Journal of Studies on Alcohol*, 45(4), 295–301.

Leedy, P.D. (1974). *Practical Research: Planning and Design*. New York: Macmillan.

McDowell, I. and Newell, C. (1987). *Measuring Health: A Guide to Rating Scales and Questionnaires*. London: Oxford University Press.

Mendelsohn, H.N. (1987). *A Guide to Information Sources for Social Work and the Human Services*. Phoenix, AZ: Oryx Press.

Milner, J.S. (1986). *The Child Abuse Potential Inventory: Manual*. Webster, NC: Psytec Corp.

Munson, C. (1983). *An Introduction to Clinical Social Work Supervision*. New York: Haworth Press.

Nurius, P.S. and Hudson, W.W. (1993). *Human Services Practice, Evaluation, and Computers*. Pacific Grove, CA: Brooks/Cole.

Piliavin, I., Sosin, M., Westerfelt, A.H., and Matsueda, R.L. (1993). The duration of homeless careers: An exploratory study. *Social Service Review*, 67(4), 576–598.

Polansky, N.A. (1986). There is nothing so practical as a good theory. *Child Welfare*, 65(1), 3–15.

Powers, G.T., Meenaghan, T.M., and Toomey, B.G. (1985). *Practice Focused*

Research: Integrating Human Service Practice and Research. Englewood Cliffs, NJ: Prentice-Hall.

Reid, W.J. (1978). *The Task-centered System.* New York: Columbia University Press.

Robertson, J.F. (1989). A tool for assessing alcohol misuse in adolescence. *Social Work*, 34(1), 39–44.

Robinson, J.P. and Shaver, P.R. (1973). *Measures of Social Psychological Attitudes.* Institute for Social Research. University of Michigan, Ann Arbor.

Rosen, A. and Proctor, E.K. (1978). Specifying the treatment process: The basis for effectiveness research. *Journal of Social Service Research, 2,* 25–26.

Rosenberg, M. (1965). *Society and the Adolescent Self-Image.* Princeton, NJ: Princeton University Press.

Royse, D. (1987). Homelessness among trash pickers. *Psychological Reports,* 60, 808–810.

Royse, D. and Rompf, E.L. (1992). Math anxiety: A comparison of social work and non-social work students. *Journal of Social Work Education,* 28(3), 270–277.

Seltzer, M.M. and Bloksberg, L.M. (1987). Permanency planning and its effect on foster children: A review of the literature. *Social Work,* 32(1), 65–68.

Solkoff, N. (1992). Children of survivors of the Nazi Holocaust: A critical review of the literature. *American Journal of Orthopsychiatry,* 62(3), 342–358.

Vander Mey, B.J. and Neff, R.L. (1986). *Incest as Child Abuse: Research and Applications.* New York; Praeger.

Wiehe, V. (1986). Empathy and Locus of Control in Child Abusers. *Journal of Social Service Research,* 9(2,3), 17–30.

3
Single System Designs

Imagine my dilemma: The social work department of a Veterans Affairs (VA) hospital invited me to speak to them. They wanted me, over the course of three afternoon sessions (spaced a week apart) to refresh their knowledge of research—to remind them of everything that they needed to know. I was supposed to help them remember what they had forgotten and teach them what they had never learned, preparing them to meet the hospital's new emphasis on accountability and evaluation. Although I was flattered that they had confidence in my ability to condense possibly more than a semester's course into six hours of instruction, I had to think long and hard about where to start and what content to give them. Most of the social workers had been out of school for fifteen years or longer. What did they know? What would they be likely to retain and use after I left? Where should I start?

I started with single system designs. This tool can be used even with very little research expertise. In fact, these designs are attractive to social workers because they are so easy to use and understand, even with a limited understanding of research methodology. Single system designs provide practitioners with immediate, inexpensive, and practical feedback on whether their clients have improved.

Unlike the quantitative approaches that we will study later that involve groups of clients and compel us to understand the "average" client, single system designs focus on an individual client and his or her situation. Single system designs are easiest to explain when the client has a specific behavior, like binge eating, that will be the focus of intervention. However, social work practitioners are not limited to applying these designs only to individual clients. Single system designs can be used to evaluate the progress being made by a community, an organization, a family, or even a couple receiving marital counseling.

Advocates of single system designs argue that information about specific clients is often obscured in studies where clients are grouped together, that one might learn little about an individual client—perhaps only whether a client did better or worse than average. Single system designs "personalize" the research by looking at a client's particular behavior over time. Before we learn how to develop single system designs (also known as N = 1 research, single case evaluation, case studies, and single subject designs) for our clients, let's first consider a little of the history about them.

The Origin of Single System Designs

The study of individual cases has long been a part of the richness of the social sciences. Thomas (1978) noted that for over a century case studies have been conducted in behavioral research. Bromley (1986) has stated that, in fact, the case study method goes back even further, to "remote origins in human social history" (p. 39). Prior to the development of statistics for group comparisons, research in the social sciences consisted almost entirely of descriptive case studies and reflections upon them. Case studies were useful for illustrating to one's colleagues and students how problems requiring remedial action could be approached or solved with specific theories or interventions.

Although these studies seldom employed any quantification of dependent variables, a number of important discoveries have come, not from the use of large groups of subjects commonly associated with social science research, but from the observations of single individuals. Several examples will serve to demonstrate this. Using nonsense syllables and himself as the subject, Ebbinghaus made major discoveries regarding principles of human learning. (We learn more efficiently in the morning than in the evening, for instance.) Pavlov's basic findings were obtained from single organisms and later reproduced (replicated) with other organisms (Hersen and Barlow, 1976). Piaget's theories derived from observations of his own children. From Freud's discussion of specific cases to eleven-month-old little Albert becoming conditioned to fear a white rat, generalizations from single subjects have played significant roles in helping us understand human behavior.

50

Individual case studies have appeared with some frequency all through the social science literature (Dukes, 1965), and case examples or vignettes of cases are not uncommon today in medical and other journals, such as the *American Journal of Psychiatry, Hospital and Community Psychiatry,* the *Journal of Nervous and Mental Diseases,* and in social work journals such as *Families in Society* and the *Clinical Social Work Journal.* However, case studies have tended to vary greatly in their format, content, and organization. As statistical tests of comparison were developed and widely accepted, case studies fell out of favor with "sophisticated" researchers in the social sciences. This led to an era when research with single subjects was viewed by many as being elementary and somewhat inferior. The use of control groups and group statistical comparisons has now become firmly established in the social sciences, and the objective or quantitative methods of measurement used with these group studies have led to changes among those conducting case studies.

The emergence of single system designs in the 1960s and 1970s has been attributed to their use by B. F. Skinner and other practitioners of behavior modification (Zimbalist, 1983; Kazdin, 1982). With a focus on a specific target behavior, single system designs were well-suited for practitioners interested in demonstrating that their interventions were effective. Unlike the descriptive case studies of prior years, which relied heavily upon subjective assessments of change, single system studies today often use objective measures to document that change has occurred. In fact, they may be very quantitative in appearance, and do not resemble the heavily narrative case studies of previous years except for the fact that they focus on one individual.

Single system designs were developed primarily in response to dissatisfaction with group research designs for clinical practice situations (Nelsen, 1988). Single system designs today provide a needed alternative to the group research designs usually associated with the conduct of research in the social sciences.

Single System Designs and Practice

Single system designs have been said to bridge the gap between research and practice (Dean and Reinherz, 1986). How is this possible? Imagine for a moment that it is sometime in the future. You have made it through the social work program and are now employed as a therapist in a mental health agency. Your next appointment is a college student in her twenties. As she explains why she has sought counseling, you begin to see a pattern of symptoms suggestive of depression. You have worked with depressed persons before and feel that you can work with this woman. Go forward in time another ten weeks. The young woman is now interested in terminating treatment. How would you determine whether your counseling was successful? Would you calculate the number of times she smiled during your last several sessions? Would her body posture indicate her level of depression? Her plans for the future? While you might have an intuition that you had helped her, could you empirically document this for a supervisor or program director? How would you go about evaluating your own practice?

This example of the depressed young woman comes from Berlin's (1983) description of a practitioner involved in both research and practice with the same client. In her article, Berlin describes how a single system design was employed by the practitioner to evaluate intervention with a twenty-two-year-old part-time graduate student with overwhelming feelings of sadness and despair.

Because the client's symptoms suggested depression, the therapist asked the client to complete a short, twenty-item standardized scale (the CES-D) that measured depression. The client scored forty-five on this scale, suggesting that she was clinically depressed. Treatment goals were then developed within the context of trying to understand the client's despair. Berlin was able to track the client's progress by administering the CES-D each time she met with the client. When one views these test results on a graph over the several weeks of treatment, it is easy to see that the client's level of depression fell dramatically during this time and remained low one month after termination. Figure 3.1 demonstrates this visually in the graph used by Berlin.

Even a cursory glimpse at this graph or at the others in this chapter will convince you that single system graphs are intuitively obvious and easy to comprehend. This is the essence of single system designs—the visual presentation of a client's progress.

A Closer Look at the Single System Design

If you look closely at figure 3.1, the several component parts needed for a single subject design can be detected. Note that a single **target behavior** (the dependent variable) was identified. In this instance, the problem was the client's depression, and the practitioner's interventions were oriented toward reducing that depression. Of course, depression may manifest itself in many forms. Berlin chose an objective instrument to measure the level of depression being experienced by the client. It would also have been possible to have monitored improvement with behavioral measures of depression, depending upon

FIGURE 3.1: A Graph from a Single System Study

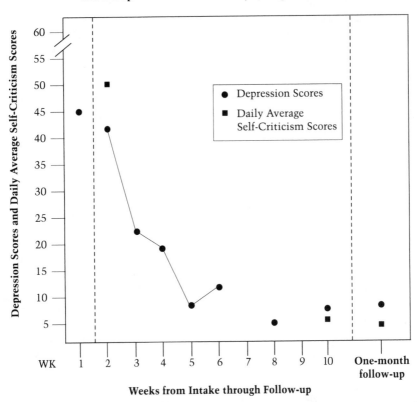

CES-D Depression Scores and Daily Average Self-Criticism Scores

Source: Berlin, S. (1983). Single-case evaluation: Another version. *Social Work Research and Abstracts*, 19(1), 9. © National Association of Social Workers, Inc. Reprinted with permission.

the client's presentation of the problem and the worker's assessment. The client may have had crying spells, restless sleep, poor appetite, and loneliness. The selection of a target behavior, such as frequent crying spells, could have been used had there been no objective instrument available for detecting changes in the depression.

Note that no complicated statistical procedures were used—just a simple graph to record (with repeated measurements) the client's improvement over time. (Although it is possible to use statistical procedures to check for statistically significant differences in improvement, this is not a requirement or a necessity for most single system designs.) The arrangement of the data chronologically on the graph is easy to interpret and follows from the research design. Ideally, data are collected before the intervention begins. The preinterventive data are called the **baseline** and allow for comparisons to be made with the behavior during and after intervention.

Retrospective (or reconstructed) baselines are estimates of the severity of a problem based upon memory, or in some instances upon prior data that already exist, such as a report card indicating grades or absences from school. Concurrent baselines are measurements of the problem that are begun sometime after intake assessment.

Starting a Single System Study

The first step in developing a single system study is to choose a behavior to monitor. This may be a difficult decision, but sometimes it is obvious which behavior needs to be targeted: If you have a client who has been arrested for driving while intoxicated and this is the second arrest in six months, it is clear that you have a client who needs to change his or her drinking behavior. Similarly, it would be apparent that a child with school phobia needs to decrease the number of days absent from school. Some clients need to demonstrate greater assertiveness; others need to learn to handle their destructive anger. Generally speaking, you will be working with clients to either increase or decrease certain behaviors. However, there can be as many as five different ways to think about how to modify behavior. Sundel and Sundel (1993) have suggested that we can help the client: (1) acquire a behavior; (2) increase the strength or frequency of a behavior; (3) maintain a behavior; or (4) decrease a behavior.

There will not be one target behavior that can be selected for all clients. Behling and Merves (1984) have provided fifty suggestions of behaviors that can be monitored (e.g., increasing positive interaction with co-workers, reducing fear of being alone, increasing positive use of time, maintaining therapy). Behaviors to be monitored in a single system study must necessarily follow from the treatment plan prepared for that individual client. Even though most social workers are not behaviorists, and the goals for their clients are fairly global or long-range, single system designs can be used in nonbehavioral treatment providing that the client's final goals can be stated in measurable terms (Nelsen, 1981).

The selection of the appropriate problem to be influenced by the intervention is obviously very important. When choosing a target behavior, there are several considerations that should be kept in mind:

1. *Target behaviors should come from the client.* As Hepworth and Larsen (1986) have noted: "the presenting problem . . . is the focal point of clients' motivation for seeking help" (p. 173). To select problems that are not attuned to clients' perceptions of their problems risks premature termination. Although some clients may have a secret agenda for seeking help or other problems that may be revealed after a trusting relationship has been established, the best place to start is with the problem the client has identified as being most significant. This may require some prioritizing of the client's problems.

Along this line, it may be helpful to use the following criteria to help rank the problems mentioned by clients: (1) problems that are the most immediate expressed concern of the client; (2) problems that have the most negative consequence for the client, significant others, or society if not handled immediately; (3) problems that have the highest probability of being corrected quickly, thus providing an experience of success; and (4) problems that require handling before other problems can be dealt with (Sundel and Sundel, 1993). Ideally, there should be mutual agreement between the social worker and the client regarding the major concern and focus of the intervention.

2. *Vaguely stated problems are difficult to measure.* Select behaviors that are concrete and observable. Avoid any behavior that might be difficult to detect or about which there might be disagreement as to whether it was happening or not (e.g., Johnnie says his parents don't respect his individuality). Choose behaviors that can be counted, observed, or quantified. You may have to help your client move from an ambiguous description of the problem to a more precise definition. For instance, "nervousness" is a vague complaint, but associated with it may be several observable behaviors such as nail biting, overeating, stuttering, episodes of gastro-intestinal attacks, or excessive use of antacids, that could be used as surrogate measures of the nervousness. One could count the number of antacids consumed in a day, the number of stuttering episodes, or the number of calories ingested per day. Whenever possible, target behaviors should be so well defined that others would have little difficulty in observing or recording them.

Start with the presenting problem, and then explore how that problem manifests itself. Let's say that a woman tells you that her husband doesn't respect her. You cannot use "lack of respect" as a target behavior, because the term is too broad and not immediately associated with any specific behaviors. You need to find how this problem is expressed or detected by the client. What specific behaviors illustrate the problem of lack of respect? It could mean that her husband walks away while she is talking. It might seem that he is always late for supper. You want to identify the actions that indicate to the woman that her husband does not respect her. From these specific behaviors, choose one or two to focus on during the intervention.

In Berlin's example, a short standardized instrument was available for use. What happens if the therapist knows of no instrument suitable for measuring a problem like depression, anxiety, or other vaguely stated concerns? The therapist has only two choices: review the literature and attempt to find such an instrument or work without an instrument and select specific target behaviors suggested by the client's particular set of problems.

For instance, suppose a married couple comes to you because they are arguing almost daily. They are interested in saving their marriage; however, both are assertive, strong-willed individuals. The obvious target behavior is the number of arguments that they have. What led the couple to therapy? The wife (who happens to be a bookkeeper) kept a record of the number of arguments that the couple had over the past fourteen days. The frequency of these arguments was disturbing to both of them, and they agreed to seek help.

In this instance, the baseline was readily available to the therapist, and the couple were in agreement that they wanted to reduce the number of arguments that had been occurring. While an instrument would not be needed, one that measured marital satisfaction (Hudson, 1982) could be used if it were known to the therapist. If the marital counseling is successful, then it is reasonable to assume that a graph illustrating the number of arguments would show fewer arguments after intervention than during the baseline period.

Sometimes clients describe problems like fear of dying or loneliness that seem to be more of a mental state, more attitudinal than behavioral. In instances like these, you may want to consult Corcoran and Fischer's (1987) *Measures for Clinical Practice* to obtain scales to objectively measure their death anxiety or loneliness. However, even these conditions are likely to be associated with problem behaviors. The person who is afraid of dying may be having panic attacks or insomnia or be unable to concentrate at work or school. The individual who is experiencing loneliness may need to change introverted, reclusive behaviors and increase social contacts by joining clubs, bowling leagues, co-ed volleyball teams, hobby groups, and so on. As a practitioner you have quite a choice of what behaviors to monitor and how to monitor improvement. The challenge is always to operationalize so specifically that there is little doubt when change or improvement is occurring.

Not only will vaguely stated problems create difficulties when you attempt to measure them, but so can rather specific events (e.g., hearing voices or having delusions) if your client doesn't always report these and if they are not observable by others. Certainly, clients are able to self-report on behaviors or problems that are not noticeable to others, but I would not select these for measurement with a single system design unless the client was strongly motivated to alleviate the problem and could be trusted to report with accuracy. The easiest problems to measure are those that are easily recognized by others and repetitive. (For instance, I once heard of a client in a residential treatment program who took ten or more showers a day. It could be difficult to monitor growth in the amount of consideration shown for the other residents, unless you associated this improvement with the number of showers taken each day.)

Frequency of an event is not the only way of measuring problem behavior like a couple's arguments. In a different situation the therapist might have suggested that the length (or duration) of the arguments be monitored.

FIGURE 3.2: Incomplete Single System Graph

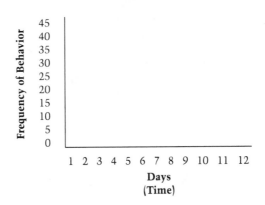

Or the intensity (magnitude) of the arguments might have been recorded. Minor verbal disagreements might not be counted; only those of the foot-stomping, door-slamming variety would qualify. Residents of a group home who live with someone showering ten times a day might be just as unhappy if "Mr. Clean" took fewer showers but stayed in thirty-five minutes each time, using up all the hot water.

The practitioner has quite a bit of freedom in choosing what to measure, how to measure, and even who should do the recording. However, the target behavior should always suggest itself from the client's description of the problem. The behavior should be an activity that a client agrees is important to count or record. Clients should be able to see how change in the target behavior contributes to improving their problem situation.

3. *Target behaviors are monitored over time.* Graphs are useful tools to portray changes in behavior. Graphs need not be drawn on engineering or graph paper; you can draw vertical and horizontal lines that intersect at a right angle and calibrate or demarcate the lines in a way that has meaning and indicates how much of the activity is occurring during the observation period (See figure 3.2).

On the vertical line (or axis), plot the number of times (frequency) the target behavior occurs. You need to have a rough idea how often the behavior is occurring in order to devise a scale to show its pattern.

For instance, if little Pablo misses his morning bus three times in one week, the vertical axis should be constructed to record the lowest and greatest number of these incidents. It is likely that he couldn't miss his bus more than five mornings a week, so the range would be 0 to 5.

Some thought needs to go into the selection of the behavior or the problem being counted on the vertical axis. Because missing a bus might be a matter of oversleeping, you might want to target the number of times that little Pablo gets to bed on time the night before. Or, if he is a little older and sets his own alarm clock, the number of times that he oversleeps. Both of these could be legitimate target behaviors for intervention.

Notice the emphasis on counting behaviors. It would be less useful to chart the actual times (e.g., 7:04 A.M.) that little Pablo actually awakens since his problem might be one of procrastination and not oversleeping. On the other hand, if his difficulty is getting to bed on time, the vertical axis might be constructed to show the number of minutes *past his bedtime* that he is late each evening. Counting intervals of time such as minutes past bedtime and hours spent doing homework are also appropriate for the vertical axis.

The horizontal line is used to portray the behavior as it occurs over time. Whether you decide to use hours, days, or weeks as the unit of time is dependent upon the behavior itself. If you were working with a twelve-year-old who was having stomachaches because of school phobia and this tended to happen once a day (ten minutes before the school bus arrived), it would be better to count the number of times a week that the stomachaches occurred than to keep hourly records. A baseline graph of the stomachaches in a month prior to the intervention might resemble the one in figure 3.3.

This graph shows that the child had stomach problems five times (corresponding to the five school days) the first week that a record was kept, five times the second and fourth weeks, but only four times in the third week when there was a school holiday because of snow. In this example, we know that the symptoms are occurring every schoolday. The child missed having a stomachache only once on a schoolday during a twenty-eight-day period. This is a well-established or *stable pattern* of behavior. If intervention is effective, a pattern of improvement will be readily observable. Contrast this with a target behavior that is unpredictable (where there is no discernible pattern). Suppose that the child had one stomachache the first week, none the second week, five stomachaches during the third week, and none during the fourth week. This would be an erratic pattern. In this case, we might want a longer baseline to help us understand what is going on. Instead of school phobia, the child's stomach problems might be due to food allergies that are triggered by specific foods that are not eaten every week.

It is difficult to provide a rule about how long the baseline period should be. Much depends on how often the behavior is occurring and how stable this pattern is. A behavior that occurs relatively infrequently probably is not a useful behavior to choose for monitoring because it will be hard to see any patterns. Similarly, behavior that varies a great deal will not make a good target behavior. Choose a behavior that is fairly dependable in its occurrence. There can be some variation in the frequency of the behavior, but this variation should not have "wild swings." It would be ridiculous to monitor a behavior that occurred twenty times in one day and then did not occur at all during a three week observation period. Stable patterns are sometimes evident by the sixth or seventh observation period. However, the length of the baseline must be tempered by the availability of data and concern for not unduly delaying intervention.

You don't have to wait five or six weeks before you can begin interven-

---

FIGURE 3.3: An Example of Developing a Baseline

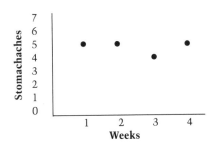

tion. Suppose a mother comes to you because she is concerned that her five-year-old is still wetting the bed. You ask, "About how often does this happen?" If the mother says, "About every night" or "Almost every night," then the baseline is established and you can begin with the assumption that bed wetting is occurring about thirty times a month. Even if it is actually happening only twenty-seven or twenty-five times a month, the obvious goal is to decrease these incidents to zero times a month.

As a rule, it is necessary to document the behavior prior to intervention (the baseline) only long enough that you can understand how often it occurs, on average. Remember, the purpose of the baseline is to provide the data necessary for "before and after" comparisons.

Baseline data can come from various sources. You might find that there is ample reference to the occurrence of the target behavior in progress notes, the client may have kept some informal records or have a good memory, or there may be official records (e.g., elementary school absences). In our society, documentation is often readily available. A baseline for a spouse whose drinking behavior results in days missed from work, for example, might be obtained by looking at paycheck stubs. In some instances, clients can keep logs or self-report on the occurrence of the target behavior. In other situations, someone else will need to monitor the behavior. These are individually determined by a knowledge of the client's abilities and situation.

The argument for using existing records or data for the baseline is that the very act of counting or measuring a behavior during the baseline phase may begin to change the client's behavior (especially if the client is self-reporting and motivated to improve) even before the intervention is implemented. Self-reporting, though generally regarded as reliable, does have a reactive effect in that clients' behavior might change when they know they are being observed. (See Kopp, 1988, for a thorough discussion of the self-monitoring literature.) Needless to say, self-monitoring data will give a false picture if the client is motivated to misrepresent the extent or severity of the problem.

As can be seen in the graph in figure 3.4, the behavior during the base-

---

FIGURE 3.4: Essential Components of a Single Subject Design

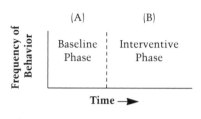

line period is usually separated from the behavior during the intervention phase by a vertical dotted line.

4. *The last step in developing a single system study is selecting a design.* Of the many single system designs from which to choose, only a few of those judged to be the most useful to practitioners are presented here. As you read the balance of this chapter, you may find yourself liking some designs because you feel that you could comfortably use them. Other designs may strike you as impractical (or worse) because they seem more suited for experimental labs and require greater control over the client system than you feel that you have or ought to have. One design (the AB) is likely to meet most of your needs. But other designs may be more appropriate for specific cases or when you want greater assurance that it was your intervention that had the desired effect.

The Case Study or B Design

The case study (which has already been briefly discussed) is the design most familiar to students because it is used frequently in the social sciences. Case studies are sometimes called uncontrolled case studies because they lack baseline measures and use anecdotal information rather than objective measures of the target behavior. These designs are therefore seriously limited in that they do not permit conclusions that the intervention caused the change in the client's behavior. (There may have been other forces or influences at work in addition to the intervention.)

However, these designs are simple to conceptualize, don't require preplanning, and are possible to use once intervention has begun. In spite of their limitations, they are able to show that the client has made progress. (It is just that they can't rule out competing explanations.)

The practitioner begins keeping records with the beginning of intervention regarding how the client changes or improves. No attempt is made to compare the behavior at the end of the intervention with its baseline (because there was none). This design can be used with any theoretical orientation, and its value is the feedback it provides. For the reasons previously discussed—lack of systematization, no baseline measures or objective measurement, and little control of the treatment variable (e.g., the intervention may involve several simultaneous procedures)—this is a weak design that does not allow confidence in drawing conclusions about the effect of the intervention.

Case studies generally are not regarded as formal research strategies (Yin, 1989). A good example is the case described by Ashley Montagu (1971) in his book *The Elephant Man: A Study in Human Dignity*. A case study is interesting to read and to discuss because of the rich description it provides about generally rare or uncommon occurrences. As a research strategy, its weakness comes from the fact that there is no basis for comparison. However, we can take an interesting case and construct a basis for comparison. This approach is discussed next.

The AB Design ✳

The basic **AB** design is the "workhorse" of the single system designs and the one most often used by beginning social work practitioners and researchers (Nelsen, 1988, p.367). There are two main features to this design: observation of the behavior prior to treatment (the baseline) and observation of the behavior after intervention has begun. The **A** portion of the design is the baseline measurement (e.g., administration of an instrument at intake to measure depression). The **B** part of the design is the data collected during the treatment phase. Because of its simplicity, the **AB** design is virtually unlimited in its applicability in social work. This is perhaps its greatest strength. It reveals changes in behavior—if they occur. Unfortunately, changes in behavior that are detected with this design do not "prove" that the intervention was responsible. There could be alternative explanations such as the occurrence of other events during intervention (e.g., leaving a stressful job, the birth of a child, over-the-fence counseling by a neighbor, or maturation of the client) for changes in the client's behavior. These alternative or rival explanations are difficult to rule out with the basic **AB** design. Most practitioners, however, would be happy with the client's success and would not worry about alternative explanations. While the **AB** design may not adequately control for competing explanations, it provides a useful way of examining whether there has been an improvement since intervention began.

FIGURE 3.5: Illustration of an *AB* Design Graph

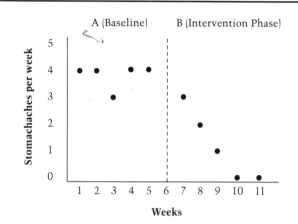

Weeks

The ABA and ABAB Designs

These two designs are sometimes called withdrawal, reversal, or experimental single system designs because they allow the client's behavior to return to its preinterventive level (the baseline condition) in order to show that the intervention was responsible for the observed effect on the target behavior. These designs are concerned with whether the effect of the intervention will continue or be maintained. After the intervention (**B**) has been completed or substantially delivered, treatment is withdrawn or stopped, and the target problem is monitored to see what direction it takes.

The second (**A**) phase in an **ABA** design is like the first **A** phase in that behavior is recorded during a period of no intervention. This is not to suggest that you as a practitioner should purposely withdraw treatment for "research" purposes; that would be an unethical practice. The second **A** phase could legitimately come about following termination (Berlin mailed a depression scale to the client as a follow-up measure one month after treatment. Look back to figure 3.1 for an example of this graph).

Because of practice-related concerns about ending client contact during a nonintervention phase, Bloom and Fischer (1982) do not recommend this design for most practice situations. However, if the second **A** phase comes about as a follow-up to intervention, or for other therapeutically sound reasons, this design might be useful and ought not be overlooked.

Each phase of the classical single system design (**AB**) is repeated twice in the **ABAB** design. As in the **ABA** design, treatment is withdrawn or removed in the second baseline (**A** phase) in order to see if the target behavior will return to its original level (prior to intervention). There may be valid reasons for a second period of nonintervention, both practical—for example, the therapist's vacation—and therapeutic—for example, a trial period of three weeks between appointments to wean a "dependent" client away from intervention. After the second baseline period, the treatment is reintroduced. Unlike the **ABA** design, the study ends during an intervention phase, which makes it more appealing from an ethical standpoint.

Because the client serves as his or her own control, the **ABAB** design is an experimental design and provides some assurance that the intervention actually was responsible for any changes in behavior. In this sense, the **ABAB** design is a stronger and more powerful design than the **AB** and **ABA** designs. If the same effects are shown during the second **AB** (replication) phase, then there is less likelihood that outside influences (alternative explanations) were responsible. The **ABAB** is an "ideal" design for those who are interested in contributing to our knowledge base by experimentally demonstrating that some intervention is effective—especially if they want to show generality by replicating the treatment with other clients (Howe, 1974).

However, use of the **ABAB** design is not always practical. In fact, if the first treatment phase reduced the behavior to acceptable levels for the client and others concerned, it is likely that all involved persons would feel that the intervention was a success. Termination would occur, and the therapist would be given a new client to add to his or her caseload. There would be little reason to introduce intervention again unless the client made another request. In fact, the more successful the intervention, the less likely it will be that the behavior would return to its initial baseline (**A**) level.

The **ABAB** design may not feel comfortable to many practitioners because they are painfully aware of the shortage of staff or the long lists of clients patiently waiting for help with their problems. Even though the second baseline could come about naturally (vacations, hospitalizations, etc.), the **ABAB** design may still seem excessive or a luxury unavailable to many practitioners.

The **ABAB** design is best thought of as a design to be used for knowledge-building. It is a design that enables thorough testing of an intervention and reduction of alternative explanations for the client's improvement. This design is what you would use if you were sure that a given intervention worked and you wanted to document or publish your success in some sort of formal way.

The ABC and ABCD *Designs*

Practitioners know well that sometimes the intervention that you start with doesn't work, is not valued by the client, or does not appear to be working as fast as it should. In these situations, major changes are made in the treatment plan. Another intervention might be started or multiple modalities employed.

The **ABC** or "successive interventions" design allows the practitioner to respond with different interventions when needed and still allows for monitoring the effects of these interventions. In this scheme, the effects of the second intervention are identified as (**C**). The effects of the third intervention are (**D**), and so on. (It is also possible to think of the **C** phase as a period when the client is taught how to maintain the behavior achieved during the intervention [**B**] phase.)

Since there is no return to a baseline between the second and third (or even fourth) interventions, these successive intervention designs do not allow the practitioner to determine which interventions caused the changes in the behavior. Even though it might appear that the first intervention (**B**) didn't work, but that the second intervention (**C**) did, it could be that the accumulative or interactive effects of both **B** and **C** resulted in the change. Although one's colleagues and the client may be duly impressed with these changes, strictly speaking, conditions were not controlled enough for any sort of formal statement of causality.

Even if this design tends to fall short of the experimenter's expectations, it is appealing to practitioners, because intervention is often modified in practice and different techniques are used in the course of therapy. If everyone is happy that the behavior has changed in the desired direction, and success is in the air, neither client nor practitioner may need greater "proof" that the interventions worked. Figure 3.6 shows an example of an **ABCD** design found in the social work literature (Nuerhring and Pascone, 1986).

Multiple Baseline Designs

Single system designs known as **multiple baseline designs** may be used when you want to apply the same intervention with a client having two, three, or more problems. For instance, Taber (1981) has described the use of a multiple baseline design with an eleven-year-old boy who was referred to a residential treatment center for impulsive fighting, hitting, and swearing. When there is more than one target behavior, a baseline is needed for each. After the desired change has been achieved with the first behavior, the intervention is then ap-

---

FIGURE 3.6: Treatment Progress of a Businesswoman with Early-Phase Alcoholism

---

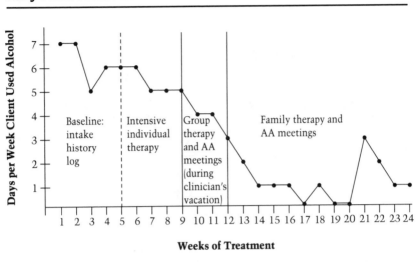

Weeks of Treatment

Source: Nuehring, E.M. and Pascone, A.B. (1986). Single-subject evaluation: A tool for quality assurance. *Social Work*, 31(5), 361. © National Association of Social Workers, Inc. Reprinted with permission.

plied to the second behavior, and so on. The shorthand notation for a **multiple baseline design across behaviors** for two problems and one intervention would be **A₁A₂B**. The design for three target behaviors and one intervention would be **A₁A₂A₃B**.

The multiple baseline designs are variations of the basic **AB** design, except that monitoring of all the behaviors continues until the desired change has been reached with the last target behavior. Practitioners may find these designs more useful than the **ABA** or **ABAB** designs because no withdrawal of intervention is required.

The multiple baseline design can also be used when you are working with several clients having the same problem and receiving the same intervention. (Then it is called a **multiple baseline across subjects design**.) For instance, you might be a social work consultant to several nursing homes and find similar cases in need of intervention at three different homes. Treatment is begun with one individual at a time, and baseline data are gathered on the other clients. When the first individual begins to show a change in behavior, intervention is applied to the second client.

A recent example of a multiple baseline across subjects design is

FIGURE 3.7: Illustration of Multiple Baselines Across Subjects

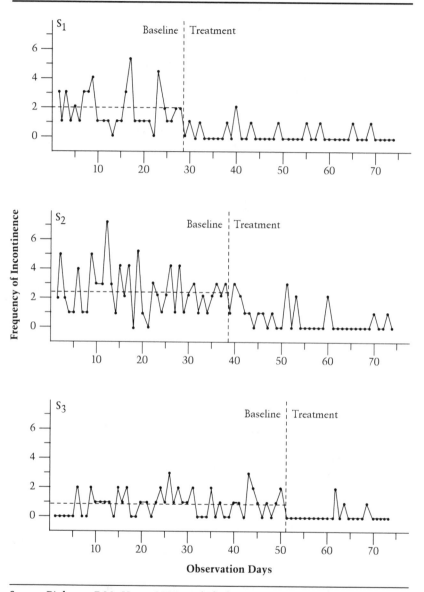

Source: Pinkston, E.M., Howe, M.W., and Blackman, D.K. (1987). Medical social work management of urinary incontinence in the elderly: A behavioral approach. *Journal of Social Service Research*, 10 (2,3,4), 188. © Haworth Press, Inc. Reprinted with permission.

found in Pinkston, Howe, and Blackman's (1987) description of a treatment procedure for the problem of urinary incontinence in three wheel-chair-bound nursing home residents with organic brain disorders. Following the intervention of praise and cookies for appropriate urination, there was a decrease in urinary incontinence and an increase in appropriate toilet behavior.

You can see in figure 3.7 that multiple baseline designs have baselines of unequal length and that intervention does not begin in the second graph until change has been recorded in the first. This holds true whether the design involves one subject with multiple target behaviors (the Taber example) or multiple subjects having a single target behavior (the Pinkston, Howe, and Blackman example). One of the strengths of the multiple baselines design is that it is useful in testing the external validity (generalizability) of an intervention (Behling and Merves, 1984) and for demonstrating causality (Bloom and Fischer, 1982). This is because multiple baselines show that specific changes in problems or in clients are related to the onset of intervention. Change is produced only after intervention and is not due to other factors.

Statistical Analysis

Cooper (1990) has demonstrated the use of one of the simplest statistical approaches. She uses a celeration line to analyze data from a client with obsessive-compulsive disorder. The client was a young woman with pervasive ritualistic behavior, such as rinsing in the shower for forty-five minutes and counting gulps of liquid when swallowing. Figure 3.8 shows how Cooper used a celeration line to understand the behavior was accelerating and to reveal where it would have been without intervention.

You can construct a celeration line easily once an adequate baseline is obtained (there are ten baseline points in the example above). Begin by dividing the baseline in half, and then divide each of these in half so that the baseline has four equal quarters. If you have an even number of baseline points you will need to draw your lines between data points. If there is an odd number, draw through the middle point.

Once this is done, compute an average or mean frequency for each half of the baseline. These means are then marked on the one-quarter and third-quarter indicator lines and a line is drawn connecting them and extending in both directions.

The celeration line that crosses the line indicating when intervention begins shows what you could expect of the behavior or event

FIGURE 3.8: Number of Twists, Presses, and Clicks of Make-Up Case by Client Each Morning at Baseline (7/2 to 7/15) and After Intervention (7/17 to 8/21)

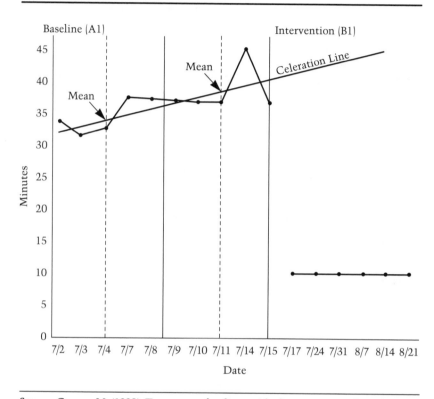

Source: Cooper, M. (1990). Treatment of a client with obsessive-compulsive disorder. *Social Work Research and Abstracts*, 24(2), 29. © National Association of Social Workers, Inc. Reprinted with permission.

if there were no intervention. Bloom and Fischer (1982) explain further procedures and provide reference tables so that interested practitioners can determine if a statistically significant change has occurred.

Statistics usually are not needed with single system designs. Because these designs rely upon graphs and visual inspection, "eyeballing" and clinical significance are all that is usually needed to establish that improvement occurred. However, for those situations where it is important to establish that there was a statistically significant change in behavior, or where it is impossible to determine whether there was a change by visual inspection, there are a number of statistical tests that can be computed fairly easily. These procedures are outlined elsewhere (Jayaratne, 1978; Jayaratne and Levy, 1979; Bloom and Fischer, 1982; Kazdin, 1982; Gingerich, 1984). These sources provide detailed presentations on the use of statistical tests with single system designs.

It should also be noted that computer software exists to store single subject data, draw graphs, and perform statistical analysis (Nurius and Hudson, 1993; Bronson and Blythe, 1987). Not only available for assessment and diagnosis, but also these software allow the social worker to aggregate data gathered on individuals for evaluation of service effectiveness.

Advantages and Disadvantages of Single System Designs

Single system designs are popular with social workers for several reasons. Some of these may be more apparent than others. Bloom and Fischer (1982) have listed twelve advantages, and I have condensed these into what I think are the major advantages. First of all, single system designs readily lend themselves to clinical practice situations. If a social worker wants to objectively evaluate his or her practice, single system designs do not require either control groups or large groups of clients in order to demonstrate that the intervention is working.

Secondly, single system designs are not disruptive to the treatment process. In fact, they support and complement practice nicely by focusing on specific treatment goals or problems. Often, they serve to clarify or confirm a worker's initial assessment of a client. Further, these designs are constructive in that they provide continuous feedback to the practitioner as well as the client. There is no need to wait until the treatment has ended to determine progress. Many clients have "failure" identities and need to be reassured that they are progressing. Single system designs can visually demonstrate the progress that has been made.

Thirdly, single system designs do not normally require computers, knowledge of statistics, or clerical help in compiling data. These designs do not require that you develop a hypothesis to test. In short, they are not burdensome to one's practice. They are easy to use and understand. Lastly, they are theory-free. That is, they can be applied regardless of the worker's theoretical application. For social workers who are interested in some form of accountability, but not in larger empirical research projects, there is much to recommend single system studies.

69

Nuehring and Pascone (1986) have suggested that single system designs should be used by social work department heads for peer reviews. If a client is not making progress, this is readily detected, and suggestions for corrective action can be made.

On the other hand, these designs have some major limitations. A considerable one is the problem of generalization. Even though one uses a rigorous single system design and clearly demonstrates that the intervention worked, there will still be those skeptics who say, "So? Maybe you worked well with this one client. Show me that your approach works with lots of clients." The skeptic makes a good point. A social worker or counselor could be very effective with a single client and yet ineffective with the rest of the caseload. It is possible to make your results have greater generalization by replicating (repeating) single subject designs with other clients. However, practically no replications have been reported in the literature (Reid, 1987).

A number of practical problems sometimes emerge during the use of single system designs. Ideally, all phases should be of equal length, yet realistically an intervention might be longer than the baseline or longer in one phase (the **B** phase) than another phase (the **C** phase). In actual practice, it is unlikely that all phases would be the same length. Other problems are encountered when we know the baseline behavior is not stable but must start intervention immediately or when several interventive techniques have to be applied simultaneously. Another problem is that even experienced practitioners may be hard-pressed to think of situations in which they would deliberately withdraw or remove an intervention that is working just to show that it is the intervention that was responsible for the change in behavior. As a consequence, some of the more experimental single system designs (e.g., **ABAB**) may be viewed by practitioners with disdain or lack of interest.

The Choice and Use of Single System Designs

This chapter has presented several different single system designs. Some of these designs are more powerful (e.g., the **ABAB** design) than others (e.g., the **AB** design) for demonstrating that the intervention and not some other factor was responsible for the change in behavior.

The single system design that is "best" to use depends upon how much evidence you feel that you need to rule out alternative explanations for improvement; it is also dictated by the target behaviors or problems identified in the treatment plan. Knowledge of the client and his or her problems is an important consideration in the choice of a design. For instance, you wouldn't want to attempt an **ABAB** design with a client who agrees to a maximum of three contacts. With another client, you may feel that it is important to monitor three or more target behaviors. Sometimes you might combine such behaviors as hitting and fighting and refer to the commission of either as "assaultive acts"; then you could use only one graph instead of two. With single subject designs, you have a great deal of flexibility. As a general guideline, however, let your knowledge of the client dictate the design rather than choosing a design and attempting to find a client who conforms to it. If we were all to wait for the "ideal" client to come along before beginning to evaluate our practice, not much evaluation would get done.

It is important not to forget that the purpose and best use of single system designs is to identify whether a client is progressing. These designs cannot explain why an intervention isn't working. Their purpose is only to inform you whether the intervention is working.

Recent developments in the creation of objective measures to document the severity of our clients' problems make the use of single subject designs even more exciting. Besides the over 100 scales available in Corcoran and Fischer's book (1987), you'll find other useful instruments to use in Nurius and Hudson's book (1993). Some of the scales contained in their book are:

Index of Self-Esteem	Partner Abuse Scale (Nonphysical
Clinical Anxiety Scale	abuse)
Index of Peer Relations	Partner Abuse Scale (Physical
Index of Alcohol Involvement	abuse)
Index of Marital Satisfaction	Generalized Contentment Scale

Each of these scales is twenty-five items and is constructed so that a score of thirty or higher indicates a clinically significant problem. Further, each of these scales can be purchased relatively inexpensively in pads of fifty or you can buy the computer software so that clients can complete the scales you select for them on a computer in your agency.

It requires a certain amount of self-discipline to conduct research. One has to be conscientious about keeping records or monitoring changes in behavior. For many practitioners whose agencies do not require formal evaluation, it is easier to use subjective determinations ("I think the client is doing better"; "The client is acting more appropriately"; "I feel that the couple is getting along better.") However, subjective determinations do not advance the profession or build practice knowledge. Single system designs can allow you to discover what works under which circumstances. A study by Campbell

(1988) indicates that clients prefer the use of some single system evaluation procedure over practitioners' opinions of effectiveness of treatment. Campbell went on to note that "concern over client reactions to the use of single system evaluation procedures does not appear to be a valid reason for not using them" (p. 22).

Single system designs have practical value and can benefit you and your clients. You may find that if you make use of them, you gain an appreciation for empirical research and are more willing to engage in it.

As a practicing social worker, you will surely find that you are too busy to attempt a single system design for every client. That's understood. However, unless you make an effort to evaluate some clients, you'll soon forget how to go about it. What do I recommend? Simply that you use a single system design with your most difficult clients. You'll keep your skills fresh and your supervisor happy, and you'll be able to determine objectively whether or not these clients are making progress.

Questions for Class Discussion

1. Think again about the discussion of the twelve-year-old who had stomachaches. Why wouldn't you want to graph the behavior in terms of times per day? (Hint: make a graph on the blackboard showing the reduction from one episode a day to none per day at the end of the intervention.)
2. Is there more than one way graphs can show lack of improvement? Choose a target behavior and draw suggestions from the class that demonstrate lack of improvement.
3. Why is the ability to operationalize target behaviors important for single subject designs?
4. What would be a good argument for monitoring more than one target behavior with a client?
5. Think about how to set up a graph for a particular target behavior. Would there be advantages in graphing positive behaviors (e.g., number of days on the job) rather than negative behaviors (e.g., days of work missed)?
6. A co-worker tells you that she has just completed a single system design on a family that has received intervention for seven months. She is pleased with what she has done and brings a graph to show you.
   a. What would be your initial reactions about her competence?
   b. Can the single subject design "prove" that your co-worker is an excellent social worker? Why not?

7. With a multiple baseline across subjects design, what is the reason for waiting for a change in the behavior of the first subject before beginning intervention on the second? Can you think of any reasons why intervention shouldn't be started on all three subjects at the same time?

8. Odette is failing the ninth grade. At a conference with her mother, Odette's teachers said that she simply was not studying or turning in any homework. The family's social worker wants to develop a single subject design to monitor the effect of requiring Odette to study two hours every afternoon before the television could be turned on. The social worker is planning to have the vertical axis show "yes" or "no" regarding the completion of two hours of study time every afternoon. Could this design be improved? How?

9. What is wrong with the single subject design presented below?

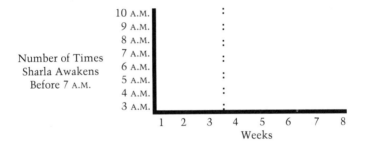

(If you don't see any problem, try making up some fictitious data and recording it on the graph.)

10. What is wrong with this single subject design?

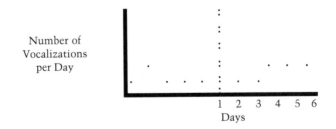

Mini-Projects for Experiencing Research Firsthand

1. Choose a client with whom you have worked or are working. (Or make up a fictitious client.) Describe the presenting problem, and then select a target behavior that follows from the cli-

ent's description of major concerns. Construct a graph for a single system design to monitor the client's progress. Be sure to address the following:
  a. What is the target behavior?
  b. How long a baseline will you need? What units will you use to measure the time intervals? How will you measure the target behavior (e.g., frequency of the behavior)?
  c. What design would you use? It should be apparent on the graph.
  d. Have the graph show that the intervention was successful.
  e. What other explanations for the change could there be?
2. Find an article that reports the use of a single system design.
  a. What additional information do you think should have been included? Do you have enough information to replicate the study?
  b. Could another design have been used? If so, what design?
  c. How convincing were the findings? Do you think replication should be attempted?
  d. Were alternative explanations adequately discussed?
  e. What are the implications for social work practice?
3. Using the scenario below, construct a graph or graphs to use with a single system design to monitor the couple's progress.

> Mr. and Mrs. Jones have been having terrible arguments. Mrs. Jones, a college graduate, has quite a bit more education than her husband (a high school graduate). He has been spending time away from home, and often finds excuses to work late and on weekends. They are not having meaningful discussions. Generally, the arguments start when Mr. Jones finds fault with something that Mrs. Jones has either done or not done. Sometimes she doesn't get up when the alarm clock rings, and he must fix breakfast for their kids. She does not like to do housework, and clutter greatly bothers Mr. Jones.
>
> On the other hand, Mr. Jones does not often sit down and listen when his wife is talking. Mr. Jones is very conscious of time and most often will be doing something else while she is talking. She complains that he doesn't spend enough time with the family, but Mr. Jones feels that it is more stressful than enjoyable when they do something together. When she complains about this, Mr. Jones finds some problem with her housekeeping. The zip seems to have gone out of this marriage, and the number of arguments each week is escalating.

With your single system design, be sure to address:
a. the target behavior(s)
b. the design
c. the baseline
Briefly summarize the intervention and the client's progress after eight weeks.
4. Using the scenario below (modified from Taber, 1981), construct a graph or graphs for monitoring the client's progress.

> Steve, an eleven-year-old boy living in a residential treatment center, was referred there because of his outbursts of temper, which involved fighting, hitting, and swearing. Steve verbally abused or hit his peers in response to slight provocations. When child-care workers tried to direct his activities, Steve would become enraged, grabbing and hitting workers with intensity. Steve showed no sign of thinking before he acted. These problems persisted during his first year in residence, despite the efforts of child-care workers to modify his anger through "life-space interviews," use of time-outs, and a token economy system. Steve was anxious to go to a foster home. Since this was contingent upon control of his anger, he was eager to work on the problem.

With your single system design, be sure to address:
a. the target behavior(s)
b. the design
c. the baseline
Briefly summarize the intervention and the client's progress after eight weeks.
5. Particularly for students interested in working with populations where behavior modification techniques are commonly employed (e.g., autistic children and populations with serious behavioral and mental challenges), *The Journal of Applied Behavior Analysis* provides a plethora of articles containing single subject designs. Choose an article from this journal to read and then write a one-page summary of what you learned.

Resources and References

Behling, J.H. and Merves, E.S. (1984). *The Practice of Clinical Research: The Single Case Method.* New York: University Press of America.

Berlin, S.B. (1983). Single-case evaluation: Another version. *Social Work Research and Abstracts,* 19, 3–11.

Bloom, M. and Fischer, J. (1982). *Evaluating Practice: Guidelines for the Accountable Professional*. Englewood Cliffs, NJ: Prentice-Hall.

Blythe, B.J. and Briar, S. (1985). Developing empirically based models of practice. *Social Work*, 30, 483–488.

Bromley, D.B. (1986). *The Case-Study Method in Psychology and Related Disciplines*. New York: Wiley.

Bronson, D.E. and Blythe, B.J. (1987). Computer support for single-case evaluation of practice. *Social Work Research and Abstracts*, 23(3), 10–13.

Campbell, J.A. (1988). Client acceptance of single-system evaluation procedures. *Social Work Research and Abstracts*, 24(2), 21–22.

Cooper, M. (1990). Treatment of a client with obsessive-compulsive disorder. *Social Work Research and Abstracts*, 26(2), 26–32.

Corcoran, K. and Fischer, J. (1987). *Measures for Clinical Practice*. New York: The Free Press.

Dean, R.G. and Reinherz, H. (1986). Psychodynamic practice and single system design: The odd couple. *Journal of Social Work Education*, 22, 71–81.

Dukes, W.F. (1965). N + 1. *Psychological Bulletin*, 64(1), 74–79.

Gambril, E. and Barth, R. (1979). Single-case study designs revised. *Social Work Research and Abstracts*, 16(3), 15–20.

Gingerich, W.J. (1978). Procedure for evaluating clinical practice. *Health and Social Work*, 4, 104–130.

Gingerich, W.J. (1984). Generalizing single-case evaluation from classroom to practice. *Journal of Education for Social Work*, 20, 74–82.

Gingerich, W.J. (1984). Meta-Analysis of applied time series data. *Journal of Applied Behavioral Science*, 20, 71–79.

Hepworth, D.H. and Larsen, J.A. (1986). *Direct Social Work Practice: Theory and Skills*. Chicago, IL: Dorsey.

Hersen, M. and Barlow, D. (1976). *Single Case Experimental Designs*. Elmsford, NY: Pergamon Press.

Howe, M.W. (1974). Casework self-evaluation: A single-subject approach. *Social Service Review*, 48, 1–24.

Hudson, W.W. (1982). *The Clinical Measurement Package: A Field Manual*. Homewood, IL: Dorsey.

Jayaratne, S. (1977). Single-subject and groups designs in treatment evaluation. *Social Work Research and Abstracts*, 13(3), 35–42.

Jayaratne, S. (1978). Analytic procedures for single-subject designs. *Social Work Research and Abstracts*, 14(3), 30–40.

Jayaratne, S. and Levy, R. (1979). *Empirical Clinical Practice*. New York: Columbia University Press.

Kazdin, A.E. (1982). *Single-Case Research Designs: Methods for Clinical and Applied Settings*. New York: Oxford University Press.

Kopp, J. (1988). Self-monitoring: A literature review of research and practice. *Social Work Research and Abstracts*, 24(4), 8–20.

Levy, R. and Olson, D. (1979). The single-subject methodology in clinical practice: An overview, *Journal of Social Service Research*, 3, 25–49.

Montagu, A. (1971). *The Elephant Man: A Study in Human Dignity*. New York: Dutton.

Nelsen, J. (1981). Issues in single-subject research for nonbehaviorists. *Social Work Research and Abstracts*, 17, 31–37.

Nelsen, J. (1984). Intermediate treatment goals as variables in single-case research. *Social Work Research and Abstracts*, 20, 3–10.

Nelsen, J. (1985). Verifying the independent variable in single-subject research. *Social Work Research and Abstracts*. 21(2) 3–8.

Nelsen, J. (1988). Single-subject research. In Richard M. Grinnell (Ed.), *Social Work Research and Evaluation*. Itasca, IL: Peacock.

Nelson, J.C. (1978). Use of communication theory in single-subject research. *Social Work Research and Abstracts*, 14(4), 12–19.

Nuehring, E.M. and Pascone, A.B. (1986). Single-Subject evaluation: A tool for quality assurance. *Social Work*, 31(5), 359–365.

Nugent, W.R. (1991) An experimental and qualitative analysis of a cognitive-behavioral intervention for anger. *Social Work Research and Abstracts*, 27(3), 3–8.

Nurius, P. S., and Hudson, W.W. (1988). Computer-based practice: Future dream or current technology? *Social Work*, 33(4) 357–362.

Nurius, P. S., and Hudson, W. W. (1993). *Human Services Practice, Evaluation, and Computers*. Pacific Grove, CA: Brooks/Cole.

Orme, J.G. (1991). Statistical conclusion validity for single-system designs. *Social Service Review*, 65(3), 468–491.

Pinkston, E.M., Howe, M.W., and Blackman, D.K. (1987). Medical social work management of urinary incontinence in the elderly: A behavioral approach. *Journal of Social Service Research*, 10, 179–183.

Reid, W.J. (1987). Research in social work. In Ann Minahan (Ed.), *Social Work Encyclopedia*. 18th ed. Silver Spring, MD: National Association of Social Workers, p. 482.

Richey, C.A., and Hodges, V.G. (1992). Empirical support for the effectiveness of respite care in reducing caregiver burden: A single-case analysis. *Research on Social Work Practice*, 2(2), 143–160.

Robinson, E.A.R., Bronson, D.E., and Blythe, B.J. (1988). An analysis of the implementation of single case evaluation by practitioners, *Social Service Review*, 62, 287–301.

Ruckdeschel, R., and Farris, B. (1981). Assessing practice: A critical look at the single-case design. *Social Casework: The Journal of Contemporary Social Work*, 62, 413–419.

Sundel, M., and Sundel, S.S. (1993). *Behavior Modification in the Human Services: A Systematic Introduction to Concepts and Applications*. Newbury Park, CA: Sage.

Taber, S.M. (1981). Cognitive-behavior modification treatment of an aggressive eleven-year-old boy. *Social Work Research and Abstracts*, 17(2), 13–23.

Thomas, E. (1978). Research and service in single-case experimentation: Conflicts and choices. *Social Work Research and Abstracts*, 14(4), 20–31.

Thyer, B.A. and Thyer, K.B. (1992). Single-system research designs in social work practice: A bibliography from 1965 to 1990. *Research on Social Work Practice,* 2(1), 99–116.

Welch, G. (1983). Will graduates use single-subject designs to evaluate their casework practice? *Journal of Education for Social Work,* 19, 42–47.

Witkin, W. and Harrison, D. (1979). Single-case designs in marital research. *Journal of Social Service Research,* 3, 51–66.

Yin, R.K. (1989). *Case Study Research.* Beverly Hills, CA: Sage.

Yin, R.K. (1993). *Applications of Case Study Research.* Newbury Park, CA: Sage.

Zimbalist, S.E. (1983). The single-case clinical research design in developmental perspective: Mainstream or tangent. *Journal of Education for Social Work,* 19, 61–66.

4
Research Designs for Group Comparisons

Some years ago an educator described a series of events he had undoubtedly observed firsthand, events you may also have observed. He characterized the events by what he called the "law of the hammer": if you give a young child a hammer, the child will find many things that "need" hammering. Few of us would want to hire a carpenter who has only a hammer in his toolchest. While it is important to know what and when to hammer, it is also essential to have the various tools that different jobs require as well as knowledge of how to use them.

Single system designs may not always be the right "tool" for every research occasion. They provide only one tool to use in a very complex world of clients and their problems and agencies and their programs. There are times when we need to aggregate our data in order to understand phenomena or to conduct an evaluation at a group, program, or community level. When we move beyond a single client focus, we use research designs that allow us to make comparisons with groups or clusters of individuals.

Hudson (1978) suggests that the teaching of single system designs should be targeted to those students who wish to have careers in counseling or direct-service delivery (microsystems), but that those wanting to work with macrosystems (administration, social policy, planning, and community organization) ought to know the traditional research methodologies. He states that these methodologies (the experimental and quasi-experimental designs, field studies, and social surveys) are more useful for dealing with the types of problems experienced when one works with institutions, systems, agencies, communities, and advocacy groups. Macrosystem practitioners, he argues, need to know methodologies that use group comparisons and data aggregation.

While all of this may be sobering news for those interested in macrosystems, microsystem practitioners are not off scot-free. Many who never considered the possibility of doing anything but direct practice while they were in school often are promoted to management positions and find themselves having to evaluate their staff, to determine whether one treatment modality is better than another, to decide whether one group of clients averages a longer length of stay than others, or to conduct surveys of clients or of the community. Some phenomena are best studied not on the individual level, but with group data. Evidence to support the notion that social workers need to know more than single subject designs comes from a study by three social workers (Gentry, Connaway, and Morelock, 1984) who mailed questionnaires to members of the National Association of Social Workers asking about their involvement with research. They found that 91 percent engaged in at least one research activity. Eighty-five percent had given a formal presentation; 81 percent had planned a new program; 73 percent had evaluated an agency program; 66 percent had conducted a needs assessment; 58 percent had prepared a paper; 49 percent had systematically compared a group of cases; 36 percent had written a grant proposal; 35 percent had conducted a research project; 31 percent had developed a research proposal; 28 percent had submitted a manuscript for publication; and 19 percent had had an article published.

Still not convinced that you'll ever need to know more research than single system designs? Consider the following scenario: You are a medical social worker assigned to the oncology (tumor) unit in a local hospital. Let's further imagine that you have been running a support group for women with breast cancer. Women who participate in this group not only seem to have fewer medical problems after they leave the hospital but also seem to have less anxiety and depression and more energy and vigor than those who don't participate. You mention your observations to one of the medical doctors who treats patients on the unit and he scoffs. In such a situation, wouldn't you like to have data from a large number of patients who benefited (not just two or three single subject designs) to show him? Wouldn't he be contrite if your experiment showed that cancer patients who participate in a support group develop healthier immune systems and live longer than patients without the intervention? Actually, exciting studies with cancer patients are beginning to show these very benefits. (See, for example, Spiegel, 1990, and Fawzy et al., 1990.)

Is there a need for studies based on groups of clients, to test the effectiveness of receiving or not receiving our interventions? You bet! Without the experiments and other designs in this chapter, the social sciences would consist more of opinions than of science.

You may find it somewhat comforting to learn that students in sociology, psychology, education, and the allied health disciplines learn the same designs when they study research methodology.

Choosing the Right Design

Numerous research designs can be used to guide research projects. Choosing the right design is somewhat analogous to picking out a new car. The primary consideration when deciding on a car is how much money you have or how big a monthly payment you can manage. The researcher must also consider how much has been budgeted for the research. Design issues related to finances are: use of staff time (e.g., making follow-up contacts with clients in person or by phone); postage, telephone, or travel expenses; purchase of copyrighted instruments or scales; computer processing of the data; use of consultants; and so on. These and other variables contribute to the cost of the project.

While the car buyer considers whether the car's optional equipment is really necessary, the researcher decides which facets of the study are essential. Some procedures or features of the proposed study, the researcher may believe, are definitely needed. The investigator may have firm ideas about how the "success" of the intervention should be determined. This could require expensive personal interviews or involve less costly examination of existing data.

Having made decisions to this point, the car buyer usually begins to choose among models. Some models may strike the buyer as having more quality or more prestige than others. Some cars are chosen because they provide the basics without any frills. Similarly, some research designs are more respected than others; these are the classic experimental research designs. However, because social workers almost always view experimentation with clients with great suspicion, no-frill designs (pre-experimental or quasi-experimental designs) with less rigorous requirements may have greater appeal or relevance.

In summary, various motives or considerations have a bearing on the choice of a research design. No one design will be applicable or correct in every situation. The design is dependent upon the nature of the problem being investigated, the availability of clients or other data, monetary and staff resources, the amount of time one has to complete the project, and the purpose of the research (is it for internal agency use or do you need to convince skeptical colleagues outside of the agency?).

Research strategies are most often developed from the specific objectives of the study and the nature of the presenting problem. Social work researchers generally move from interest in a problem to the selection of a design. Seldom would one choose a design and then look for a problem to investigate.

Experimental Research

The classic experimental design is the "ideal," the model to which other research designs are compared. Even though the opportunities to conduct true experiments may not often come your way, the experimental design remains the standard when it is important to be as scientific as possible. Other designs in this chapter are discussed in terms of how close they come to the "ideal."

For many social workers, the notion of experimentation involving human subjects brings to mind misconceptions about unethical, painful, or presumably painful stimuli (e.g., the controversial Milgram experiments) being inflicted upon unsuspecting persons in a climate-controlled laboratory. These notions are best forgotten. Today there is much greater concern for and widespread protection of the rights of persons participating in research than there was twenty-five to thirty years ago. For instance, the federal government requires institutional review boards to oversee research being funded with federal money and involving human subjects. (See chapter 12 for a discussion of ethical guidelines for researchers.) Further, these old stereotypes do not facilitate our thinking about how experimental designs can be of benefit to us in our practice.

It will be helpful at this point to briefly discuss several examples of experimental research to broaden our understanding of the practical benefits of experimentation. Since the concept of the medical community testing the effects of medication on persons with certain illnesses is probably familiar to you, let's start with an example from a medical experiment.

With the rapid adoption of aspartame (NutraSweet) by food

processing companies as a substitute for sugar came a number of complaints of headaches, which supposedly were caused by the sweetener. The Duke University Medical Center enrolled forty people with these complaints in a carefully controlled study. Subjects were given identical capsules that contained either aspartame or inert cellulose (a placebo). Two days later, those who received the aspartame were given the placebo and vice versa. A double-blind procedure was used so that neither the researchers nor the subjects knew who got the placebo. Subjects were monitored for the onset of headaches during the course of the study. The investigators found that fourteen of the subjects who got the aspartame did get headaches; however, eighteen subjects reported headaches when they got the placebo (which would not have caused the headaches). The experiment showed that it was not the aspartame that caused the headaches (Schiffman, Buckley, Sampson, Massey, Baraniuk, Follett, and Warwick, 1987).

In the field of social work, experiments have made valuable contributions to practice and have affected the way services are delivered to clients. Cox, Brogan, and Dandridge (1986) reported on a study that attempted to find the best way to reduce payment errors to recipients of Aid to Families with Dependent Children. Clients were randomly assigned to one of three groups. One group was never visited by a caseworker; those in the second group were visited only during the application process; and those in the third group were visited at both intake and in the fourth month of program participation. The authors found that there were no statistically significant differences in error rates or payment amounts among the three groups.

Applegate (1992) has described an interesting experiment designed to assess the therapeutic reactive effects of filling out subjective self-ratings during an eight-session psychodynamic clinical social work intervention. Clients of a family agency were randomly assigned to a control or self-report group. Between appointments those in the self-report group completed the Index of Self-Esteem, the Cantril Ladder, and the Multiple Affect Adjective Checklist. Applegate found that those clients completing self-ratings of subjective states did not improve more in personal and social adjustment and on six dimensions of mood than did those who did not complete the self-ratings, even though anecdotal comments by most clients filling out the self-ratings indicated a substantial impact.

In another study using an experimental design, Edleson and Syers (1990) examined the effectiveness of three different treatment models (in twelve- and thirty-two-session program formats) for men who batter. Six months after intervention, their interviews revealed that twelve-session treatment groups were as effective as thirty-two-session groups in reducing repeat incidents of violence and terroristic threats. Also, men in the self-help groups were less successful than those in the structured education group or groups that combined the features of these two.

Some social policies have been shaped by the outcomes of social experiments. Hausman and Wise (1985) estimate that the government spent over $500 million on social experiments during the 1970s. These experiments ranged from Experimental Housing Allowance Program (EHAP) to negative income tax experiments and prevention of coronary heart disease.

One of the longest and most sophisticated social experiments ever carried out in the United States, the New Jersey Graduated Work Incentive Experiment, ran from 1968 to 1972 and cost $8 million. This experiment was set up to determine if a negative income tax (cash paid to those below the poverty line to bring them up to a guaranteed income level) would reduce the incentive to work. As families' incomes rose from outside earnings, the negative tax would be reduced, but always less than the earnings, so that there was an incentive for a family to improve its financial situation. The experiment found that the negative tax did not reduce the participants' propensity to work. In fact, black families in particular worked harder and earned more as a result of the guaranteed income. There were no significant effects on health, fertility, marital dissolution, or school attendance (Bulmer, 1986).

The Classic Experimental Research Design

Experimental designs are the most rigorous of research designs and the ones that best permit casual inferences to be made. These designs have two main features that distinguish them from other designs: clients (or subjects) who participate in the experiment are randomly selected (defined as the absence of bias; allowing chance to play the role of selecting clients) and assigned to either the group that gets the intervention (the *experimental group)* or the group that gets no intervention (the *control group).*

The shorthand notation for the classic **Pretest-Posttest Control Group Design** is often written as follows:

$$R \quad O_1 \quad X \quad O_2$$
$$R \quad O_3 \quad \quad O_4$$

The **R** in this notation scheme stands for the random assignment of clients to either the experimental or the control group; the **X** represents the intervention. Observations, measurements, or assessments of each group are made twice. The first observation (O_1) is called the **pretest,** and the second observation (O_2) is called the **posttest.** This design provides information not only about changes in the group that receives the intervention, but also comparable information from the group that does not get intervention. What kind of changes would the experimental design pick up? This depends entirely on the dependent variable or variables the researcher has chosen and the way they have been operationalized.

As an example of this design, suppose you are a medical social worker assigned to a dialysis clinic. Let's further assume that the management of anxiety is a major problem for patients in the clinic. You decide to start a support group for anxious patients because you believe it will help alleviate some of their health concerns. Because you are limited in the amount of time you can allocate for this project, you want to start small with about twenty-five patients. Since this is a large dialysis clinic with hundreds of patients, there is no problem in finding willing participants. In keeping with the experimental Pretest-Posttest Control Group Design, you randomly select twenty-five dialysis patients for the support group and randomly assign an approximate number to the control group. Next, you use a standardized measure like the Clinical Anxiety Scale (Thyer, 1984) to determine the anxiety level of both groups prior to the start of the intervention. The support group begins and runs its normal course (six to eight weeks). Afterwards, you administer the instrument a second time to both groups and make comparisons. Has the average level of anxiety in the experimental group decreased? Has the average amount of anxiety in the control group remained about the same or increased? Finally, is the level of anxiety in the experimental group less than in the control group? If so, then you have some evidence that the intervention was effective.

This is a strong design because the group that receives no intervention provides a "control" for possible alternative explanations for the effect on the experimental group. Random selection of subjects makes the groups equivalent before the intervention begins. For instance, if clients tend to make better decisions because they grow wiser with the passage of time (maturation) and not because of the intervention, then the control group would also show similar improvement or outcome. There would be little reason to believe that the intervention was responsible for any changes if the same changes were also found in the control group.

The Posttest Only Control Group Design

A second experimental design, the **Posttest Only Control Group Design,** is handy for those situations where a pretest might affect the posttest results or when it is not possible to conduct a pretest. This design is also useful in situations where anonymity is paramount—so it would not be possible to compare an individual's pretest and post-test scores.

Campbell and Stanley (1963) note that there is a common mis-conception that pretests are always needed in an experimental design. Not so, they say. Early experimental designs in agriculture did not make much use of pretests. As with the previous design, random selection and assignment of subjects establish the initial equivalence between the experimental and control groups. Measurement of the control group (O_2) then serves as a pretest measure for comparison with the experimental group's posttest (O_1).

$$R \quad X \quad O_1$$
$$R \qquad O_2$$

As an example of this design, consider the following problem. Counseling agencies often find that 30 percent or more of scheduled appointments result in "no-shows" or last minute cancellations. Productive or "billable" time is lost, which can seriously affect the revenue needed to operate an agency. Suppose you have a hypothesis that the 30 percent no-show rate could be reduced by the agency's receptionist calling clients to remind them of their scheduled appointments. The group receiving the phone calls would constitute the experimental group. Those clients who do not receive a reminder constitute the control group. Membership in either the experimental or control group would be randomly determined. (For instance, even-numbered clients scheduled for an appointment during the first week of March would be assigned to the experimental group and would get a reminder. Odd-numbered clients would be assigned to the control group.) At the end of the study period, the cancellation rates for the two groups could be compared.

The Solomon Four-Group Design

The third experimental design is called the **Solomon Four-Group Design.** As you can see from the notation below, it is composed of the basic experimental design plus the Posttest Only Control

Group Design. This is an elaborate, sophisticated design that social workers may not often have the opportunity to utilize.

This design provides two opportunities for the treatment effect to be demonstrated. The design's strong point, however, is that the investigator can maximally control for alternative explanations and thus increase the confidence that can be placed in the findings. While this is a rigorous design and provides greater confidence that the intervention produced any observed changes, the tradeoff for this certainty is greater difficulty in coordinating and implementing the design.

$$R \quad O_1 \quad X \quad O_2$$

$$R \quad O_3 \quad \quad O_4$$

$$R \quad \quad X \quad O_5$$

$$R \quad \quad \quad O_6$$

Internal and External Validity

To keep the explanation of the single system design in chapter 3 uncomplicated, I used the terms *alternative explanations* and *competing explanations* to refer to those unplanned or unexpected variables that might have had an effect upon the observed outcome. However, now we will examine the internal and external validity of studies to more fully understand the strengths and weaknesses of the various research designs for group comparisons. The following section is presented to help you think about the variables that can influence your study and make it difficult to determine if your intervention was effective. As you learn more about research, you will develop an appreciation for factors (not limited to those below) that can interfere with your study. Keep in mind that this discussion of internal and external validity is equally applicable to the single system designs.

Campbell and Stanley (1963) and Cook and Campbell (1979) are prominent in social science research because of their conceptualization of research designs. Their books are classic texts on the topic, and few research methodology texts have not cited their work. Besides identifying a host of experimental, quasi-experimental, and pre-experimental research designs (more about these a little later), these authors contributed to our understanding of internal and external validity.

Threats to the **internal validity** of a study (that is, whether the intervention was truly responsible for the observed differences in the experimental group) come from extraneous variables (those not purposely incorporated into the experiment).

1. *Maturation:* Growing older or different rates of growth within two comparison groups are examples of an influence that researchers should be cognizant of and attempt to control as much as possible. A client's criminal activities may cease not because of intervention from a concerned therapist, but because the client has grown too old to hustle or no longer has the athletic quickness needed to avoid capture.

2. *History:* This refers to the specific events that occur between the pretest and posttest that were not part of the researcher's design and that could influence the results (e.g., national crises, tragedies, or historical events; or, on a local level, a large factory laying off hundreds of employees—including some of those in your study). For instance, if you were trying to evaluate the impact of an AIDS prevention program, and Magic Johnson made his public announcement during the study period, this would constitute a threat to the internal validity.

3. *Testing:* Taking a test on more than one occasion can affect later test scores. Repeated testing provides practice and is in itself a unique experience that may influence subsequent scores (e.g., the subject gets bored with the test and does not pay as much attention to the test the second time, or the subject's score improves not because of an intervention, but because of the results of practice on the test).

4. *Instrumentation:* This refers to changes in the use of the measuring instrument, in the way the instrument is scored, in procedures during the study, or in the way the dependent variable is counted or measured (e.g., as a result of becoming tired, the observers are less attentive to and accurate in the behavior they are counting).

5. *Selection of respondents:* This threat to internal validity stems from any bias that causes the control and experimental groups to be different because of the way they were selected (e.g., your experimental subjects volunteer to participate, while an incentive is used to attract the control group).

6. *Statistical regression:* This refers to the selection of subjects who were chosen because of extreme scores. There is a tendency for extreme scores to move toward the group average on a second testing.

7. *Mortality:* Also known as attrition, this threat to internal validity refers to the loss of respondents (e.g., they terminate services, move out of town, get sick, or simply just drop out of the study). The loss of subjects may change the overall group complexion (especially if a large number of clients are involved or if

they have extreme scores) and may produce differences in the data at the posttest that have nothing to do with the intervention.

8. *Interaction effects:* This occurs when any of the extraneous variables interact with one another. In a selection and maturation interaction, the subjects in one group may mature at a faster rate than those in the comparison group. The example Powers, Meenaghan, and Toomey (1985) use of a maturation and mortality interaction is clients who improve from maturation and then drop out of the control group. In such situations, the researcher would have difficulty in understanding the true effect of the intervention.

Threats to the internal validity of a study are like viruses that can infect and weaken it. They sap the confidence that you as a researcher have in the finding that it was the intervention, and only the intervention, that was responsible for any improvement in clients' lives.

The use of any experimental design will help you gauge the extent of any of these threats to the internal validity of your study. It is the use of randomization and a control group that allows the investigator to determine if any extraneous variable has exerted an unexpected influence. For instance, if you notice an unexpected improvement in the control group, you might suspect that an extraneous variable (such as history, maturation, or testing) had an effect upon the study. You might want to correct for that influence by subtracting the gains made by the control group from those of the experimental group when computing the benefits of intervention.

When you have considered these eight threats and ruled them out as having produced an effect, then you have established that your study has internal validity. You can now conclude with some confidence that the intervention was responsible for (caused) the observed changes. Then, if you want to ensure that the findings from your study can be generalized to different subjects or settings, you should consider the threats to the external validity of the study.

Campbell and Stanley (1963) must also be given credit for identifying several ways in which the **external validity** (the generalizability or representativeness of the study) can be threatened.

1. *Reactive or interactive effect of testing:* This occurs when a pretest affects the respondent's sensitivity or awareness to important variables associated with the study. The pretest could make the subjects unrepresentative of the population from

which they were drawn by raising their consciousness or by stimulating new learning, or simply because they realize that they are involved in a study. This threat should seem familiar to you because it is the same as the internal validity threat of testing.

2. *Interaction effects of selection biases and any research stimulus:* These occur when there are problems getting a random sample. If you are conducting a study that requires in-depth interviews of two or three hours in duration, the majority of persons you contact might turn you down and not participate. Those who agree to the interview may not be representative of the larger population—they have volunteered when most others have not. They may have some traits or characteristics (e.g., they are lonely) that make them less representative and therefore affect the generalizability of the study.

3. *Reactive effects of arrangements:* This has to do with the experiment being conducted in a setting that is different from the subject's usual experience. Subjects' behavior may change because of the different environment. Subjects may be more productive or more wary and nervous. They may behave in a way not indicative of their normal style. (Would your behavior change if you knew that you were being videotaped or observed through a two-way mirror?)

4. *Multiple-treatment interaction:* This becomes a problem when there is more than one intervention. The researcher needs to be sure that the same timing, sequence, or order is followed for each subject. Multiple treatments may have a cumulative effect, which could make reaching conclusions about a specific intervention difficult.

External validity is important if you want to convince others that your study or experiment has produced a major scientific discovery. For instance, suppose I play country music beside a baby's crib twenty-four hours a day for four years. Let's assume that the child is overheard plunking out a recognizable tune on the piano sometime after his fourth birthday. Because the child has never had a music lesson, I conclude that he is a musical prodigy and am prepared to go on talk shows recommending that parents all over America play country music beside their babies' cribs.

As you mull over the potential impact of my findings, you consider the small sample size, the obvious problem of selection bias and representativeness of the sample, the ability of the intervention to create a musical prodigy, and the operational definition of musical

90

talent and its assessment. It is very likely that you would feel that my pronouncement about how to produce musical prodigies was a little premature and unconvincing, whether you live in Peoria, Chicago, Miami, or Little Rock.

In those situations where you are evaluating a local or specific program, it might *not* be important to you to demonstrate external validity. In this instance, you are concerned only with whether treatment worked in a specific program—you may not be interested in generalizing your results to their communities or subjects because your program is not like any others.

On the other hand, if you are concerned with generalization and obtaining maximum credibility, you'll want to use an experimental design and attempt to anticipate all the potential threats to the internal and external validity of your study. For additional information on threats to external validity you may want to consult Grinnell and Stothers (1988), who cite six threats; Kazdin (1982), who discusses nine; or Cook and Campbell (1979), who cite thirteen.

In summary, there are always distinct threats to a study's internal and external validity. Think of the threats to the internal validity as the alternative explanations that can be offered to explain why it wasn't the intervention that produced the observed changes. Experimental research designs use random selection and assignment of subjects to comparison groups to help the researcher monitor and understand the threats to internal validity. As a rule, the more control you have over the situation or experiment, the greater the internal validity. However, there is a corresponding cost in terms of external validity.

With more control comes the problem of making the experimental setting or situation unlike those familiar to the subjects. Even the best research project has some weaknesses, and the researcher must realize that every study has its limitations. While generalizability may be more limited than you had initially hoped, your study may still reveal that an innovative procedure worked with your clients!

Pre-Experimental Designs

Suppose you are a counselor in an agency and are working with a group of shy individuals. You have developed an approach that, over the course of ten meetings, significantly alleviates shyness. You administer a shyness inventory to the group on its first meeting, and the average score for the group is 135. From the scores and your clinical impressions, you know that this group is extremely shy. Your group meets ten times, and you administer a posttest on the last session.

You find that the group's average score has gone down to 62, which indicates major improvement.

This type of design does not have the complexity of an experiment. Since subjects are not randomly selected or assigned to either a treatment or a control group, this design is popular and often used in evaluations of social service programs. This design (which is similar to the **AB** design) is called the **One-Group Pretest-Posttest Design** and can be designated with the notation:

$$O_1 \quad X \quad O_2$$

Here, again, the (O_1) represents the pretest measurement or observation and the (O_2) the posttest.

Even though you, as a clinician, have seen major improvement in the individuals of the group, this design cannot rule out alternative explanations for the changes. It cannot rule out the internal validity threats of history, maturation, testing, instrumentation, or the interaction of selection and maturation. Any of these extraneous variables may have produced the changes in the shyness inventory. Without a control group, it is impossible to say that these threats did not have an effect. The researcher, however, may be able to rule out some of these threats because of the particular situation or context within which the study occurred. Although this is a weak design, it serves a purpose when no control group is available for comparison.

If there were no pretest data associated with the earlier study of shy individuals, the resulting design would be the **One-Group Posttest Only Design.**

$$X \quad O_1$$

With this design, an intervention is delivered, and later, observations are recorded in order to determine the intervention's outcome. This design stipulates only that you take a reading or observation after the intervention. If you were working with the group of shy individuals described above, this design would require only a posttest after the intervention. Since there would have been no pretest for comparison, the average posttest score of sixty-two does not provide much information. With no data available for comparison, any perceptions of a reduction in shyness are unsubstantiated. Instead of the intervention having an effect on shyness, extraneous variables such as selection, history, maturation, or mortality may have contributed to any perceived effect after treatment.

With the One-Group Posttest Only Design there is the presumption of an effect. Sometimes, however, you can see an effect more clearly—especially if you are conducting a study of a problem that is behavioral (e.g., you have a group of clients who are trying to quit drinking). If the group reported after ten weeks that they weren't drinking, you would be pleased and willing to take the credit. Indeed, your colleagues probably would have no difficulty attributing the cessation of drinking to the intervention. However, the "success" might have been due to spouses or mates threatening to leave if loved ones didn't stop drinking, bosses threatening to fire inebriated employees, court appearances for driving while intoxicated, or a combination of several factors. Again, without a control group, it is difficult to know the extent to which extraneous factors are influencing the outcome.

A third pre-experimental design is called the **Posttest-Only Design with Nonequivalent Groups.** It is expressed:

$$X \quad O_1$$
$$O_2$$

This design is an improvement over the previous two in that the control group functions as a pretest condition and can be compared with the group that receives the intervention. While it may seem logical to infer that any observed differences are due to the intervention, this is debatable, since we cannot assume that the two groups were similar prior to the intervention (there was no random assignment to the groups). As a consequence, differences between O_1 and O_2 may be due to their nonequivalence in the beginning and not to the effect of intervention.

By way of example, think of the population of women who have been battered by husbands or boyfriends. Assume we want to know if service programs connected with a shelter for battered women are instrumental in helping these women avoid returning to abusive situations. Of the battered women who contact the shelter, some request shelter services, while others request information about child custody, jobs, police protection, etc. and attempt to leave abusive situations on their own without spending time in the shelter. There are, then, two groups of women with the same basic problem. One group gets the intervention (the shelter), while the other group does not. For the purpose of follow-up research to determine how many women were living in abusive situations one year from their contact with the shelter, would these two groups be equivalent? I think not. They may differ in the amount of financial resources at their disposal (those who don't stay at the shelter may have more money), in the extent of

93

family or social support systems, and possibly with regard to the severity of the abuse experienced.

These two groups of women may seem to be convenient groupings in terms of trying to determine the impact of a battered women's shelter. If it were later found that a greater proportion of the women who used the shelter's services than of women who didn't were still in abusive situations, what does this say about the shelter's services? It would be risky to conclude that the shelter was in some way responsible for its clients returning to abusive situations. While it may appear that women who avoid the shelter are more successful in not returning to abusive situations, we must keep in mind that the two groups of women may not have been equivalent even though they shared a common problem. If we were to select these two groups for our study, we might expect differences in the two groups even before our data are aggregated. Of course, the more similar (or homogeneous) the two groups are, the more comfortable everyone will be that the intervention did have an effect. The absence of randomization makes this design weak; we are unable to rule out such internal validity threats as those of selection, mortality, and interaction among variables (such as selection and maturation).

Kidder and Judd (1986) say that these three pre-experimental designs are examples of how *not* to do research if there are alternatives. Fortunately, alternatives exist—they are called quasi-experimental designs.

Quasi-Experimental Designs

Quasi-experimental designs are those that fall a little short of the "ideal." Often in agency settings, it would not be acceptable or possible to randomly assign clients to one of several treatment modalities (or to a control group receiving no intervention). When randomization cannot be done, the researcher should consider quasi-experimental designs.

The **Nonequivalent Control Group Design** has been called the "archetypal quasi-experimental design" because it is the most internally valid design that can be implemented in most applied settings (Judd and Kenny, 1981). It is also one of the most commonly used quasi-experimental designs.

The notation for Nonequivalent Control Group Design is:

$$O_1 \quad X \quad O_2$$
$$O_3 \quad \quad O_4$$

94

In this design, a control group is used, just as with the experimental design. However, there is no randomization. Usually a convenient natural group (e.g., another class of fifth graders, another AA group, another group of shy clients) is selected that is similar but may not be equivalent to the group receiving the intervention. Just as with the previous design, the control group consists of clients who have the same characteristics. The control group can come from those clients on a waiting list for service, clients receiving alternative services from the same agency or from another similar agency, or even from nonclients.

Researchers often attempt to match the two groups on important variables (e.g., age, socio-economic status, drinking experience). As you can imagine, matching is difficult because of the number of variables that could be involved. A major problem with matching is that observed differences between the control and intervention groups at the end of the experiment may have been due to the influence of unmatched variables. When you must match, the best advice is to match the groups on as many of the relevant variables as possible. Equivalence is not guaranteed with matching, but it does serve to approximate equivalency. When random assignment is not possible, matching is a good alternative.

With this design, it is usually plausible to assume that the treatment produced the effect. Like the experiment, this design does provide the investigator with the ability to monitor internal validity threats such as those from testing, maturation, instrumentation, history, and mortality. The main threat to this design's internal validity comes from interaction of selection with maturation, with history, or with testing, since random assignment wasn't used (so there was no guarantee of equivalency). Still, this design is better than the pre-experimental designs because of the use of a control group. The more similar the control and the experimental groups, the more confidence you can have in your findings.

As an example of this design, consider the problem of relapse among the chronically mentally ill. You want to know whether those patients who are served by your state-run hospital stay as long in the community as those in a similar institution in a different part of the state. With the cooperation of both hospital administrators, you make comparisons of such variables as staff-to-patient ratios, percentage of first-time admissions, and average age of patients in order to establish that the patients and the facilities are roughly equivalent.

Suppose you find out that the patients from your hospital do seem to have longer stays in the community than patients of the other hospital. You might conclude that the programming or staff at your hospital is better. However, this design cannot unequivocally demonstrate this. It could be that more of the clients in the other hospital return to rural areas, where there is not the same level of community support services (aftercare) as are available to the patients from your hospital (who tend to remain in an urban area). There could be differences in staff morale at the two hospitals (which might affect the treatment received by patients) or in the ease of readmission or screening procedures. Could differences in the physical facilities be a factor? (What if one hospital had been built in 1894 and the other in 1984?) So, while you can be somewhat reassured that your hospital is more successful than another, the lack of control over potentially very important factors prevents you from *conclusively* determining that the intervention at one hospital is the main reason for the patients' longer stays in the community.

Another quasi-experimental design is called **Time-Series** or **Interrupted Time Series.** This design is one of the older designs used in the natural sciences, but it has not been utilized extensively in the social sciences. The Time-Series design is an extension of the One-Group Pretest-Posttest design, where there are a series of measurements taken before and after an intervention. This allows the researcher to understand trends and patterns in the data before the intervention is applied and then provides for continued monitoring for major changes. Notation for a Time-Series design is:

$$O_1 \quad O_2 \quad O_3 \quad X \quad O_4 \quad O_5 \quad O_6$$

With this design, the researcher is able to get a grasp on incremental changes (if any) in the study group's behavior prior to the intervention and then to determine if the change after intervention is greater or not. When possible, an equal number of measurements should be made before and after the intervention. Also, the period of time between the measurements should be comparable. Note that the period of time between intervals is determined by the researcher; it is not imposed from the design. The amount of time between O_1, O_2, and the other observations could be seven days, two weeks, or three months. This design is particularly well-suited for research in social policy when historical or archival data is available. Each observation could then represent a year's data. For instance, you might monitor the number of suicides or homicides from handguns in a city three years before and three years after passage of a new ordinance requiring a five-day "cooling off" period before purchase of a handgun.

On a smaller scale, one might use the Time-Series design to

look at such agency productivity before and after the executive director implements a new four-day, forty-hour workweek. When using the Time-Series design in this way, it is important to watch for seasonal variations. Would it be all right to compare January (O_1), February (O_2), and March (O_3) with June (O_4), July (O_5), and August (O_6)? This wouldn't be a fair comparison if there were lower productivity in the summer months. To protect against making a conclusion influenced by seasonal or other natural fluctuations in data, include enough observation periods to get a stable baseline. This may require going back more than just the three observation points suggested by the design.

When the data from time series are graphed (recall the **AB** designs in the last chapter), the slope of the line is often of assistance in understanding whether the observed effect was caused by the intervention. On a graph, you can readily determine if the magnitude or frequency of a behavior is increasing prior to and after an intervention. Because the measurements are obtained over an extended period of time, history is the chief threat to the internal validity of this design. A threat from instrumentation might also be apparent in some instances.

This Time-Series design provides even better information if a corresponding control group can be added:

$$O_1 \quad O_2 \quad O_3 \quad X \quad O_4 \quad O_5 \quad O_6$$

$$O_1 \quad O_2 \quad O_3 \quad \quad O_4 \quad O_5 \quad O_6$$

This new design with a control group is called the **Multiple Time-Series Design.** It resembles a stretched out Nonequivalent Control Group Design. Campbell and Stanley (1963) recommend this design for research in school settings. It is a strong quasi-experimental design with no serious internal validity threats. The investigator can use the control group to check for the influence of history and to understand the effects of testing, maturation, mortality, and instrumentation.

For instance, prior to the passage of the Brady Law, which requires a five-day "cooling off" period before purchase of a handgun, an investigator could examine the number of homicides in a sample of cities or states with such legislation and compare this data to a control group of cities or states that did not have such legislation. You would expect fewer homicides, over time, in the sample having the greater regulation of handgun sales. Use of a control group allows the investigator to determine whether a decrease in homicides is part of a national trend toward less violence or whether it could be attributed to the legislation.

Design and Validity Considerations

The main reason that researchers often choose experimental over pre-experimental or quasi-experimental designs is that they make causal inference easier (Cook and Campbell, 1979). As a social work practitioner, you may have a notion that a certain intervention employed by you or your agency is more effective with clients than others. To test this hypothesis, you would probably choose one of the designs described in this chapter. Sometimes, however, social workers have questions like "Are parents of disabled children more likely to abuse their children than other parents?" Or "Is alcoholism primarily responsible for the problem of homelessness?" Such basic research questions as these do not require experimental research designs. Rather, they are more likely to be explored using secondary data analysis (chapter 8) or a survey research design (chapter 6). The designs in this chapter are commonly used to determine the impact or effect of an intervention used with groups.

As previously discussed, pre-experimental and quasi-experimental designs are susceptible to problems of internal validity. Yet, useful information and valuable studies can come from designs that are not truly experimental.

For example, if you are hired as a school social worker in an alternative school providing group therapy and support groups for adolescents with chemical dependency problems, random assignment may not be possible—the groups were started at the beginning of the school year. If you want to evaluate the success of these groups, the best design remaining might be the nonequivalent control group design. Even though experimental designs are the best, quasi-experimental designs should not be summarily dismissed, particularly when you are engaged in what I call "salvage" research (when you're trying to rescue data that otherwise might be lost).

In order to make your study as strong as possible, careful planning is required. Some threats to the internal validity of your study can be eliminated or minimized by following the suggestions of Mitchell and Jolley (1988):

1. Keep the time between the start and the end of the study short. This helps minimize the threat of *history*. (Note that this suggestion does not apply to time-series designs.) Also, keeping the study period short can help minimize the threat of *matura-*

tion (especially a problem when studying children and youth), as well as any interaction of maturation with selection.

2. Test subjects only once, use different versions of the same test, or give the subjects opportunity to extensively practice prior to collecting the pretest data so that any gains occurring at the posttest are not an effect of the second test. This helps minimize the threat of *testing*.

3. Administer the instrument the same way every time. (This helps minimize the threat of *instrumentation*.)

4. Use innocuous or placebo treatments, brief treatments, or mild incentives so that subjects do not drop out of the study. Keep in touch with those participating in your study—especially with those in the control group when there is a long period between observations. (This helps minimize the threat of *mortality*.)

5. Be careful with choosing subjects on the basis of one extreme test score. (This helps minimize the threat of *statistical regression*.)

6. Randomly assign where possible. If you must match, match on as many key variables as is practical. (This helps minimize the threat of *selection*.)

Thinking about ways of preventing extraneous variables from influencing (or explaining away) the effect of your intervention will result in a stronger study. While the selection of a good research design is important, it is no substitute for good planning. Even a strong design can be poorly implemented and go awry when little attention is paid to details. If, for instance, you lose most of your control group through neglect, even an experimental design will be of little assistance in helping you infer that the intervention caused the observed changes in the treatment group.

Research designs are only guides to the research process. They structure a problem-solving process and provide an outline for how data will be collected. Choice of a particular design is a complex decision often hinging upon feasibility considerations. Should you be faced with having to use a group research design sometime in the future, remember that there are numerous other designs (and multiple variations of the designs in this chapter) available to you. Regardless of the design you choose, devote time to considering how extraneous variables may affect the internal and external validity of your study.

Finally, some social workers say that they have ethical problems with experimental designs because these designs deny clients needed services. These same individuals overlook the fact that most agencies have waiting lists and that natural control groups can be found in those who are queued up, waiting for their turn.

Another way to think about the problem is that control group members would not be denied anything; they would receive the usual or customary services. The experimental group would also receive these services plus an additional boost of something more intense. What's more intense? Meeting twice a week with a case manager or therapist is more intense than meeting once a week. Individual counseling may be more intense than group therapy. Individual counseling is more intense than distributing reading material or videotapes (educational intervention). Who says that everyone benefits from the same approach?

Even the lowly pre-experimental designs have a role. As exploratory or pilot studies, they attempt to expand our knowledge about the interventions we use and their effects upon our clients. They may not be great studies, but they have the potential of providing some new knowledge that can be explored in greater depth and precision with a more powerful and rigorous design. In some instances, they provide all the evidence necessary to convince a foundation or funding source to underwrite a more extensive and scientific study.

However, randomization is not always possible and when it is not, groups for comparison should be sought within one's agency or from other agencies that provide similar treatment, or even from similar populations in a different locality.

Sometimes people naturally form themselves into control groups. Some men who batter would rather go to jail than attend a psycho-educational treatment program. Some men are released with community service, fined, or put on probation. Even if random assignment is not possible, comparison to some of these other groups can still reveal cogent and compelling information.

Questions for Class Discussion

1. What are the different pretest-posttest comparisons that can be made with the Solomon Four-Group design?
2. What kinds of experimental research do you think are needed or would you like to see conducted? Make a list of these.
3. Consider the threats to internal validity as presented in this chapter and discuss how they also may pose threats to single system designs.
4. Discuss how pragmatic considerations (the agency setting, its

clientele) influence the choice of a research design. How do the possible implications or findings of the study affect the choice of a design?

5. Which two designs discussed in this chapter are identical except for the use of randomization?

6. How might the use of experimental designs in social service agencies involve ethical considerations?

7. Do you think practitioners who want to do research start with a specific research design that they want to use or start with an intervention they want to evaluate and then seek a research design that fits the situation?

8. A social work student in a psychology course was assigned the project of conducting an exhaustion study with a white rat on a small treadmill. A piece of cheese was hung in front of the rat to keep it running. The student's lab partner, feeling sorry for the rat, fed it pieces of cheese until the rat became so full that it quit running. Feeding the rat was most like what threat to the internal validity of the lab exercise?

9. Discuss the arguments for choosing an experimental design over a quasi-experimental design to evaluate an intervention.

Mini-Projects for Experiencing Research Firsthand

1. Briefly describe a feasible experiment that could be conducted in a social service agency using one of the three experimental designs. Be sure to address each of the following:
   a. your hypothesis
   b. how you will acquire your subjects and how they will be randomly assigned
   c. your intervention
   d. your dependent variable (How would you operationalize it?)
   e. the number of observations or measurements required

2. Think about some controversial social problem (e.g., homelessness, teen pregnancy, drug abuse) and describe a grand social experiment that might test a hypothesis or a notion you have about how to ameliorate the social problem. Specify a hypothesis, the research design, and threats to the internal validity of your study.

3. Identify some recent legislation and describe how a time-series quasi-experimental design could be used to study the effects of the legislation. Be sure to identify the type and source of the data that you would need for the study.

4. Imagine you are the new director of a small agency that is not well-known in the community. You direct a staff member to coordinate a number of activities that worked in your former agency and that you think will increase contacts and referrals from the community in your new agency. How will you know if the public relations intervention made any difference? Specify a research design.

5. Read the reports of the Milgram (1963, 1965) experiments and write a brief report arguing why you think the experiments were or were not important and whether they were ethical.

Resources and References

Applegate, J.S. (1992). The impact of subject measures on nonbehavioral practice research: Outcome vs. process. *Families in Society*, 73(2), 100–108.

Bulmer, M. (1986). *Social Science and Social Policy*. London: Allen & Unwin.

Campbell, D.T. and Stanley, J.C. (1963). *Experimental and Quasi-Experimental Designs for Research*. Skokie, IL: Rand McNally.

Cook, T.D. and Campbell, D.T. (1979). *Quasi-Experimentation: Design and Analysis Issues for Field Settings*. Skokie, IL: Rand McNally.

Cox, G.H., Brogan, D.R., and Dandridge, M.A. (1986). The effectiveness of home visitation in reducing AFDC case payment errors. *Social Service Review*, 60(4), 603–618.

Edleson, J.L. and Syers, M. (1990). Relative effectiveness of group treatments for men who batter. *Social Work Research and Abstracts*, 26(2), 10–17.

Fawzy, F., Cousins, N., Fawzy, N., Kemeny, M., Elashoff, R., and Morton, D. (1990). A structured psychiatric intervention for cancer patients. *Archives of General Psychiatry*, 47, 720–725.

Gentry, M.E., Connaway, R.S., and Morelock, M. (1984). Research activities of social workers in agencies. *Social Work Research and Abstracts*, 20(4), 3–5.

Grinnell, R.M. and Stothers, M. (1988). Utilizing research designs. In Richard M. Grinnell (Ed.), *Social Work Research and Evaluation*, Itasca, IL: Peacock.

Hausman, J.A. and Wise, D.A. (1985). *Social Experimentation*. Chicago, IL: University of Chicago Press.

Hudson, W.W. (1978). Research training in professional social work education. *Social Service Review*, 52 (March), 116–121.

Judd, C.M. and Kenny, D.A. (1981). *Estimating the Effects of Social Interventions*. Cambridge: University Press.

Kazdin, A.E. (1982). *Single-Case Research Designs: Methods for Clinical and Applied Settings*. New York: Oxford University Press.

Kidder, L.H. and Judd, C.M. (1986). *Research Methods in Social Relations.* New York: Holt, Rinehart and Winston.

Milgram, S. (1963). Behavioral study of obedience. *Journal of Abnormal and Social Psychology, 67,* 371–378.

Milgram, S. (1965). Some conditions of obedience and disobedience to authority. *Human Relations, 18,* 57–76.

Mitchell, M. and Jolley, J. (1988). *Research Design Explained.* New York: Holt, Rinehart and Winston.

Powers, G.T., Meenaghan, T.M., and Toomey, B.G. (1985). *Practice Focused Research.* Englewood Cliffs, NJ: Prentice-Hall.

Schiffman, S.S., Buckley, C.E., Sampson, H.A., Massey, E.W., Baraniuk, J.N., Follett, J.V., and Warwick, Z.S. (1987). Aspartame and susceptibility to headache. *New England Journal of Medicine, 317* (19), 1181–1185.

Spiegel, D. (1990). Can psychotherapy prolong cancer survival? *Psychosomatics, 31*(4), 361–363.

Thyer, B. (1984). The clinical anxiety scale. In Kevin Corcoran and Joel Fischer (Eds.) *Measures for Clinical Practice.* New York: The Free Press.

5
Understanding and Using Research Instruments

Social work researchers use (and design) scales and instruments to measure concepts that concern them. For instance, take the problem of determining if a drug prevention program had the effect intended upon its seventh, eighth, and ninth grade target population. Assume that the intervention and curriculum are already established. The presenters are ready, the school administrators are eager for the program to start. What happens next?

Let's further assume that the goals of the intervention can be clearly established and all that is needed is some sort of instrument to measure any changes that occur from the pretest to the posttest. When I was presented with this problem several years ago, I immediately thought about going to the literature and trying to find an instrument to help me gauge the results of the intervention.

One of my first dilemmas was how to operationalize the success of the program. Ideally, the best test of the program's success would be if these middle schoolers didn't abuse drugs or alcohol as adults. Since we would be unable to lurk in the shadows and follow over one thousand participants over that span of time, success had to be viewed a little differently.

We could have chosen to ask students about their current drug use prior to the intervention and then some time later (e.g., six months after the program ended). However, school administrators tend not to be very comfortable with asking about current drug use. Plus, there was come concern that students might be prone to falsify statements of their drug use in order to appear "cool."

Maybe we could have envisioned success as improvement in knowledge on a test of different drugs and their effects. However, the presenters would not be teaching that red pills do this and that blue pills have this other effect.

Having considered and rejected students' current *behavior* (drug usage) and *knowledge* about drugs and alcohol, we decided to measure changes in students' *attitudes* about drugs. And as a first step, we quickly surveyed the literature. Not finding any instrument that excited us, we had to design our own.

Now, assuming that you've approached this task after thoroughly studying the previous chapter, how would you know if the instrument you have created is any good?

Instruments and scales are evaluated along two primary dimensions: reliability and validity.

Reliability

Reliability is an easy term to understand because its usage by researchers is very close to its use in the everyday world. When a watch keeps time accurately, it is said to be reliable. If, on the other hand, your watch gained a half hour in one week, lost seventeen minutes the second week, and gained three hours at the end of the third week, you would suspect that something is wrong with it—that it is not reliable. Similarly, a scale or instrument that consistently measures some phenomenon with accuracy is said to be **reliable.** The instrument is dependable and has a certain amount of predictability associated with it. If an instrument is reliable, then administering it to similar groups under comparable conditions should yield similar results. This is one of the principles upon which standardized tests (such as I.Q. tests) are developed.

One of the ways we evaluate standardized instruments is by their reliability. Generally this information resembles a correlation coefficient and is reported in a journal article or in a manual describing the characteristics of the instrument. Reliability coefficients are numeric values between 0 and 1. Nunnally (1978) says that in the early stages of research one can work with instruments having modest reliability, by which he means .70 or higher; that .80 is needed for basic research; and that a reliability of .90 is the minimum when important decisions are going to be made with respect to specific test scores. If there is no reliability data on a scale and it is not well known, reliability cannot be assumed—the scale could have poor reliability.

Researchers want their instruments to have a form of reliability known as **internal consistency.** This means that individual items correlate well with the full scale. If this doesn't happen, the items have very little in common. For example, say you were constructing a scale to measure assertiveness. You write the following items:

THE SLAP-TOGETHER ASSERTIVENESS SCALE
Agree   Disagree

Agree	Disagree	
_____	_____	1. I always speak my mind.
_____	_____	2. I am frank about my feelings.
_____	_____	3. I take care of myself.

After creating these three items, you develop writer's block. As you try to think of additional items to include, you recall your friend Henry, who was the most assertive individual you have ever known. You ponder Henry's distinctiveness and remember how fanatical he was about baseball. Maybe knowledge of baseball and assertiveness are somehow related, you think. So, you write a new item:

4. I believe professional baseball is superior to all other sports.

These four items complete our scale, and we administer the Slap-Together Assertiveness Scale to a large cross section of adults. One of the ways we can obtain information about our scale is by running the Reliability procedure available through the *Statistical Package for the Social Sciences* (SPSS). SPSS is computer software installed on most universities' mainframe computers (and versions for personal computers are also available).

After you've entered the way each individual responded to the items on the scale, the computer program will produce a reliability coefficient and indicate those items that do not correlate well with the rest. By dropping these items, it is often possible to improve a scale's internal consistency.

For example, a simplified printout might show something like this:

	Item-Total Correlation	Alpha If Item Deleted
Item 1	.5350	− .3501
Item 2	.5103	− .2894
Item 3	.2556	.1150
Item 4	− .5383	.7165

The item-total correlation from the printout reveals that item 4 is inversely related to the rest of the scale. In other words, assertive individuals (as measured by the first three items) in our sample often disagreed with item 4. Should we keep it anyway? The Reliability procedure informs us that we have the makings of a promising scale (an Alpha of .72, rounded) if we delete item 4. Dropping this item would be a good decision and would leave us with a three-item scale. If we wanted to improve our internal consistency even more, we would need to try out additional items with another group of subjects.

Sometimes researchers measure internal consistency by dividing their longer scales in half (either top and bottom or even versus odd items) and examining how well the two halves correlate with each other. This is known as the *split-half* technique. Another approach is to devise *parallel* or *alternate* versions of the scale and administer both forms to similar groups. Again, one would hope that both versions would correlate with each other—the higher the correlation coefficient, the stronger the reliability.

Once a scale has been shown to have internal consistency, researchers next want to demonstrate that its capability is not impaired by differences in space and time. Would those individuals who were identified as being assertive on the fifteenth of October still be assertive two weeks later? What about in January? To determine stability, researchers will often administer a scale to the same group on more than one occasion (*test-retest reliability*) to see if persons with high test scores at the first administration maintain high scores at the second administration.

Over short periods of time, scores (of assertiveness or whatever) should remain fairly consistent. While it is expected that some individuals will increase or decrease in assertiveness, possibly as a result of an intervention or some personal event that happened only to them, there would be no logical explanation for why the majority of a large group should experience extreme changes in their assertiveness scores. Should this happen, and if the researcher can find no other explanation, it is reasonable to assume that there is some problem with the instrument.

With the example of the Slap-Together Assertiveness Scale, there could be too few items to give it stability over time. Similarly, it would have reliability problems if it showed internal consistency with subjects from one part of the United States but not from another geographical area. What good would such an instrument be?

Internal consistency cannot be computed on a single item. As a general rule, fewer items usually equate to lower reliability. All else being equal, a scale of twenty-five items stands a better chance of having acceptable reliability than one of three or four items.

Validity

An instrument is said to be **valid** when it measures what it was designed to measure. An intelligence test should measure intelligence. An instrument designed to measure anxiety should provide an accurate assessment of anxiety but probably would not be valid for measuring such concepts as social responsibility, dogmatism, and paranoia. Validity research demonstrates what an attitudinal or psychological measure can and cannot do—its limitations as well as its advantages. No test or scale is applicable in all circumstances. The purpose of validity research is to identify situations in which the instrument is valid.

There are numerous ways to go about establishing the validity of an instrument. Research texts generally discuss the types of validity efforts in terms of the following categories:

1. Content validity
2. Criterion validity
   a. Concurrent approaches
   b. Predictive approaches
3. Construct validity

In order to have **content validity**, an instrument needs to sample from the entire range of the concept that it was designed to measure. For instance, it could be difficult for a scale measuring anger in children under the age of eight to be valid if the scale did not consider pouting, hitting, or temper tantrums as manifestations of anger. Likewise, a scale measuring anxiety in adolescents might not have content validity if it did not include such behavior as nail-biting, crying, stomachaches, and sleeplessness. To the extent that an instrument contains a representative sampling of the universe of behaviors, attitudes, or characteristics that are believed to be associated with the concept, then it is said to have content validity. Content validity could be established when a panel of experts examines the scale and agrees that the items selected are representative of the range of items associated with the concept to be measured. However, there are no standardized procedures for assessing content validity.

While the terms *content* and *face validity* are sometimes used interchangeably, they do not have the same meaning, even though a similar process is used to establish both. An instrument is said to have **face validity** when colleagues are asked to examine an instrument and express their opinions about whether the proposed instrument measures what it was intended to measure. While it is necessary to ensure that a new instrument has face validity, this term refers to what the instrument "appears" to measure and therefore is not technically a form of validation. Both face validity and content validity are necessary for acceptance of the scale by others; however, they are not sufficient for establishing that the scale will allow generalizability, a test for "true" validity.

Once content validity is established, the instrument is ready to be put to use. One begins to establish **criterion validity** when positive correlations are obtained between the test or scale values and some external criteria that are assumed to be indicators of the concept. Criterion validity, the second major category of validity research activities, is based upon the scale's ability to correspond with other test results that are thought to be indicative of the attitude, trait, or behavior being measured. There are several ways to establish criterion validity. We will quickly discuss two approaches.

Concurrent validity is demonstrated by administering your scale simultaneously along with another scale that has documented validity to the same subjects. If the two scales correlate well in the direction expected, then your scale has demonstrated one form of concurrent validity. As an example, suppose you had developed the Drug Attitude Questionnaire (Appendix C). How would you go about showing that it had concurrent validity? One way would be to administer it along with another "proven" instrument that also measures attitudes about drugs. In fact, this is what we did. We correlated the Drug Attitude Questionnaire (DAQ) with a similar but shorter (fourteen-item) instrument. This meant that some students in our study had to complete both instruments.

We found that the DAQ correlated .76 with the shorter instrument at posttest using a sample of ninth grade students and correlated .79 using a sample of college students. These relatively high correlations show that low scores on one test correspond to low scores on the other and vice versa. When high correlations are obtained between two tests presumed to be measuring the same concept, then concurrent validity is demonstrated.

Predictive validity is the second form of criterion validity and is demonstrated when scores on a test or scale predict future behavior or attitudes. The Drug Attitude Questionnaire has predictive validity if, years later, you find that within your study group of middle school students, those who had pro-drug attitudes were suspended from school or arrested for drug possession, while those with anti-drug attitudes were not suspended or arrested for drug possession.

The third major category in validity research is **construct validity**. A well-constructed scale ought to be able to discriminate among individuals along the lines you would expect. For instance, think about individuals who would likely have positive attitudes regarding drugs. Where would you find these people? In drug treatment programs? In jail? Where would you find individuals with negative attitudes about recreational drug use? In church groups? A scale with construct validity should show statistically significant differences in the scores between, say, students attending a conservative Baptist college and clients of an outpatient drug treatment agency. These were the two samples we used to demonstrate that the Drug Attitude Questionnaire had construct validity (Royse, Keller, and Schwartz, 1982).

What if we had found no differences? The DAQ wouldn't have had any construct validity, although it still may have had some face or content validity. What does this tell you? That it is the ability of an instrument to distinguish among individuals who have a lot of, some of, or none of the characteristic being measured that makes the instrument useful. When it can discriminate along the lines you hypothesize it should, then you have evidence that it can do what it was constructed to do.

Establishing validity is not a one-time or a single-shot deal, but rather an ongoing process. Different uses of the instrument become opportunities to show its ability to discriminate among different populations, which adds to the accumulative evidence of its validity. For example, even though the DAQ was designed for middle school students, it might be employed with inpatients or outpatients in drug treatment programs to determine if attitudes about drugs changed as a result of intervention.

For the purpose of instruction, reliability and validity are usually presented as separate concepts. However, these two concepts are interrelated in a complex fashion. On the one hand, when we can empirically demonstrate that an instrument is valid, it can generally be assumed to have adequate reliability. On the other hand, a reliable instrument may not be valid. That is, an instrument may provide dependable measurements but of some concept unrelated to what we thought we were measuring. Both reliability and validity ought to be demonstrated as evidence that an instrument is psychometrically strong.

As you come across various instruments in practice or in your reading, it is important to realize that if you know nothing about the reliability and validity of a scale, then any results that are obtained from its use may have very little meaning. The scale may not provide consistent results (poor reliability) or it may measure something quite different from what was intended (poor validity). The importance of knowing a scale's reliability and validity cannot be emphasized enough.

Locating Research Instruments

While complete scales are sometimes reproduced in journal articles, this is a fairly rare occurrence because of space limitations. Commonly what is found are examples of items from the scale and information about the scale's reliability and validity. This usually means that the reader will have to consult the bibliography and may have to search through several other articles to find the actual scale or more specific information about where to obtain it.

Some instruments may be protected by copyright. More than likely, you will have to purchase copies of these instruments before you can use them. Other instruments are in the public domain. That means that they belong to you, the public, and can be used without special permission.

Instruments that you find in journal articles are not likely to be protected by copyright. However, good research etiquette dictates that you contact the author anyway and request permission to use the instrument. This can be a useful contact to make. Most authors want to keep informed of research conducted with their instruments. They'll be interested in yours. As you discuss your proposed research with them, they may be able to help in ways that you didn't expect. Sometimes they have prepared shorter or newer versions of old instruments or may share a bibliography of recent applications and findings with the instrument.

Finding an appropriate instrument without immersing yourself completely in the literature can be a bit like chasing a rainbow. However, there are several good sources for scales that may contain just the instrument you require. A listing of some resources that may be of use to you includes:

Brodsky, S.L. and Smitherman, H.O. (1983). *Handbook of Scales for Research in Crime and Delinquency.* New York: Plenum Press.

Corcoran, K. (1994). *Measures for Clinical Practice: A Sourcebook, Volume 2, Adults.* New York: Free Press.

Corcoran, K. and Fischer, J. (1987). *Measures for Clinical Practice: A Sourcebook.* New York: Free Press.

Fredman, N. and Sherman, R. (1987). *Handbook of Measurements for Marriage and Family Therapy.* New York: Brunner/Mazel.

McDowell, I. and Newell, C. (1987). *Measuring Health: A Guide to Rating Scales and Questionnaires.* New York: Oxford University Press.

Miller, D.C. (1991). *Handbook of Research Design and Social Measurement.* Newbury Park, CA: Sage.

Nurius, P.S. and Hudson, W.W. (1993). *Human Services Practice, Evaluation, and Computers.* Pacific Grove, CA: Brooks/Cole.

Robinson, J.P., Shaver, P., and Wrightsman, L.S. (1991). *Measures of Personality and Social Psychological Attitudes.* San Diego: Academic Press.

Touliatos, J., Perlmutter, B.F., and Straus, M.A. (1990). *Handbook of Family Measurement Techniques.* Newbury Park, CA: Sage.

Other references, although somewhat dated, may help you to locate a specific test or instrument:

Chun, Ki-Taek, Cobb, S., and French, J.R., Jr. (1975). *Measures for Psychological Assessment: A Guide to 3000 Original Sources and Their Applications.* Ann Arbor, MI: Institute for Social Research.

Goldman, B.A. and Busch, J.C. (1982). *Directory of Unpublished Experimental Mental Measures.* New York: Human Sciences Press.

Hamill, D.D. (1989). *A Consumer's Guide to Tests in Print.* Austin, TX: Pro-ED.

Keyser, D.J. and Sweetland, R.C. (1984). *Test Critiques.* Kansas City, MO: Test Corporation of America.

Keyser, D.J. and Sweetland, R.C. (1987). *Test Critiques Compendium: Reviews of Major Tests from the Test Critiques Series.* Kansas City, MO: Test Corporation of America.

Lake, D.G., Miles, M.B., and Earle, R.B., Jr. (1973). *Measuring Human Behavior: Tools for the Assessment of Social Functioning.* New York: Teachers College Press.

Robinson, J.P., Athanasiou, R., and Head, K.B. (1969). *Measures of Occupational Attitudes and Occupational Characteristics.* Ann Arbor, MI: Institute for Social Research.

Sweetland, R.C. and Keyser, D.J. (1986). *Tests: A Comprehensive Reference for Assessments in Psychology, Education, and Business.* Kansas City, MO: Test Corporation of America.

When You Can't Find the Instrument You Want

Most often when students complain that they can't find an instrument they need, they've had a problem narrowing down exactly what they want to measure. Not too long ago, a student told me she had spent hours in the library and reviewed about a hundred abstracts without finding the kind of instrument she was looking for. As we talked more, she revealed that she'd been searching under "children" and "families" when it would have been more profitable for her to look for literature on parenting programs.

If, however, you have conducted an exhaustive literature search and consulted with knowledgeable people and still can't find the instrument you want, two avenues lie before you. First, you can take an existing instrument and modify it to meet your needs. It is reasonable to take such drastic action if, for instance, you've found a potentially useful scale but it's too long for the group you intend to use it with (e.g., persons with short attention spans).

In such a situation, write to the author of the instrument to ask if any short forms have been developed, and if they have not, if you may have permission to use her other items to create a brief version. Most authors, particularly if their scales have appeared in professional journals and are not copyrighted, will likely be interested in your research and grant you permission. The only caution here is that anytime you modify an existing instrument, the burden is upon you to prove that the resulting instrument is reliable and valid. Because the longer instrument was psychometrically sound does not guarantee that the shorter instrument will be. You will have to demonstrate reliability and validity.

A colleague and I once modified the social distance scale created by E.S. Bogardus in 1925. In an attempt to measure acceptance of different nationalities or races, Bogardus asked respondents if they would admit someone different from themselves into such situations as:

1. Kinship by marriage
2. Club membership
3. Neighbors
4. Employment in one's occupation
5. Citizenship in one's country
6. Visitors to one's country

Our social distance scale asked some of these same questions, providing *Strongly Agree, Agree, Undecided, Disagree,* and *Strongly Disagree* as response choices:

SA A U D SD   I would be opposed to a person having AIDS living on the same street with me.

SA A U D SD   I would be uncomfortable if I had to work in the same department or office as a person having AIDS.

SA A U D SD   I would allow a person having AIDS to become a citizen of the United States.

SA A U D SD   I would exclude a person having AIDS from visiting my country.

Even with just these four items, the reliability was quite strong (.82). Since this was an exploratory study, we didn't attempt to establish the validity of the instrument, but we did find that our Social Distance Scale correlated .67 with our Fear of Aids Scale and −.68 with our Empathy for AIDS Victims Scale, which at least suggests that our measure might have more than just face or content validity. (For further information about the research we conducted with this instrument, you might want to see Royse and Birge, 1987.)

When would it be important to establish that a scale has validity? This would be something you would want to do if you were planning further research with the instrument or if you were thinking about getting a copyright in order to market it. Perhaps your scale could help social service employers screen out applicants who have the least empathy for clients or who would be too fearful to work with AIDS patients. Or, if your responsibility with an organization is to provide in-service training, you might want a valid scale to help you evaluate what the participants acquired from the in-service training.

If you find no instruments you want to modify, a second option is to create your own scale. Once again, it will be your responsibility to establish that the instrument measures what was intended and does so reliably. Just because you think it has content or face validity does not make it a good instrument. Take, for example, questions 7 through 15 of the Attitudes about Research Courses Questionnaire (from Appendix A).

FEAR ITEMS FROM THE ATTITUDES ABOUT RESEARCH QUESTIONNAIRE

7. T or F   I dread speaking before a large group of people more than taking a research course.

8. T or F   I would rather take a research course than ask a waitress to return an improperly cooked meal to the chef.

9. T or F   My fear of snakes is greater than my fear of taking a research course.

10. T or F My fear of spiders is less than my fear of taking a research course.
11. T or F I would rather take a research course than ask a total stranger to do a favor for me.
12. T or F My fear of research is such that I would rather the university require an additional two courses of my choosing than require one research course.
13. T or F I dread going to the dentist more than taking a research course.
14. T or F I fear a statistics course more than a research methodology course.
15. T or F I have always "hated math."

Can you guess what I was trying to measure with this scale? Although I had high hopes for it, the scale's reliability was so poor that I've never attempted any further research with it. What struck me as a clever way to measure fear of research simply didn't work. I suspect that individual responses to such things as spiders and dentists interfered with rather than facilitated the concept I was trying to measure. Oh, well, this is the way research moves forward. Sometimes there's considerable trial and error involved.

How does one go about constructing a scale? Normally, you begin with creating a pool of items that you think will measure different dimensions or degrees of the behavior, knowledge, or attitude that you have in mind. Sometimes experts in the field are invited to contribute items. Then some weeding out of items occurs, and a draft of an instrument is prepared. This version is then administered to a large group. From the data the group supplies, the evaluator uses computer software to identify which items correlate well. The items that correlate most poorly are thrown out.

Depending on the reliability coefficient obtained, the researcher might, at that point, decide that the refined list of items is adequate. If the reliability coefficient is lower than desired, the researcher will add new items and administer the second version to another set of people, dropping and adding new items until he or she is satisfied with the internal consistency of the instrument. Only then does the researcher begin to assess the validity of the instrument and to become concerned with its ability to be reliable over time.

There's more to know about scale development than can be quickly conveyed in this introductory text. For instance, factor analysis (an advanced statistical procedure performed on the computer) is often used to demonstrate the relatedness of items and that "factorial validity" exists (when the items and scales are statistically acting as though they are measuring what they were designed to measure).

Also, five- and seven-choice item formats tend to be more reliable than two- (Agree/Disagree) or three-choice item formats and create fewer distortions in computed correlations. The novice scale developer will need to do some additional reading, perhaps starting with Comrey (1988) and continuing with some of the references in his bibliography.

To see how social work researchers have gone about demonstrating that their scales are valid and reliable, consult such articles as those on the Index of Clinical Stress (Abell, 1991), the Index of Self-Esteem (Nugent and Thomas, 1993), the Protective Services Questionnaire (Combs-Orme, Orme, and Guidry, 1991), the Attitude Toward the Provision of Long-Term Care (Klein, 1992), and others found in the references at the end of this chapter.

A Sampling of Instruments

Throughout this chapter we've been talking about instruments and scales. For the section that follows, I've secured the permission of several authors to reproduce all or portions of their instruments. Even with this small sample, you'll see some of the great variety of instruments that have been created by social workers. Instruments contained in this section are:

The Community Living Skills Scale

The Social Work Empowerment Scale

The Prosocial Tendencies Scale for Children

Attitude Toward the Provision of Long-Term Care

The Maternal Characteristics Scale

Helping Behavior Checklist

Role Strain Index

Job Satisfaction Scale

The Community Living Skills Scale (CLSS)

Description

The CLSS is a scale designed to measure level of functioning within a psychiatric population. This self-rating scale is distinctive in that the consumers of a psychosocial rehabilitation agency played a major role in helping develop it. Using the Denver Community Mental Health Questionnaire as a model, a group of consumers participated in brainstorming sessions that identified activities within the broad areas of personal care, social relations, and activities/vocational skills in which a mental health consumer living in the community would be engaged. Later, these were restated in behavioral terms and a pretest was conducted with fifty clients. It has been proposed that the CLSS could be used to measure community living skills of individuals in psychiatric hospitals or residential facilities and for outcome evaluation.

Psychometric Data

Internal consistency (Cronbach's Alpha) ranged from .79 to .84 on four retained subscales, showing them to have adequate reliability. Validity of the scale was examined by comparing CLSS scores from consumers in the pretest group with ratings on the Global Assessment Scale (GAS). Results were mixed. The Personal Care subscale was significantly correlated ($r = .41$) with the GAS scores, but none of the other three subscales were significantly correlated. The authors explain this by stating that the GAS is geared more toward appearances and behaviors usually associated with psychosis, whereas the CLSS does a better job of measuring subjective distress.

In terms of discriminant validity, the CLSS was administered to a comparison group of fifty social work graduate students. As was expected, the student group had significantly higher (more functional) scores and smaller standard deviations on all the subscales.

Availability

Smith, M.K. and Ford, J. (1990). A client-developed functional level scale: The Community Living Skills Scale (CLSS). *Journal of Social Service Research,* 13(3), 61–84.

For further information about the instrument, contact Mieko K. Smith, Ph.D., Dept. of Social Work, Cleveland State University, Euclid Ave. at E. 24th Street, Cleveland, OH 44115, or Janet Ford, Ph.D., College of Social Work, University of Kentucky, Lexington, KY 40506-0027.

Scoring

Responses are scored as follows: "Almost always" (4), "Usually" (3), "Sometimes" (2), "Hardly ever" (1). However, reverse scoring must be used for items 7, 20, 21, 28, 31, 33, 34, 35, and 46. Additionally, some items (particularly in the socialization/relationship area) were not applicable to everyone—for example, those who are not married. For the "Not applicable" responses, the authors used an average of the other items from that subscale to replace the missing value.

FIGURE 5.1: The Community Living Skills Scale

Please mark an X on the answer that is the closest to how often you accomplish each act.

	Almost Always	Usually	Some-times	Hardly Ever

Personal Care

1. I (can) do (food) shopping.
2. I bathe enough to keep myself clean.
3. I (can) do my own laundry.
4. I eat balanced meals.
5. I get dressed daily.
6. I am capable of finding ways to solve my own problems.
7. I have difficulty in getting up daily.
8. I get to the dentist when I need to.
9. I keep my appearance presentable.
10. I fight depression when it comes.
11. I get to the doctor when I need to.
12. I go to bed at a reasonable hour.
13. I keep my hair neat.
14. I manage my money.
15. I get the amount of sleep I need.
16. I keep my living quarters decent.
17. I control my alcohol/drug problems.
18. I take my medications (if any) as prescribed.
19. I find transportation as needed.

Socialization/Relationships

20. I am afraid of being with others.
21. I avoid meeting new people.
22. I devote time to my family.
23. I get along with the people I live with.
24. I control my anger.
25. I cope with my anxiety.
26. I show consideration for others.
27. I am respectful of other peoples' rights.
28. My relationship with my child(ren) interferes with my life.
29. I get along with my neighbors.
30. I have trusting relationships.
31. My relationship with my spouse interferes with my life.
32. I behave in an acceptable manner.
33. I have difficulty in listening to others.
34. My relationship with my parent(s) interferes with my life.
35. I get into trouble with people in authority (parents, bosses, teachers, doctors, etc.).

FIGURE 5.1 Continued

	Almost Always	Usually	Some- times	Hardly Ever
Activities/Leisure Skills				
36. I participate in activities with others.	___	___	___	___
37. I do things I enjoy.	___	___	___	___
38. I walk or do some other exercise.	___	___	___	___
39. I do things that make me feel good about myself.	___	___	___	___
40. I find emotional support when I need it.	___	___	___	___
Vocational Skills				
41. I organize my tasks daily.	___	___	___	___
42. I am thorough when I work.	___	___	___	___
43. I have difficulty completing tasks as required.	___	___	___	___
44. I manage my time successfully.	___	___	___	___
45. I learn skills required to do my work.	___	___	___	___
46. I have difficulty in concentrating on the task at hand.	___	___	___	___

Source: Smith, M.K. and Ford, J. (1990). A client-developed functional level scale: The Community Living Skills Scale (CLSS). *Journal of Social Service Research*, 13(3), 73–75. © Haworth Press, Inc. Reprinted with permission.

The Social Work Empowerment Scale (SWES)

Description

The Social Work Empowerment Scale was designed to measure social workers' perceptions of personal and professional power. This thirty-four-item instrument has five subscales (Collective Identity, Knowledge and Skills, Self-Concept, Critical Awareness, and Propensity to Act). Although empowerment is a condition that social workers try to create for their clients, even professionals can feel powerless, unable to initiate effective action, alienated from a collective identity, and lacking in self-validation and self-esteem. The author suggests that the SWES may be useful as a process evaluation tool for group or organizational interventions. The original use of the instrument was to determine if use of information technology influenced levels of personal empowerment. The author found that the more experience workers had with computers, the more empowered they seemed to be.

Psychometric Data

From a random sample of 520 NASW members who completed mailed SWESs, the internal consistency for all thirty-four items was

FIGURE 5.2: The Social Work Empowerment Scale

In this questionnaire you will be asked about some of your opinions and beliefs as they relate to you and your profession. Please provide only one response to each question.

The response codes are as follows:

Strongly agree = SA		Disagree	= D
Agree	= A	Strongly disagree	= SD
Uncertain	= U		

1. I enjoy spending time with other people in my profession.   SA A U D SD
2. It is helpful to join with others to solve problems.   SA A U D SD
3. The workers in my agency all have a common purpose.   SA A U D SD
4. I identify strongly with my profession.   SA A U D SD
5. I consider myself a joiner.   SA A U D SD
6. I enjoy using a team approach.   SA A U D SD
7. I have frequent contact with other specialists in my field.   SA A U D SD
8. I usually know what response to take to situations that arise at work.   SA A U D SD
9. My education prepared me for my job.   SA A U D SD
10. I have adequate information resources to solve most professional problems.   SA A U D SD
11. I am aware of all the pertinent issues related to my field of practice.   SA A U D SD
12. I rarely run into unfamiliar problems at work anymore.   SA A U D SD
13. I often read professional journals.   SA A U D SD
14. I attend frequent conferences and training sessions to improve my skills.   SA A U D SD
15. If I don't have the answer to a question, I always know where to get it.   SA A U D SD
16. I am frequently told that I am a very knowledgeable worker.   SA A U D SD
17. I feel that I am important to the people I work with.   SA A U D SD
18. I feel as competent as anyone else I work with.   SA A U D SD
19. I feel pretty sure of myself even when people disagree with me.   SA A U D SD
20. I think I serve a valuable role in my professional capacity.   SA A U D SD
21. I generally make a good impression with others.   SA A U D SD
22. I feel self-assured around my superiors.   SA A U D SD
23. I don't doubt my self-worth even when I think others do.   SA A U D SD
24. I am usually able to think through all the relevant issues.   SA A U D SD
25. I always know who has the power in different situations.   SA A U D SD
26. My place in the world is always very clear to me.   SA A U D SD
27. I usually know exactly where I stand.   SA A U D SD
28. My intuitions and hunches prove to be right most of the time.   SA A U D SD
29. I volunteer to take on extra work in areas of concern or interest to me.   SA A U D SD
30. When I become aware of activities to address a problem of interest, I try to find out how to get involved.   SA A U D SD
31. I am often the one to initiate responses to problems.   SA A U D SD
32. I have organized co-workers or others to offer new programs or interventions.   SA A U D SD
33. One of the things I like in a job is to have multiple involvements in different areas of interest.   SA A U D SD
34. I would rather take action than trust that things will work out.   SA A U D SD

Source: Frans, D.J. (1993). A scale for measuring social work empowerment. *Research on Social Work Practice, 3*(3), 326–327. © Sage Publications. Reprinted with permission.

.89, with the five subscales attaining alpha scores ranging from .71 to .86. In order to establish concurrent validation, the author found an empowerment index from another study and administered it and the SWES to a nonrandom sample of forty-three social work practitioners and nineteen MSW students. Fifty-one subjects completed both instruments, and a significant correlation of .51 was obtained.

Availability

Frans, D.J. (1993). A scale for measuring social work empowerment. *Research on Social Work Practice*, 3(3), 312–328.

The scale has also been revised and a number of new items have been incorporated for use with alcoholics and addicts. For further information, contact Doug Frans, Ph.D., Decision Point, 301 Holcomb, P. O. Box 1174, Springdale, AR 72765.

Scoring

There are no reverse scored items in this scale. "Strongly agree" responses are coded as 5, "Agree" items 4, "Uncertain" 3, "Disagree" 2, and "Strongly Disagree" 1.

Prosocial Tendencies Scale for Children (PTS-C)

Description

Child development researchers have begun to study altruistic behavior in children. Prosocial behavior includes sharing, helping, comforting, and giving information that aids or benefits another without expectation of external reward. Along the lines of Kohlberg's use of hypothetical vignettes to study moral development, the Prosocial Tendencies Scale is a multidimensional pencil-and-paper measure of children's tendencies to act in a prosocial manner. Each of twenty-four brief vignettes asks subjects to make a responsibility attribution by judging if the individual had a good reason for being in need. These responses contribute to an attributed responsibility subscale. Then subjects indicate the likelihood they would offer a particular form of help (the second subscale).

Psychometric Data

During pretesting, a panel of expert raters determined that the PTS-C vignettes were largely free of ethnic and class bias. A Raygor

Readability Estimate indicated that the PTS-C had a difficulty level of grade 6.5. Cronbach's alpha coefficient was computed for the subscales and was found to be .74 for attributed responsibility (PTS-CA) and .78 for children's reported tendencies to behave in a prosocial manner (PTS-CH).

A sample of 142 children ages ten through seventeen from two-parent families was drawn from a community center in a major Midwestern city. In addition to the PTS-C, the children completed the Social Self-Peers subscale of the Coopersmith Self-Esteem Inventory, the Index of Peer Relations, and the Children's Loneliness Questionnaire. The authors found that items on the two subscales of the PTS-C tended to correlate better with their own total scores than with the total scores of other instruments and that there were no significant relationships between social self-esteem or peer relations and prosocial tendencies. However, a significant relationship was found between prosocial tendencies and loneliness ($r = .14$). Because of the lack of hypothetical convergent instruments, a similar analysis was not undertaken for the PTS-CA. However, the authors report the PTS-C subscales to have good to excellent factorial validity and good convergent and discriminant qualities on the item level of analysis.

Availability

Abell, N., McDonell, J.R., and Winters, J. (1992). Developing a measure of children's prosocial tendencies: An initial validation of a self-report instrument. *Journal of Social Service Research*, 16(3/4), 19–37.

For further information, contact Dr. Neil Abell, School of Social Work, Florida State University, Tallahassee, FL 32306-2024. Dr. Abell is interested in following any potential applications of his instrument. Please contact him if planning one.

Scoring

Subscales of the PTS-C are scored by computing the mean of item responses where items (corresponding with vignettes as numbered in the instrument) are:

PTS-CH (Stranger):	1,4,5,6,16,17,18,20,21,22,23
PTS-CH (Friend):	2,3,8,9,10,11,12,13,14,15,19,24
PTS-CA (External):	1,4,6,7,10,11,12,15,18,19,21,24
PTS-CA (Not External):	2,3,5,8,9,13,14,16,17,20,22,23

FIGURE 5.3: Prosocial Tendencies Scale for Children

The stories below are examples of situations people may find themselves in. First, read each story and think about how good or bad you believe the person's reason was for doing what he or she did. Show how much you believe the reason was good or bad by circling whether you think the reason was:

    1 = very good   2 = a little good   3 = a little bad   4 = very bad

Next, read the sentence after each story and think about how much you believe that you would do the same thing that is suggested. Show your answer by circling whether you:

    1 = really would   2 = probably would   3 = probably would not   4 = really would not

This is not a test, so there are no "right" or "wrong" answers. Please begin.

1. Someone you just met called and said, "If I don't finish my chores before dinner, my parents won't let me go out tonight. I could have started sooner, but my cousin got hurt in an accident and I decided to help him. By the time he was taken care of it was pretty late."

   The person's reason for not finishing the chores was (circle one):

       1 = very good   2 = a little good   3 = a little bad   4 = very bad

   If this happened, I would go over and help that person finish the chores (circle one):

       1 = really would   2 = probably would   3 = probably would not   4 = really would not

2. A friend left some important books at another friend's house. The friend said, "I know I should go get them but I decided not to because I have a chance to go swimming instead."

   The friend's reason for not going to get the books was (circle one):

       1 = very good   2 = a little good   3 = a little bad   4 = very bad

   If this happened, I would go get the books for my friend (circle one):

       1 = really would   2 = probably would   3 = probably would not   4 = really would not

3. A friend called and said, "I don't know the way to Sandy's party. I knew Sandy was going to give out directions after school, but I didn't want to hang around so I decided to go home."

   The friend's reason for not getting the directions was (circle one):

       1 = very good   2 = a little good   3 = a little bad   4 = very bad

   If this happened, I would tell my friend the way to the party (circle one):

       1 = really would   2 = probably would   3 = probably would not   4 = really would not

FIGURE 5.3 Continued

4. Someone you just met did not bring any lunch to school. The person said, "I couldn't fix anything because we're out of food. My Mom's been sick and no one has been able to go to the store."

   The person's reason for not bringing any lunch was (circle one):

   1 = very good   2 = a little good   3 = a little bad   4 = very bad

   If this happened, I would share the food I had with that person (circle one):

   1 = really would   2 = probably would   3 = probably would not   4 = really would not

5. Someone you just met had a car stuck in the mud on a dirt road. The person said, "I knew this road was a mess, but I wanted to go down it anyway."

   The person's reason for going down the dirt road was (circle one):

   1 = very good   2 = a little good   3 = a little bad   4 = very bad

   If this happened, I would help that person get the car out of the mud (circle one):

   1 = really would   2 = probably would   3 = probably would not   4 = really would not

6. Someone you just met was standing in line to buy some tickets. The person said, "If I don't get home soon to look after my little brother, my mother will be late for work. I'm going to have to go."

   The person's reason for leaving the line was (circle one):

   1 = very good   2 = a little good   3 = a little bad   4 = very bad

   If this happened, I would offer to stand in line for that person (circle one):

   1 = really would   2 = probably would   3 = probably would not   4 = really would not

7. Someone you just met was stuck in the mud on a dirt road. The person said, "I knew the road was a mess but I decided to try it because I was taking someone home and it was the only way to get there."

   The person's reason for going down the dirt road was (circle one):

   1 = very good   2 = a little good   3 = a little bad   4 = very bad

   If this happened, I would help that person get out of the mud (circle one):

   1 = really would   2 = probably would   3 = probably would not   4 = really would not

8. A friend said, "My Mom's birthday is tomorrow and I really want to buy her a present. I had a chance to make some money but I decided not to because I wanted to play basketball instead."

   The friend's reason for not making the money was (circle one):

   1 = very good   2 = a little good   3 = a little bad   4 = very bad

   If this happened, I would lend my friend some money to buy a present (circle one):

   1 = really would   2 = probably would   3 = probably would not   4 = really would not

FIGURE 5.3 Continued

9. A friend was late going home and stopped by your house. The friend said, "I knew I was late but I wanted to finish the game I was playing. I'm really going to get it if I go home alone."

   The friend's reason for not going home on time was (circle one):

       1 = very good   2 = a little good   3 = a little bad   4 = very bad

   If this happened, I would go home with my friend to help my friend stay out of trouble (circle one):

   1 = really would   2 = probably would   3 = probably would not   4 = really would not

10. A friend called and said, "I don't know the way to Sandy's party. I knew Sandy was going to give out directions after school but I decided not to stay because I knew I'd miss my bus."

    The friend's reason for leaving was (circle one):

        1 = very good   2 = a little good   3 = a little bad   4 = very bad

    If this happened, I would tell my friend how to get to the party (circle one):

    1 = really would   2 = probably would   3 = probably would not   4 = really would not

11. A friend did not finish all of last night's homework. The friend told you, "I decided not to do the work because my little sister got really sick and my Mom needed help taking care of her."

    The friend's reason for not doing the homework was (circle one):

        1 = very good   2 = a little good   3 = a little bad   4 = very bad

    If this happened, I would help my friend finish the homework (circle one):

    1 = really would   2 = probably would   3 = probably would not   4 = really would not

12. A friend missed a ride to swimming practice and called you sounding very upset. The friend said, "The kid next door got hurt pretty bad playing and his parents weren't home. I knew I'd miss my ride but I decided to help out anyway. What can I do?"

    The friend's reason for missing the ride was (circle one):

        1 = very good   2 = a little good   3 = a little bad   4 = very bad

    If this happened, I would help my friend find a ride (circle one):

    1 = really would   2 = probably would   3 = probably would not   4 = really would not

13. A friend missed a ride to swimming practice and called you sounding very upset. The friend said, "I knew I might miss my ride but I was messing around outside and didn't want to stop. What can I do?"

    The friend's reason for missing the ride was (circle one):

        1 = very good   2 = a little good   3 = a little bad   4 = very bad

    If this happened, I would help my friend find a ride (circle one):

    1 = really would   2 = probably would   3 = probably would not   4 = really would not

FIGURE 5.3 Continued

14. A friend did not finish all of last night's homework. The friend told you, "I decided not to do the work because there was a TV program on that I wanted to watch."

    The friend's reason for not doing the homework was (circle one):

    1 = very good   2 = a little good   3 = a little bad   4 = very bad

    If this happened, I would help my friend finish the homework (circle one):

    1 = really would   2 = probably would   3 = probably would not   4 = really would not

15. A friend was late going home and stopped by your house. The friend said, "I knew I was late, but some kids said they were going to beat me up and I had to take the long way home to stay out of their way."

    The friend's reason for not going home on time was (circle one):

    1 = very good   2 = a little good   3 = a little bad   4 = very bad

    If this happened, I would go home with my friend to help my friend stay out of trouble (circle one):

    1 = really would   2 = probably would   3 = probably would not   4 = really would not

16. Someone you just met did not bring any lunch to school. The person said, "I couldn't fix anything because I was late. I knew it was time to get up but I decided to stay in bed anyway."

    The person's reason for not bringing any lunch was (circle one):

    1 = very good   2 = a little good   3 = a little bad   4 = very bad

    If this happened, I would share the food I had with that person (circle one):

    1 = really would   2 = probably would   3 = probably would not   4 = really would not

17. Someone you just met went to the store and forgot to buy diapers for the baby. After getting home the person said, "I really need some diapers but my feet are tired and I just don't want to go back to the store."

    The person's reason for not going back to the store was (circle one):

    1 = very good   2 = a little good   3 = a little bad   4 = very bad

    If this happened and that person gave me some money, I would go to the store and get some diapers for the baby (circle one):

    1 = really would   2 = probably would   3 = probably would not   4 = really would not

127

FIGURE 5.3 Continued

18. Someone you just met borrowed a bike from Tony. The person said, "I was told not to leave it anywhere because it doesn't have a lock, but I had a flat tire and had to go into a store to call for help. I was only gone for a minute, and when I came out the bike was gone. Now I'm afraid to tell Tony what happened."

The person's reason for leaving the bike outside the store was (circle one):

    1 = very good   2 = a little good   3 = a little bad   4 = very bad

If this happened, I would go with that person to tell Tony what happened (circle one):

1 = really would   2 = probably would   3 = probably would not   4 = really would not

19. A friend left some important books at another friend's house. The friend said, "I know I should go get them but I decided not to because if I don't get a good grade on tomorrow's math test I won't pass this year. I really have to study."

The friend's reason for not going to get the books was (circle one):

    1 = very good   2 = a little good   3 = a little bad   4 = very bad

If this happened, I would go and get the books for my friend (circle one):

1 = really would   2 = probably would   3 = probably would not   4 = really would not

20. Someone you just met called and said, "If I don't finish my chores before dinner, my parents won't let me go out tonight. I would have started sooner, but some friends came by and I decided to hang out instead."

The person's reason for not finishing the chores was (circle one):

    1 = very good   2 = a little good   3 = a little bad   4 = very bad

If this happened, I would go over and help that person finish the chores (circle one):

1 = really would   2 = probably would   3 = probably would not   4 = really would not

21. Someone you just met went to the store and forgot to buy diapers for the baby. After getting home, the person said, "I really need some diapers but the baby started getting sick and there is no one else to watch her if I go back out."

The person's reason for not going back to the store was (circle one):

    1 = very good   2 = a little good   3 = a little bad   4 = very bad

If this happened, and that person gave me some money, I would go to the store and get some diapers for the baby (circle one):

1 = really would   2 = probably would   3 = probably would not   4 = really would not

FIGURE 5.3 Continued

22. Someone you just met was standing in line to buy some tickets. The person said, "If I leave my place in line, the tickets might sell out, but this is so boring I think I'm going to leave."

The person's reason for leaving the line was (circle one):

1 = very good   2 = a little good   3 = a little bad   4 = very bad

If this happened, I would offer to stand in line for that person (circle one):

1 = really would   2 = probably would   3 = probably would not   4 = really would not

23. Someone you just met borrowed a bike from Tony. The person said, "I was told not to leave it anywhere because it doesn't have a lock, but I wanted something to eat from the store. I was only gone for a minute, and when I came out the bike was gone. Now I'm afraid to tell Tony what happened."

The person's reason for leaving the bike outside the store was (circle one):

1 = very good   2 = a little good   3 = a little bad   4 = very bad

If this happened, I would go with that person to help tell Tony what happened (circle one):

1 = really would   2 = probably would   3 = probably would not   4 = really would not

24. A friend said, "My Mom's birthday is tomorrow and I really want to buy her a present. I had a chance to make some money but I decided not to because my school work has been really hard lately and I had to spend time on that."

The friend's reason for not making the money was (circle one):

1 = very good   2 = a little good   3 = a little bad   4 = very bad

If this happened, I would lend my friend some money to buy a present (circle one):

1 = really would   2 = probably would   3 = probably would not   4 = really would not

Source: Abell, N., McDonell, J.R., and Winters, J. (1992). Developing a measure of children's prosocial tendencies: An initial validation of a self-report instrument. *Journal of Social Service Research*, 16(3/4), 38–47. Copyright 1990, Abell, McDonell, and Winters. Reprinted with permission of Haworth Press.

Attitude Toward the Provision of Long-Term Care (ATPLTC)

Description

The ATPLTC was developed to measure an individual's attitude about providing long-term care to a disabled family member, whether because of chronic illness, accidental injury, or a developmental disability. This operationalization of long-term caregiving allows direct-practice social workers to assess caregiver attitudes and beliefs so that care plans and intervention can be designed to support or replace their involvement. This self-report instrument is intended for use in practice settings in which the client is seeking assistance or self-change. It is not recommended for those situations where the client has a strong self-interest in representing a particular attitude.

Psychometric Data

The internal consistency of the ATPLTC (coefficient alpha), at .863 for the twenty-six items, was found to be more than adequate for basic research.

To show validity, the author incorporated four items that were theoretically related to attitude about provision of long-term care and correlated these as a composite criterion with individual scores on the ATPLTC. A statistically significant correlation of .32 was obtained, showing some beginning evidence of criterion-related validity. Using the four-item composite scores, the author then divided the respondents into those who were most positive and those who were least positive. The ATPLTC was found to differentiate between the two groups. Evidence of construct validity was seen in that each item in the ATPLTC correlated more highly with the scale itself than with other unrelated variables, and the ATPLTC correlated more highly with the composite score than with other variables.

Availability

Klein, W. (1992). Measuring caregiver attitude toward the provision of long-term care. *Journal of Social Service Research*, 16(3/4), 147–161.

For further information contact: Dr. Waldo Klein, School of Social Work, 1798 Asylum Avenue, West Hartford, CT 06117–2698.

Scoring

Lower scores indicate a more positive attitude toward caregiving. Responses are scored as indicated on the instrument. Items 1, 5, 9, 11, 12, 18, 20, 21, 22, 23, and 25 are reverse scored. Once this adjustment has been made, ATPLTC is scored using the following formula:

$$\text{Score} = 100 \ (Y-N)/4N$$

where Y = the item responses, and N = the number of appropriate responses provided. Any item responses beyond the range of 1–5 are treated as missing. This formula provides scores that range from 0 to

FIGURE 5.4: Attitude Toward the Provision of Long-Term Care

The following statements refer to personally providing care on an ongoing basis to a family member who is unable to meet all of his or her own needs in performing various activities of daily living. These activities include such things as preparing meals, bathing, going to the bathroom, and dressing. This disability may result from a birth defect, an accident, a stroke, a chronic disease, or growing old. Please respond to each statement by placing the number of the statement that best expresses your attitude on the line provided.

1. **Strongly Agree**
2. **Moderately Agree**
3. **Neither Agree nor Disagree**
4. **Moderately Disagree**
5. **Strongly Disagree**

_____ 1. It is not fair that adult children should have to give up so much to care for frail elderly parents.

_____ 2. Families should not place severely retarded children in institutions.

_____ 3. A parent should look after his or her child even if that child is severely disabled.

_____ 4. Families that really want to provide care for a disabled relative will find a way to do so.

_____ 5. Nursing homes or institutions can provide better care for disabled relatives than families.

_____ 6. The physical demands of providing care to a disabled family member are manageable.

_____ 7. It is the responsibility of families to care for their disabled members.

_____ 8. This society will collapse if family members do not provide care for their disabled members.

_____ 9. Family members who cannot bathe or dress themselves are better off in nursing homes or institutions.

_____ 10. Providing care for a disabled family member is one of the basic responsibilities of a family.

_____ 11. It is not fair that young parents should have to give up so much to care for retarded children.

_____ 12. Any right-thinking person would have second thoughts about providing care to a disabled family member.

_____ 13. People should be willing to quit their jobs in order to provide care to impaired family members.

_____ 14. Providing ongoing care for a disabled relative would be one of the most meaningful things a person could do.

_____ 15. Providing care to a disabled family member is a basic human responsibility.

_____ 16. Families should plan for the possibility of providing care for an elderly disabled family member.

_____ 17. Families should rearrange their schedules in order to provide care to disabled family members.

_____ 18. Providing care for disabled family members at home is useless since most of them will end up in institutions or nursing homes anyway.

FIGURE 5.4 Continued

_____ 19. Although medical advances have increased the need for extended care, family members should continue to provide this care to dependent family members.

_____ 20. Disabled children over the age of six years who cannot bathe or dress themselves are an unfair burden to their parents.

_____ 21. When people can no longer care for themselves, it would be better for them to die than to be dependent on family to provide care.

_____ 22. Providing care for a disabled family member is mentally exhausting.

_____ 23. It should be the responsibility of government programs rather than families to provide care for disabled people.

_____ 24. Families are just as good at providing care to dependent family members as organizations that specialize in providing those kinds of services.

_____ 25. Older family members who cannot bathe or dress themselves are an unfair burden to their children.

_____ 26. Humankind is benefited by families that care for their disabled members.

Source: Klein, W. (1992). Measuring caregiver attitude toward the provision of long-term care. *Journal of Social Service Research*, 16(3/4), 151–152. © Haworth Press, Inc. Reprinted with permission.

100 regardless of the number of items completed. (However, the author cautions against interpreting scores that are based on less than 75 percent of the data.)

The Maternal Characteristics Scale (MCS)

Description

The MCS was originally constructed by a group of social workers to investigate personality features that might be associated with child neglect. Caseworkers use knowledge of their clients to complete the thirty-five items of the MCS that comprise four different character dimensions (relatedness, impulse-control, confidence, and verbal accessibility). A replication found that the subscales distinguished neglectful mothers from other low-income women in similar life circumstances. The authors hope that the MCS can be used preventively to assess those who may be likely to neglect their children.

Psychometric Data

Internal consistency was found to range from .63 to .88 among the four subscales. Cronbach's Alpha exceeded .75 for three of these scales. The instrument has been cross-validated with samples from

FIGURE 5.5: Maternal Characteristics Scale

Caseworker _____   *Study No.* _____

Date _____

This is a scale on which we ask you to summarize some features of the mother's personality we have found to be important. Circle one answer for each item. *YES* means this statement would apply to this mother. *NO* means I have no reason to believe it applies and I'm rather sure it does not. When answering these statements, go with your *best available* evidence. Please write *DK* next to any item you cannot answer.

YES *NO*   1. Frequently and appropriately expresses herself in abstractions.

YES *NO*   2. Sets and maintains control of her own behavior.

YES *NO*   3. Takes pleasure in her children's adventures.

YES *NO*   4. Shows warmth in tone when talking with her children.

YES *NO*   5. Plans realistically for herself, children, family.

YES *NO*   6. Speaks in a faint voice or voice fades away at end of sentence.

YES *NO*   7. Shows belligerence toward interviewer from time to time.

YES *NO*   8. Answers questions with single words or phrases.

YES *NO*   9. Keeps virtually the same posture throughout the interview.

YES *NO* 10. Mentions she is aimless, or getting nowhere.

YES *NO* 11. Shows warmth in gestures with interviewer.

YES *NO* 12. Usually states opinion reasonably directly.

YES *NO* 13. Has shown defiance toward authorities in word and deed.

YES *NO* 14. Shows tolerance of routine.

YES *NO* 15. Seems incurious about the inner feelings of others.

YES *NO* 16. Shows interest in, and knowledge of, larger world scene.

YES *NO* 17. Apparently married to escape an unpleasant home situation.

YES *NO* 18. Often buys things impulsively.

YES *NO* 19. It is hard for her to consider a new way of looking at the same thing.

YES *NO* 20. Belongs to a church.

YES *NO* 21. Says she enjoys living.

YES *NO* 22. Shows warmth in tone when discussing her children.

YES *NO* 23. Has a sad expression or holds her body in a dejected or despondent manner.

YES *NO* 24. Follows through on plans that have been made for herself, children, family.

YES *NO* 25. Speaks with pride of personal achievement or possessions.

YES *NO* 26. Has engaged in behavior not acceptable in her own community (subculture).

YES *NO* 27. Shows enthusiasm.

YES *NO* 28. Evidences (some verbalization) negative or discouraged attitude toward future accomplishments or attainments.

YES *NO* 29. Talks of her situation with practically no outward sign of emotion.

FIGURE 5.5 Continued

YES   NO   30. Verbalizes embarrassment.
YES   NO   31. Expresses awareness of complexities in others' decisions; that they
have to weigh alternatives.
YES   NO   32. In discussing children, client frequently adverts to self.
YES   NO   33. Evidences sense of humor.
YES   NO   34. Discusses her children's behavior as if from the outside.
YES   NO   35. Can laugh at herself.

Source: Courtesy of Norman A. Polansky and James M. Gaudin, Jr.

rural Southern Appalachia and Philadelphia, showing that it can differentiate groups of neglectful mothers from nonneglectful mothers in otherwise similar situations. However, it has not been used widely enough at this point to make critical judgments about individuals.

Availability

Polansky, N.A., Gaudin, J.M., and Kilpatrick, A.C. (1992). The maternal characteristics scale: A cross-validation. *Child Welfare,* 71, 271–280.

For further information contact James Gaudin, Ph.D., Director, Child Welfare Training Program, School of Social Work, University of Georgia, Athens, GA 30602–7016.

Scoring

Each of the thirty-five items is rated as true or not true (or more one than the other). If a personality facet thought to be "healthy" or "positive" is true, it is scored (1); if not true, a zero (0). A negative feature earns a zero if true, a plus if not true. Items 1–5, 11–12, 14, 16, 20–22, 24–25, 27, 30–31, 33, and 35 are considered positive items; the others are negative.

Helping Behavior Checklist

Description

The Helping Behavior Checklist was designed to measure parents' opinions and views of mental health professionals who have provided services to their children. In preparing the thirty-one-item instrument, six different codes of ethics were examined and sixteen principles extracted.

Psychometric Data

A preliminary version of the instrument was reviewed by a panel of thirty-four experts on professional ethics identified by NASW. Nineteen of thirty-one items were matched to the same ethical principle by more than 90 percent of the experts. Eleven other items were matched by more than 70 percent. The remaining item was matched to the same principle by 60 percent of the judges. Seventy-four percent of the experts agreed that the questions as a whole adequately covered ethical conduct.

Reliability and discriminant validity were tested by mailing questionnaires to parents on mailing lists of organizations for parents of children with mental, emotional, or learning problems. Half of the parents were asked to rate the mental health professional they found most helpful; the other half rated the professional they found least helpful.

The authors calculated one-month test-retest correlations on the individual items and found that twenty-two correlations were significant and ranged from .30 to .86. The authors describe these as being only moderate.

In terms of discriminant validity, twenty-one items correlated with the parents' overall satisfaction with the child's progress since treatment had begun. Only one item correlated with a global satisfaction question that asked parents to rate satisfaction with the child's current functioning.

Availability

Cournoyer, D.E. and Johnson, H.C. (1991). Measuring parents' perceptions of mental health professionals. *Research on Social Work Practice*, 1(4), 399–415.

For additional information contact David E. Cournoyer, Ph.D., School of Social Work, University of Connecticut, 1798 Asylum Avenue, West Hartford, CT 06117.

Scoring

The instrument uses two- and four-point scales with "Don't know" and "Unsure" categories. Mean ratings in the article are reported only for individual items, not for the scale as a whole.

FIGURE 5.6: Helping Behavior Checklist

Instructions: This questionnaire is about the kinds of things professional helpers may do and your opinions about services you have received. Decide if these statements are true of the helper being rated. Indicate your choice by placing an "X" in the brackets under your choice. Try to rate each statement. If you don't understand or can't rate any item, check the column "Don't Know."

	Almost Always True	Often True	Seldom True	Almost Never True	Don't Know
The Professional Helper:					
1. Was courteous.	[ ]	[ ]	[ ]	[ ]	[ ]
2. Explained clearly what I needed to do to help my child.	[ ]	[ ]	[ ]	[ ]	[ ]
3. Suggested that my skills as a parent contributed to my child's problem.	[ ]	[ ]	[ ]	[ ]	[ ]
4. Understood what I have been going through.	[ ]	[ ]	[ ]	[ ]	[ ]
5. Treated me like an expert about my own child.	[ ]	[ ]	[ ]	[ ]	[ ]
6. Took time to answer my questions or listen to my ideas.	[ ]	[ ]	[ ]	[ ]	[ ]
7. Didn't involve me in important decisions concerning my child's treatment.	[ ]	[ ]	[ ]	[ ]	[ ]
8. Provided services that didn't help.	[ ]	[ ]	[ ]	[ ]	[ ]
9. Valued my opinion about my child.	[ ]	[ ]	[ ]	[ ]	[ ]
10. Blamed me for my child's problem.	[ ]	[ ]	[ ]	[ ]	[ ]
11. Didn't seem to know very much about my child's problem.	[ ]	[ ]	[ ]	[ ]	[ ]
12. Provided services which helped my child.	[ ]	[ ]	[ ]	[ ]	[ ]
13. Indicated to me that I was doing my best for my child.	[ ]	[ ]	[ ]	[ ]	[ ]
14. Cared about how I felt.	[ ]	[ ]	[ ]	[ ]	[ ]
15. Was honest and up-front with me.	[ ]	[ ]	[ ]	[ ]	[ ]
16. Implied that my emotions were harming my child.	[ ]	[ ]	[ ]	[ ]	[ ]

	Yes	No	Unsure
Did the professional helper do any of the following?			
17. Describe costs and payment plans clearly and accurately	[ ]	[ ]	[ ]
18. Inform me about risks associated with treatment	[ ]	[ ]	[ ]
19. Bill me for services that I thought had not been provided	[ ]	[ ]	[ ]
20. Help me make decisions about treatment	[ ]	[ ]	[ ]
21. Help me find other services when he/she couldn't help	[ ]	[ ]	[ ]
22. Refuse to provide reasonable access to records I asked to see	[ ]	[ ]	[ ]

FIGURE 5.6 Continued

	Yes	No	Unsure
23. Do something that harmed my child	[ ]	[ ]	[ ]
24. Discriminate against me because of my race, religious beliefs, or sexual orientation	[ ]	[ ]	[ ]
25. Encourage me to purchase unneeded goods or services in which he/she had a financial interest	[ ]	[ ]	[ ]
26. Give me accurate information about how services would help my child	[ ]	[ ]	[ ]
27. Charge more than I could afford	[ ]	[ ]	[ ]
28. Give information about my child or me to someone without my permission	[ ]	[ ]	[ ]
29. Encourage me to enter into a sexual relationship with him/her	[ ]	[ ]	[ ]
30. Refuse to serve my child when I complained about something	[ ]	[ ]	[ ]
31. Continue to provide services even when they were no longer helpful	[ ]	[ ]	[ ]

Source: Cournoyer, D.E. and Johnson, H.C. (1991). Measuring parents' perceptions of mental health professionals. *Research on Social Work Practice*, 1(4), 412–413. © Sage Publications. Reprinted with permission.

Role Strain Index

Description

This instrument is designed to measure stepparent role strain and conflict associated with the gain or loss of roles, feelings of exclusion, lack of emotional support from spouse, unclear family boundaries, and ambiguous role expectations often brought about by divorce and remarriage. Stepchildren and nonresidential parents can influence the stepfamily household even though they are not physically present. Stepparents can find themselves instant fathers or mothers and experience self-role incongruence. This instrument measures different dimensions of role strain frequently associated with being a stepparent.

Psychometric Data

Factor analysis revealed eight factors (role captivity, role ambiguity, role conflict, self-role incongruence, emotional spouse support, boundary ambiguity, inclusion/exclusion, and resources). Internal consistency of these factors ranged from .60 (inclusion/exclusion) to .94 (self-role incongruence). Overall, the Index achieved an internal reliability of .91.

FIGURE 5.7: Role Strain Index

SA = **Strongly Agree**   MD = **Moderately Disagree**
MA = **Moderately Agree**   SD = **Strongly Disagree**
N   = **Neither Agree nor Disagree**

	SA	MA	N	MD	SD
1. I clearly *know* what my spouse expects of me in regard to his/her children in terms of the following:					
a) Discipline	4	3	2	1	0
b) School/homework	4	3	2	1	0
c) Chores	4	3	2	1	0
d) Nurturance	4	3	2	1	0
e) Spending time together	4	3	2	1	0
2. My career demands sometimes interfere with my role as a wife/husband.	4	3	2	1	0
3. Sometimes my time away at work conflicts with family time.	4	3	2	1	0
4. I feel that I am constantly juggling my different roles (e.g., spouse, job, parent) to meet all the different demands of those roles.	4	3	2	1	0
5. Sometimes I wish I could escape from all the demands I am asked to meet.	4	3	2	1	0
6. At times I feel that my own needs get lost trying to meet everyone else's.	4	3	2	1	0
7. I wish I felt the way I *think* I should feel about loving my stepchild.	4	3	2	1	0
8. I wish I felt the way I *think* I should feel about spending more time with my stepchild.	4	3	2	1	0
9. I want to feel more positive about my stepchild than I actually feel.	4	3	2	1	0
10. I wish I could give more of myself emotionally to my stepchild than I do.	4	3	2	1	0
11. Living arrangements are inadequate to meet the needs of our family.	4	3	2	1	0
12. No matter how hard we work, there never seems to be enough money to meet all our expenses.	4	3	2	1	0
13. The visiting schedule is hard for me in terms of having to adapt to other people's needs.	4	3	2	1	0
14. At times I feel left out of the relationship between my spouse and his/her child.	4	3	2	1	0
15. I would like to be included more in decision making.	4	3	2	1	0
16. I would like my spouse to talk to me more about his/her feelings about his/her former spouse.	4	3	2	1	0
17. I am not sure how to act in regard to my spouse's former wife/husband.	4	3	2	1	0
18. I feel that my spouse's former husband/wife interferes with my relationship with him/her.	4	3	2	1	0
19. I resent having to spare my spouse's time with his/her child(ren).	4	3	2	1	0

FIGURE 5.7 Continued

	SA	MA	N	MD	SD
20. I believe my stepchild feels a conflict of loyalties between me and his/her natural parent.	4	3	2	1	0
21. I feel that my spouse's former husband/wife interferes with my relationship with my stepchild.	4	3	2	1	0
22. I feel that stepparenting would be easier if my spouse helped out more.	4	3	2	1	0
23. I feel that stepparenting would be easier if my spouse supported how I discipline his/her children.	4	3	2	1	0
24. I wish I could lean on my spouse more.	4	3	2	1	0

VS = Very Strongly	**RS = Rarely Strongly**
MS = Moderately Strongly	**NS = Never Strongly**

	VS	MS	RS	NS
25. When you think of your experiences as a stepparent, overall how strongly do you feel angry?	3	2	1	0

Source: Whitsett, D. and Land, H. (1992). The development of a role strain index for stepparents. *Families in Society*, 73(1), 19. © Families International, Inc. Reprinted with permission.

Availability

Whitsett, D. and Land, H. (1992). The development of a role strain index for stepparents. *Families in Society*, 73(1), 14–22.

For further information contact Doni Whitsett, Ph.D., or Helen Land, Ph.D., School of Social Work, University of Southern California, Los Angeles, CA 90089-0411.

Scoring

Items are scored as they appear on the instrument. The higher the score, the more the role strain in the relationship; however, instrument norms have not been established. Total mean scores reported in their article are based on a fifty-one-item instrument before factor analysis and elimination of items.

Job Satisfaction Scale (JSS)

Description

The authors began using measures of job satisfaction in 1980 while exploring the antecedents and consequences of job stress and

---

FIGURE 5.8: Job Satisfaction Scale

Instructions: Please rate each of the aspects of your work listed below according to the **degree of satisfaction or dissatisfaction** it provides you. Circle a number between 1 (Very Dissatisfied) and 11 (Very Satisfied) for each aspect.

	Very Dissatisfied							Very Satisfied			
1. Working with your clients	1	2	3	4	5	6	7	8	9	10	11
2. The amount of authority you have been given to do your job	1	2	3	4	5	6	7	8	9	10	11
3. Your salary and benefits	1	2	3	4	5	6	7	8	9	10	11
4. Opportunities for promotion	1	2	3	4	5	6	7	8	9	10	11
5. The challenge your job provides you	1	2	3	4	5	6	7	8	9	10	11
6. The quality of supervision you receive	1	2	3	4	5	6	7	8	9	10	11
7. Chances for acquiring new skills	1	2	3	4	5	6	7	8	9	10	11
8. Amount of client contact	1	2	3	4	5	6	7	8	9	10	11
9. Opportunities for really helping people	1	2	3	4	5	6	7	8	9	10	11
10. Clarity of guidelines for doing your job	1	2	3	4	5	6	7	8	9	10	11
11. Opportunity for involvement in decision making	1	2	3	4	5	6	7	8	9	10	11
12. The recognition given your work by your supervisor	1	2	3	4	5	6	7	8	9	10	11
13. Your feeling of success as a social worker	1	2	3	4	5	6	7	8	9	10	11
14. Field of specialization you are in	1	2	3	4	5	6	7	8	9	10	11

Source: Courtesy of Gary F. Koeske.

strain. The preliminary measure was a short seven-item scale, which has evolved over the years and is now made up of fourteen items. The Job Satisfaction Scale, in one form or another, has been used with over six hundred social service professionals in diverse human service settings.

Psychometric Data

Several studies reveal the JSS to have good internal consistency, ranging from .83 to .91. From factor analysis of the fourteen job satisfaction items, three different dimensions were found. The first was called Intrinsic Job Satisfaction and reflected intrinsic qualities of the work role. The second dimension was called Organizational Job Satisfaction and depicted satisfaction with supervision and other elements of agency operation. The third factor contained two extrinsic items dealing with salary and promotion. Internal consistency of these subscales ranges from .75 to .90. Test-retest reliabilities on the full scale ranged from .80 (nine months) to .64 (fifteen months).

In terms of predictive validity, a study of intensive case managers found that JSS scores were inversely related to later depression and emotional exhaustion scores, and were positively related to intention to quit the job. Supportive findings suggest convergent and construct validity. In one study, the Moos Work Environment Scale correlated .61 with the Job Satisfaction Scale, and the JSS correlated .76 with a global item that asked, "All things considered, how satisfied or dissatisfied are you with your job?" The authors found that this instrument was significantly correlated with each of the widely used Maslach Burnout Inventory dimensions (e.g., −.59 with emotional exhaustion). In a 1984 study the authors found that job satisfaction was inversely related to the percentage of "difficult" clients in one's active caseload. The JSS appears to be a short, reliable, and valid measure of job satisfaction in the human services.

Availability

The Job Satisfaction Scale is available for use without securing special permission. A description of the development of this scale can be found in Koeske, G.F., Kirk, S.A., Koeske, R.D., and Rauktis, M.B. (1994). Measuring the monday blues: Validation of a job satisfaction scale for the human services. *Social Work Research*, 29(4), 27–35.

For additional information contact Gary Koeske, Ph.D., School of Social Work, University of Pittsburgh, 2217H, Pittsburgh, PA 15260.

Scoring

Overall and subscale scores are simple sums, corrected for missing and any "not applicable" responses. The author has used seven- and nine-step responses scales in the past but says it appears to make little difference because of scale length.

Questions for Class Discussion

1. How could an instrument you create be reliable but not valid?
2. How would you show that the Slap-Together Assertiveness Scale has construct validity?
3. Why is internal consistency an important quality for a scale to have?
4. The term *discrimination* usually has a negative connotation,

such as when it is associated with sexism or racism. However, does the term have a positive or negative connotation when we think about a scale with construct validity being able to discriminate well?

5. Suggest ways to improve the individual items comprising the Fear of Research Scale (questions 7 through 15) from the Attitudes about Research Courses.

6. What type of validity were Smith and Ford trying to demonstrate with the Community Living Skills Scale by correlating it with the Global Assessment Scale?

Mini-Projects for Experiencing Research Firsthand

1. Read one of the articles on the development and validation of a scale referenced in this chapter. Summarize, in a short paper, all the steps the authors went through.

2. With a partner, attempt to create a scale measuring some concept of your choice. Then present the scale to the class for a discussion of its face and content validity.

3. Using either a scale that you've developed or one with known psychometrics, collect a small sample of data. Enter the data into a computer with statistical analysis software so that you can compute the scale's internal consistency. Discuss what you found and possible explanations.

4. Skim one of the books containing multiple scales referenced in this chapter. Make a list of at least five scales that you might be able to use sometime in the future as a social work practitioner. Explain how each could be used.

References and Resources

Abell, Neil. (1991). The Index of Clinical Stress: A brief measure of subjective stress for practice and research. *Social Work Research and Abstracts*, 27(2), 12–15.

Camasso, M.J. and Geismar, L.L. (1992). A multivariate approach to construct reliability and validity assessment: The case of family functioning. *Social Work Research and Abstracts*, 28(4), 16–26.

Combs-Orme, T.D., Orme, J.G., and Guidry, C.J. (1991). Reliability and validity of the Protective Services Questionnaire (PSQ). *Journal of Social Service Research*, 14(1/2), 1–20.

Comrey, A.L. (1988). Factor analytic methods in scale development in personality and clinical psychology. *Journal of Consulting and Clinical Psychology*, 56, 754–761.

Congdon, D.C. and Holland, T.P. (1988). Measuring the effectiveness of substance abuse treatment: Toward a theory-based index. *Journal of Social Service Research,* 12(1/2), 23–48.

DeVellis, R.F. (1993). *Scale Development: Theory and Applications.* Newbury Park, CA: Sage.

Harrison, D.F. and Westhuis, D.J. (1990). Rating scales for sexual adjustment. *Journal of Social Service Research,* 13(3), 85–100.

Hudson, W.W., Nurius, P.S., Daley, J.G., and Newsome, R.D. (1990). A short-form scale to measure peer relations dysfunction. *Journal of Social Service Research,* 13(4), 57–69.

Klein, W.C. (1992). Measuring caregiver attitude toward the provision of long-term care. *Journal of Social Service Research,* 16(3/4), 147–161.

Koeske, G.F. and Koeske, R.D. (1992). Parenting Locus of Control: Measurement, construct validation, and a proposed conceptual model. *Social Work Research and Abstracts,* 28(3), 37–46.

MacNeil, G. (1991). A short-form scale to measure alcohol abuse. *Research on Social Work Practice,* 1(1), 68–75.

Nasuti, J.P. and Pecora, P.J. (1993). Risk assessment scales in child protection: A test of the internal consistency and interrater reliability of one statewide system. *Social Work Research and Abstracts,* 29(2), 28–33.

Nugent, W.R. and Thomas, J.W. (1993). Validation of a clinical measure of self-esteem. *Research on Social Work Practice,* 3(2), 191–207.

Nunnally, J.C. (1978). *Psychometric Theory.* New York: McGraw-Hill.

Poertner, J. (1985). A scale for measuring clients' satisfaction with parent education. *Social Work Research and Abstracts,* 21(3), 23–28.

Polansky, N.A., Gaudin, J.M., and Kilpatrick, A.C. (1992). The Maternal Characteristics Scale: A cross validation. *Child Welfare,* 71(3), 271–282.

Royse, D. and Birge, B. (1987). Homophobia and attitudes toward AIDS patients among medical, nursing, and paramedical students. *Psychological Reports,* 61(3), 867–870.

Royse, D., Keller, S., and Schwartz, J.L. (1982). Lessons learned: The evaluation of a drug education program. *Journal of Drug Education,* 12(2), 181–190.

Schondel, C., Shields, G., and Orel, N. (1992). Development of an instrument to measure volunteers' motivation in working with people with AIDS. *Social Work in Health Care,* 17(2), 53–71.

Shields, J.J. (1992). Evaluating Community Organization Projects: The Development of an Empirically Based Measure. *Social Work Research and Abstracts,* 28(2), 15–20.

Smith, M.K. and Ford, J. (1990). A client-developed functional level scale: The community Living Skills Scale (CLSS). *Journal of Social Service Research,* 13(3), 61–84.

6
Survey Research

If the topic of experimental design was strange or alien to you, survey research should be familiar. Social work literature abounds with surveys. Surveys have been conducted to explore such varied problems as why battered wives return to their husbands, teen dating violence, menopause, and shoplifting. Our understanding of the human condition and of human diversity has been extended by such surveys as those exploring stress in black, low-income, single-parent families, effectiveness of casework services with Chicanos, the marital and parental behavior of lesbian wives and mothers and gay husbands and fathers, and coverage of women's issues in social work journals.

Pick up a social work journal and browse through it to see if you find any surveys. I picked up an issue of *Social Work in Health Care* and found an article that described surveys conducted in a New York City municipal hospital to ascertain the extent of hunger reported by patients and its possible causes (e.g., physical inabilities to buy or prepare food). The authors of an article in the *Journal of Child Sexual Abuse* conducted surveys of parents' behaviors, attitudes, and beliefs regarding sexual abuse prevention for preschoolers. Practically every issue of *Social Work* contains at least one article that uses survey methodology.

Most Americans are familiar with surveys, and even if they've not participated in one recently, they know that surveys are attempts to understand our interests, values, knowledge, and preferences. In years when there are presidential elections, newscasts, newspapers, and news magazines bombard us with the results of numerous surveys. Sometimes surveys show conflicting results—the incumbent appears to be ahead in one survey, but a second shows the contender out front. When this happens, we sometimes scratch our heads and wonder what good are surveys. But they are important.

In a report for the National Research Council, Adams, Smelser, and Treiman claim that the sample survey is "the single most important information gathering invention of the social sciences" (cited in Fienberg, Loftus, and Tanur, 1985). We see the truth in this statement as we think about the various ways in which surveys provide us with information about the world around us.

Surveys may well be the most common research methodology used by social workers. If you think of all the times you have been asked to participate in a survey, or the numerous occasions when surveys or polls have been reported in the mass media, you know that most Americans are accustomed to the survey approach to obtaining information. Moreover, the popularity of surveys seems to be increasing. We need to understand their use.

Surveys can be thought of as photographs or portraits of attitudes, beliefs, or behaviors at one point in time. Using a predetermined set of questions or issues, they reveal what a group of respondents is thinking, feeling, or doing at the time during which the survey is conducted. Social workers and social scientists use surveys, as do market researchers, who poll the public about consumer purchases, and professional pollsters, who predict the outcomes of elections, assess the popularity of an elected official, and discover the public's views on certain issues.

Social workers use surveys to identify community needs or the needs of special client groups (e.g., chronic schizophrenics or persons with dual diagnoses). Sometimes these surveys are called **needs assessments** and may include interviewing direct-service personnel and referral sources, as well as clients or their families. Even individuals randomly selected from the larger community may be interviewed. Social workers also use surveys conducted by others (e.g., the Bureau of the Census) to understand how the population is distributed and to help determine such things as areas within a city where there are concentrations of the elderly or the impoverished.

Surveys can be used for program evaluation activities. Surveys are sometimes conducted to see how satisfied clients are with an agency's services. As an administrator, you might be interested in surveying client admission data to see if your agency is currently serving a greater percentage of minority or elderly clients than in a previous year. You might survey your staff to determine the extent of feelings of burnout, or you might have your staff evaluate you as an administrator or the agency as a whole. You might even survey the community to ask what perceptions people have of your agency.

Surveys are also conducted to gather data about special problems or concerns when little information is available. We conduct surveys to learn more about phenomena that are not well understood, for example, to determine the extent of a condition in a group or target population so that appropriate intervention can be applied. Surveys are not limited to providing basic information for research; their uses are more varied than can be fully elaborated here. For instance, public opinion surveys have been used to try to change the venue of highly publicized criminal cases and to exclude persons from jury service because of their attitudes about the death penalty.

The multiple varieties and uses of surveys can be summarized by noting that they fall into three broad categories. Where there is little data, **exploratory surveys** provide beginning information so that more rigorous studies can be implemented. **Descriptive surveys** provide information on the characteristics of a given population. For example, a descriptive survey of juvenile status offenders might examine and describe them in terms of average age, parents' income, number of prior offenses, attendance in school, and so on. Neither exploratory nor descriptive surveys require hypotheses. In **explanatory surveys** the researcher collects data in an attempt to show that some stimulus (independent variable) caused or had an effect on something else (dependent variable). However, surveys cannot definitely establish causal connections between variables.

Because they can be creative in designing questions and can easily tailor existing questionnaires to specific settings or clientele, social workers tend to like surveys. If a committee or group is developing the questionnaire, everyone can participate either by suggesting items or by pointing out ways specific items might be misinterpreted or could be improved. Other reasons for the popularity of surveys are that they are quickly implemented and convenient to administer. Once the survey instrument has been chosen or designed and a sample identified, the survey can often be handled by a clerical person (for instance, with a mail survey), thus freeing the researcher to attend to other matters until a sufficient number of survey questionnaires have come in for analysis. Sometimes, the investigator can coordinate the collection of data from personal or telephone interviews. Each of these approaches has its own set of advantages and disadvantages.

The Mail Questionnaire

The advantages of the mail questionnaire have been well expressed by Dillman (1983):

> What could be easier and more efficient than conducting surveys through the mail? The researcher simply has to write the questionnaire and then prepare it for mailing. The otherwise time-consuming legwork of locating respondents is done by the U.S. Postal Service; respondents interview themselves at their own convenience. Interviewer salaries and travel costs, the major expenditures incurred in face-to-face interviews, are thereby eliminated making it feasible to survey thousands of people for the same cost as a few hundred interviews. Further, since postage rates do not increase with geographic dispersion, the data collection costs for national surveys may approximate those for city and county surveys. (P. 359)

The mail questionnaire also allows greater anonymity for the respondents when the topic of the study involves private or sensitive issues (e.g., illegal or sexual behavior).

A final advantage of the mail questionnaire is that it reduces errors that might occur in the process of interviewing. Not all interviewers are equally skilled, and some may have traits that annoy, offend, or cause those being interviewed to be less than honest.

On the other hand, there are a number of specific disadvantages to the mail questionnaire: first of all, unlike with personal or telephone interviews, researchers experience some loss of control over the survey process once the questionnaire has been mailed. Although the questionnaire may be delivered to the proper address, there is no guarantee that the intended recipient will be the one who completes the questionnaire. An eleven-year-old child could respond for his or her mother or father even though the researcher intended the survey form to go to adults. A related problem is that the survey could be completed under less than optimal conditions (e.g., when the respondent is ill or intoxicated, or completes the questionnaire while the television is blaring or a party is going on in the living room).

Second, investigators cannot assume that all recipients of the survey will be literate or will be able to comprehend complex issues. While college students are accustomed to questionnaires and multiple choice response sets, individuals with lower levels of educational attainment may find structured response sets (e.g., "Strongly Agree," "Agree," "Undecided," "Disagree," "Strongly Disagree") confusing or too confining for the responses they want to give.

Third, mail questionnaires tend to be highly structured and relatively short. These questionnaires may not provide the detail that could emerge from a face-to-face contact. In personal interview situations, the interviewer is able to ask for additional information (to probe) if the respondent says something exceptionally interesting or if the interviewer is not sure of the response or thinks the respondent did not understand the question.

Mail questionnaires have become a popular gimmick with some businesses (e.g., an official-looking survey form arrives asking information about how much you travel or take vacations, but its real purpose is to sell real estate or vacation time-sharing plans). Consequently, some Americans see surveys as a form of soliciting or as junk mail. Even if a survey form arrives in an envelope carrying first-class postage, it can be seen as an invasion of privacy and thrown away. Individuals with good intentions can put the survey form aside until "later" with the result that questionnaires get lost, thrown out, or put in the parakeet's cage.

Another problem is that Americans are a highly mobile population and are constantly changing addresses, last names, and places of employment. Your survey will be seriously disadvantaged if your mailing list is inaccurate or out of date. The post office may not be able to deliver or to forward mail—especially if the intended respondent is trying to avoid creditors or legal authorities.

These factors directly affect the number of people who complete and return survey questionnaires. It is not uncommon for only 25 to 35 percent of those who were mailed a questionnaire to return it. (Alreck and Settle, 1985, say that the response rates for mail surveys are often only 5 to 10 percent, and response rates over 30 percent are rare.) Of course, if your addresses are recent and the topic is one that interests the respondents, response rates will improve, but will seldom reach response rates of telephone or face-to-face interviews. However, these rates apply only to those who receive one mailing. With a reminder postcard and the mailing of a second questionnaire to those who did not initially respond, these rates can be improved quite a bit—to 50 percent or more. This is discussed in the next section.

Getting the Most Out of Mail Questionnaires

Designing a mail questionnaire is not so simple as it may first appear. Extensive research exists on all aspects of the mail survey. It is known, for instance, that using first-class postage results in better re-

FIGURE 6.1: An Example of Items from a Questionnaire

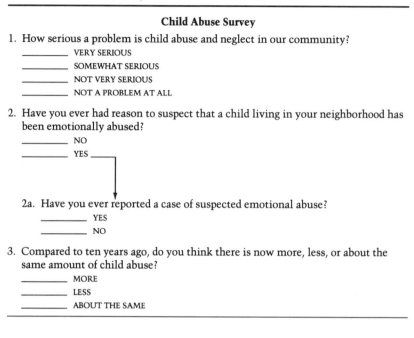

Child Abuse Survey

1. How serious a problem is child abuse and neglect in our community?
   _____ VERY SERIOUS
   _____ SOMEWHAT SERIOUS
   _____ NOT VERY SERIOUS
   _____ NOT A PROBLEM AT ALL

2. Have you ever had reason to suspect that a child living in your neighborhood has been emotionally abused?
   _____ NO
   _____ YES

   2a. Have you ever reported a case of suspected emotional abuse?
   _____ YES
   _____ NO

3. Compared to ten years ago, do you think there is now more, less, or about the same amount of child abuse?
   _____ MORE
   _____ LESS
   _____ ABOUT THE SAME

sponse rates than using bulk mail. Similarly, personalized cover letters are thought to provide better response rates than "Dear friend" or comparable salutations.

Dillman (1983) has provided an overview of steps that contribute to what he calls the "Total Design Method." He suggests that the questionnaire be photo-reduced and designed as a booklet to make it more appealing and less imposing (preferable size is 6.5 inches by 8.25 inches). The first page is designed as a cover with an interesting title and illustration; the back page is left blank for additional comments. The booklet should be printed on white paper (preferably sixteen-pound weight) and arranged so that the most interesting questions appear first. The whole questionnaire should be designed so that lowercase letters are used for questions and uppercase letters for responses. Visual clues (arrows, indentations, and spacing) are used to their fullest advantage to help respondents answer in a straight vertical line rather than going back and forth across the page. (See figure 6.1.)

Considerable thought and research have also gone into the implementation of the survey procedures. Dillman (1983) suggests a one-page cover letter on letterhead stationery explaining that a socially useful study is being conducted and why each respondent is important. Individual names and addresses are typed on the cover letter and the envelope (which are then mailed first class). One week after the first mail-out, a reminder postcard is sent to all recipients. Three weeks after the first mail-out, a second cover letter, questionnaire, and return envelope are sent to all those who have not responded. Seven weeks after the first mail-out, another cover letter and questionnaire are sent by certified mail to all those who have not responded.

The Total Design Method greatly improves the response rates ordinarily found with mail surveys. Dillman (1978) states that the average response rate for forty-eight surveys using his procedures was 74 percent, with no survey receiving less than a 50 percent response. Response rates of 77, 79, and even 92 percent have been reported in social work literature in connection with the use of prepaid postcard surveys and a single follow-up letter (Weinbach, 1984). Another study reported that an overall response rate of 66 percent was obtained with a seven-page questionnaire when social workers used a lottery approach with incentives to reward respondents (Blythe, 1986).

Incentives are sometimes necessary to increase response rates. The good news, however, is that monetary inducements don't have to be very large. One study (James and Bolstein, 1992) found that a prepaid incentive of $1 almost doubled the response rate. Further, a $5 check produced almost the same response rate (52 percent) as a $40 check (54 percent). Promising even as much as $50 did not improve response rates over providing no incentive at all.

Recently, Wilk (1993) reported a systematic random survey of 400 names chosen from the NASW *Register of Clinical Social Workers*. She found that a $1 incentive improved her response rate from 43 percent to 63 percent.

I've used incentives when adolescent subjects in a control group needed to complete several instruments that we were using as a posttest. They had limited contact with the agency, but a promised check of $15 helped improve our response over what it was when we offered no incentive. Would the response rate have been improved still more if we had offered them cash instead of promising to mail them a check within two weeks? I believe so. Unfortunately, the agency's fiscal policies prevented us from testing that notion.

Whether or not you use an approach like the one advocated by Dillman, the success of your mail survey will rest largely upon three considerations: (1) ensuring that the mailing list is current and accurate; (2) keeping the questionnaire as short and interesting as possible (preferably one to two pages); and (3) following up with another copy of the questionnaire to all nonresponders.

The Telephone Survey

The chief advantage of the telephone survey over the face-to-face interview is that it is less expensive (one avoids all expenses associated with traveling to the respondent). Telephone surveys can also be conveniently run from an office. Bulk user rates (WATS lines) help reduce the costs of numerous calls. Telephone surveys allow the interviewer to have control over the choice of the respondent and give the interviewer the ability to probe when questions or responses are not understood. (However, Blankenship, 1977, has noted that too much probing can be a source of annoyance to the respondent and result in a terminated interview.)

Telephone surveys allow interviewers access to individuals who cannot or will not open their doors to strangers for the purpose of an interview (e.g., persons confined to bed because of illness or injury). Another advantage is that when timeliness is important, special issues can be explored and data gathered almost immediately. A final advantage is that telephone interviewers can be closely monitored and the quality of their work frequently evaluated to ensure that questions are asked correctly and responses are coded satisfactorily.

A disadvantage of the telephone survey is that the interviewer cannot see the respondent. This means that some items such as the person's race or the condition of the house cannot be observed. If these are important to the investigator, they must be asked of the respondent. When the phone is used, the interviewer misses facial expressions, which indicate such states as confusion or the beginning of an emotion like anger or sadness. Not everyone can be a successful telephone interviewer; he or she must be articulate, personable, and a good conversationalist. The quality of the interviewer's voice ("telephone voice") is important (Blankenship, 1977). An interviewer must quickly interest the potential respondent in cooperating and establish rapport before the respondent loses interest. If open-ended questions are used, the interviewer must be able to write down the responses quickly and accurately.

Another disadvantage of telephone surveys is that they must be kept short. Telephone interviews should be under twenty minutes long, and the shorter the better (there are exceptions—much longer surveys have been successfully completed by phone). As a general rule, the more interesting the topic is for the respondent, the greater the probability that the respondent will complete the interview even if it is lengthy.

Some believe that interviewing by telephone is unacceptable because of built-in bias associated with the inability to interview persons who do not have telephones. While telephone surveys may somewhat underrepresent the poorest of the poor, 93.9 percent of all American households have telephones (U.S. Department of Commerce, 1993). The Rand Corporation concluded in 1977 that the number of telephones in the United States was so high that exclusion of those without phones was no longer a liability for telephone surveys in most parts of the country: "For most purposes, the evidence that the universe of telephone households is an acceptable representation of all households is now rather compelling" (Lucas and Adams, 1977, p. 5).

However, the use of a telephone directory to produce samples for telephone surveys can lead to biased data. Police officers, celebrities, single and divorced women, mental health professionals, and public officials often do not have listed phone numbers. And the number of unlisted phones varies markedly by geographical area. In Lexington, Kentucky, about 11 percent of phones are unlisted, compared with 43 percent in Philadelphia, 61 percent in Los Angeles, and 62 percent in Las Vegas. Nationally, about a third of all phone numbers are unlisted (*Lexington Herald-Leader*, May 9, 1990). To compensate for unlisted numbers, most large-scale telephone surveys use such procedures as random-digit or added-digit dialing. In random-digit dialing, there is intentional selection of the first three digits for the desired local exchanges, and the last four digits are randomly generated by a computer. In added-digit dialing, a legitimate "seed number" is provided for those local exchanges from which the samples are to be drawn, and then consecutive digits are added to the last digit or the last two or three digits. While these procedures result in some phone calls to businesses or others who are not target respondents, it provides a good way of accessing households with unlisted numbers and thus getting a representative sample of all households with phones.

Although telephone response rates are often much better than those obtained from mailed surveys, recent advances in electronic technology have expanded the use of computers in telephone solicitation, resulting in many more "nuisance" calls to households with phones. As a defensive measure, many Americans have resorted to screening their calls with telephone answering machines. As many as 50 percent or more of Americans may own telephone answering machines. However, those interested in the phone as a data-gathering mechanism are studying these developments and preparing procedures to deal with the proliferation of answering machines, such as treating the call to one of these machines as a "no answer" household, which would require a call-back (Tuckel and Feinberg, 1991). In the near future, it is likely that technological innovations such as phones and answering machines that bar the entry of callers who are not "recognized" will create interesting challenges for those who use telephone survey techniques.

A spokesperson for the Gallup organization, one of the better-known survey companies in the United States, said that they were able to achieve 80 percent response rates when they first began interviewing by phone in the 1970s. Since then, Gallup's phone response rate has dropped into the 60 percent range (Farhi, 1992).

Getting the Most Out of Telephone Surveys

Interviewers need to be trained in the conduct of the survey. This training should include role-plays and interviewing other trainees to ensure that the purpose of each question is well understood. All interviewers should be given standardized introductory statements that move quickly to the survey questions. Some texts advise against asking the respondents' permission to interview them or if they have a few minutes to answer some questions (Alreck and Settle, 1985; Institute for Social Research, 1976). A brief introduction might go something like this:

> Hello. My name is _____. I'm calling from the _____ Survey Research Center. We're conducting a survey this month of people randomly selected from across the state. The survey will take about fifteen minutes. We have only a phone number and not any names, so all of your responses will be anonymous. If I have your permission, let me begin by asking how many years you have lived in this state . . . .

It is strongly recommended that the questionnaire and interview procedures be tested (a pilot survey) to determine if there are any unforeseen problems.

Personal Interviews

The personal interview provides the interviewer with more control than either mail or telephone surveys. The interviewer can read facial expressions and moods, monitor environmental distractions, and determine if the interview should move to a quieter room or be continued at a later date. See for example, the following report from an interviewer:

It was a three-ring circus—the respondent had five children ranging from one to eight years and they all had a great time climbing all over the furniture. One child stood on her head on the couch next to me. I managed to hang onto my pencil, the questionnaire, my purse—but it wasn't easy! (Converse and Schuman, 1974, p. 3)

Observational data (such as the respondent's race or affect) can also be determined from the personal interview without requiring questions to be asked of the respondent. Further, visual aids can be used to help a respondent. This is particularly advantageous if there is a need for a complex response set. In such situations, the respondent can be handed a card from which to choose a response. Another advantage is that the personal interview usually achieves a higher response rate than either mail or telephone surveys.

The prime disadvantage of the interview is that it is much more expensive than the two other approaches. While interviewers can be paid either by the hour or by the number of interviews completed, there must also be allowances for travel time to the respondents' homes. Occasionally, multiple trips must be made when appointments are broken (because they have been forgotten, friends drop in, or minor emergencies arise). Interviewers can get lost, find it difficult to locate the respondent's residence, or have car trouble. Further, comments hurriedly scrawled in the margin of the questionnaire can become difficult to discern hours later in the office. The safety of interviewers can also be a major concern, and sometimes interviewers must be assigned in teams of two. Supervision and quality control of the interview process can be more difficult to assure than with the telephone survey.

In order to avoid the great expense of selecting a random sample of households, going door-to-door, and then personally interviewing those selected, another approach is called intercept surveying. Typically, these surveyors position themselves in malls or on busy streets and attempt to interview those persons who are willing to stop and talk to them.

Intercept surveys are convenience samples (often of the worst kind) where surveyors seek to fulfill certain quotas or to capture information from persons with certain apparent characteristics (e.g., executives carrying briefcases). Even if they strive to reach a cross-section of persons, there's always a problem with self-selection (some people don't like to be stopped on the street). These surveys are limited by the location and times chosen to do the interviewing.

Because they draw nonprobability samples, there is no way to tell whether the data they obtain is representative of the larger population. On the other hand, as survey methods tend to go, there can be savings in the amount of time required to conduct the study, and in cost.

Getting the Most from Personal Interviews

The Survey Research Center at the University of Michigan is one of several well-known institutions that have many years of experience in conducting surveys. (Another is the National Opinion Research Center at the University of Chicago.) Anyone seriously considering conducting a large number of personal interviews for research purposes should start by reading the Survey Research Center's *Interviewer's Manual: Revised Edition*. This very practical publication outlines, in a step-by-step format, what the interviewer should and should not do. Suggestions are provided for such concerns as securing the interview and responding to such questions as "How did you pick me?" and "What good will all this do?" With regard to the first question, the interviewer briefly explains the sampling process. To answer the second question, it is helpful to pull out newspaper or periodical clippings to show the respondent how information from surveys is used.

The Survey Research Center also recommends that the interviewer ask questions exactly as they are worded and in the order in which they appear on the questionnaire. Interviewers are not to assume that they know the respondent's position or response. Every question should be asked, even if a preface is needed ("I know that we have already touched on this, but . . ."). The Center recommends that the interviewer repeat questions that are misunderstood or misinterpreted, and probe when necessary. (You can probe by repeating the question, by being silent for a few seconds and giving the respondent time to expand on his or her thoughts, by repeating the respondent's reply, by making a neutral comment such as "Can you tell me a little more?" "Anything else?" or by simply stating that you do not understand.)

Babbie (1986) has composed a list that he calls general rules for interviewing. His recommendations are: the interviewer should dress in a fashion similar to what would be found in the respondent's neighborhood; he or she should not over- or underdress. He says that middle-class neatness and cleanliness are expected by the largest number of respondents. Further, the interviewer must be familiar with the questionnaire so that he or she doesn't stumble over words or phrases. Responses should be recorded exactly. He also recommends that an interviewer's first five completed questionnaires should be reviewed by a supervisor to ensure that there are no major problems, and that some random reviewing and checking should be employed later on.

Comparison of the Three Approaches

Mail surveys have the advantage of generally being less expensive than telephone or personal interviewing. Tradeoffs are the low response rate and the tendency for respondents to skip questions they don't understand, that seem to require too much thought or writing, or for which they don't want to give a response. On the other hand, both mail and telephone surveys can allow the respondent to reply somewhat anonymously. Respondents may not feel anonymity to the same extent in personal interviews.

Complicated questions are more easily handled by a personal interview than with the other two approaches, but when time is an important consideration, the telephone survey has the advantage. Mail surveys and face-to-face surveys can easily take three to four months to complete (Frey, 1989). Both telephone and face-to-face surveys are labor-intensive and require personnel with good social and conversational skills.

Which is the best approach to use? Each approach has its own particular set of strengths as well as weaknesses. Dillman (1978) has listed twenty-four factors that could be considered in choosing among the three approaches. These range from the obvious desire to keep costs low, to speed of implementation, and to such issues as contamination by others in the household and success with boring or tedious questions. Dillman concludes by stating that any final decision "requires the subjective weighing of one consideration against another" (p. 76). In short, the best approach is the one that has the fewest limitations and the most advantages at a cost you can afford. See table 6.1 for further assistance with the decision of which approach is best for your project.

Sampling Theory

Virtually every day you are involved in sampling. On cold winter days you may stick your foot out from under the covers and decide that it is too cold to get up right then. Later on, you test your bath or shower water to see if the temperature is right. You might take a sip of coffee and decide it is too strong. You sometimes walk into a clothing store, glance at a few price tags, and decide the store has more ex-

TABLE 6.1   Comparison of Mail, Face-to-Face, and Telephone Survey Methods

Factor	Mail	Face-to-Face	Intercept	Telephone
ADMINISTRATION				
1. Cost	1	4	2	2
2. Personnel requirements: interviewers	n/a	4	4	3
3. Personnel requirements: supervision	2	3	3	4
4. Time for implementation	4	4	1	1
SAMPLE				
5. Sample coverage	3	1	4	1
6. Response rate—general public	4	2	2	2
7. Refusal rate	unknown	3	3	3
8. Noncontact/nonaccessibility	2	3	1	2
9. Ability to obtain response from elite population	4	1	unknown	2
10. Respondent within household	4	1	n/a	1
11. Sampling special subpopulation	4	2	4	2
DATA QUALITY				
12. Interview control	n/a	3	3	1
a. Control consultation	4	1	2	1
13. Obtaining socially desirable responses	1	4	2	3
14. Item nonresponse	3	2	2	3
15. Impact of questionnaire length on response	3	1	4	2
16. Confidentiality	4	4	2	3
17. Ability to ask sensitive questions	2	1	3	2
18. Ask complex questions	3	1	2	3
a. Ability to clarify	4	1	1	2
b. Use of visual aids	3	1	4	4
19. Use of open-ended questions	4	1	3	2
a. Ability to probe	4	1	1	2

Key: 1 = Major advantage
      2 = Minor advantage
      3 = Minor disadvantage
      4 = Major disadvantage
      n/a = not applicable

Source: Frey J.H. (1989). *Survey research by telephone.* Newbury Park, CA: Sage, p. 76. © Sage Publications, Inc. Reprinted with permission.

pensive items than you can afford. If you donate blood, a tiny sample of your blood is tested to see if it has sufficient iron content.

In each of these instances sufficient information came from sampling. It was not necessary to experience the *whole* of the phenomenon. You didn't have to drink the whole cup of coffee to realize it was too strong. One sip served as a sample of the whole cup. You didn't have to examine every article of apparel in the clothing store to know that the store catered to an exclusive (and rich) clientele. The people at the blood center didn't have to draw blood from every part of your body, because your blood (whatever its characteristics) is pretty much the same regardless of whether it is in your arm or foot or ear.

The notion behind sampling theory is that a small number of **sampling units** (a few price tags) can tell you something about the total population (all the items of apparel sold by the clothing store).

Let's say that you have been elected to a school board in a town with 50,000 registered voters. If there is a movement to raise taxes to build a new high school, you wouldn't have to talk to all 50,000 registered voters to get an accurate notion of whether the majority of the adults in the community were in favor of this tax. A telephone poll of several hundred randomly selected registered voters could provide you with an accurate assessment of support for a new tax. Polling 50,000 individuals is impractical, if not impossible. But more importantly, it is unnecessary. Sampling is best applied when large populations or numbers are involved and when economy is a consideration.

Sampling works because trends or tendencies within a large population can be discovered from a much smaller number of individuals. For instance, if 90 percent of the registered voters in the above example were going to vote for an increase in their taxes, an indication of support for the tax issue should be apparent whether you sample 75 or 475 of the registered voters (if these voters were randomly selected). The larger sample merely allows for greater confidence and precision in estimating the "true" level of support or nonsupport for the tax issue. It is possible that if you sample only a handful of individuals, these few may not feel, act, or believe as the majority of the larger population. But if the sample is large enough (something akin to a critical mass), and there is no bias in the selection of the individual sampling units, then the pattern or characteristics found in the sample should match what you would find if you could contact everyone in the total population.

Surveyors employing scientifically selected samples (known as **probability samples**) are meticulous about how their respondents are selected. Their attention to random selection and sample size gives these surveys a great deal of accuracy in their findings.

The Accuracy of Probability Samples

The Gallup organization is one of several nationally recognized professional survey research organizations. Even though the population of the United States is in excess of 200 million, Gallup is able to develop representative samples of the U.S. adult civilian population with interviews of approximately fifteen hundred respondents. That sample size allows them to be 95 percent confident that the results they obtain are accurate within plus or minus 3 percentage points. Their accuracy is impressive. As can be seen in table 6.2, in twenty-eight national elections, their samples differed from the actual election results by an average of only 2 percentage points.

Although there may be times when a researcher would want to interview every person in a given population, it rarely would be necessary. If sampling is conducted without bias, then smaller representative samples can be used quite adequately to gauge or predict the larger population. A sample is representative when all individual units of the population have an equal chance of being selected.

With probability sampling the investigator has a good idea of both the number of people or units in the target population and their characteristics. With these parameters the researcher can determine if a sample is representative. There are several probability sampling designs to consider. The first one we will examine is the **simple random sampling design**, where each sampling unit in the population has the same probability (an equal chance) of being chosen.

Suppose the president of your university is retiring, and the board of trustees is interested in selecting a former governor for the new president. You think it is a good idea, but you want to know what the rest of the student body thinks. You find out from the registrar that there are 19,787 students enrolled in the university. Knowing the population of university students, you can begin to make some decisions about how many to contact and which survey approach to use.

If the registrar provides you with a listing of all the enrolled students as well as their phone numbers and addresses, you could use a table of random numbers (see Appendix B) to find a starting place and randomly select a sample of students to contact. This listing would be known as the **sampling frame**. You choose to contact a sample of 100 students. If you have a good list and you randomly select from it, the names you draw for your sample should be representative of the population enrolled at the university. Your sample should be a microcosm of the population of university students. The proportion of males and females in the sample should reflect

TABLE 6.2 Gallup Poll Accuracy Record

Year	Gallup Final Survey		Election Results		Deviation
1992*	49.0%	CLINTON	43.2%	CLINTON	+ 5.8
1990	54.0	Democratic	54.1	Democratic	− 0.1
1988	56.0	BUSH	53.9	BUSH	− 2.1
1984	59.0	REAGAN	59.1	REAGAN	− 0.1
1982	55.0	Democratic	56.1	Democratic	− 1.1
1980	47.0	REAGAN	50.8	REAGAN	− 3.8
1978	55.0	Democratic	54.6	Democratic	+ 0.4
1976	48.0	CARTER	50.0	CARTER	− 2.0
1974	60.0	Democratic	58.9	Democratic	+ 1.1
1972	62.0	NIXON	61.8	NIXON	+ 0.2
1970	53.0	Democratic	54.3	Democratic	− 1.3
1968	43.0	NIXON	43.5	NIXON	− 0.5
1966	52.5	Democratic	51.9	Democratic	+ 0.6
1964	64.0	JOHNSON	61.3	JOHNSON	+ 2.7
1962	55.5	Democratic	52.7	Democratic	+ 2.8
1960	51.0	KENNEDY	50.1	KENNEDY	+ 0.9
1958	57.0	Democratic	56.5	Democratic	+ 0.5
1956	59.5	EISENHOWER	57.8	EISENHOWER	+ 1.7
1954	51.5	Democratic	52.7	Democratic	− 1.2
1952	51.0	EISENHOWER	55.4	EISENHOWER	− 4.4
1950	51.0	Democratic	50.3	Democratic	+ 0.7
1948	44.5	TRUMAN	49.9	TRUMAN	− 5.4
1946	58.0	Republican	54.3	Republican	+ 3.7
1944	51.5	ROOSEVELT	53.3	ROOSEVELT	− 1.8
1942	52.0	Democratic	48.0	Democratic	+ 4.0
1940	52.0	ROOSEVELT	55.0	ROOSEVELT	− 3.0
1938	54.0	Democratic	50.8	Democratic	+ 3.2
1936	55.7	ROOSEVELT	62.5	ROOSEVELT	− 6.8

NOTE: No Congressional poll done in 1986.

*The Ross Perot candidacy created an additional source of error in estimating the 1992 presidential vote. There was no historical precedent for Perot, an independent candidate who was accorded equal status to the major party nominees in the presidential debates and had a record advertising budget. Gallup's decision to allocate none of the undecided vote to Perot, based on past performance of third party and independent candidates, resulted in the overestimation of Clinton's vote.

TREND IN DEVIATION

Elections	Average error
1936–1950	3.6
1952–1992	1.6

Average deviation for 28 national elections: 2.2 percent
Reprinted with permission. *The Gallup Poll Monthly*, November 1992

their proportion at the university, as should the proportion of freshmen, sophomores, juniors, and seniors. (For example, if you find that 42 percent of your sample are seniors and yet seniors make up only 18 percent of the student body as a whole, then you should suspect something is wrong with either your sampling procedure or your list of students.)

Sometimes researchers talk about **systematic sampling.** What they mean by this is best explained by way of example. Let's say that you plan to take a 10 percent sample of the 19,787 university students. However, a quick calculation shows that this would require almost 2,000 interviews. Since you plan to conduct the telephone survey in a week's time, you decide that 2,000 would be far too many students to attempt to contact. As you think about the realistic constraints on your time, you decide that 200 interviews is much more feasible. If you divide the proposed sample size of 200 by the university's population of 19,787, you get a **sampling ratio** of .01—which means that your sample will draw one name for every hundred students enrolled in the university.

In this example of systematic sampling, the next thing you need to do is to number all of the students on the listing you received from the registrar. Then you refer to the random number table (Appendix B) and find a random starting place (any number between 1 and 19,787), for example 6. The first student selected from the list would be 6, followed by 106, 206, 306, 406, 506, 606, 706, 806, 906, 1,006, 1,106, 1,206, and so on through the entire list of 19,787 students. If the list was not numbered and since numbering all 19,787 students would be very time-consuming, you could count out the first 100 names, measure that distance with a ruler, and then use that distance to locate the next name to be selected.

Both systematic and simple random sampling approaches tend to provide representative samples as long as the lists you work from are not organized in such a way as to bias the sample. For example, suppose you choose the first name on the list, then the one hundredth, the two hundredth, and so on, but you aren't aware that a computer program inadvertently placed students with the highest grade point averages in every hundredth position. In this case, your sample would contain only those students most likely to make Phi Beta Kappa and would not be representative of the larger student body.

While probability sampling is the best insurance against a sample being unrepresentative, it is no guarantee that every group will be well represented. Sometimes bad luck or some form of bias will produce a random sample that is not representative. For example, 48 percent of the university population may be female, but 54 percent of those drawn for your sample could be female. If you play cards, you understand how this could happen. Even though the deck is shuffled many times, luck (chance) plays a role in which cards you are dealt— it is possible to get all hearts or four aces. Similarly, any sample from a population is by definition only an approximation of the total population. Numerically large samples are the best guarantee against obtaining unrepresentative samples.

Some researchers try to guard against a freak or fluke sample by using **stratified random sampling.** When certain important characteristics of the population (e.g., the percentage of men and women) are known, exact proportions are obtained by dividing the study population into subgroups or subsets called strata and sampling the appropriate proportion from each stratum.

For instance, suppose that instead of sampling from the whole student body, you want to interview only seniors and freshmen. You already know that there are twice as many freshmen as seniors and that you want to interview 200 students. You again approach the registrar and ask for a listing of just freshmen and seniors. Once again you number each of the freshmen and seniors, choose a random starting place, and begin selecting from each strata. Since there are twice as many freshmen as seniors, you decide to select 65 seniors to interview and 130 freshmen. This keeps the proportion of seniors to freshmen in your sample the same as it is in the university, and you have retained the sample size that you think is manageable. This is not simple random sampling because sampling was done within each strata.

When it is not possible to obtain or feasible to construct a complete list of all the individuals who make up a population, (for example, the names and addresses of all social work majors in the United States), researchers sometimes employ a **cluster sampling design.**

Used primarily for convenience and economy, cluster sampling randomly selects individuals from natural groupings or clusters. Because human beings are social creatures, we tend to belong to numerous groups like civic organizations, clubs, fraternities, sororities, and churches.

For example, if you want to know how the parents of children with emotional, mental, or learning problems view helping professionals, you might go to your local mental health center and ask for their cooperation. If you wanted a more geographically diverse sample, it might occur to you to contact such national organizations as the National Alliance for the Mentally Ill, Children with Attention Deficit Disorder, and the Learning Disabilities Association of America. These organizations were the clusters from which Cournoyer and Johnson (1991) drew random samples from their mailing lists.

An example of a **one-stage cluster sampling** is dividing the population of a town into households (households would be the clusters because they usually contain more than one individual) and then taking a sample of households and obtaining information from *all* the members of the household. **Two-stage cluster sampling** involves dividing the population into households or clusters and then taking a *sample* of members from each selected household (Jolliffe, 1986).

One of my students used a **multistage cluster sampling design** in connection with a research project. She had been reading about transracial adoption and found that there was little information about blacks' attitudes toward this topic. Since she was not interested in whites' attitudes, but only in blacks' attitudes, a random community survey would have been inefficient. Instead, a multistage cluster sampling design was selected.

We first identified the nine census tracts in the city containing the highest concentrations of blacks. From these nine tracts, three were randomly selected (since she was doing the interviewing all by herself, there was no need to walk her legs off). From these three tracts, forty city blocks were randomly chosen. Finally, every sixth household was selected from these blocks (after getting a random starting place) until 150 interviews had been completed (Howard, Royse, and Skerl, 1977).

Because the individuals within a cluster tend to be more homogeneous than individuals in different clusters, the researcher typically wants to maximize the number of clusters for greater representativeness. This may mean that few individuals are selected from any one cluster. However, because of the efficiency permitted with random sampling, there is no obligation to sample from each cluster. Oftentimes it makes sense to combine stratification techniques (e.g., to stratify by geographical area) with cluster sampling.

Determining Sample Size

How big a sample is necessary for a good survey? This is a major question in the minds of many would-be researchers. Unfortunately, there is no simple response to this question. Sample size is related to the researcher's objectives, monetary and personnel resources, and the amount of time available in which to conduct the research. A precise sample size cannot be determined until you are able to state your expectations in terms of the accuracy you need and the confidence that you would like to have in the data.

You may have heard that a minimum sample size is 10 percent of the population. But the accuracy of your survey is much more dependent upon the size of the sample than on the population size. In order to be confident that your findings are reasonably accurate, you need to interview proportionately more of those who compose small populations than of those making up large populations.

Before you determine sample size for a study where statistical probability statements can be made about the findings, you must understand several terms. **Margin of error** refers to the precision needed by the researcher. A margin of error of five percent means that the actual findings could vary by as much as five points either positively or negatively. A consumer satisfaction survey, for instance, with a 5 percent margin of error associated with a finding of 65 percent of clients "highly satisfied" with services would mean that the true value in the population could be as low as 60 percent (65 − 5 = 60) or as high as 70 percent (65 + 5 = 70). If you believe that greater precision is needed (e.g., plus or minus two points), then you must plan on obtaining a larger sample to support that precision. This can be seen in table 6.3 by comparing the sample sizes in the .05 column with those in the .02 column.

The other term that is important to understand is **confidence level.** A confidence level (or level of confidence) is a statement of how often you could expect to find similar results if the survey were to be repeated. Since every survey varies slightly (depending upon who is selected to be in the sample), the confidence level informs about how often the findings will fall outside the margin of error. For example, in a sample developed to have a 95 percent confidence level with a 5 percent margin of error, the findings could be expected to miss the actual values in the population by more than 5 percent only five times in one hundred surveys. (In the example above, findings that less than 60 percent or more than 70 percent of the clients were "highly satisfied" would be expected to occur no more than five times in one hundred surveys.) The use of a 95 percent confidence level and 5 percent margin of error is pretty standard in the social sciences.

Table 6.3 will help you decide how large a sample to select in your own surveys. This table is used when you do not have a firm notion about the proportion of a population that would be in favor of or opposed to a specific issue. In order to be confident that the same findings would have occurred in 95 surveys out of 100, and to be accurate to within plus or minus 5 percentage points, you would need to interview 79 persons in a population of 100. However, in a population of 1 million, you would have to interview only 384 persons. The greater the precision you require, the larger your sample must be. Note that

TABLE 6.3   Appropriate Sizes of Simple Random Samples for Specific Permissible Errors Expressed as Absolute Proportions When the True Proportion in the Population Is 0.50 and the Confidence Level Is 95 Percent

Population Size	Sample size for permissible error (Proportion)				
	0.05	0.04	0.03	0.02	0.01
100	79	86	91	96	99
200	132	150	168	185	196
300	168	200	234	267	291
400	196	240	291	343	384
500	217	273	340	414	475
600	234	300	384	480	565
700	248	323	423	542	652
800	260	343	457	600	738
900	269	360	488	655	823
1,000	278	375	516	706	906
2,000	322	462	696	1,091	1,655
3,000	341	500	787	1,334	2,286
4,000	350	522	842	1,500	2,824
5,000	357	536	879	1,622	3,288
6,000	361	546	906	1,715	3,693
7,000	364	553	926	1,788	4,049
8,000	367	558	942	1,847	4,364
9,000	368	563	954	1,895	4,646
10,000	370	566	964	1,936	4,899
15,000	375	577	996	2,070	5,855
20,000	377	583	1,013	2,144	6,488
25,000	378	586	1,023	2,191	6,938
30,000	379	588	1,030	2,223	7,275
40,000	381	591	1,039	2,265	7,745
50,000	381	593	1,045	2,291	8,056
75,000	382	595	1,052	2,327	8,514
100,000	383	597	1,056	2,345	8,762
500,000	384	600	1,065	2,390	9,423
1,000,000	384	600	1,066	2,395	9,513
2,000,000	384	600	1,067	2,398	9,558

Source: *Sampling and Statistics Handbook for Research in Education* (National Education Assn., 1980). Copyright by Chester McCall. Reprinted with permission.

for a permissible error of 1 percent with the same population of 1 million, you would need a sample of 9,513. Few issues are worth the increase in sample size necessary when one goes from plus or minus 5 percentage points to plus or minus 1 point. For example, if you are 95 percent confident, plus or minus five percentage points, that 80 percent of the sample supports a tax increase, then it really doesn't matter whether the "true" level of support is 75 percent or 85 percent. The tax issue would pass comfortably with anything over a 51 percent majority.

It is possible to find other tables that allow you to use smaller samples if you can accept less confidence (e.g., permissible error of 10 percent), or if you have some evidence (prior surveys) of how the sample might respond (e.g., 90 percent opposed to a tax increase).

Sample size is obviously much more of a concern if you are planning a probability sampling design than if you are planning a sample of convenience. With a probability design, you will need to consult a table to arrive at the appropriate sample size. In nonprobability studies, sample size is dictated more by considerations of convenience and appearance. It may be relatively easy, for instance, to interview 30 to 40 clients, but interviewing a sample of 260 or so might be virtually impossible unless you have help.

Would it be wise to enlist the aid of a co-worker or friend and attempt to go from 30 to 100 interviews? The more data you can collect, and the more respondents you can interview, the more likely you are to understand the phenomenon you are studying. Generally speaking, 100 interviews would be seen as having more credibility than 30 or 40. Thirty of anything is beginning to be a large number and smaller samples "feel" inconsequential.

Here's a small example to demonstrate sampling:

Katie's mother complained that her seventh grader, Katie, watched too much television. "But Mom," Katie protested, "my grades are good. And besides, all my friends watch more than me." Katie's mother got on the phone that afternoon and began calling other mothers of seventh grade students. This is what she learned:

	Amount of TV Watched Daily	GPA
Katie	4 hours	3.0
Jake	3 hours	2.5
Rochelle	3 hours	2.0
Martha	1 hour	4.0
Tim	5 hours	2.8
Shawna	2 hours	3.3
John	3 hours	3.0

Susie	0 hours	3.4
Glenna	1 hour	2.6
Matthew	5 hours	2.0

The average amount of television watched by this sample of students was 2.7 hours (total of 27 hours divided by 10). Katie's mother concluded that Katie was watching more television than her peers. However, would she have come to the same conclusion if she had taken a smaller sample of one or two students? Suppose she called only Matthew's mother. What if she contacted the mothers of Jake, Tim, John, and Matthew? Does Katie watch as much television as the other honor roll students? From this exercise, you can see that many different samples could be selected. Some smaller samples would not be very representative of the larger group. However, as the sample size increases, values obtained from the sample begin to look much more like the average of the larger group.

Nonprobability Sampling Designs

Nonprobability sampling designs are generally regarded as unscientific because there is no way of knowing how accurate or representative their findings are. At the same time, these designs are often employed as straw polls—unofficial estimates of opinions or concerns about issues. In actual practice, it is likely that social workers employ more of the nonprobability than probability designs because they are generally cheaper, faster, and more easily conducted. If you were, for instance, to poll ten friends about some matter instead of randomly selecting a sample from the 50,000 registered voters in your town, you would be taking a **sample of convenience**. When we draw a convenience sample, we do so because it is easy or quick, and we think it will provide us with some information as to what the larger population might think. But this type of sampling is prone to error. Your friends, for example, knowing how strongly you feel on an issue such as the tax for a new high school may not be completely honest in telling you how they would vote. Since there is some reason they are your friends, the common interests you have (your friends may all be social workers, have about the same income, and have children in school) may also influence how they would vote. In other words, your ten friends may not be representative of the other 49,990 voters in your town who are not social workers, who make more or less than you do annually, and who may or may not have children.

If you were to skim a wide variety of professional journals, you would find that many surveys with college students are conducted each year. Why do you think that is? Could it have anything to do with the convenience with which researchers might access them? At the same time, how well do college students represent the other adults in our population? Could they be younger, more educated, more liberal in their views? Although college students may not be representative of our adult population, often researchers are willing to assume that patterns or relationships found with convenience samples of college students might also be discovered within more scientific probability samples. In this sense, they may use convenience samples as exploratory studies before they commit to a larger-scale investigation.

Nonprobability sampling is often done when the extent of the population is not known. For instance, in my exploratory research to find out how much money trash pickers make each day from gathering and selling aluminum beverage cans (Royse, 1987), I did not know the true population (the actual number) of trash pickers in the city or the state, so I arbitrarily chose a nonprobability sample of fifty. This group may have been somewhat unrepresentative of the larger population of all trash pickers, but there was no way of knowing this. (I tried to make the study a little more representative by interviewing trash pickers in two different cities.) This type of sampling is also known as **purposive sampling**, because the respondents had to have certain characteristics in common in order to be selected for an interview (in my study, they all had to be trash pickers).

One respondent leading you to another respondent (e.g., the mother of an autistic child gives you the name of another mother of an autistic child) is sometimes referred to as **snowball sampling**. The sample grows by referrals to other potential respondents.

The snowball sample is used when you can't find respondents any other way. Wolf (1989), for instance, used this approach after he mailed out 100 questionnaires to a random sampling of Catholic priests and got only eighteen respondents—even though they could respond anonymously. With an 82 percent nonresponse rate, Wolf couldn't conclude anything about homosexuals in the priesthood. Changing his approach, Wolf mailed questionnaires to five priests whom he knew to be homosexual and asked them to send surveys to other homosexual priests whom they knew.

With the snowball approach Wolf got back 101 surveys. While he couldn't make any definitive conclusions about the proportion of gay priests, he was able to study several important issues about whether they had disclosed, their views about celibacy, and their plans about remaining in the priesthood. He concluded that homosexuality was not incompatible with the priesthood.

Quota sampling involves knowing certain characteristics of a population (e.g., the proportion of an agency's clientele who are under thirty, middle aged, and sixty or older) and then striving to obtain the same proportions in the selected sample. With this approach, screening is often done early in the interview so that interviewers will not have to continue with those who do not have the desired characteristics. Although the final sample may match the population in terms of the proportions of respondents having certain characteristics, the sample may be unrepresentative in other areas because of characteristics for which they were not screened. For example, although the quota sample may resemble the population by containing an identical proportion of those who are over age sixty, a poorly designed quota sample could reveal that the majority of the respondents over sixty were retired or disabled, while in actuality this characteristic was found in only 20 percent of those sixty and older in the actual population. With this approach, interviewers have greater flexibility in deciding whom to reject or include, and for this reason the potential for interviewer bias is a major concern.

In a study of fifty social work majors, a quota sampling design might specify that a quota of half of the respondents would be African American or that half would be male. If males and African-American students did not make up 50 percent of all social work majors, then more attention is being given to obtaining a certain number or percentage of respondents with a given characteristic than to the representativeness or precision that would be obtained with a probability design.

The problem with all nonprobability sampling designs is not knowing how representative the sample is or how closely it resembles the "true" population. The nonprobability sample could be very biased, yet it would be difficult for the investigator to know this without drawing additional samples.

Additional Survey Designs

In addition to the probability and nonprobability survey designs, several other designs may be useful. The term **cross-sectional survey design** is used to refer to the probability sampling designs. The term indicates that a one-time survey is made with a randomly selected sample. The cross-sectional design allows a broad representation of the population and thus involves persons of all ages, incomes, and educational levels.

In contrast, **longitudinal surveys** may not be representative of the population. These surveys are conducted on multiple occasions over

TABLE 6.4   **Comparison of Trend, Cohort, and Panel Longitudinal Surveys**

Type	Subjects' Ages in 1990	Subjects' Ages in 1995	Subjects' Ages in 2000
Trend	15 yrs. old	15 yrs. old	15 yrs. old
Cohort	15 yrs. old	20 yrs. old	25 yrs. old
Panel	15 yrs. old	20 yrs. old	25 yrs. old

an extended period of time. Change is measured through a succession of surveys. There are three types of longitudinal surveys: **trend surveys, cohort surveys,** and **panel surveys.** Trend studies require multiple samplings from the same population over months or years in order to monitor changes or trends. The same individuals are not repeatedly interviewed. For good examples of trend survey research, see *Trends in Public Opinion: A Compendium of Survey Data* (Niemi, Mueller, and Smith, 1989) or Young, Savola, and Phelps (1991).

A cohort is a group of persons who have some critical or significant experience in common (e.g., Vietnam veterans). Cohort studies involve only persons who fit into these subgroups. Persons who are born, married, or graduated from high school in a given year could be used to form cohorts by birth, marriage, or graduation, respectively. Cohort studies involve multiple samples from the cohort(s) of interest. Comparisons by cohorts are most commonly found in sociological studies of the population.

Panel studies are studies of the *same* group of persons over an extended period (e.g., the survivors of Hiroshima). Panel studies are used to detect changes in individuals over time.

Table 6.4 shows the three types of longitudinal surveys. Each study began with interviewing fifteen-year-old runaways in Chicago. In a trend survey, the investigator is interested in differences in fifteen-year-old runaways over time. Do their characteristics change? Do the reasons they run away change? An investigator using a cohort survey would want to interview any person who was fifteen years old and a runaway in 1990. The panel surveyor would want to interview the 1990 runaways in 1995 and 2000.

Mistakes to Avoid

If you have the time and resources, choose a probability design over a nonprobability sampling design. Even then, be alert to any limitations that could result in your sampling frame being less inclusive than you had planned. Be particularly alert to sample selection bias that could occur because of the order in which the sample units are listed, incomplete listings (e.g., the omission of employees who work fewer than forty hours per week), and the tendency of respondents to self-select.

For instance, I once watched a television camera crew approach individuals for "person-in-the-street" interviews. What was of interest to me was the number (perhaps the majority) of individuals who, seeing the camera, crossed to the other side of the street to avoid it. While the process of indiscriminately stopping people and asking for their opinions seemed random, actually there was a severe bias in that everyone did not have an equal chance of being chosen. Some deliberately avoided giving their opinions. Did the more vocal individuals represent the views of the shy ones? This cannot be determined in a sample of convenience.

Similarly, if you stand outside of a supermarket at 4:00 A.M. on Friday your respondents may be quite different from those who show up at 10:00 A.M. or even 8:00 P.M. Might there be a difference in the supermarket shoppers at 11:00 A.M. on Sunday and those at 3:00 P.M. on the same day? There is a good reason that samples of convenience are also known as **accidental** and **available samples**.

No matter which approach you select to conduct your survey, it is important to **pilot test** (or pretest) your procedures and instrument. Generally, pilot testing is informal and can involve giving the survey instrument to a few friends or co-workers to see if they understand the questions and respond in the ways you anticipate. Even better, administer the survey instrument to a group of persons as similar as possible to the population that you will be surveying. The major purpose of the pilot test is to determine if the type of information you want is supplied by the respondents. Pilot testing need not involve more than twenty persons if the respondents have no problems understanding the questions or recording their responses. Pilot testing provides estimates of the time required to complete the questionnaire and, in the case of telephone and face-to-face interviews, provides useful data for estimating the cost of the survey.

Allow sufficient time to follow up on nonrespondents. Reminder postcards and mailing second and third questionnaires to nonrespondents greatly increase response rates. In telephone and face-to-face interviewing, unless you follow up on those who are not home when you call, you run the risk of having a bias against those who work during the hours that you attempt to reach them.

A low response rate is just as problematic as too small a sample. If less than a majority of the respondents reply, one is left wondering about the attitudes or characteristics of those who chose not to respond. Are the data biased when only 20 percent respond? Would a different pattern of findings emerge if the response rate could be raised from 35 percent to 70 percent by following up on the nonresponders? There is no way of knowing unless nonresponders are given more than one opportunity to reply. It has been said that the response rate is "probably the most important single indicator of the reliability of a survey" (Shipman, 1981, pp. 67–68). If you have a response rate of 50 percent or less, it is not possible to extrapolate the findings with any confidence to the larger population (Posavac and Carey, 1985).

If you need to employ interviewers, train them well to prevent careless errors in the field or in the recording of responses. Let them know that you will be recontacting a portion of their respondents to validate their answers. A nationally prominent sociologist once told me that as a student he sat in a coffee shop and made up information for a community directory when he should have been going door-to-door to obtain accurate data. However, falsification of data is not a major difficulty with most surveys, particularly if you screen your interviewers well.

A Final Note about Surveys

I started off this chapter describing the confusion that sometimes results when seemingly similar surveys (like voters' polls during election years) yield conflicting results. How is this possible? I bet many of you can already explain this phenomenon. There are several possible explanations that will occur to you as I share an amusing account.

I once received a survey from the Beer Drinkers of America. (And no, I don't belong nor do I drink so much beer that they should have my address.) Anyway, this "survey" opened my eyes to the many ways in which surveys have been abused and could be used to mislead. The cover letter informed me that a federal excise tax on beer had gone into effect and that an article in *Time* magazine "claimed" that 72 percent of the American people support the tax increase.

The next sentence asked, "Were you included in the survey?" The obvious implication is that most Americans were not consulted. The letter goes on to state that "only" five hundred people were asked to participate and then asks for my help to stop our politicians from using surveys like "that one" to justify higher taxes on beer. The Beer Drinkers of America developed a questionnaire to reach "thousands of people across the country" in order to "counter the effects of misleading surveys that manipulate the American people—and our public officials—into supporting unfair tax increases on beer drinkers."

Question two on their questionnaire asked, "Do you agree or disagree that beer drinkers should suffer even greater tax increases in the future?" Question four asked, "Should beer advertising on television be outlawed or restricted even if the result if to force major sporting events onto cable and pay-per-view systems?" Then, the "National Taxpayers Opinion Poll" provides a convenient box for those interested in "joining the fight" and who want to include a "membership acceptance check" of $5 to help the cause.

Suppose for a moment that you compare the result from the *Time* magazine poll and the results from the Beer Drinkers of America. The results from these efforts probably would be different. Why?

First of all, the Beer Drinkers of America are likely to galvanize the opinions of only those respondents who are concerned about the excise tax on beer. If you were unconcerned, you wouldn't go to the trouble to complete their questionnaire or mail back any cash contributions. Do you think their sample will be fair and impartial, representative of the way most Americans would respond? Or would it lead to a biased sample?

Second, some of their questions are worded in such a way as to influence the respondent's thinking in a certain direction. The word *suffer* in question two, for example. Most of us don't want to make anyone suffer. And quite a few Americans would not want to see major sporting events "forced" onto cable or pay-per-view systems. It may be erroneous, however, to assume that this course of events would occur even if beer advertising were restricted. Do you see how the wording of these questions could lead respondents to disagree with the excise tax?

Finally, because the organization solicits members at the same time that it is conducting the "poll," one can't help but wonder whether the Beer Drinkers of America is more interested in the results or the contributions that might be obtained. Of course they would hope for a high response rate (no pun intended), but for what purpose—to acquire statistics or lobbying power?

When you experience conflicting results from surveys that appear to be examining the same topic, you need to investigate:

a. How the sample was drawn. (Is it representative, unbiased, employing a probability design?)

b. How the questions are worded. (Are the questions leading, or likely to influence a certain response?)

c. Sample size and margin of error.

d. Response rate.

e. When the survey was conducted.

Surveys, particularly political polls, can appear to be at odds with one another when in fact they were conducted at different times or used different questions or different sampling procedures. Attitudes can and do change over time—sometimes on a national level almost overnight when a president does something decisive or unpopular. We'll discuss the effect of wording questions in more detail in the next chapter, but you can already see how a questionnaire can influence the respondent's thinking. And finally, it is important to know about the sample—who was included and who was excluded. Knowledge of these factors will help you to understand how seemingly similar survey efforts can produce dissimilar conclusions.

You shouldn't necessarily be persuaded by a large sample size. I recently read an article in our newspaper about a survey that had been mailed to 5,000 families. "Interesting," I thought to myself. "I wonder how they arrived at that number? Don't they know about random sampling?" As I read further into the article, I became convinced that the researchers didn't know much at all about survey methodology. What were the clues? The researchers got back less than half (43 percent) of their questionnaires (was the questionnaire too long or uninteresting, or maybe they didn't follow up with the nonresponders?), 78 percent of the respondents were women (what happened to the men?), and they used telephone books to construct their sample frame (we already know what bias that interjects into a study).

"Happy Families Abundant in State, Survey Says" proclaimed the headline. "Yeah, right," I thought to myself again. "How happy are the 57 percent of the sample who didn't respond? And how about those who weren't included because they were too poor to own a phone or because they had an unlisted number?" How a survey is planned and conducted must be understood before its findings can be given any credence.

Questions for Class Discussion

1. You want to conduct a national survey of social workers. What are three ways in which you might stratify the sample? Why might you want to stratify the sample?

2. Assume that you have a budget of $3,500 (exclusive of your own

time) with which to conduct a national survey of social workers. What survey approach would you use? Why?

3. Give an example of a topic that might best be explored with the following:
   a. Snowball sampling
   b. Cluster sampling
   c. A longitudinal design
4. Assume that you are the director of a staff of twenty-five. You suspect that they are so overworked that they are fast approaching burnout. You decide to conduct a survey of the staff. How many of the staff should you interview?
5. How have surveys advanced our understanding of human nature or improved our lives? Cite examples if possible.
6. Cite examples of surveys in which you have participated or personal encounters you have had with surveys.
7. Your agency has asked you to conduct a random sampling of clients to determine how satisfied they are with the agency's services. After some discussion, it is decided that a telephone survey is the most sensible approach. If the agency closed approximately three thousand cases last year, how big a sample would be needed in order to have 95 percent confidence in the findings, plus or minus 5 percent? If the agency decides to use a mail approach, how many persons would you have to contact in order to get the same level of confidence and accuracy? (Keep in mind that about 30 percent of the respondents in a mail survey respond on the first mailing.)
8. Let's pretend that *Money* magazine prints a questionnaire. One of the questions asked is "What do you think about most—money or sex?" Can the findings from this study be considered to represent the thinking of most American adults? If you wanted to investigate that question, what would be a better way to do it? Would you expect the findings from the *Money* magazine survey to be different from findings from the same questionnaire in an issue of *Playboy*?
9. In his book *The Superpollsters*, David Moore discusses criticisms of books written by Shere Hite. He mentions that for one book she distributed approximately 100,000 questionnaires through women's organizations and got back approximately 3 percent. Further, she instructed respondents that they didn't have to answer every single question but only those that interested them. And she didn't standardize her questionnaire, but used multiple versions. Could she claim a representative sample? Did her methodology deserve criticism?

Mini-Projects for Experiencing Research Firsthand

1. List the steps you would go through to draw a random sample of 50 from a population of 350 using the table of random numbers. Draw the sample of 50 and record the numbers of those who would be selected.

2. Look through past issues of the *Gallup Report* and find an example of survey research. Respond to the following questions:
   a. What is the topic of the research?
   b. What does the survey data show?
   c. What period of time is covered?
   d. What was the sample size?

3. Browse through back issues of *Social Work* and find five articles that report the use of a survey methodology. What is the average size of the samples reported? In how many instances did the sample size seem to be too small to allow 95 percent confidence and plus or minus 5 percent accuracy? Were most of these studies exploratory studies?

4. Skim through old magazines in order to locate survey data. Try to find an article citing or using survey data. Discuss what it reveals with regard to how the survey was conducted. What else would you like to know? How much confidence do you place in the survey findings?

Resources and References

Alreck, P.L. and Settle, R.B. (1985). *The Survey Research Handbook.* Homewood, IL: Irwin.

Babbie, E. (1986). *The Practice of Social Research.* Belmont, CA: Wadsworth.

Blankenship, A.B. (1977). *Professional Telephone Surveys.* New York: McGraw-Hill.

Blythe, B.J. (1986). Increasing mailed survey responses with a lottery. *Social Work Research and Abstracts,* 22 (3), 18–19.

Bradburn, N.M. and Sudman, S. (1988). *Polls and Surveys: Understanding What They Tell Us.* San Francisco: Jossey-Bass.

Converse, J.M. and Schuman, H. (1974). *Conversations at Random: Survey Research as Interviewers See It.* New York: Wiley.

Cournoyer, D.E. and Johnson, H.C. (1991). Measuring parents' perceptions of mental health professionals. *Research on Social Work Practice,* 1(4), 399–415.

Dillman, D.A. (1978). *Mail and Telephone Surveys: The Total Design Method.* New York: Wiley.

Dillman, D.A. (1983). Mail and other self-administered questionnaires. In P.H. Rossi, J.D. Wright, and A.B. Anderson (Eds.), *Handbook of Survey Research.* New York: Academic Press.

Dillman, D.A. (1991). The design and administration of mail surveys. In W. Richard Scott and Judith Blake (Eds.) *Annal Reviews of Sociology.* Palo Alto, CA: Annual Reviews, Inc., 225–249.

Farhi, P. (1992). Pollsters looking at who's not talking. *Lexington Herald-Leader,* April 15, p. A3.

Fienberg, S.E., Loftus, E.F., and Tanur, J.M. (1985). Cognitive aspects of health survey methodology: An overview. *Milbank Memorial Fund Quarterly/Health and Society,*63 (3), 547–564.

Frey, J.H. (1989). *Survey Research by Telephone.* Beverly Hills, CA: Sage.

Howard, A., Royse, D., and Skerl, J.A. (1977). Transracial adoption: The black community perspective. *Social Work,* 22(3), 184–189.

Institute for Social Research, Survey Research Center. (1976). *Interviewer's Manual.* Rev. ed. Ann Arbor: University of Michigan Press.

James, J.M. and Bolstein, R. (1992). Large monetary incentives and their effect on mail survey response rates. *Public Opinion Quarterly,* 56(4), 442–453.

Jolliffe, F.R. (1986). *Survey Design and Analysis.* New York: Halsted.

Lavrakas, P.J. (1993). *Telephone Survey Methods: Sampling, Selection, and Supervision.* Newbury Park, CA: Sage.

Lucas, W.A. and Adams, W.C. (1977). *An Assessment of Telephone Survey Methods.* Prepared under a grant from the National Science Foundation (Report R-2135-NSF). Santa Monica, CA: Rand Corp.

Moore, D.W. (1992). *The superpollsters: How they measure and manipulate public opinion in America.* New York: Four Walls Eight Windows.

Niemi, R.G., Mueller, J. and Smith, T. (1989). *Trends in Public Opinion: A Compendium of Survey Data.* New York: Greenwood Press.

Posavac, E.J. and Carey, R.G. (1985). *Program Evaluation: Methods and Case Studies.* Englewood Cliffs, NJ: Prentice-Hall.

Rosenberg, A.S. (1990). 'The number you have dialed' . . . is often unlisted. *Lexington Herald-Leader,* May 9, p. A2.

Rosenberg, E. and Bernabo, L. (1992). Hunger: A hospital survey. *Social Work in Health Care,* 16(3), 83–95.

Rossi, P.H., Wright, J.D., and Anderson, A.B. (1983). *Handbook of Survey Research.* New York: Academic Press.

Royse, D. (1987). Homelessness among trash pickers. *Psychological Reports,* 60, 808–810.

Schuman, H. (1985). *Racial Attitudes in America: Trends and Interpretations.* Cambridge, MA: Harvard University Press.

Shipman, M. (1981). *The Limitations of Social Research.* New York: Longman.

Tuckel, P.S. and Feinberg, B.M. (1991). The answering machine poses many questions for telephone survey researchers. *Public Opinion Quarterly,* 55, 200–217.

U.S. Department of Commerce, Bureau of the Census. (1993). *Statistical Abstract of the United States: 1992.* Washington, DC: U.S. Government Printing Office.

Weinbach, R.W. (1984). The prepaid postcard survey: Enhancing brief research. *Social Work Research and Abstracts*, 20(4), 5–6.

Wentland, E.J. and Smith, K.W. (1993). *Survey Responses: An Evaluation of Their Validity*. San Diego: Academic Press.

Wilk, R. (1993). Research note: The use of monetary incentives to increase survey response rates. *Social Work Research and Abstracts*, 29(1), 33–34.

Wolf, J.G. (1989). *Gay Priests*. New York: Harper & Row.

Wurtele, S.K., Kvaternick, M., and Franklin, C.F. (1992). Sexual abuse prevention for preschoolers: a survey of parents' behaviors, attitudes, and beliefs. *Journal of Child Sexual Abuse*, 1(1), 113–128.

Xu, M., Batu, B.J., and Schweitzer, J.C. (1993). The impact of messages on survey participation in answering machine households. *Public Opinion Quarterly*, 57(2), 232–237.

Young, C.H., Savola, K.L., and Phelps, E. (1991). *Inventory of Longitudinal Studies in the Social Sciences*. Newbury Park, CA: Sage.

7
Designing Questionnaires
for Surveys and Agency Use

Social workers are familiar with the use of questionnaires. In almost every social service agency, initial data collection is conducted before new clients are admitted for services. This process is called "intake," "screening," completing the "face sheet," or "taking the client's history." To collect data, social workers follow a set of previously determined questions in an established order and sequence. Although most agencies' admission forms may not have been designed for research purposes, they have enough in common with research questionnaires that we can use them to increase our knowledge about questionnaires.

Think for a moment about an agency's admission form (or any other questionnaire with which you are familiar). Someone (or perhaps a committee) may have spent a considerable number of hours in deciding which questions were important to ask and which ones were not. One of the purposes of the questionnaire is to ensure that the same set of questions is asked each time information is required. From the agency's perspective, this standard set of questions provides the minimal level of information required of each client. The social worker does not have to guess or anticipate what information the agency needs, because it has already been predetermined on the printed form. The social worker is also freed from worrying about wording the question the same way each time. If the social worker had to decide with each new client how to phrase the questions, there is the possibility that these questions would be unclear or confusing and not generate the same type of information each time. With a standard set of pretested questions in a carefully designed admission form, problems with clients providing erroneous information are minimized.

Similarly, research questionnaires use a set of carefully selected questions that standardize the way the information is asked for and structure the respondents' responses (e.g., instead of asking the respondent to state his or her age, the questionnaire asks for year of birth). Through careful wording and attention to such matters as the sequence and order of questions, researchers attempt to remove opportunities for recording inaccurate data.

Questionnaire design requires more precise statements and questions than we use in ordinary conversation. In casual conversation between two individuals, vague areas either become clear later in the conversation, or more specific information is not needed. One person may say to another, "I've noticed that Martha has a pretty low self-esteem." Seldom will the other party say, "How are you operationalizing self-esteem?" However, in the conduct of research the concepts we use must be operationalized and focused. Ambiguities and vague terms in questionnaires can cause problems for respondent and researcher alike. Such problems will be discovered and eliminated during pretests of the questionnaire. The resulting final product should provide each respondent with a clear notion of what is being asked.

DeVaus (1986) articulates well the importance of specificity in developing useful items for questionnaires:

> It is not enough to say, "I'm interested in getting some answers about inequality." What answers to what questions? Do you want to know the extent of inequality, its distribution, its causes, its effects, or what? What sort of inequality are you interested in? Over what period? (P. 27)

Designing research questions that are clear and concise and that result in data that can be used by the researcher is not an easy task. Questions that seem to be straightforward to their developers might be described as confusing or circuitous by others. In an effort to become precise, it is possible to become too wordy so that the intent of the question is hard to comprehend. Questions may also inadvertently omit important response choices or contain overlapping response choices. And there is always the problem of unconsciously biasing the responses simply by the way the questions are phrased.

Beginning the Development of a Questionnaire

First and foremost, you must have a clear idea of what data the questionnaire should provide. What is it that you want to find out? What are the specific content areas to be covered? Concurrently, you must decide which survey approach will be used to present the questions to the respondents. Some formats (e.g., questions requiring many response options) work better in mail surveys than in telephone surveys. In mail surveys, respondents can simultaneously view all of the response categories (e.g., "Strongly agree," "Agree," "Undecided," "Disagree," "Strongly disagree") before choosing one. In telephone surveys, respondents find it difficult to keep the question as well as all of the response options in mind. Sudman and Bradburn (1982) have noted that even five categories can stretch a respondent's ability to keep a whole scale in mind at once. Consequently, respondents may remember some but not all of the responses, and their responses may have a narrower range of variation ("Agree" or "Disagree"). Another consideration is that when recall and recognition questions are vital to the survey, interviews work better than mail surveys (Berdie, Anderson, and Niebuhr, 1986).

The nature of the content, the intended survey approach, and the nature of the population being surveyed affect the final form that the questionnaire takes (Blankenship, 1977). Only after consideration has been given to these areas should further conceptualizing of the questionnaire begin.

A review of the literature can provide questions or examples of ways that researchers have approached the topic of interest. It is not unethical, but rather good research practice, to use questions that have worked well for other researchers (Sudman and Bradburn, 1982). Do not, however, "borrow" items that are protected by copyright without the author's permission. Customarily, one writes the author of the instrument for permission to use it and requests any additional information that the author may have on the instrument. Sometimes the author can refer you to other researchers who have recently modified or used the instrument with interesting results. Besides the possibility of saving time in questionnaire design, another advantage of using questions that have already been employed by other researchers is that you can then compare your findings to those from existing studies. The literature review may also reveal methods or approaches that were not successful.

As you begin selecting and composing questions for the first draft of a questionnaire, you will have to give some thought to whether your research topic requires **closed-ended questions** (multiple choice type responses) or **open-ended questions** (unstructured responses).

Closed-Ended Questions

Closed-ended questions are those that have their own predetermined response set. (Look again at the items on the Drug Attitude Questionnaire in the Appendix.) The major advantage of closed-ended questions is that a great deal of time is saved in the tabulation of the data and coding it for computer analysis. Since the response choices are supplied (e.g., "Yes," "No," or "Strongly agree," "Agree," etc.) the person who is tabulating the responses does not have the problem of deciphering lengthy, illegible responses. Virtually no interpretation is required of what the respondent intended or whether a response is more like an existing set of responses or deserves a whole new category. Another advantage is that since closed-ended questions list response options, their greater specificity communicates the same frame of reference to all respondents (Converse and Presser, 1986).

Closed-ended questions are used when it is known how respondents might reply. If their responses are difficult to anticipate, open-ended questions can be used in a pilot study to find out what terms or language respondents tend to use in responding. It is then possible to identify frequent or common responses as well as the range of responses so that closed-ended questions can be developed.

Closed-ended questions can be used effectively in practically all areas of interest to social workers. For example, perhaps you are interested in specific dimensions of nursing home life. One area that you feel is important is how the residents evaluate the food prepared by the nursing home. You might construct a closed-ended question that allows for ratings of "Excellent," "Good," "Fair," or "Poor." However, a "fair" rating does not provide a wealth of information about the food. It doesn't tell you, for instance, whether hot oatmeal is served every day for breakfast, whether it arrives barely warm, or whether there is a wide variety of breakfast foods available. A number of closed-ended questions might be used to follow the initial question and to further help assess the quality of meals provided at the nursing home. Additional closed-ended questions can be used to examine residents' perceptions of other facets of nursing home life.

Open-Ended Questions

Open-ended questions have no prepared response choices. This form of question allows respondents to communicate without having to choose from a set of prepared response categories. Open-ended questions are best suited for those occasions when the researcher intends that direct interviewing be employed. Few respondents take the time to elaborate on their thoughts or feelings when they must write them out on paper. Whether respondents are self-conscious about their writing skills or do not wish to create so personal a written document, mailed questionnaires that rely heavily on open-ended questions have a poorer response rate than those that use closed-ended questions. There is some evidence (Sudman and Bradburn, 1982) that open-ended questions result in greater reporting of sensitive or socially disapproved behavior than closed-ended questions. One possible explanation for this is that respondents will avoid placing themselves in categories that include high levels of socially unacceptable behavior when there are categories with more acceptable levels of behavior from which to choose.

There are times when the researcher wants greater detail than closed-ended questions typically provide. For example, if you wanted to know more about the quality of life in a nursing home as the residents experience it, closed-ended questions are not likely to provide you with much insight into their personal reflections. Open-ended questions supply you with quotes from residents—if this is of interest. On the other hand, a respondent can ramble; it requires a skillful interviewer to bring the respondent back to the topic of interest.

In any given survey, it is possible to combine both closed-ended and open-ended questions. In the example of an evaluation of a nursing home, one could rely chiefly upon closed-ended questions for rating various facets of the nursing home (e.g., courteousness of the staff, noise level, social and recreational opportunities) and still employ an open-ended question such as: "Is there anything else you would like to tell us about how it feels to live in this nursing home?" Alternatively, you could use these open-ended questions: "What is the *best* thing about living in this nursing home?" and "What is the *worst* thing about living in this nursing home?" Your use of open- or closed-ended questions (or a mixture of the two) is dependent upon the goals of your research and the type of information you require. Keep in mind that open-ended questions are easier to develop than closed-ended ones, but they are harder to analyze. For instance, suppose you ask a group of volunteers this question: "What kinds of things did you do as a Big Brother or Big Sister?" You might get back a list of such activities as:

Went out to eat	Played Monopoly and board games
Played basketball	Worked on my car
Went to movies	Went fishing
Tutored	Watched television
Visited the mall	Went bicycling
Visited the zoo	Visited friends
Went shopping	Went to the library
Built model planes	Baked cookies
Talked on the phone	

Now suppose you want to summarize these into one or two categories to understand what kinds of activities Big Brothers and Big Sisters favored. Would you use the category of athletic/nonathletic activity? If so, is fishing athletic? Would you create categories for those activities that required spending money (e.g., going to a movie or to a restaurant) versus those that didn't (e.g., watching television)? But then, couldn't making cookies involve an expense (if you had to buy chocolate chips and sugar)? Does fishing involve an expense? (It does if you have to buy a license and bait.) A visit to the mall doesn't have to be expensive, but would you know if the Big Brother bought a soft drink and a taco for himself and his Little Brother?

Take my word for it, closed-ended questions are a great deal easier to analyze. The only problem is that with them you have to anticipate how the respondents would answer. However, a small pilot test with open-ended questions can often suggest the categories or response set that you need for the same item to be converted to a closed-ended question.

Whether you adopt questions that have been used by other researchers or write your own, circulate a rough draft of the proposed questionnaire among your colleagues for comments and suggestions. Use their responses to revise the questionnaire before it goes out for a pilot test. After the pilot test, scrutinize the questionnaire again for questions that might have been misunderstood, biased items that suggest responses, insufficient response categories, typographical errors, and similar problems. Only after several revisions should the questionnaire be printed and distributed.

To assist you in developing good questionnaires, a number of specific guidelines have been elaborated. These guidelines are suggested in order to help you recognize the subtle ways in which bias can creep into your questionnaire items. Ill-conceived questions can produce error. However, more important than memorizing a series of rules is that you understand why hastily constructed questions can result in worthless data. Examples of poorly phrased or constructed questions appear in this chapter; consider each of the examples and decide for yourself why it is flawed before reading the discussion accompanying it.

Pitfalls in Writing Good Questions

Double-Barreled Questions

Example: Have you donated blood or gone to the dentist this month?

( ) Yes
( ) No
( ) Don't know

This question is poorly constructed because it asks about two different behaviors (donating blood and visiting the dentist) but is structured so that only one response is expected. In the minds of most people, these two events are not connected in any way. A response of "Yes" could mean that the respondent had donated blood and been to the dentist. It is also possible that some respondents might respond "Yes" when they had visited the dentist but not donated blood, and vice versa. Some respondents will indicate "No" when they have done one but not the other. Some "No" responses will mean that the respondent has neither donated blood nor gone to the dentist. In this example, it is impossible to interpret what any response means.

As a rule, a question should ask about one issue, thought, or event at a time. If more information is desired, more questions should be asked. In this example, two separate questions should be constructed—each one focusing upon a single issue. Avoid asking two questions in one item.

However, sometimes a single item might be used when the focus is on the similarity of two different events. For instance, if we were interviewing abuse victims it could be acceptable to ask, "Were you threatened with a gun or a knife?" If the intent was to discover how often these weapons were used, there may not be any reason to break this item into two different questions.

On the other hand, a question like "Have you ever been called names or threatened with harm?" is poorly constructed because being called names is a fairly common occurrence and doesn't imply the same order of danger as being threatened with harm.

Leading Questions

Example: Don't you agree with the president that the federal government should not overspend?

( ) Agree
( ) Disagree
( ) Don't know

This question clearly leads the respondent into thinking along certain lines. Most of us want to be agreeable and to get along with others. And most Americans believe it is important to respect the office of the president and would generally want to support that office (by agreeing with the president when possible). This example is a leading question because it suggests the desired response.

The question "Don't you agree that the federal government should spend more on social services and less on germ warfare research?" is an example of a double-barreled leading question. Besides begging for an "Agree" response, it also asks for information about two different items. First, it wants to know if the government should spend more money on social services. Second, it wants to know if the respondent thinks the government should spend less on germ warfare. Again, the respondent could agree with one of these two thoughts and disagree with the other and be confused about how to respond. The two separate ideas can be constructed in the format: "As you think about the amount the federal government spends on social services programs in this country, would you say that amount is: (a) adequate, (b) inadequate, or (c) excessive?"

Unavailable Information

Example: How many hours of television did you watch last year?

Respondents should not be asked for information that is not available to them. Since most of us do not keep records of this kind of thing, it would be unlikely that the response we give would be anything more than a wild estimate. It would be better to ask about the average number of hours of television watched daily (and perhaps on weekends).

Another example of asking for information not generally available to the respondent would be: "What was your favorite color when you were five years old?" The flaw in this question is that it asks for information that most people could not reasonably be expected to have. Recall of distant events is always problematic, because human memory is subject to error. Converse and Presser (1986) note that recall of even important events, such as hospitalizations, can erode with time. When one asks questions about events or situations several years after they have occurred, one should not assume that reliable information has been given. Avoid asking for information that is unavailable to the respondent.

Asking for information that might not be available to *all* respondents can present another problem. Consider the following question: "Do you agree or disagree with the philosophy of the state's Commission on Literacy?" This question is a poor one *if* the philosophy of the state's Commission on Literacy is not well known. If, on the other hand, the Commission has recently been in the news because of some unusual or controversial philosophy, then it would be quite reasonable to ask this question. However, it might be better to ask in one question if there is a Commission on Literacy; then ask those respondents who answer "Yes" to describe the Commission's philosophy. A third question in this series might ask if they agree or disagree with the Commission's philosophy. This approach involves the use of **contingency questions** (branching questions). Those respondents who answer "Yes" to the first question are directed to the second and third subquestions. Those who respond "No" to the first question are guided to another set of questions. See figure 7.1 for an example of a contingency question.

FIGURE 7.1: Illustration of a Contingency Question in a Personal or Telephone Interview Schedule

---

We have discussed several self-help groups found in our area. Now we would like to examine some additional services that may be available statewide.

11. Can you tell me if the state funds a Commission on Literacy?
  ( ) Yes, it does _____
  ( ) No, it doesn't
     (GO TO QUESTION 12.)

  11a. Can you briefly describe the Commission's philosophy?
     _____ Has an aggressive philosophy in promoting literacy classes
     _____ Is not aggressive in promoting literacy classes
     _____ Respondent not informed
  11b. Do you agree or disagree with the philosophy of the Commission on Literacy?
     a. Agree
     b. Disagree
     c. Undecided

Use of Jargon and Technical Terms

Example: Do you feel that Freud's structural hypothesis is an improvement over his topographic hypothesis?

Like the previous question relating to respondents' favorite color when they were five years old, this question asks for information that most people could not be expected to have. Furthermore, it uses terms that are not familiar to most adults. In fact, even those who are familiar with psychoanalytic theory may not know how to answer this question. It is too technical, and it uses jargon.

Use the simplest terms and vocabulary possible—the language that we use in everyday speech (sometimes called Standard English). Avoid slang, colloquialisms, abbreviations, and foreign phrases. Some texts (Alreck and Settle, 1985) recommend using words that an average eighth grader would understand. Sentences should not be long and complex; keep them short and simple.

Insensitive Language

Example: How do you people feel about Jesse Jackson?

You may be interested in discovering how a certain ethnic or racial group feels about an issue. But a question like this may make some people uneasy because it is suggestive of racial bias. It accentuates differences among respondents by saying, in effect, that the respondent is a member of a group that is dissimilar from others (possibly the majority of Americans). Instead of asking questions in the format of "How do *you blacks* (or *you Indians*) . . . ," simply ask, "How do *you* feel about . . . ?" Or, present a statement and ask the respondent to choose a response that reflects his or her feelings about the subject. Later, when analyzing the data, you will be able to determine if racial groups differ in their attitudes (if you collect data on the respondent's racial group as part of your questionnaire). Avoid using any language in a questionnaire that is suggestive of racism, sexism, or insensitivity.

Inflammatory or "Loaded" Terms

Example: Are you a religious fanatic?

Social desirability is a term used to describe the tendency of people to want their behavior to be perceived as socially acceptable.

It is a strong motivation, and response bias can easily occur as respondents avoid categories or labels that are stigmatizing. Few of us want to be labeled fanatic, zealot, or any other term that has socially undesirable connotations. Even though a respondent may have very strong convictions, he or she would likely deny having tendencies toward fanaticism. Examples of loaded terms that should be replaced with more neutral terms include *crisis, innocent, victim, forced,* and *coerced.*

Just as the term *fanatic* is loaded, few people would want to be labeled alcoholic. Questions that get the information without labeling or stigmatization should be employed. A better way to explore the extent of problem drinking is to ask respondents about specific behaviors; for example, "How many times a week do you have a drink in the morning?" You might also provide a series of categories that give a respondent an opportunity to describe his or her pattern of drinking in more socially acceptable terms. Consider the set of response choices in the next example.

Mutually Exclusive Response Choices

Example: "Teetotaler," "Social Drinker," "I occasionally drink to excess," "I frequently drink to excess."

In our quest to avoid socially unacceptable labels, we create another problem. Consider the two response choices of "social drinker" and "I occasionally drink to excess." Are they mutually exclusive? Is it possible to be a social drinker and to occasionally drink to excess? If you agree, then this response set will not provide "clean" data. Since the categories overlap, some respondents will think of themselves as social drinkers even though they drink to excess. Being a social drinker is a more attractive response to some individuals than the more unacceptable possibility of revealing how often they drink to excess. Measuring the number of times a person drinks and the amount (volume) of alcohol he or she consumes in an average weekday are more precise ways of developing categories that help the investigator separate light drinkers from moderate or heavy drinkers. Behavioral measures such as these are much more useful than stigmatizing or labeling terms.

The problems of overlapping response categories and finding good behavioral measures are obvious examples of why you need to refer to the literature as part of the research process. It is very likely that other researchers have struggled with these problems and have developed response sets or categories (if not whole questionnaires) that you could use in your research. If your literature review is thorough, you may find that someone has already done the very research that you are proposing. This being the case, you may decide to go no further, or you may make modifications to pursue a slightly different hypothesis.

We're not always aware of overlapping response choices. Can you detect any problems with the response below?

"How often do you date?"

a. almost every night   d. 3 to 4 times a week
b. once or twice a week   e. once every 2 weeks
c. a few times a month   f. a few times a year

Vague and Ambiguous Terms

Example: How many times in the past year have you seen a social worker?

The problem with this question is that it contains language that is vague. Is the intent of this question to find out how many social workers are observed (seen) by nonsocial workers in a year's time? Or to learn the number of appointments or sessions the respondent had with a social worker last year? To rephrase the question to "How many times in the past year have you talked with a social worker?" is not an improvement, since one can talk informally or socially with social workers (for instance, at a party or conference). It would be better to ask, "How many appointments have you made with your social worker in the last thirty days?" Or, since it is possible to make appointments but not keep them, "How many office visits have you had with your social worker in the last thirty days?" Even these two questions could be refined since an office visit could last ten minutes or two and a half hours. But these questions omit the whole dimension of home visits. A more exact approach would be to ask, "In the past thirty days, about how much time (in hours and minutes) have you spent talking about your problems face-to-face with your social worker?"

The following question also uses a vague term that may cause problems: "Do you attend Alcoholics Anonymous (AA) meetings regularly?" The problem with this sentence is that "regularly" is one of those terms that means different things to different individuals. Some respondents may attend AA regularly—at the beginning and end of each school year. Other respondents may attend regularly the first Wednesday of the month. Some respondents may attend twice a week every week. A better way to ask for information of this type would be: "How many times a month do you attend Alcoholics Anonymous meetings?"

Another example of the use of vague terms is the question: "What is your income?" This question is problematic because the respondent must figure out whether the information sought has a yearly, monthly, or weekly referent. It also is unclear whether the respondent should report annual salary (gross income) or the amount after all the deductions have been made (net income). A further problem is that the question does not indicate whether combined family income is expected or whether the respondent should report only his or her personal income (even though others in the household may be working).

Similarly, "Are you employed?" may be difficult to answer because there are several responses that can be made in addition to "Yes" or "No." The status of being employed could include those who work full-time and those who work part-time. There may be respondents who have retired from one career and work sporadically in order to help out when other employees take vacations or when others are on sick leave. Respondents could be employed seasonally (e.g., migrant workers or college students who work full-time in the summer but not at all when school is in session). Finally, there are those who help with a family business (e.g., a spouse who keeps the books) but who do not receive a paycheck.

Vague and ambiguous terms do not convey the same frame of reference to all respondents. For instance, some respondents will read "Has your child missed a lot of school?" and think in terms of the whole school year. Other parents may think only about absences in the past month or week. Parents may also respond to this question in terms of their own experience in missing school or compare one child to another so that even though Hugh has missed fourteen days of school in the first grading period, that's not a "lot" compared to his sister Edna who missed six weeks due to illness. It would be far better to ask, "How many days of school did your child miss during the first grading period?"

Even when we think an item is not vague, pretesting or reliability scaling may show that respondents have different impressions of what it is asking. Agreeing to the item "I have difficulty getting up in the morning" may mean either that the respondent needs assistance because of a physical disability or that the individual tends to oversleep, perhaps because of not hearing the alarm clock. It would be a mistake to plan a large-scale survey without pilot testing your questionnaire to eliminate confusing and vague items.

All-Inclusive Terms

Example: Are you always in bed by 11:00 P.M.?

The use of such terms as *always* and *never* creates problems for the respondent and for the researcher attempting to interpret the data. Does *always* allow for exceptions? For instance, what if you are in bed by 11:00 P.M. every night of the year except for New Year's Eve, when you stay up until 12:01 A.M.? Does that mean that you should respond with a "No" to the above question? *Always* and *never* imply that there are no exceptions. In my experience, researchers are more concerned with general patterns; for example, "On most week nights, about what time do you usually go to bed?"

Negatively Constructed Items

Example: Marijuana should not be decriminalized.

This item, borrowed from DeVaus (1986), is a good example of how the word "not" confuses the meaning of the statement. In this instance, it reverses the meaning of decriminalized so that a person agreeing to the statement is saying in effect that marijuana usage should be illegal. A respondent disagreeing with the statement is saying that marijuana use should be made legal. It is much more clear and straightforward to ask, "Should the private use of marijuana be made legal?" Where possible, the term *not* should be avoided in questionnaires.

Kidder and Judd (1986) have suggested that **acquiescence,** a tendency some respondents have to agree with items regardless of their content, can be countered by constructing items so that the respondent will respond positively (e.g., "Agree") and negatively (e.g., "Disagree") in roughly equal proportions. With a little creativity, items can be prepared so that the respondent does not know which response is the one desired by the researcher. Figure 7.2 provides an example of wording questions so that a respondent sympathetic to AIDS victims could not respond either "Strongly Agree" or "Agree" to all four questions.

Sequence of Questions

There is general agreement that the first questions to be asked should be of interest to the respondent. Respondents need to "warm up" to the survey process and establish a sense of trust or rapport

---

FIGURE 7.2: Phrasing Questions to Avoid Acquiescence

	Strongly Agree	Agree	Undecided	Disagree	Strongly Disagree
1. Children with AIDS should be allowed to attend school.	( )	( )	( )	( )	( )
2. Persons having AIDS should be quarantined.	( )	( )	( )	( )	( )
3. Persons having AIDS should be allowed to eat in public restaurants.	( )	( )	( )	( )	( )
4. Persons who contract AIDS deserve what they get.	( )	( )	( )	( )	( )

---

with the researcher or the researcher's representative (which could be the mailed questionnaire). Accordingly, the first several questions should be applicable to all respondents. Respondents seem to prefer closed-ended questions at the start of mailed questionnaires but open-ended questions when interviewed in person or over the phone. Information about potentially sensitive areas such as age and income should occur at the end of the questionnaire. Such information, if asked at the beginning of the interview or questionnaire, may result in a lower response rate. More important questions should be asked earlier than less important ones in case the respondent decides to terminate the interview or stop working on the questionnaire before all questions have been completed. Respondent fatigue can be a problem with especially long questionnaires.

There also seems to be consensus that topically related questions should follow one another in some sort of recognizable sequence as opposed to being interposed and spread throughout the questionnaire. Usually, some sort of "funnel sequence" is used, in which general questions are followed by more narrowly focused questions. A problem may occur if a question has an effect on subsequent responses because it creates some sort of expectancy or "mind-set." Some topics seem to be immune to this sort of problem, and others are sensitive to it. Little experimental research is available to help us anticipate this problem in advance. Frey (1983) has noted that broad, summary-type questions are more susceptible to contextual redefinitions than specific questions that have concrete responses. The best advice that can be offered regarding order effects is to be alert to the possibility that questions can affect later responses.

Thinking about Guidelines

The problem with guidelines is that sometimes it makes sense to violate them. There are times when one might use a loaded question to try to determine the extent of some socially undesirable behavior. For instance, the implication that "everyone does it" may be useful in reducing the threat of reporting some behaviors. This approach is illustrated in the following example from Sudman and Bradburn (1982): "Even the calmest of parents get angry at their children some of the time. Did your child(ren) do anything in the past seven days to make you, yourself, angry?" (p. 75).

Other instances come to mind of when guidelines are best ignored. If you are interviewing members of a street gang, you may want to use terms that they commonly use instead of those terms common to Standard English.

It is difficult to cover every situation with a guideline. Potential problems arise for which there seem to be no guidelines. However, it is possible to learn more about questionnaire construction than the space limitations of this chapter allow: When you, as a professional, have the responsibility of developing a questionnaire for a research project, you may want to consult some of the references at the end of this chapter for further assistance. Dillman (1978) has a particularly useful discussion of the questionnaire's format.

It has been shown, for example, that crowded, cluttered, or difficult-appearing questionnaires result in lower response rates than those that appear interesting, inviting, or simple to complete. Mailed questionnaires should be visually attractive. Blank or white space should be used to full advantage. The responses should appear in the same area of the questionnaire so that the respondent can easily locate them. Instructions, questions, and response categories should be kept brief, and diagrams used to visually direct the respondent where necessary. Numbering the questions is also useful to both respondents and those who must process the data. Where there are various components or parts to the study, a sentence or two to indicate that a shift is occurring smoothes the transition (e.g., "Now we would like to change the subject just a bit and ask some health related questions").

In Appendix C of this book you'll find a shortened version of the Drug Attitude Questionnaire, the instrument we designed to measure the effects of the drug education program I described at the beginning of chapter 5. As it turned out, a longer version than I've shown had excellent reliability (.93 to .97). You might want to review the

Drug Attitude Questionnaire to review some of the items. If you look closely, you'll note that this reliability came despite some items that I would change if I were to write them again. For instance, what about items 9 and 17? Do they violate any guideline that we have learned in this chapter? What do you think would be the scale's reliability if we were to measure attitudes about drugs using only one or two of these items?

Self-Anchored Scales

Another option available to you when you are developing research instruments is to generate self-anchored, single-item scales for obtaining measurements (particularly about clients' problems). Self-anchored scales are especially valuable when you need to quickly estimate the magnitude or severity of a problem. A chief advantage is that they can be used to assess thoughts and feelings (such as security in a relationship, self-perceptions of stupidity or attractiveness to others) that may be unique to a client or group of clients and for which there may not exist a standardized measurement tool.

While many self-anchored scales are based on 10 equal intervals, it is not unusual to find scales based on 5, 7, 9, or even 100 points. The only thing tricky about designing these scales is keeping in mind that only one dimension of a concept should be presented. For instance, "angry" and "not angry" represent only one dimension and would be acceptable at opposite ends of a continuum. However, "angry" at one end and "happy" at the other involves two concepts instead of one and may make the scale less accurate because of different feelings associated with anger and happiness.

Self-anchored scales can also be used in single subject designs as a repeated measure to keep track of progress resulting from intervention. When self-anchored scales are designed for specific clients, their own actions and feelings—described in their own words—can be used to anchor the ends of the continuum.

To demonstrate what self-anchored scales look like, I've created several examples below.

THE AMOUNT OF ANGER I FELT TODAY

0	1	2	3	4	5	6	7	8	9	10

None	*Moderate*	*Extreme*
(Had pleasant conversation)	(Slammed the door and walked away)	(Shouted obsceni-ties, punched wall)

HOW SATISFIED I AM WITH MY LIFE

| 0 | 10 | 20 | 30 | 40 | 50 | 60 | 70 | 80 | 90 | 100 |

No Satisfaction   *Average Satisfaction*   *Very Satisfied*

COMMUNITY INVOLVEMENT

| 1 | 2 | 3 | 4 | 5 | 6 | 7 | 8 | 9 |

Not Involved   *Medium Involvement*   *Very Involved*

FEELINGS OF EMOTIONAL INTIMACY WITH LOVED ONE

| 1 | 2 | 3 | 4 | 5 | 6 | 7 | 8 | 9 |

Not at All Close (Unhappy;   *Very Close (Happy with*
not much sharing)   *relationship; lots of sharing)*

While there is not a lot of empirical evidence attesting to the psychometric characteristics of self-anchored scales, Thyer et al. (1984) have reported data showing criterion validity of the Subjective Anxiety Scale. Hersen and Bellack (1988) have discussed the reliability and validity of the Fear Thermometer, and Nugent (1992) obtained a criterion validity index of .82 when he correlated a self-anchored depression scale with a standardized measure of nonpsychotic depression. However, although he found evidence for some convergent and discriminant validity for a self-anchored scale measuring self-esteem, the reliability was quite low, and Nugent (1993) recommended extreme caution when trying to use a single item to measure self-esteem. He concluded that some constructs may be well measured by self-anchored scales while others are not.

The Role of Questionnaires in Generalizing Results

Substantive generalization of survey results is dependent upon various assumptions. Jaeger (1984, p. 19) has identified these as:

1. the questions were "construct valid";
2. the respondents understood the questions;
3. the questions were interpreted as intended;
4. the respondents were cooperative and willing to respond;
5. the respondents had the knowledge or information needed to respond;
6. the respondents were honest in their responses;
7. responses were recorded accurately;

8. responses were interpreted accurately;
9. responses were transcribed and aggregated accurately.

As you can see, developing a good questionnaire is necessary if one hopes to generalize the survey results. Even if the sampling design is sound, a poorly constructed questionnaire will result in little useful information. Good questionnaires do not result from a single draft. They come about from polishing, revising, pretesting, and revising again. If a concept is not operationalized well, the questionnaire needs to be redone. Dillman (1978) talks about doing eight, ten, or even twelve revisions before sending the final questionnaire to the printer. Don't be afraid to circulate your drafts among those whose opinions you respect. More times than not, they will be flattered that you asked for their assistance! Be sure to pilot test your questionnaire with persons who are similar to those who will be participants in your study. Make sure that the items are understood and that this is indicated in the responses they make. Pilot testing and revising are crucial steps in the construction of a good survey instrument.

This advice applies even to faculty. I learned this lesson once again this past summer when the information coming from a questionnaire I had designed didn't provide me with the data I needed to know.

One section of the questionnaire dealt with additional education that a group of mothers on welfare might have attained while participating in a project that provided them with intensive case management. The item went something like this:

PLEASE CHECK BELOW THE EDUCATIONAL EFFORTS YOU HAVE MADE SINCE ENTERING THE PROJECT:

_____ finished high school
_____ attained GED
_____ completed vocational training
_____ began college (indicate hours completed _____)

This item appeared by itself at the top of the second page of the questionnaire. What's the problem? When all the questionnaires were returned, about half of the respondents did not check any categories on the top of page two. Did this mean that they didn't attain any additional education? Or did they just forget to fill out the second page? Since the questionnaires were completed anonymously, it's a question that I can never answer. A pilot test might have identified this problem for me and I could have fixed the item by providing a response choice for those who had not attained any additional schooling.

Finally, it is vital that your questions not only be technically correct but also provide you with the information you need to prepare a response to some problem. Each question should give you some essential information, and all of the questions taken together should help you conclude something about the topic of your investigation. Research is much more than formulating questions or devising questionnaires. Perhaps my relating of an actual experience will serve to reinforce this point: A group of local citizenry asked for my assistance in conducting a mental health needs assessment of their community. "Okay," I said, "tell me more." Their spokesperson indicated that they had found a book about needs assessment that included, in its appendix, a complete set of questions that could be photocopied and used with very little modification. As I looked at the needs assessment instrument, I saw a question that asked the respondents to list three problems in their neighborhood and another that asked for a ranking of the most serious problems in the community. In my mind, I saw respondents being concerned with street lights and potholes, police protection, and a great many other community concerns. I did not, however, believe the use of that particular questionnaire would produce much usable information about the mental health needs of the community. I asked the spokesperson, "What do you hope to learn from the community needs assessment?" "Well," she said, "we want to know about all the mental health needs in the community." Further questioning revealed that there wasn't anything more specific that they hoped to learn.

At that point I tactfully asked the group to meet together to determine what, exactly, they wanted to know about the mental health needs in the community. They met and discussed what they wanted to know, and to the best of my knowledge, that group never did conduct a community needs assessment. I strongly suspect that one of the reasons they didn't was that there was no agreement among them on what was important to learn about their community's mental health needs—or how the information would be used. As you can see, the point is not just to develop a set of questions—the questions we ask must have a clear focus and purpose. Each question should add another increment to that sum of information that we require. The well-designed questionnaire asks no less and no more than is needed for our research. Anyone can develop a questionnaire or conduct a survey. The "test" of a good survey is whether it produces useful data. Genuinely useful information seldom comes about just because someone happens to find a set of already prepared questions.

Questions for Discussion

1. Why is it important that the questionnaire communicate the same frame of reference to all respondents?
2. Construct a closed-ended question (complete with response set) to record marital status.
3. Why is it important to decide upon the survey methodology before designing the questionnaire to be used?
4. What is wrong with each of the following questions? (Hint: watch for terms that are not operationally defined and may not mean the same to everyone.) Suggest a better way to phrase each question.
   a. Do you feel that individuals who are forced to have life support systems in order to continue existence should be given the choice to die?
   b. Do you feel that the feminization of poverty has come about due to the increasing divorce rate?
   c. What effect does dropping out of school have on employment opportunities?
   d. Is there a higher incidence of suicide among upper-middle-class teens than in the lower income levels?
   e. Are older men or women more likely to be abused?
   f. Is abuse of the elderly related to the emphasis of youth on television?
   g. Among teens who later become pregnant, why do you think they do not consistently use birth control?
   h. Do you think that higher levels of education result in a decrease in racist attitudes?
   i. Do you think there is not any more drinking among college students who live at home than among those who live away from home?

Mini-Projects for Experiencing Research Firsthand

1. Iacono-Harris and Nuccio, in an article entitled "Developing the Macro Pool: Turning Undergraduates on to Macro Practice" (*Administration in Social Work*, 11(2), Summer, 1987), state in their conclusions (p. 85), "We believe that macro practitioners are developed, not born."
   a. How would you test this hypothesis?
   b. What kinds of questions would you develop? Develop a ten- to fifteen-item questionnaire that would help you test this hypothesis.

c. Share your questions with another student who has also developed questions. Examine all of the group's questions and decide which ones could be used for research into this topic and which ones should be purged.

2. Develop a set of questions to use to interview nursing home residents to find out about the quality of their lives.
   a. List the important dimensions to be covered.
   b. Construct five open-ended and five closed-ended questions along with the corresponding response set.
   c. As you reflect on the questions you would ask, what would you learn about life in a nursing home? What wouldn't you learn from this set of questions?

3. Conduct a twenty-minute interview with a neighbor, friend, grandparent, or someone else you know. Explore a significant experience (e.g., living through the Depression, recovery from major surgery, running for political office). Use only open-ended questions. Keep notes, and transcribe your interview. Be sure to include the questions that were asked of the respondents and any remarks (such as transitional statements) you made along the way. Share in class what you learned from the experience. Be sure to include a brief description of the person whom you interviewed (e.g., female, eighty-three years of age, former journalist, etc.).

4. Develop a questionnaire that will help you learn why your fellow students have become social work majors.
   a. What hypothesis do you want to test?
   b. Develop ten to fifteen closed-ended questions and one open-ended question.
   c. Interview ten social work majors.
   d. What did you learn from this experience? Did you learn more from the open-ended or the closed-ended questions?

5. Review the article "Student Satisfaction with Field Placement" (Fortune, Feathers, Rook, Scrimenti, Smollen, Stemerman, and Tucker, 1985) in *Journal of Social Work Education*, 21 (3), pp. 92–112. Look especially at the items used on their questionnaire (p. 95). If it were your responsibility to revise this instrument, what modifications would you make? Prepare a revised questionnaire to measure students' satisfaction with their field placements.

Resources and References

Alreck, P.L. and Settle, R.B. (1985). *The Survey Research Handbook*. Homewood, IL: Irwin.

Berdie, D.R., Anderson, J.F., and Niebuhr, M.A. (1986). *Questionnaire Design and Use.* Metuchen, NJ: Scarecrow Press.

Blankenship, A.B. (1977). *Professional Telephone Surveys.* New York: McGraw-Hill.

Bradburn, N. and Sudman, S. (1979). *Improving Interview Method and Questionnaire Design.* San Francisco, CA: Jossey-Bass.

Converse, J.M. and Presser, S. (1986). *Survey Questions: Handcrafting the Standardized Questionnaire.* Beverly Hills, CA: Sage.

DeVaus, D.A. (1986). *Surveys in Social Research.* London: George Allen and Unwin.

Dillman, D.A. (1978). *Mail and Telephone Surveys: The Total Design Method.* New York: Wiley.

Fink, A. and Kosecoff, J. (1985). *How to Conduct Surveys: A Step-by-Step Guide.* Beverly Hills, CA: Sage.

Frey, J.H. (1983). *Survey Research by Telephone.* Beverly Hills, CA: Sage.

Hersen, M. and Bellack, A. (1988). *Dictionary of Behavioral Assessment Techniques.* Elmsford, NY: Pergamon Press.

Jaeger, R.M. (1984). *Sampling in Education and the Social Sciences.* New York: Longman.

Kidder, L.H. and Judd, C.M. (1986). *Research Methods in Social Relations.* New York: Holt, Rinehart and Winston.

Nugent, W.R. (1992). Psychometric characteristics of self-anchored scales in clinical application. *Journal of Social Service Research,* 15(3/4), 137–152.

Nugent, W.R. (1993). A validity study of a self-anchored scale for measuring self-esteem. *Research on Social Work Practice,* 3(3), 276–287.

Nugent, W.R. and Thomas, J.W. (1993). Validation of a clinical measure of self-esteem. *Research on Social Work Practice,* 3(2), 191–207.

Rossi, P.F., Wright, J.D., and Anderson, A.B. (1983). *Handbook of Survey Research.* New York: Academic Press.

Schuman, H. and Presser, S. (1981). *Questions and Answers in Attitude Surveys.* New York: Academic Press.

Sudman, S. and Bradburn, N.M. (1982). *Asking Questions: A Practical Guide to Questionnaire Design.* San Francisco, CA: Jossey-Bass.

Thyer, B., Papsdorf, J., Davis, R., and Vallecorsa, S. (1984). Autonomic correlates of the subjective anxiety scale. *Journal of Behavior Theory and Experimental Psychiatry,* 15, 3–7.

8
Unobtrusive Approaches to Data Collection: Secondary Data and Content Analysis

The research approaches we have discussed thus far have one thing in common—they involve interaction with respondents in order to collect the needed data. Unfortunately, anytime interviewers interact with respondents there is the potential for producing unintended changes in them. For example, imagine that you are involved in presenting a workshop to your co-workers on the avoidance of sexism in language. A week before the workshop you send each participant a small questionnaire that asks if he or she uses certain terms or phrases in conversation. Suppose Robert Doe reads the questionnaire, briefly considers how he will respond, and then indicates on the form that he does not use any of those terms in his normal conversation. However, driving home from work that night, he reflects back upon the questionnaire and realizes that there are several other ways in which his choice of words or phrasing might be considered sexist. As a result of thinking about the pretest, he resolves to eliminate these terms and phrases from his speech and writing.

Your workshop is conducted as scheduled, and you administer the posttest. An examination of the data reveals a decrease in the use of sexist language at the time of the posttest. But if others in the agency had the same experience as Robert Doe, how would you know which had the most impact, the workshop or the pretest? Perhaps any reduction in sexist language was merely the result of respondents' reactions to the pretest questionnaire. It is conceivable that even as mild an interaction as testing can bring about changes in attitudes, behavior, or knowledge.

Even if we are considerate and polite about it, asking respondents to give us information about themselves is intrusive. This can be seen in the number of respondents who refuse to cooperate with interviewers or complete survey forms. Even with cooperation, there is the possibility that merely asking questions may have some inadvertent effect upon respondents.

One of the more famous examples of an unanticipated effect on research subjects has come to be known as the **Hawthorne Effect**. Prior to World War II, researchers at a Western Electric plant in Chicago found that employees in the study raised their production—no matter what physical changes were made in their work environment (e.g., the lighting was both increased and decreased). What researchers learned is that subjects may be significantly influenced by the knowledge that they are taking part in a research study. In fact, knowing that they have been chosen to participate in a research project had more influence on them than the independent variables.

One way to avoid having to rule out the Hawthorne Effect is to utilize data that already exist instead of collecting new data from respondents. Using existing data that do not involve interaction with research subjects fits into the category called **unobtrusive research**. The classic work in this area is that of Webb, Campbell, Schwartz, and Sechrest (1966), *Unobtrusive Measures: Nonreactive Research in the Social Sciences.*

Whether they are aware of it or not, social workers in performing their routine tasks help collect mountains of data each year. The vast majority of these data come from the ordinary processing of clients into and out of service delivery systems—in admission forms, social histories, and progress notes. Data available for unobtrusive research are also contained in the records of institutionalized persons, in the portfolios of immigrants, and in the files of persons who've enrolled in community educational presentations. Sometimes these data are kept in "hard copy" form and stored in filing cabinets, or they may be contained in the electronic memory of a computer. These data are not collected with research purposes in mind. However, collections of such data represent a wealth of research opportunities for interested social workers.

Researchers who rely upon public documents, reports, and historical data are said to be engaged in a type of unobtrusive research called **archival research** or **secondary data analysis**. This type of research involves the analysis of an existing data set that results in knowledge, interpretations, and conclusions beyond those stated in the original study (Hakim, 1982). The intent is not to find fault with another's study, but rather to test new hypotheses or explore questions not examined in the original report. While the original study may have collected data on the attitudes of a cross-section of Americans, a secondary analysis might examine only the attitudes of a minority subgroup. Secondary analysis extends or goes beyond what the initial investigators reported.

For instance, I once took coal production data from one state agency and matched up suicide data from another department. I had the hypothesis that coal tonnage and suicides would be inversely related—that as miners were laid off and fewer tons of coal were mined, suicides would increase. What I found was that there was virtually no correlation. However, I can't help but wonder what might have been uncovered if homicides had been correlated with coal tonnage. Secondary data analysis has a certain flexibility in that new hypotheses can be easily spun off and tested without a great deal of extra work. Investigators are not limited to a single data set or source document and may utilize several data sets from different sponsors or agencies.

In a fascinating article on the history of child protection efforts, Lindsey (1994) has used multiple sources of data to show that reports of child abuse in the United States have risen from approximately 6,000 in 1963 to almost three million by 1992. During approximately the same period of time, child murder victims 15 to 19 years of age have increased from under 500 per year in 1962 to over 2,500 by 1991. Increased reporting of abuse has not reduced child fatalities, and Lindsey speculates as to why this might be. One possibility could be that child welfare professionals are using inadequate technology to assess the risk faced by children. Another possibility is inadequate funding of child protective services. What other explanations might this secondary trend data suggest to you?

Secondary data analysis should not be considered as a research approach to be employed only when a researcher does not want to collect his or her own data. In fact, Stewart (1993) argues that

> it is hard to conceive of a research effort that does not begin with at least some secondary research. Existing information provides a foundation for problem formulation, for the design of new research, and for the analysis and interpretation of new information. There is little point in rediscovering that which is already known.

A good use of secondary data is to identify trends. For example, a student once approached me with some concern because she had heard from a relative that her home county had the highest suicide rate in the state. I was somewhat skeptical about this, but when I had the opportunity, I went to the Government Documents section of the library and examined several of the Department of Health's *Vital Statistics* annual reports. I found that in the most recent year the county in question, with a population of approximately 12,000, had 7 suicides. This gave it a rate of 52.5 suicides per 100,000 population. (This is a standard base for comparison so that urban counties can be compared with rural counties.) This was in fact one of the highest suicide rates in the state, as the overall average for the state was 14.3 suicides per 100,000 population.

However, a look at the previous year's statistics revealed no suicides. Thus, in the span of two years, the county had one of the lowest and one of the highest rates in the state. This is not uncommon when the actual number of events (such as suicides) is relatively small. Looking at the statistics for one additional year revealed that there were only 2 suicides, but that the rate for the county (15.2 per 100,000 population) again exceeded that state's average.

As you can tell by looking at table 8.1, there is a noticeable trend for the suicide rate in this rural county to exceed the state's average. In fact, in five of seven years, the county's suicide rate was higher than the average rate for the whole state.

Had the student looked at the rates for only the last two years, or just one of those two years, a mistaken impression might have been obtained. There is a certain inherent danger in misinterpreting real trends or patterns whenever one selectively draws from a study. By looking at a longer span of time, we can have greater confidence that a trend is real and well established.

Advantages and Disadvantages of Unobtrusive Approaches

Right away, some exciting advantages of unobtrusive research are apparent. First, if you discover that someone else has already collected data that you can use for a study, you can save considerable time and effort in your data collection phase. Once an interesting data base has been identified, it is often possible to move rapidly into data analysis. Secondary data sources may already be held by the library or university, or you may be able to purchase them for a nominal fee.

Second, any bias associated with the collection of the data may be generally known and accepted. It may be known, for instance, that the data tend to underestimate the true incidence of a social problem (as in the case of suicide data). Other data sets may overestimate the incidence of a problem. For example, data on psychiatric hospital ad-

TABLE 8.1   Seven-Year Suicide Rate in One Rural County (per 100,000 population)

	Number of Suicides	County Rate	State Rate
1980	1	8.1	13.3
1981	2	15.7	12.1
1982	2	15.4	13.5
1983	4	31.0	13.2
1984	2	15.2	13.7
1985	0	0	13.2
1986	7	52.5	14.3

missions that combined new patients with those who had previous admissions could overestimate incidence of the most severe form of mental illness. (Incidence is the number of *new* cases or events during a given period of time.) Since all studies have some limitations, the secondary data analyst may choose to use a data set even though it has several known problems. Problems with the data set are not a reflection upon the researcher using secondary data analysis. After all, the secondary data analyst is only borrowing the data set.

Third, since you are not interviewing clients or patients or interacting with them in any way, you need not worry that your inquiries will put them at risk or have any harmful effects. If the data are in the public domain, you may not need consent or permission from institutional review boards or other research and review committees to conduct your research.

The final but best reason for conducting secondary data analysis is that it provides an opportunity to study social problems in terms of long-term change and enables comparative study. Secondary data analysts can make comparisons across localities, states, and nations (presuming, of course, that the data are available).

On the other hand, there are some disadvantages associated with relying upon secondary or archival data. Sometimes the important historical records you need have been destroyed by fire, flood, tornadoes, or rodents. Sometimes researchers, well into their projects, find gaps in the data because of changes in procedures or policies that affected the data collection. With the passage of time, conditions such as laws change, which can affect the definitions of variables. Categories can suddenly become more or less inclusive.

I once discovered that a set of child abuse archival data I wanted to explore was compartmentalized. The data were recorded in two different computers in two different formats because the data collection forms had been redesigned. There was no way to combine the data sets into one large file without going to the expense of hiring computer programmers to prepare the data in a more usable form. As a result, I did no research with that data.

If the data were reported more or less voluntarily (there was no penalty for not reporting), it may not be as reliable as when 100 percent of the units were required to report.

Several years ago I was examining one state's outpatient admissions to community mental health centers and found that not all centers were fully cooperating in returning their monthly reports. While the vast majority of these centers did, perhaps 5 percent didn't. These tended to be small, rural centers without a lot of staff.

While their failure to report on a timely basis didn't have a huge effect in terms of the total number of admissions in the state, it did raise questions about the reliability of the data set. Could there have been other, larger agencies that failed to report their admissions on occasion? Did anyone monitor the data to make sure there were twelve reports from each agency at the end of each year? Researchers using secondary data have to be concerned about the reliability of the data that they intend to analyze. The researcher should be alert to potential problems with the completeness of the data, the ease with which data can be manipulated, and the way data are collected and presented.

Finally, recent data may not be available as soon as the researcher may desire it. It is not unusual for some agencies or departments to take six to twelve months (or longer) to produce their most "current" annual report of the previous year's data.

In summary, while there are many advantages associated with secondary data analysis, the researcher should be alert to changes in the way the data were collected, completeness of data, and the ease with which data can be manipulated.

State-Maintained Data Sets Are Useful for Secondary Analysis

Secondary analyses can be conducted in both private and public agencies. However, private agencies tend to be protective of their data. Even though researchers agree not to divulge personal data, private agencies often feel that any research within their agencies may endanger the privacy of individual clients. Another argument often heard from both public and private agencies is that the proposed research will require too much clerical support to locate archival records or selected cases. Unlike private agencies, public agencies and departments are often required to keep certain statistics that are viewed as public information and available to all. While public agencies are not always as cooperative as many researchers would like, they generally do provide some form of aggregated data each year in the form of annual reports.

Table 8.2 contains examples of variables or **social indicators** (they tell us something about trends within social problems) that are commonly collected by all states. Generally these data are reported by county.

These examples are only some of the variables that are routinely collected and reported each month, quarter, or year. Public and university libraries often will be designated as state depositories and will have recent reports as well as more historical reports. If the reports you need are not found in the library, contact various departments in your state capital. Eventually you will locate the appropriate depart-

---

TABLE 8.2   Examples of Variables for Secondary Research

Indicator	Source
Marriages	Department of Health
Divorces	Department of Health
Suicides	Department of Health
Live births	Department of Health
Infant deaths	Department of Health
Deaths (all ages)	Department of Health
Deaths from cirrhosis of the liver	Department of Health
Inpatient admissions	Department of Mental Health
Outpatient admissions	Department of Mental Health
General relief cases	Department of Public Welfare
Aid to dependent children	Department of Public Welfare
Motor vehicle injury accidents	Department of Highway Safety
Motor vehicle deaths	Department of Highway Safety
Motor vehicle accidents	Department of Highway Safety
Dependency and neglect cases	Department of Child Welfare
Delinquency cases	Juvenile Court Statistics
Arraignments	Supreme Court Statistics
School dropouts	Department of Education
School enrollment	Department of Education
Unemployment	Bureau of Employment
Average weekly earnings	Bureau of Employment
Retail alcohol sales	Department of Liquor Control

ment from which to collect the data. Departmental names vary across the states. For example, in some states the Department of Highway Safety is known as the Transportation Department.

Applications of Secondary Data Analysis

If information is power (Francis Bacon noted that "knowledge itself is power"), then the possibilities of being able to effect change are enormous when one has access to secondary data.

Example 1: Suppose you are a school social worker, and a number of children have been injured because there is no traffic light at a busy intersection they must cross before they can get to school. Let's further suppose that "officials" are dragging their feet, saying that a traffic light is not needed. You obtain a list of all the locations where vehicular and pedestrian-injury accidents have occurred in your city in the past year. What if the intersection that you feel needs a light was the site of more injury accidents than any other location in the city not only for the previous year, but also the past three years? Isn't that powerful information that you could use to help advocate for a traffic light?

Example 2: You are a state employee, the supervisor of a child abuse investigation team. You are painfully aware that your unit is understaffed. In talking with others, you sense that your unit may investigate more reported cases of abuse and neglect than any other unit in the state. Yet, when you talk to the agency director about this problem, he or she is not sympathetic about your need for additional staff. The director indicates that cases of abuse are increasing over the whole state—that it isn't just a problem in your county.

However, because you occasionally have the opportunity to talk to other social workers from across the state, you learn that some investigation units are adding staff, while your unit has added no new staff in three years. A research question forms in your mind. Which county has the highest incidence of child abuse/neglect cases in the state? When you look at the data you discover that while the more populous counties have significantly more cases of abuse and neglect, your county has more cases of child abuse and neglect *per thousand population* than any other county in the state. Would this information be enough to use for leverage to get some additional staff? If not, a next step might be to gather data on how many staff the other investigation units have and which units have the lowest ratio of cases to staff. If your county has the highest ratio (the most cases but fewest staff), this would be compelling objective information that could influence the decision to allocate additional staff to your unit.

This example could be carried further. If the data were available, you could examine the ratio of cases to child protective services staff in your state to those of surrounding states. This type of information might be used to influence your legislators to increase appropriations at the state level. You could also compare salaries of child protective workers in your state with those in other states. If workers in your state are paid below the average, lobby for increased pay.

Example 3: You become concerned about adolescents' use of illegal drugs in your community. You suspect that a new street drug is the cause of a rash of fatal overdoses, but you have no "hard" data to support this assumption. Since you want to conduct a drug education campaign for adolescents, you feel that local data are needed. You learn that the data are not obtainable from the state Health Department or from the police department. You find, however, that the hospital emergency room keeps this sort of data. Even if the hospital does not make these records available, you may find that the county's ambulance service keeps this data and would be happy to share it.

There is no shortage of ways that secondary data can be used. You could investigate whether the high school dropout rate has decreased within your community over the past five years. Has the dropout prevention program had an impact? Most school systems have good records on the number of dropouts. It would be relatively easy to determine if there has been a dramatic change in the dropout rate. Other uses of social indicators include examining how your state compares with other states in terms of unemployment, teen pregnancies, or some other social problem.

Additionally, you might want to formally test hypotheses—for example, that concern about AIDS will result in fewer divorces. You might want to conduct correlational studies to see if increases in unemployment are associated with increases in mental hospital admissions or if high school dropout rates are associated with juvenile delinquency rates. You could be interested in whether relations among the races are improving. (See, for example, Steech and Schuman (1992), who examined twelve racial policy questions from surveys conducted in the time period 1984–1990 to evaluate the contention that racism among young white adults increased during the 1980s.)

Social indicators can also be used to make national comparisons. How does the United States compare with other industrialized countries on such indicators as infant deaths or literacy rates? Have we made advances in the last five years, or have these indicators remained at about the same level?

There is virtually no end to social indicators that may be gleaned from state and federal departments, bureaus, agencies, and offices. And there are thousands of organizations that collect information on their membership and the services provided to members. Social service agencies across this nation have fascinating questions they would like explored—if only someone with the right combination of research skills and interest would come along.

As you have seen from these illustrations, secondary data analysis is versatile and can be used with problems that vary from those with a macro focus to those with a micro concern. One of the main strengths of secondary data analysis is that there are generally multiple sources of data relevant to the topic in which you are interested. If you cannot obtain data from one source, there is almost always another, sometimes better, data set.

Secondary Analysis of Survey Data

With the advent of computer processing has come a proliferation of large-scale surveys. These surveys, often with thousands of respondents, are generally available to a broad range of researchers because of the ease with which the data can be shared via computer tape, disk, or diskette. These surveys differ in several ways from the occasional surveys conducted by social workers.

First of all, these surveys are coded so that they can be easily manipulated by computer processing. This greatly facilitates their use by researchers other than the original investigators. In fact, some of the surveys (e.g., the General Social Survey) were designed particularly for secondary analysis (Glenn, Converse, Cutler, and Hyman, 1978).

Second, these surveys tend to use large, national, cross-sectional samples. Some of these surveys (or at least portions of their questions) are repeated at regular intervals, so that trends can be observed over time.

Finally, these surveys often are indexed, and copies are made available so that the entire data set can be purchased at nominal cost. Catalogs may also be produced so that researchers have a good idea of the data available before purchasing the data set.

Secondary analysis of survey data usually comes about in one of two ways: (1) a data base is discovered that contains information not fully reported or examined; or (2) a hypothesis is generated and then a search is conducted to find an appropriate data base. Normally, hypotheses occur before data collection; however, in the case of archival research and secondary survey analysis, the researcher needs to know beforehand that the type of data needed does exist. He or she could spend several months requesting catalogs, reviewing existing data bases, and contacting various research centers only to learn that the type of data needed is not available. Consequently, some researchers develop hypotheses *after* they come across (perhaps accidentally) a particularly exciting data base. Hyman (1987) has written, "Among investigators with *broad* interests, serendipity is a likely occurrence. By chance, they are likely to find some of what they are seeking, and also to discover fortuitously in the course of one search valuable bodies of data that are strategic for the study of other problems" (p. 83).

Secondary Survey and Additional Secondary Data Sources

The federal government conducts more than two hundred surveys and censuses every year (Turner and Martin, 1984). Perhaps the best known of these is the decennial Census of Population and Housing. The U.S. Bureau of the Census also conducts special purpose surveys that supply statistical information on social, economic, and demographic characteristics (e.g., *The Hispanic Population in the United States: March 1986 and 1987*), as well as national information on such topics as employment and unemployment, income, and adult education.

To identify recent publications of the U.S. Bureau of the Census, see the *Census Catalog and Guide* (annual) and *The American Statistics Index: A Comprehensive Guide and Index to the Statistical Publications of the United States Government* (ASI). The ASI is a comprehensive annual index that contains abstracts of publications issued by all the departments and agencies of the federal government. These publications can include such items as special surveys of health care costs and reports of AFDC demonstration projects.

The U.S. Bureau of the Census is just one source of good secondary data; there are many more. For instance, the Federal Bureau of Investigation prepares the *Uniform Crime Reports for the United States* based on crimes cleared by arrests and reported by local police departments across the country. Five-year trend data are reported in addition to the annual statistics. The U.S. Department of Education (National Center for Education Statistics) provides data on enrollment, number of teachers, sources of revenue, years of schooling completed by state, and even unemployment rates of persons sixteen and older by the number of years of school completed. Their report is entitled *Digest of Educational Statistics*.

The Department of Health and Human Services compiles such data as births by age of mother and birth order, mortality rates by age, race, sex, and cause of death for each state and the fifty largest standard metropolitan statistical areas. Its publication is entitled *Vital Statistics of the United States.* The Department of Labor produces a *Monthly Labor Review* that monitors trends such as employment in the civilian labor force, unemployment rates by age, sex, race, duration of unemployment, employment by type of industry (e.g., mining, government, retail), average weekly earnings, and consumer price indexes.

The National Institute of Justice (NIJ) maintains numerous data sets available to researchers, corrections professionals, and students. NIJ also published *Data Resources of the National Institute of Justice,* a resource directory describing and listing each of its data sets.

A depository for social science data collected by academic survey research organizations in this country is held by the Interuniversity Consortium for Political and Social Research (ICPSR) at the University of Michigan. The consortium's holdings can be identified through its publication *A Guide to Resources and Services.* These holdings are voluminous and vary from census data to special surveys of health and crime to the historical voting records of all the members of Congress. Archives are held also at the Louis Harris Political Data Center at the University of North Carolina, which publishes the *Directory of Louis Harris Public Opinion Machine-Readable Data.*

The Roper Center for Public Opinion Research at the University of Connecticut is a public opinion research library. The Center's library contains complete data files and documentation for over ten thousand surveys conducted over the past sixty years. It houses collections of surveys taken by the Roper and Gallup organizations, as well as those commissioned by ABC, CBS, and NBC news and such papers as the *New York Times, Washington Post, Wall Street Journal,* and *Los Angeles Times.* And there are other sources too numerous to mention.

The Roper Center has periodic publications to announce its holdings and is also a depository for annual surveys known as the General Social Surveys, which have been conducted just about every year since 1972 by the National Opinion Research Center. Each survey is an independently drawn sample of English-speaking persons 18 years of age or over, not living in an institutional setting. The 1993 *Cumulative Codebook* reports the cumulative file contains over 2,000 variables and 29,388 completed interviews from 19 separate surveys. By obtaining the latest cumulative codebook from the Roper Center, you can identify questions that have been replicated over several surveys. Permanent questions as well as rotating questions and some occasional questions occur on each survey. Data can be obtained from the Roper Center directly or through the International Survey Library Association (ISLA), in which many colleges and universities hold a membership. By acquiring the latest codebook from the Roper Center (Box 440, Storrs, CT 06268), you can begin identifying questions of interest.

Table 8.3 shows how the survey data is presented in the codebook. Because each of the surveys obtains comprehensive demographic information from the respondents, the General Social Survey questions can be analyzed in great detail. For example, you could test the hypothesis that persons over sixty are more supportive of the death penalty than younger persons. Or, you could look at responses by level of education, race, geographic region, family income, and so on. These data are useful for finding trends over time. Notice how questions evolve over time. Question 81, for instance, has not been used since 1982. You'll understand why when you compare it to Question 82—which is more balanced. Question 90 allows you to see that strongly held opinions tend to be maintained over time.

For information about studies conducted in countries other than the United States, the *Index to International Statistics* is a helpful resource. Also, the United Nations has the *Demographic Yearbook*, an annual publication with statistics such as estimates by country of population by age and sex, rates of population increase, birth and death rates, marriage and divorce rates, and life expectancy at birth. The United Nations' *Monthly Bulletin of Statistics* contains mid-year population estimates by country, as well as birth, death, and marriage rates for selected countries, paid employment, unemployment rates, hours worked in manufacturing, production from mines, textile mills, rubber, chemical and other manufacturing, motor vehicles, electricity produced, and trade data. The *United Nations Statistical Yearbook* provides information on unemployment, housing conditions, persons per household, households with inside water, government disbursements (e.g., expenditures for social welfare and defense, and total government expenditures), hospitals, health personnel, schools, pupils, teachers, agricultural production, world trade, and tourist arrivals.

Content Analysis

Content analysis is another unobtrusive research process that objectively examines the content of communications. This objectivity is made possible by reliance upon quantification. Accordingly, content analysis involves searching for and counting key words, phrases, or concepts in communications. These may be counted (frequencies of

TABLE 8.3   Survey Data Presented in the Codebook

80.C.   If some people in your community suggested that a book he wrote in favor of homosexuality should be taken out of your public library, would you favor removing this book, or not?

[VAR: LIBHOMO]

DECK 5
COLS. 33–36
Qs. 79C-80C

Response	Punch	Year						COL. 36 All
		1972–82	1982B	1983–87	1987B	1988–91	1993	
Favor	1	3,707	153	1,768	159	1,272	313	7,372
Not favor	2	4,987	162	2,567	182	2,512	713	11,123
Don't know	8	276	35	122	12	121	45	611
No answer	9	21	4	16	0	15	4	60
Not applicable	BK	4,635	0	3,069	0	1,987	531	10,222

81. Are you in favor of the death penalty for persons convicted of murder?
[VAR: CAPPUN2]

DECK 5
COLS. 37–40
Qs. 81-84

Response	Punch	Year						COL. 37 All
		1972–82	1982B	1983–87	1987B	1988–91	1993	
Yes	1	1,750	0	0	0	0	0	1,750
No	2	1,151	0	0	0	0	0	1,151
Don't know	8	200	0	0	0	0	0	200
No answer	9	16	0	0	0	0	0	16
Not applicable	BK	10,509	354	7,542	353	5,907	1,606	26,271

82. Do you favor or oppose the death penalty for persons convicted of murder?
[VAR: CAPPUN]

| | | Year | | | | | | COL. 38 |
Response	Punch	1972–82	1982B	1983–87	1987B	1988–91	1993	All
Favor	1	6,933	154	5,410	154	4,274	1,151	18,076
Oppose	2	2,936	165	1,696	165	1,242	337	6,541
Don't know	8	607	32	399	33	364	112	1,547
No answer	9	33	3	37	1	27	6	107
Not applicable	BK	3,117	0	0	0	0	0	3,117

DECK 5
COLS. 44–46
Qs. 88-90

90. In general, do you think the courts in this area deal too harshly or not harshly enough with criminals?
[VAR: COURTS]

| | | Year | | | | | | COL. 46 |
Response	Punch	1972–82	1982B	1983–87	1987B	1988–91	1993	All
Too harshly	1	482	29	245	30	206	54	1,046
Not harshly enough	2	9,546	119	6,253	255	4,822	1,300	22,295
About right (Vol.)	3	1,227	17	694	43	573	156	2,710
Don't know	8	834	8	318	21	288	88	1,557
No answer	9	47	3	32	4	18	8	112
Not applicable	BK	1,490	178	0	0	0	0	1,668

occurrence), measured (e.g., the size of a newspaper article in column inches or the amount of time allocated to a specific topic in a speech), or otherwise categorized in a manner that others could replicate. Content analysis can be used either retrospectively (to examine materials already in existence) or prospectively (to analyze impending events or narratives). However, the major use of content analysis is to provide a framework so that a quantitative approach can be used to analyze communications after they have been spoken or printed.

Examples of materials that can be content analyzed include: newspapers, magazines, journals, books, television programs, audio and video tapes, minutes from agency board meetings, congressional records, presidential addresses, and historical documents such as letters, diaries, and so on.

While the first dictionary definition of content analysis appeared in 1961, its intellectual roots go back considerably further. In 1910, Max Weber proposed a large-scale content analysis of newspapers at the first meeting of the German Sociological Society. Also, around the turn of the century in this country, quantitative newspaper analyses (measuring the column inches devoted to specific subjects) were conducted because of concern that newspapers were not providing as much factual content as they were gossip, sports, and scandals (Krippendorff, 1980).

During World War II, content analysis was used to analyze propaganda. After the war, the value of content analysis as a research tool was widely recognized, and interest in it spread beyond the field of communications to the disciplines of political science, psychology, history, sociology, and literature.

Several interesting applications of content analysis have been made by social workers. McMahon and Allen-Meares (1992) have asked, "Is Social Work Racist?" and examined the articles about minorities contained in four major social work journals during the 1980s.

Jenkins et al. (1982) used content analysis to review 712 abstracts of social work dissertations published from 1975 to 1979. They found that 44 percent of the dissertations were focused on direct practice with individuals, families, groups, and communities; 36 percent concerned the method of social policy and administration; and 3 percent involved social work education. Further, when they looked at fields of specialization, they found that almost two-thirds of all the dissertation abstracts fell into five main fields. The largest, "professional issues," made up more than 19 percent of all theses. The other main specializations were: family and child welfare, 14 percent; mental health, 13 percent; personal social services, 11 percent; and aging, 8 percent.

Wilson (1982) reported on the use of computer software to conduct content analysis of debates contained in the Congressional Record specific to a policy focus, the Employment Act of 1946. Wilson was able to find that the categories of "role of organized social welfare" and "role of families and individuals" received almost no mention in the debates. In other words, social services were not seen as being instrumental in affecting employment nor was there any emphasis on the "rights, or responsibilities of families and individuals" (p. 41.)

Billups and Julia (1987) used a content analysis of position-vacancy descriptions in *Social Casework and NASW News* to find out how social work practice was represented in these position descriptions. Among their findings were that family and child welfare position vacancies decreased from 58.9 percent in 1960 to 21.3 percent in 1980, while mental health related descriptions went from 11 percent to 45 percent in 1980. The titles "clinical social worker" and "therapist" constituted less than 2 percent of the total in 1960 but about 20 percent of the titles in 1980.

Other uses of content analysis have been suggested by Allen-Meares (1984):

> to analyze the recorded interactions of social work students before and after a training program in order to evaluate the efficacy of the training: "Did students who participated in the training use more reflective listening statements after training?" Content analysis might also be used to study social work texts: "Do recent texts present gays and lesbians in a more positive context than older texts? Are blacks more likely than women or other minority groups to be presented in a negative context in social work texts?" (P. 52)

Content analysis lends itself well to other techniques employed by social workers. For instance, Barry (1988) has discussed the use of autobiographical writing with elderly adults. Content analysis could be used to show that this technique is successful in ameliorating depression, improving self-acceptance, and helping older adults focus on the present. As a research tool, content analysis would allow social workers to measure older adults' progress by quantifying the positive themes in their writings.

Include Martin Seligman (1990) among those researchers who have recognized the power of content analysis. Seligman has done some absolutely fascinating work, demonstrating from diaries that older adults kept as teenagers that explanatory styles for bad events are highly stable over forty and fifty years. Those who self-blame as teenagers (as opposed to finding other explanations) continue assuming responsibility for bad events in old age.

Further, his content analyses have shown that health at age sixty is strongly related to optimism at age twenty-five and that we Americans have elected the more optimistic-sounding candidate in eighteen of twenty-two presidential elections that he examined. Seligman believes that individuals who are depressed do a lot of self-blaming but that their depression can be reduced by teaching them to think more optimistically. Doesn't this again make the point that practice and research are vitally connected?

Examples of the use of content analysis abound. Morrow (1991) examined the explanations given by female adolescent incest victims for their molestation. It was found that those who attributed the molestation as due to something about self were more depressed and had lower self-esteem. Content analysis has even been used by parents' groups interested in documenting the amount of sex and violence on television and movies. (Did you know that the movie *GoodFellas* contains 282 expletives and fourteen bloody death scenes?) Can you think of some way you could use content analysis to advocate for some policy change?

There has been a recent resurgence of interest in content analysis. Although it may sometimes be referred to as conversational analysis (Gale and Newfield, 1992), or even contextual analysis, and used to "deconstruct" meaning, these are essentially variations of the content analysis method.

Advantages and Disadvantages of Content Analysis

Like secondary data analysis, content analysis has the advantages of being (1) unobtrusive, (2) generally inexpensive to conduct, and (3) able to deal with large volumes of data. No special training or expertise is required—all that is needed is a research question or hypothesis and a set of communications or body of materials from which to begin developing categories.

One of the disadvantages of content analysis is that coding or categorizing the items can be a problem if several individuals are involved in the process. Reliability must be maintained throughout this phase of the project. If categories are vaguely defined, more mistakes will be made than if classification rules are clearly defined. However, it is not difficult to determine the reliability of the categorization process (the consistency among coders). See, for instance, Allen-Meares's (1984) description of computation for reliability.

The most common units of analysis are individual words or terms. However, if you search for selected key words, you may miss other terms that could also refer to the concept you are studying. Thus, if you instruct reviewers to search for the number of times "clinical social worker" is used in the newspaper, they might overlook references to "mental health worker." The term "mental health worker" could be an indirect reference to a clinical social worker. Reference can be made to the subject directly or indirectly. Indirect references might be discovered late in the project or not at all. This problem is more likely to occur when computers are used to conduct the content analysis without the investigator pretesting categories on a sample of source materials.

Essentials of Content Analysis

When you want to employ content analysis you start with a research question or hypothesis. Perhaps you want to know when the term "clinical social worker" evolved in social work literature. Or perhaps you have a notion that the newspaper you most frequently read has a negative opinion of social workers or some other definite bias that you want to document. You may want to test the hypothesis that fewer articles on the topic of community development have been written in the past five years than on private practice. Some question or assumption that can be tested through an examination of written or spoken communications occurs to you.

From that hypothesis or research question, you begin to think about what materials would provide the best source of communications for the content analysis. Will you use a local newspaper, the *New York Times*, *Social Work*, *Social Service Review*, *Families in Society*, or some combination of journals or papers? Naturally, there are pragmatic decisions to be faced. The materials should be relatively easy to obtain. It is easier to conclude your study if your library has a complete collection of the materials you need than if you have to travel out of state to examine them. Familiarity with the source materials is also needed; some journals or newsletters may be less relevant to your topic than you originally thought. Newer journals may not have the historical record in which you are interested.

Third, you will need to decide what will constitute the **units of the analysis**, or the recording units. Depending upon the amount of data to be analyzed, you may choose to examine words or terms, entire paragraphs, or the whole item itself (e.g., an entire article or speech). Most commonly, content analysis involves quantification of words or terms (counting the number of times that certain terms such as "social action" and "community organizer" appeared in social work journals during 1989).

The examination of themes and whole items can involve more complex rules for categorization. Take, for instance, the situation where newspaper editorials were analyzed for opinions of President Bush. How would such editorials be categorized? Searching for a set of specific words or phrases (e.g., "good President") may not be of much help. The editorials may not use those particular words but still be favorably impressed with Bush's performance. It is also possible that an editorial may like some of his policies but not others. A simplistic way would be to determine if the context of an editorial was basically positive (supportive) or negative (nonsupportive).

When determining units of analysis, think about what you intend to count or quantify. This generally leads to conceptualizing what categories will be needed. These categories should not be developed apart from the material being reviewed; your familiarity with the material will assist you in devising definitions and categories. As with questionnaire development, the use of a pilot test will assist you in refining the operational definitions of categories. Written rules, especially if more than one person is going to be involved in the content analysis, assist with the classifying and categorizing of data. It is important that categories be exhaustive and mutually exclusive.

Another decision that needs to be made is how much of the material to review. This issue cannot be addressed until the researcher can define the universe of items to be reviewed. This is not a problem when the universe of items is so small that all of it can be examined. However, when there are volumes of material available for examination, it is often advisable to sample those materials. (As discussed in the chapter on survey research, there are several ways to sample.) With regard to content analysis, it makes the most sense to think of sampling in terms of whether it should be random or systematic. However, there may be times when you want to have a stratified sample because magazines and journals differ in their prime audiences and in the characteristics of their subscribers. Krippendorff (1980) has also described cluster, multistage, and other forms of sampling with content analysis.

As with other methods discussed in this book, investigators who are concerned with their results meeting the test of replication must concern themselves with issues of reliability in the classification of content categories. Of chief concern is intercoder reliability. If those who are coding the content don't agree with each other very often, the coding system will not be reliable. Depending upon the extent of the project, stability of the coding effort over time can become important. Reliability is strengthened when there is training for the raters with practice sessions and clear coding instructions and rules.

More specific information on how to conduct content analysis on verbatim speech can be found in Schulman, Castellon, and Seligman (1989). Those interested in using computer software to perform content analysis should read Kronick and Silver (1992).

A Practical Application of Content Analysis

A serious problem for most mental health and social service agencies is public image. Bad publicity may affect agency admissions or the community's perception of the quality of care provided by an agency. What follows is a partially true (Royse and Wellons, 1988), partially fictionalized account of how content analysis has been used as a research tool to bring about needed change.

At one point in my career I was employed by a mental health system that was (so the administrators thought) too often in the local news. A local newspaper covered every board meeting, and much of the coverage had a negative slant to it. For instance, one editorial stated that the mental health system had "axed practically all hope of renewing the [mental health] levy with the construction of a $2.2 million building." Since the vote on the mental health levy was over two years away, such a statement by the newspaper seemed to indicate a stance that was not supportive of the community mental health system's need for the county's property tax levy. Our fear was that the newspaper had a powerful potential for influencing citizens of the community to vote against the renewal of the mental health levy. Since more than half of the revenue to operate the mental health system came from the tax levy, it became clear that effort should begin right away to counter negative perceptions held by the newspaper staff. Part of the strategy was to objectively demonstrate to them how the content of their articles and headlines was not balanced and could have a detrimental effect upon public opinion.

Every morning the director's secretary clipped articles from the local newspapers that referred to the mental health system. These were kept in a historical file. Clippings had been kept for about ten years and constituted an obvious source of material for a content analysis. Since reading ten years of newspaper clippings was a sizable task, we decided that reading headlines was much more manageable. A listing of all the headlines and captions above the news articles was made, and this constituted our units of analysis.

While our interest was in identifying the amount of negative coverage by the newspaper, this quickly became problematic. It was not difficult to identify those headlines we regarded as negative ("Hostility Erupts at Mental Health Board Meeting," "Mental Health Board in Dispute," "Mental Health Officials Squabble"). However, there were other headlines that we took to be negative, but that others who were not affiliated with the mental health system might not have interpreted that way. In addition, a headline might have been categorized as positive, but the article below it might have been negative. And some headlines were difficult to interpret ("Crisis Center May Resume Services" or "Judge Promises Fast Ruling") without reading the whole article. Consequently, it was decided to conduct the content analysis on selected key words.

It would not have been possible to anticipate every term or key word that indicated a negative reflection on the mental health system. Even clusters of negative words or phrases would have been very difficult to specify. Therefore, we decided to search for those key words that had something to do with the delivery of services or administrative issues.

Among our findings was that there were thirty-seven headlines, over the ten-year period, containing the key word "facility." This number of appearances was larger than that of any problem-specific key word, such as "divorce," "alcohol," "stress," "depression," "addiction," "domestic violence," "incest," "runaways," "death," and so on. It also occurred more times than population-specific terms, such as "aging," "elderly," "stepparent," "families," "teenagers," "juveniles," "children," and "students." Clearly, the newspaper was much more concerned with administrative issues (such as building a new facility) than with service delivery issues.

The number of square inches of newspaper coverage associated with each headline was also included in the study. We found that over 40 percent of all the coverage dealt with the mental health system's administrative board. The balance of the coverage was spread over the five local mental health agencies that actually delivered services to consumers. We also found that of the three local newspapers, the one perceived to be the most negative was providing about a third more coverage on the mental health system in terms of square inches of the articles than either of the two other papers.

When the study was finished, it was nicely typed and presented during a meeting of the agency staff and the editorial staff of the most negative newspaper. When confronted with the results of the study and examples of how the public could be interpreting their coverage, the editorial staff agreed to review their policies and coverage of the mental health system. Subsequent coverage was much more balanced and presented no opposition to the renewal of the mental health levy.

Using Unobtrusive Approaches

I recently came across a newspaper article describing a "sick-out" staged by some social workers. Twenty-three called in "sick" on the same day to protest a rise in their caseloads from an average of thirty-one to forty-three active cases and from 107 child abuse investigations to 125 per year. At the time, there were thirty-three vacant social work positions. These social workers used existing secondary data to advocate for themselves.

A little later that same day, a poster from the Handgun Control organization caught my eye. It noted that "In 1990, handguns killed 22 people in Great Britain, 13 in Sweden, 91 in Switzerland, 87 in Japan, 10 in Australia, 68 in Canada and 10,567 in the United States." It's hard to argue with persuasive data. These data define the severity of the problem in such a way that most can understand—a prerequisite step before we as a country can take the necessary steps to limit the sale and easy availability of handguns.

Given the considerable wealth of information available in this society, just for the asking, unobtrusive approaches ought to be considered first when research is required. Since unobtrusive methods do not require a lot of research expertise, even social workers who don't think of themselves as researchers can apply them. Finally, informed social workers need to be familiar with the social indicators available in the special fields in which they work. And where there is no good source of data about the problems with which we are concerned, then we need to advocate for and help establish mechanisms to collect needed data.

This chapter provides only a few examples of secondary data sources and content analyses and illustrations of how they might be used. Unobtrusive methods provide a needed alternative for those situations where resources are lacking to conduct large-scale surveys or other more rigorous forms of investigation, or where the nature of the question or problem does not lend itself to first-hand data collection. Even if we could collect the data ourselves, oftentimes there is no need to because someone else has already compiled it. Would you act differently or speak more carefully if you knew you were being videotaped? If you think you might, you've just confirmed the need for unobtrusive approaches.

Questions for Class Discussion

1. On the chalkboard, list the social service agencies where students have worked or been placed in a practicum. In a separate column, list the types of social problems with which these agencies deal. Next, make a list of the social indicators that could be used by social workers in these agencies to determine if their programs are having an impact on the social problems.
2. Using the social indicators listed in table 8.2, discuss potential bias in terms of how each might under- or overestimate the extent of a social problem.
3. Among the social service agencies with which you are familiar, what local information do they report to the state capital each year?
4. Identify a local issue or controversy in your community or on your campus. Discuss how content analysis might be used to provide some insight into how important this issue is compared to others.
5. Discuss ways that secondary data or content analyses could be used to advocate for clients or for the profession of social work.
6. Discuss the relative merits and problems with conducting a content analysis using key words as the unit of analysis.
7. What are the advantages and disadvantages associated with a content analysis that would categorize entire items such as editorials or speeches?
8. Discuss the arguments for and against using content analysis to look for themes in the drawings of preschool children.

Mini-Projects for Experiencing Research Firsthand

1. Think about the information collected by a social service agency with which you are familiar. List the different types of information that are available. Develop two hypotheses that could be tested using archival records from the agency.
2. Are higher rates of suicide found in rural counties or urban counties? Develop a hypothesis and test it using actual state data. (Hint: you will need to operationally define rural and urban counties by their population size). How would you explain your findings?
3. Read all the past month's editorials in one daily newspaper. What consistent patterns or themes emerge? If this effort constituted a pilot study for a content analysis, what hypothesis could

you develop? What kinds of categories or decision rules would you need to develop?

4. Skim through advertisements in a popular magazine such as *Newsweek, U.S. News & World Report, Time,* or *Better Homes and Gardens.* In terms of income and gender, to whom are the advertisements being pitched? Support your hypothesis by doing a content analysis.

5. Using the United Nations *Statistical Yearbook* or related materials, develop a hypothesis about some topic such as defense or social welfare expenditures. Test your hypothesis by looking at clusters of countries grouped by continent (e.g., Africa, South America).

Resources and References

Allen-Meares, P. (1984). Content analysis: It does have a place in social work research. *Journal of Social Service Research*, 7(4), 51–68.

Barry, Joan. (1988). Autobiographical writing: An effective tool for practice with the oldest old. *Social Work*, 33(5), 449–451.

Billups, J.O. and Julia, M.C. (1987). Changing profile of social work practice: A content analysis. *Social Work Research and Abstracts*, 23(4), 18–22.

Colby, A. (1982). The use of secondary analysis in the study of women and social change. *Journal of Social Issues*, 38(1), 119–123.

Davis, J.A. and Smith, T.W. (1987). *General Social Surveys, 1972–1987.* (Machine-readable data file.) Principal Investigator, James A. Davis; Senior Study Director, Tom W. Smith; NORC, ed.; National Opinion Research Center, Chicago, producer; The Roper Center for Public Opinion Research, University of Connecticut, Storrs, CT, distributor.

Davis, J.A. and Smith, T.W. (1991). *The NORC General Social Survey.* Newbury Park, CA: Sage.

Gale, J. and Newfield, N. (1992). A conversational analysis of a solution-focused marital therapy session. *Journal of Marital and Family Therapy*, 18(2), 153–165.

Glenn, N., Converse, P.E., Cutler, S.J., and Hyman, H.H. (1978). The general social surveys. *Contemporary Sociology*, 7(5), 532–549.

Hakim, C. (1982). *Secondary Analysis in Social Research: Guide to Data Sources and Methods with Examples.* London: Allen & Unwin.

Hall, O. and Royse, D. (1987). Mental health needs assessment with social indicators: An empirical case study. *Administration in Mental Health*, 15(1), 36–46.

Harris, L. (1987). *Inside America: Public Opinion Expert Louis Harris Looks at Who We Are, What We Think, Where We're Headed.* New York: Vintage Books.

Hyman, H.H. (1987). *Secondary Analysis of Sample Surveys.* Middletown, CT: Wesleyan Press.

Jenkins, S., Sainz, R.A., Cherry, A., Nishimoto, R., Alvelo, J., and Ockert, D. (1982). Abstracts as data: dissertation trends 1975–1979. *Social Work Research and Abstracts,* 18(1), 29–34.

Kielcolt, K.J. and Nathan, L.E. (1985). *Secondary Analysis of Survey Data.* Beverly Hills, CA: Sage.

Krippendorff, K. (1980). *Content Analysis: An Introduction to Its Methodology.* Beverly Hills, CA: Sage.

Kronick, J.C. and Silver, S. (1992). Using the computer for content analysis. *Journal of Social Service Research,* 16(1/2), 41–58.

Kulka, R.A. and Colten, M.E. (1982) Secondary analysis of a longitudinal survey of educated women: A social psychological perspective. *Journal of Social Issues,* 38(1), 73–87.

Lindsey, D. (1994). Mandated reporting and child abuse fatalities: Requirements for a system to protect children. *Social Work Research,* 18(1), 41–54.

McMahon, A. and Allen-Meares, P. (1992). Is social work racist? A content analysis of recent literature. *Social Work,* 37(6), 533–539.

Morrow, K.B. (1991). Attributions of female adolescent incest victims regarding their molestation. *Child Abuse and Neglect,* 15(4), 477–483.

Myers, D.E. and Rockwell, R.C. (1984). Large-scale data bases: Who produces them, how to obtain them, what they contain. *New Directions for Program Evaluation,* 22, 5–25.

Reid, W.J. and Bailey-Dempsey, C. (1994). Content analysis in design and development. *Research on Social Work Practice,* 4(1), 101–114.

Royse, D. (1988). Voter support for human services: A case study. *Arete,* 13(2), 26–34.

Royse, D. (1986). Newspaper coverage of a community mental health system: A descriptive study. *Journal of Marketing for Mental Health,* 1(1), 113–125.

Royse, D. and Wellons, K.W. (1988). Mental health coverage in newspaper headlines: A content analysis. *Journal of Marketing for Mental Health,* 1(2), 113–124.

Schulman, P., Castellon, C., and Seligman, M. (1989). Assessing explanatory style: The content analysis of verbatim explanations and the attributional style questionnaire. *Behavior Research and Therapy,* 27, 505–512.

Seligman, M. (1990). *Learned Optimism.* New York: Random House.

Steech, C. and Schulman, H. (1992). Young white adults: Did racial attitudes changes in the 1980s? *American Journal of Sociology,* 98(2), 340–367.

Stewart, D.W. (1993). *Secondary Research: Information Sources and Methods.* Beverly Hills, CA: Sage.

Turner, C.F. and Martin, E. (Eds.) (1984). *Surveys of Subjective Phenomena.* Vol. 1. New York: Russell Sage Foundation.

The United Nations. (1991). *The World's Women 1790–1990: Trends and Statistics.* New York: United Nations Publications.

Webb, E.J., Campbell, D.T., Schwartz, R.D., and Sechrest, L. (1966). *Unobtrusive Measures: Nonreactive Research in the Social Sciences.* Chicago: Rand McNally.

Weber, R.P. (1990). *Basic Content Analysis.* Newbury Park, CA: Sage.

Wilson, S.M. (1982). Objective analysis of values in a social policy debate. *Social Work Research and Abstracts,* 18(1), 35–41.

9
Preparing and Analyzing Data

Most researchers enjoy data analysis. It is at this stage that the data begin to "come alive." Patterns emerge, trends are detected, and support either is or is not found for our pet hypotheses. We may come away with the smug feeling that we were right in our predictions all along (and we now have the data to prove it!). Or, perhaps we did not learn as much as we had hoped (but ideas and questions were produced that can be tested in the next project).

The purpose of data analysis is to take the **raw data** (the completed survey forms or questionnaires) produced in the data collection stage and condense, distill, or summarize it. In a sense, the researcher is involved in a translation process. From a pile of raw data, which may seem bewildering and without any order to the untrained eye, the researcher hopes to wring something meaningful—patterns, trends, or relationships.

Analysis goes beyond displaying all the responses that were given. Simply reporting the individual responses that seventy-five people gave to a specific question or questionnaire is not analysis. The researcher seeks order within the data and tests hypotheses that have "driven" the research.

There is no single way to go about analyzing a data set. The way you analyze your data will depend upon what you want to know. However, there are some basic techniques that are frequently used by all researchers. These techniques will not only introduce you to the topic of data analysis but also assist you in understanding your data.

Before data analysis can begin, you need to examine the raw data for errors and completeness. Whenever there is a large collection of data, there will be questionnaires containing missed or inadvertently skipped items. When interviewers merely failed to record responses, they can be asked to review their notes and supply the missing items. In other instances, respondents can be recontacted and encouraged to complete vital information. When all the data have been reviewed and made as complete as possible, you are ready to code the data for computer processing.

The Use of Computers for Data Processing

The reason for using computers for data analysis will become clear to you when you consider the problems of keeping in mind the individual responses of as few as thirty different respondents. While the results of small surveys can be manually tabulated, it is almost impossible to manually tabulate large-scale surveys. Tabulating by hand even small surveys or projects can be very time-consuming if you want to know something other than how many responded one way or another. Consider how difficult it would be to tabulate the results of a survey of 525 persons when you want to know if there were differences in the responses of low-income and middle-income persons or between young and old adults. Computers can analyze data a lot faster than you can, and they can conduct statistical tests more accurately than a person using a formula and a hand calculator. Computers are such powerful tools that analysis without computer assistance makes absolutely no sense except for the smallest of surveys.

Computers are increasingly available to practitioners and researchers alike. Finn (1988) found that almost half of a group of human service agencies in North Carolina were using microcomputers. Of the agencies without microcomputers, 54 percent indicated that they planned to purchase one within the next three to five years.

Computers come in various sizes and capabilities. In addition to micro or personal computers are the "mainframe" computers, which can process multiple jobs and communicate with many users simultaneously. While mainframe computers are not commonly found in social service agencies, it is often possible to obtain a computer account and purchase processing time from a university. Personal computers can do just about everything that the mainframe computers can do except process extremely large data sets.

The collection of electronic components that make up the computer equipment is known as the "hardware." But it is not enough to have the hardware; you also need programs that instruct the computer how to perform the needed functions. Computer programs are referred to as "software."

There is no shortage of computer software that will assist the researcher in constructing charts, graphs, and tables and in conducting statistical analyses. So much software is available that it is not possible to provide detailed descriptions here. Hundreds, possibly thousands, of computer programs vary not only in the tasks they can perform, but also the computers in which they operate. For instance, programs designed for IBM personal computers will not operate in Apple computers. Before purchasing software, be sure of the functions you want the software to perform on *your* computer.

Most universities provide many choices of programs for mainframe computers. The Statistical Package for the Social Sciences (SPSS) and the Statistical Analysis System (SAS) are two of the more popular programs used by social scientists. Either of these programs can be expected to meet most users' needs for processing statistical data. Manuals for operating these programs are generally available at university bookstores. These programs can be used for such functions as listing the number and percentage of those responding to each questionnaire item, constructing tables, and conducting more sophisticated analyses (e.g., multiple regressions).

Coding Data for the Computer

When you plan a questionnaire or data collection instrument, design it for processing by a computer. Anticipate computer coding problems, and rectify them in the design phase rather than try to make sense out of raw data when response choices have overlapped or when inadequate instructions resulted in inconsistent and ambiguous data. For instance, inexperience might lead one to use the open-ended question "What is your marital status?" instead of a close-ended one with response choices. This could present a problem if a respondent answered "Single," which the interviewer took to mean never married, when the respondent meant that she was presently single having been divorced recently.

Coding is a process of taking data from the data collection instrument and putting it into a form that can be digested by a computer. Coding translates a verbal or written response into a numerical value. Table 9.1 contains examples of three demographic variables and two items from a larger survey instrument and shows how the data might be coded.

Notice that in the last two items, CHILD ABUSE AS A COMMUNITY PROBLEM and STRICTER PROSECUTION NEEDED, the coding scheme did

TABLE 9.1   Transforming Data for Coding

Variable	Code
Q1 Marital Status	
Never married	1
Married	2
Separated	3
Divorced	4
Widowed	5
Q2 Gender	
Female	1
Male	2
Q3 Age	[Actual age]
Q4 Child Abuse as a Community Problem	
Very serious problem	4
Somewhat serious problem	3
Not very serious problem	2
Not a problem at all	1
Don't know	8
Q5 Stricter Prosecution Needed	
Strongly agree	5
Agree	4
Undecided	3
Disagree	2
Strongly disagree	1

not start with 1 as it did with MARITAL STATUS. There is no rule requiring that you start coding with 1. Sometimes it is logical to code the responses so that a high value represents the seriousness of a problem or those who have the most of a given trait.

Accordingly, if we devised a scale to measure the use of corporal punishment in disciplining children, it would be logical to code the data so that those who made the most use of corporal punishment receive scores with the highest numerical values. If our scale had 20 questions with a 5-point Likert response scale, a respondent who "Always" used corporal punishment could attain a possible score of 100 (5 points times 20 questions) while the lowest possible score ("Never" uses corporal punishment) would be 20 (1 point times 20 questions).

You will make fewer mistakes in coding data if you follow a handful of simple rules. First of all, be consistent. You will find that it is much easier to remember a rule such as "yes is always coded 1" than to try to remember exceptions to this rule. If you start coding "yes" as 1 on question 15, don't change the rule later on when you are on item 37 or 45. With such a rule, it would follow that "no" would always be coded as 0—"no" indicates the absence of a trait, behavior, or attitude and "yes" indicates its presence.

Second, use one value (such as 9) for missing data. Thus, if a respondent did not indicate his or her marital status, a 9 could be used to communicate this to the computer. Similarly, if a respondent did not provide his or her age, 99 might be used to indicate the missing age. (While it is possible that a 99-year-old could be a respondent, it is unlikely. If you are interviewing older adults and have a 99-year-old as a respondent, provide a value for missing information that is not within the range of your respondents' ages, such as 00).

Third, anticipate the maximum number of response codes needed for each variable, so that you don't find that a one-column variable should have been coded with two columns after you have coded a stack of survey forms. In order to avoid this problem, "test" the coding scheme by randomly choosing several completed surveys and coding them before developing a final version of your **codebook**.

A codebook is a reference sheet or guide for coding. It tells coders what numerical values to use in transforming data to a machine-readable format and indicates the location in which the computer should record this information. You'll understand this when you think about computer cards. The 7 1/4" long by 3 1/4" wide cards were designed with an 80-column format. Computers "understand" information punched onto these cards based upon the location of the holes punched in them. Even though these cards are no longer used by researchers (having been replaced by electronic storage of data on silicon chips), information that is going to be computer processed using statistical programs must still utilize an 80-column format. Table 9.2 is an example of how the codebook indicates both location and coding instructions. Notice that the respondent's marital status is coded only in column 4. Also note that the variable of age, unlike the others, requires two columns. If the respondent is 35, a 3 would be placed in column 6 and a 5 would be placed in column 7. If the respondent is 9 years old, a zero would be placed in column 6 and a 9 in column 7.

Figure 9.1 provides an illustration of a portion of coded data obtained from persons 9, 24, and 35 years old as they might be coded for the computer.

Our codebook suggests that the values for gender should be coded 1 or 2 (respondents are either males or females). The 3 appearing in the gender column is an error. You do, however, have a lot of

TABLE 9.2   Portion of a Codebook

Variable	Code	Column
Respondent Number		1-3
Q1 Marital Status		4
Never married	1	
Married	2	
Separated	3	
Divorced	4	
Widowed	5	
Q2 Gender		5
Female	1	
Male	2	
Q3 Age		6-7
Q4 Child Abuse as a Community Problem		8
Very serious problem	4	
Somewhat serious problem	3	
Not very serious problem	2	
Not a problem at all	1	
Don't know	8	
Q5 Stricter Prosecution Needed		9
Strongly agree	5	
Agree	4	
Undecided	3	
Disagree	2	
Strongly disagree	1	

discretion to arbitrarily assign values, such as Males = 1 or Females = 3.

Note that some universities have computers that can optically scan specially designed answer sheets. If the responses to your questions fit into this format (e.g., a multiple choice format of the type used by standardized tests), it may not be necessary to manually code your data for the computer although you will still have to prepare a codebook so that the computer will know how to read your variables.

So far this discussion of coding covers only closed-ended questions. If you employed several open-ended questions and want to code the results, it may not be immediately obvious how you should proceed. At some point you will need to create categories for the responses you have obtained. Rather than establish the first category according to the first response you read, study twenty-five or so of the responses to the open-ended questions to see if there are similarities

FIGURE 9.1: A Partially Coded Data Sheet

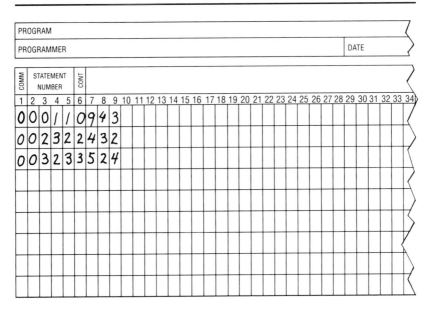

in the way respondents replied. Take, for example, the question asking why respondents dropped out of school; all of the following responses might be similar enough to fit into the category "Financial reasons": "I had no more money"; "couldn't borrow any more money"; "parents could no longer afford to send me."

When coding open-ended data, you may not know how many categories are needed to adequately reflect the responses. As a rule of thumb, too many categories (ten or more) make analysis just as difficult as too few categories. Let your choice of the number of categories be influenced by what you want to learn from the data. Draft a preliminary table with fictitious data in order to help you visualize your results. Even after data have been grouped into categories, some categories can be merged with others. This is useful when less than 10 percent of the responses are found in a category. (In table 9.3, for example, "Strongly disagree" might be merged with "Disagree.")

Univariate Analysis of Data

After the coded data have been entered into the computer, look over a printout of the raw data for data entry errors before proceeding with analysis. Examine each variable (such as gender) to see if there are any

TABLE 9.3   Example of a Frequency Distribution

Q15			**"I am well informed about AIDS."**	
Category Label	**Code**	**Absolute Frequency**	**Relative Frequency (Percent)**	**Adjusted Frequency (Percent)**
Strongly disagree	1	18	2.4	2.4
Disagree	2	228	30.6	30.7
Undecided	3	36	4.8	4.9
Agree	4	386	51.7	52.0
Strongly agree	5	74	9.9	10.0
No answer/refused	9	4	0.5	Missing data
Total		746	100.0	100.0
Q45			**Gender of Respondent**	
Female	1	477	63.9	63.9
Male	2	269	36.1	36.1
Total		746	100.0	100.0

unusual values that do not belong. This process is sometimes referred to as "cleaning" the data. If no correction is needed, the next step is preparing **frequency distributions**.

Frequency distributions present the responses obtained for each item. Data are generally displayed in ascending values. Table 9.3 provides an illustration of a frequency distribution for two items from a survey. This table displays how each response choice was coded and gives the number and percentage of respondents for each response choice. The last column provides adjusted percentages after deleting the missing data (those for whom no response was recorded) from the total respondents available. Because of the large sample size, the deletion of four respondents on item Q15 had little effect upon the figures reported under the adjusted percentages. A much greater effect would have been noticed had the sample been considerably smaller. As a rule, it is better to use the adjusted percentages, because these percentages are based on actual responses. A major difference in the relative and adjusted percentages indicates a large block of missing responses. The researcher should then consider whether too much missing data renders the item useless.

Looking at the data one variable at a time constitutes **univariate analysis**. From the frequency distribution in table 9.3 we can tell (by adding together the "Strongly agrees" and the "Agrees" and adding the "Strongly disagrees" to the "Disagrees") that two-thirds of the respondents (62 percent) believe that they are well informed about AIDS. One-third of the sample disagree with the statement (they do not feel well-informed about AIDS).

The computer programs that produce frequency distributions commonly produce other information, such as measures of central tendency (the mean, median, and mode) for each variable. Such information is much more meaningful when discussing the averages of some variables (such as age, income, and years of education) than learning that the mean of Q45, "Gender," in table 9.3 was a nonsensical 1.3.

Variables such as gender, occupation, political party, race, and marital status are **nominal variables**; their primary feature is that they allow for some categorization by name.

However, forcing individuals into one category or another sometimes doesn't work well. Take the example of baldness. The term usually makes us think of shiny-headed men without any hair. Suppose, however, that you encounter an individual who has a 40 percent hair loss. He's not completely bald, but he does have some bare patches. Into what category should we place him, bald or not bald? Nominal variables lead us to think in terms of discrete choices.

A major problem with variables measured at the nominal level is that it is not possible to average or perform many other statistical operations with them. Look at the variable of gender in table 9.3. Since we can't average male and female, the measure of central tendency used with nominal variables is the **mode**, the largest category or the most common response. In table 9.3 "Female" is the mode for the nominal variable of gender.

An improvement over the nominal level of measurement is to think of an ordered continuum or a hierarchy. At the **ordinal** level of measurement, five to seven categories might be used to rate levels of baldness. For instance, a person might be completely bald, substantially bald, moderately bald, slightly bald, or not at all bald.

Variables measured at the **ordinal** level form a scale where position and ranking are important. Variable Q15 (the statement "I am well-informed about AIDS") has response choices that are not nominal but ordinal. "Strongly agree" represents a higher level of knowledge about AIDS than an "Agree" response, which represents more knowledge about AIDS than either "Disagree" or "Strongly disagree."

The mode can be used as a measure of central tendency for ordinal variables, but the **median** is more appropriate. The median is the midpoint. In table 9.3, the median is the category that includes the next respondent past 50 percent of the data. With regard to the "I am well-informed about AIDS" item, the second category, "Agree," would represent the median value.

Obviously, both nominal and ordinal levels of measurement are frequently used, but in many instances researchers would get more accurate results by quantifying their variables and using an **interval** level of measurement. Interval data are variables that are more or less continuous and have intervals of equal length, like age or I.Q. scores.

Going back to the baldness example, it would be more accurate to record Jim as having a 40 percent hair loss, Bill as having a 30 percent hair loss, and John Ed as having a 20 percent hair loss than to try to force them into bald/not bald categories or to employ the ordinal categories of slightly or moderately bald. In this group of three, it is easy to compute and accurate to say that, on average, this group had a 30 percent hair loss.

Measuring data at the interval level allows us to talk about the **mean** or average in a way that is often useful for understanding the "typical" case. Data measured at the interval level are what is needed for most purposes, with a few exceptions, in data analysis. This is not to say, however, that the mean is "foolproof." The mean is always affected by (pulled in the direction of) extreme scores.

In the interval data shown below, the median can be easily computed to be $19,500.

EARNED SALARIES OF THIRTEEN SUCCESSFUL CLIENTS

	Yearly Salary	**Frequency**	
	$ 17,000	1	
	$ 18,500	2	
Mode	$ 19,000	3	(Most frequent)
Median	$ 19,500	1	(Middle case)
	$ 20,000	1	
	$ 21,000	2	
	$ 22,000	1	
Mean	$ 23,500	1	
	$100,000	1	
		13	

The mean, however, is $26,000 because of the inflationary effect of the one $100,000 salary. (Note that no one earned a $26,000 salary. In fact, there was only one individual who made more than $23,500.) When extreme scores are present in a frequency distribution, the median provides a better representation of the "average" value than the mean.

Other examples of dependent variables measured at the interval level can be seen in table 9.6 (Homophobia) and table 9.7 (Fear of AIDS). Also, note that scales developed with Likert-type response choices are often treated in data analysis as interval level data. In such situations, there is a presumption that the distance between ordered categories, say, "Excellent" and "Good," is the same as that between "Good" and "Fair" or between "Fair" and "Poor."

Sometimes when there is a true zero, data are measured at the **ratio** level. Temperature is a ratio-level variable because measurements below zero can be made. For most purposes in data analysis, it is not important to distinguish between interval and ratio level variables. In the social sciences, there are hardly any measurements that produce ratio-level data (Weinbach and Grinnell, 1987).

When given a choice, it is almost always better to gather data at the interval level and then, if necessary, to transform it into ordinal or nominal categories. If data are gathered at the nominal level first, it may be impossible to disaggregate the data so that means can be computed. For example, imagine a questionnaire that asked:

How many years of education have you completed?

a. 6th to 8th grade
b. 9th to 10th grade
c. 11th to 12th grade

Assume that the frequency distribution looked like this:

	f	%
6th to 8th grade	20	21%
9th to 10th grade	40	42%
11th to 12th grade	35	37%

Now, suppose you later discover that it is important to know exactly how many individuals completed the sixth grade and how many were high school graduates. Could you tell? Could you inform anyone what the average (mean) number of years of education was? This problem could have been avoided if you had not precoded the response categories but simply asked, "How many years of education have you completed?"

Whether your data are measured at the nominal, ordinal, or interval level, frequency distributions lend themselves to visual (graphic) portrayals. Graphs, pie charts, histograms, and polygrams can be prepared either manually or, many times, by the computer software that you use for data analysis. Figures 9.2 and 9.3 provide

FIGURE 9.2: "I am well-informed about AIDS"

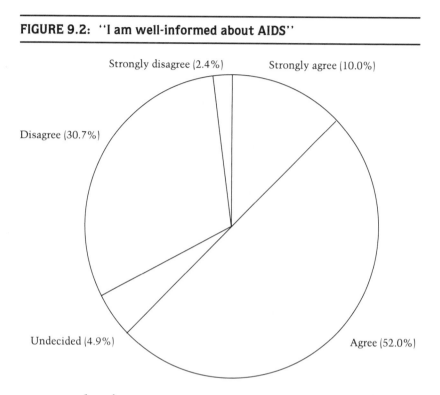

two examples of ways a computer program can present data from frequency distributions in the form of pie and bar graphs.

Bivariate Analysis of Data

After the data have been examined one item at a time, researchers often begin to look at the relationship among variables taken two at a time. A researcher may, for example, have the hypothesis that women are more knowledgeable about AIDS than men. Testing this would require using the variable of gender to analyze the responses obtained to Q15 ("I am well-informed about AIDS"). Researchers find it helpful to construct tables that allow them to examine two variables at a time. These tables may be prepared manually or by the computer; the computer version is sometimes called a **crosstabulation**, or crosstabs. Though it is not easy to determine by looking at the raw numbers, we can tell by looking at the column percentages in table 9.4 that there is virtually no difference in respondents' knowledge about AIDS by gender. Almost two-thirds of both the men and women indicated either agreement or strong agreement with the statement that they were

FIGURE 9.3: "I am well-informed about AIDS"

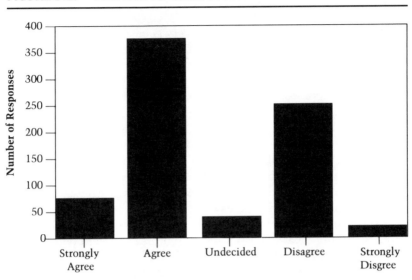

Response Choice

well-informed about AIDS. Displaying the data in this way allows researchers to easily detect patterns or relationships.

Had the results been different—had women been significantly more informed than men—further research might be required to explain this. It might then be hypothesized that women are more health conscious than men or that they more frequently read newspapers, the major source of information about AIDS. Thus, additional research might show an association between newspaper readership and knowledge about AIDS.

TABLE 9.4   Crosstabulation of Knowledge about AIDS by Gender ("I am well-informed about AIDS")

	Female	Male
Strongly agree/Agree	291 (66%)	169 (65%)
Strongly disagree/Disagree	153 (34%)	93 (35%)
Column totals	444	262

Sometimes it is difficult to tell whether or not there is any statistical association between two variables just by looking at percentages (visual inspection). Look again at the data in table 9.4, and avoid looking at the percentages. Unless you are very good at doing math in your head, you probably would not recognize that the males and females in this sample would be so similar in their responses. A statistical procedure may be needed to find out if there is a statistical difference between the two groups. The most common statistic used to test differences among categories in crosstabulations is the **chi square** (X^2) (DiLeonardi and Curtis, 1988). This is a popular test because it is widely understood; it can be easily calculated by hand or by computer, and it requires only nominal level data. These features make it particularly well-suited for social work research applications. If we were to use SPSS-X on the mainframe computer, we would learn that the computed chi square for the variables represented in table 9.4 is less than 1 and the probability level is .84. This means that there is no statistically significant difference between males and females in their perceptions of how well informed they are about AIDS.

Had there been an association between the variables, the chi square would have been much larger and statistically significant. Findings of statistical significance are represented in the following format: $p < .05$. A probability (p) level of .05 means that chance alone might have produced the same pattern of results 5 times in 100. Another way of saying this is that there are 5 chances in 100 that the hypothesis will be rejected unintentionally; in other words, males and females would have had very different opinions regarding their level of knowledge.

As useful as chi square is, it can also be misleading in those situations where there are a large number of cells with an expected frequency of fewer than five respondents or subjects. (Cells are the little boxes formed by the computer, shown in table 9.4.) Some computer programs (e.g., SPSS-X) will monitor this potential problem for you and tell you the number and percentage of cells having an expected frequency of 5 or under. These expected frequencies are generated in the process of calculating chi square. If you use some other program that does not report the number of cells with an expected frequency of 5 or fewer, be very cautious if you have a large number of blank cells. If more than 20 percent of your cells have an expected frequency of less than 5, then the produced chi square can be invalid. The procedure in such circumstances is to combine, or collapse, categories so that there are fewer cells with more respondents in them. (In table 9.4, the "Strongly agree" and "Agree" categories have been combined, as have "Strongly disagree" and "Disagree," in order to facilitate the presentation of the data.)

TABLE 9.5   Knowledge of AIDS by Community Type ("I am well-informed about AIDS")

Category	Rural	Small Town	City/Suburb
Strongly agree/Agree	121	164	174
	(57%)	(65%)	(73%)
Strongly disagree/Disagree	93	88	65
	(43%)	(35%)	(27%)
Column totals	214	252	239

Another crosstabulation is presented in table 9.5. In this example, a trend can be seen. Rural respondents rate themselves lower on knowledge of AIDS than small town or urban dwellers. When chi square is computed on this data, a value of 13.2 is obtained with a probability level less than .001 ($p < .001$). This means that there are differences in responding patterns and that these differences are real and not likely to be due to chance. A probability level of less than .001 means that chance could have distributed these two variables in this way 1 time in 1,000.

Most social scientists seek a probability level of at least $p < .05$ when reviewing the results of their statistical tests. This provides them with a reasonable amount of confidence that there are statistically significant differences between or among groups they are examining. A probability level of $p < .01$ is desirable when researchers want to be even more confident in their findings. Since most social science research does not involve life or death decisions (unlike, for instance, medical products research), it is rare to find social scientists rejecting a hypothesis because the probability that the groups were significantly different was greater than .001. Occasionally, a probability of .001 or even .0001 will be obtained, but these are not encountered as often in the literature as the .05 or the .01 probability levels.

In addition to the tabular display of data and chi square, other procedures establish differences between or among groups. Another procedure is useful with interval and ratio data. Suppose you have the hypothesis that medical students are more homophobic than social work students. You have devised a homophobia scale that provides you with interval level data. While a chi square can be performed when both variables are nominal, it would be inappropriate to use chi square if the dependent variables are continuous or interval. When you have a normally distributed dependent variable measured at the interval level, and nominal level independent variables, you can test

TABLE 9.6   Computer Printout of a T-Test

Variable	N	Mean	t value	Probability
Homophobia				
Med Students	63	6.8	2.67	.009
SW Students	60	5.7		

for statistical differences between two groups with the **t-test**. The statistical procedure, t-test, compares the mean scores for two groups and provides you with a t-value and probability statement. The t-test is appropriate even with small samples of about thirty individuals.

Practical Application of Statistics

Suppose you are conducting an AIDS educational program for medical and social work students. As part of that program you have them complete a questionnaire that measures their homophobia. Later you perform a t-test to find out if their scores are statistically different. The computer might provide information that looks something like table 9.6.

The beauty of statistical tests is that you don't have to go out on a limb and guess whether the differences in the means are substantially different. The computer will tell you if the groups are statistically different in their levels of homophobia. In this example, the medical students had higher mean scores than social work students on the homophobia scale and the probability of that finding occurring by chance was 9 out of 1000—easily below the .05 criterion level needed for statistical significance. You probably won't find the t-value terribly useful, but in the days before computer-generated printouts, the obtained t-value was necessary in order to look up the level of statistical significance on a reference table.

The SPSS-generated printout will provide a two-tailed test of significance. This is used whenever the direction of the outcome cannot be predicted in advance as when a null hypothesis has been stated. The null hypothesis is rejected whenever the difference between the means of the two groups is so large that the probability of its occurring by chance is greater than the established level of significance (for example, .05).

Assume that we do some additional research; we attempt to measure fear of AIDS among various health professionals. Since we are interested in surveying more than two groups (we want to interview medical, dental, social work, and nursing students), we would have to use a different statistical procedure. This procedure, which is almost identical to the t-test, is called the **one-way analysis of variance** (sometimes referred to as **ANOVA**). Interpretation of the one-way analysis of variance is straightforward and similar to the t-test, but, instead of a t-value, it provides an F-ratio. A computer printout of fear of AIDS by students pursuing degrees in various health careers might look like table 9.7.

Information from this one-way analysis of variance informs us that the levels of fear of AIDS among these four groups is not similar. If we were testing a null hypothesis, this ANOVA would tell us that all the means from the four groups were not equal—there were differences among these four groups of students in their fear of AIDS. This F-ratio and the associated probability does not prove that the difference between the group with the most fear and the group with the least fear is statistically significant. To test such a hypothesis, we would have to use a t-test with those two groups. The ANOVA merely indicates that among the groups being examined, there were some statistically significant differences in the pattern of responding.

Even though fear of AIDS was examined in four different career groups, only two variables were used—type of health career student and fear of AIDS.

Another way to analyze bivariate data is to use a **correlation coefficient** to summarize the relationship. A correlation coefficient is a statistic, or a numerical value, that ranges between -1.00 and $+1.00$.

In a perfect correlation, movement within one variable is matched by movement in the other. In the following example, students' exam scores increased by ten points for every hour that they studied.

**TABLE 9.7   Fear of AIDS by Health Career Orientation:
Computer Printout of a One-way Analysis of Variance**

Variable	N	Mean	F-Ratio	Probability
Fear of AIDS				
Dental Students	38	14.3		
Social Work Students	83	12.9	5.7	.001
Medical Students	79	15.2		
Nursing Students	62	13.3		
Total	262	13.9		

	Hours of Studying for Exam	Exam Score
Edna	10 hours	100
Bill	9 hours	90
Wanita	8 hours	80
George	7 hours	70
Brooke	5 hours	50

Pearson correlation coefficient = 1.00

Usually, however, it is not so easy to predict one variable from knowing the other. In the next example, the pattern of increasing scores with additional study time holds for only half of the students. For the other half, scores declined with more study time. Can you guess what the correlation will be?

	Hours of Studying for Exam	Exam Score
Martha	1	70
Micki	2	75
Waldo	3	80
Kenneth	4	85
Earl	5	90
Heather	6	90
Jennie	7	85
Bob	8	80
Nadine	9	75
Rondell	10	70

Pearson correlation coefficient = .00

In the third example, there is a slight tendency for grades to improve with additional study time for some students.

	Hours of Studying for Exam	Exam Score
Rennie	1	70
Debra	2	75
Betty	3	80
James	4	85
Edward	5	90
Pam	6	90
Donald	7	100
Robin	8	90
Glenna	9	80
William	10	70

Pearson correlation coefficient = .24

The closer the correlation coefficient is to one end or the other of the range, the stronger the relationship between the two variables. (This does not mean, however, that one variable was the cause of the other variable. A high correlation between the amount of street crime in a city and the number of social workers does not mean that the social workers caused the street crime.) A correlation coefficient hovering around .00 indicates no relationship between the two variables, while a coefficient of .24 indicates a very weak relationship. By squaring the correlation coefficient (multiplying it by itself), it is possible to determine the strength of the relationship between two variables. This tells us how much of the variance in the two variables is shared or explained. We are able to determine, then, that a coefficient of .24 explains about 6 percent of the variance, while a coefficient of .88 explains 77 percent of the variance between two variables. A coefficient of .31 would explain less than 10 percent of the variance. Correlations as high as .70 are rarely found in social science research, and the average of all correlations reported in the literature is thought to be less than .40 (Nunnally, 1978).

In the above examples, the plus sign is understood. A plus sign indicates a positive direction—as one variable goes, so goes the other variable. If one variable tends to increase, so does the other. A negative sign in front of a correlation coefficient indicates an inverse relationship—the variables go in opposite directions. As one variable increases, the other decreases.

In table 9.8, empathy for AIDS victims has an inverse relationship with fear of AIDS (– .55). In other words, individuals with greater levels of fear will tend to have less empathy for AIDS victims, and individuals with the least amount of fear will tend to have the most empathy for persons with AIDS.

Finally, keep in mind that a correlation may be statistically significant (meaning that it is likely that it did not occur by chance) but explain very little variation in the data. A correlation coefficient of .18 may be statistically significant at $p < .05$, but this isn't meaningful when you consider that only 3 percent of the variation in the data is explained. A high level of statistical significance does not automatically confer value or meaning in the sense of being clinically or practically useful to the practitioner (Schulman, Kupst, and Suran, 1976). You might be less tempted to put too much emphasis on finding a statistically significant correlation coefficient once you realize that, often, simply gathering additional respondents can produce significance. In fact, Schulman, Kupst, and Suran (1976) note that there is even a statistical test to find out how many additional subjects are necessary to get a significant difference once some preliminary data have been gathered.

TABLE 9.8   A Correlation Matrix with Four Scales

	Homophobia Scale	Empathy Scale	Fear Scale	Social Distance Scale
Homophobia Scale	1.00	−.63	.60	.66
Empathy Scale	−.63	1.00	−.55	−.68
Fear Scale	.60	−.55	1.00	.67
Social Distance Scale	.66	−.68	.67	1.00

It is entirely possible to put too much stock in statistical significance, whether it comes from a correlation or any other statistical test. For instance, suppose you are running an after-school program for delinquent youth. At the end of the school year, you find that the group's grade point average has risen, on average, from 1.45 to 1.75. A t-test reveals this to be statistically significant at $p < .05$. You feel good about this until someone points out that, practically speaking, there has been no major improvement—most of the group is still having academic problems. While their grade point average is moving in the right direction, the practical significance of the increase is educationally negligible.

Just because we have statistical tests and computers at our disposal doesn't mean that we should blindly accept findings of significant differences without investigating whether any real changes have occurred.

A correlation matrix is presented in table 9.8. This matrix resulted from correlating four scales, Homophobia, Empathy, Fear of AIDS, and Desired Social Distance from AIDS Victims, with each other. It produces some perfect correlations (when a scale is correlated with itself) as well as some positive and negative correlations. As you look at these correlations, do you understand why some have a negative sign in front of them while others do not? Why would Empathy correlate negatively with Fear of AIDS?

Multivariate Analysis of Data

The most common meaning of the term **multivariate analysis** is an analysis that involves one or more independent variables and two or more dependent variables (Glisson and Fischer, 1982). Typically, a computer is needed to perform statistical computations such as partial correlations, factor analysis, multiple regressions, and such. The appearance of these sophisticated statistical procedures in social work journals is increasing. However, at least one study has revealed numerous incidences in which multivariate statistics should have been used but were not. The authors of that study describe the problem of underuse of multivariate procedures as "severe" (Glisson and Fischer, 1982).

Such procedures as multivariate analysis of variance and covariance, canonical analysis, and discriminant analysis are beyond the scope of this chapter. However, it is possible to begin to understand multivariate analysis by constructing a table that will allow us to examine three variables at one time. Table 9.9 provides an illustration of this.

Table 9.9 provides us with a more detailed view of the pattern of data we first viewed in table 9.5. The trend shown in table 9.5 still holds: city dwellers rate their knowledge of AIDS higher than rural dwellers. However, now we observe that the difference between male urban dwellers and male rural dwellers is much more dramatic than the difference between female urban and female rural dwellers. By introducing the third variable (gender) to table 9.5, we are better able to explain the relationship between knowledge of AIDS and community of residence. With the use of statistical multivariate analysis it is possible to determine which of your variables makes the better predictor. Using this example, we could determine whether gender or type of community is the better predictor of knowledge about AIDS.

Although this illustration can help you see the value of going beyond bivariate analysis, multivariate analysis usually involves multiple regression techniques or, at least, crosstabs involving more than two dimensions. SPSS allows you to specify a maximum of ten different dimensions or variables. For example, you might want to examine Fear of AIDS by sex and by race, where race is used as a control variable. The crosstabs produced would look at Fear by sex for each of the racial groups identified.

TABLE 9.9 **Knowledge of Aids by Community Type and Gender ("I am well-informed about AIDS")**

	Female respondents			Male respondents		
	Rural	Small town	City/ Suburb	Rural	Small town	City/ Suburb
Strongly agree/Agree	73	105	112	48	59	60
	(59%)	(65%)	(71%)	(53%)	(65%)	(76%)
Strongly disagree/Disagree	51	56	45	42	32	19
	(41%)	(35%)	(29%)	(47%)	(35%)	(24%)
Totals	124	161	157	90	91	79

For an example of a social worker using stepwise multiple regression, see Lechner's (1993) study that sought to understand support systems and stress among workers caring for frail elderly parents by employing the dependent variables of role strain, mental strain, impact of caregiving, and physical conditions.

Final Thoughts

PERCENT OF MALES ARRESTED FOR SERIOUS CRIMES

Under 15 years	Under 18 years	18–24 years	25–44 years	45–64 years	55–64 years	65 yrs. and over
5.2	15.5	30.5	46.8	4.7	1.8	0.7

One caution when reading tables or data prepared by someone else: don't put your mind in neutral and assume that some authority is going to do all your thinking for you. If you do, you might arrive at some erroneous conclusions. A student brought me this example from a source book containing national statistics.

Which group of males is most responsible for serious crime? The largest category by far is the 25–44 year old males. Does that make any sense in terms of what you know about the youthfulness of most offenders? Notice, though, that the span of years 25 to 44 is considerably larger than the interval 18 to 24 years—more than three times larger. Might we have come to a different conclusion if the data had been grouped in equal intervals—say, 16–20, 21–25, 26–30, 31–35, 36–40?

Lastly, this chapter has provided an overview of the processes researchers use to analyze their data. (This is not to suggest, however, that this chapter contains all that you need to know about the use of statistics. A reading of this chapter is not a substitute for a course in applied statistics.) As you become more involved with research, you will want to know more about statistical applications.

If you are comfortable with your knowledge of statistics, test your recognition of the following statistical symbols:

1. $\underline{SD}$, S
2. $\overline{X}$
3. r
4. $p < .05$
5. F
6. t
7. X^2
8. df

Several articles have been written on social workers' knowledge of statistics. Weed and Greenwald (1973) reported in a small study that less than half of the social workers they surveyed knew any of six commonly used statistical symbols. Witkin, Edleson, and Lindsey (1980), using a larger sample, corroborated the earlier findings of Weed and Greenwald. More than a decade has passed since this last study. Are social workers now any more knowledgeable of statistics? How many of the statistical symbols did you recognize?

Answers: (1) standard deviation; (2) mean (or average); (3) correlation coefficient; (4) probability of happening by chance is less than 5 times in 100; (5) an F-value (from an F-ratio or F-test, as with one-way analysis of variance); (6) a t-value (from a t-test); (7) the symbol for chi square; (8) degrees of freedom.

Questions for Class Discussion

1. A student who had not been attentive during a lecture on coding data for the computer used two columns to code the variable for gender. This student coded males in column 4 and females in column 5. Why won't this approach work?
2. Explain how the computer "knows" that in a frequency distribution from a recent survey a "1" under MARITAL STATUS indicates "never married," while a "1" under "GENDER" indicates "female."
3. Do you notice any pattern in the correlations presented in table 9.6?
4. What does the correlation between the Social Distance and Fear scales indicate in table 9.8?
5. What are some limitations associated with correlation research?
6. While charts or graphs can simplify complex findings, what limitations are associated with trying to understand a study solely from its charts or graphs?
7. Suggest a dependent variable and have the class come up with logical independent variables to use for bivariate analysis. Discuss the most appropriate statistical procedure to be used.
8. Janice has designed a new intervention to help children who've experienced the death of a close family member. Using a standardized instrument that measures depression and an experimental design, Janice captures pretest and posttest data on both the control and intervention groups. She uses a t-test to compare the means of the two groups at pretest. Does she want to find

statistical significance? Should she hope to find statistical significance with the posttest data?

Mini-Projects for Experiencing Research Firsthand

1. Using any of the instruments described in chapter 5, collect a small sample of data (e.g., from 15–20 students), code it, and enter the data into a computer for statistical analysis. Report to the class your hypotheses, how you constructed your sample, and your findings.
2. Skim through several issues of a professional journal until you find an example of statistical analysis of data. How does the author interpret these statistics in terms of the theoretical or practical significance and the statistical significance of the relationships?
3. Find a frequency distribution reported in a magazine, newspaper, or journal, and prepare a bar or pie chart to display the data.
4. Read the articles by Weed and Greenwald and by Witkin et al. Design a small project to determine if social workers (or social work students) are now more knowledgeable about statistical symbols than reported in these articles.
5. Find a program evaluation reported in a journal. Summarize what you learned about the success or failure of the program by reviewing what the author reports in statistics and tables. How were the data analyzed? What didn't you understand? Be sure to give a full citation for the article so that it can be found by others.

Resources and References

Benbenishty, R. and Ben-Zaken, A. (1988). Computer-aided process of monitoring task-centered family interventions. *Social Work Research and Abstracts*, 24(1), 7–9.

Clark, C.F. (1988). Computer applications in social work. *Social Work Research and Abstracts*, 24(1), 15–19.

DiLeonardi, J.W. and Curtis, P.A. (1988). *What to Do When the Numbers Are In.* Chicago: Nelson-Hall.

Finn, J. (1988). Microcomputers in private, nonprofit agencies: A survey of trends and training requirements. *Social Work Research and Abstracts*, 24(1), 10–14.

Gibson, J.W. (1992). Compensating for missing data in social work research. *Social Work Research and Abstracts*, 28(2), 3–8.

Glisson, C. and Fischer, J. (1982). Research notes: Use and nonuse of multivariate statistics. *Social Work Research and Abstracts*, 18(1), 42–44.

Kanji, G.P. (1993). *100 Statistical Tests.*Newbury Park, CA: Sage.

Lechner, V.M. (1993). Support systems and stress reduction among workers caring for dependent parents. *Social Work,* 38(4), 461–469.

Lindsey, D. (1977). General-purpose computer packages in the social sciences. *Social Work Research and Abstracts,* 13(4), 38–42.

Mitchell, M. and Jolley, J. (1988). *Research Design Explained.* New York: Holt, Rinehart and Winston.

Nunnally, J.M. (1978). *Psychometric Theory.* New York: McGraw-Hill.

Pilcher, D.M. (1990). *Data Analysis for the Helping Professions.* Newbury Park, CA: Sage.

Royse, D. and Birge, B. (1987). Homophobia and attitudes towards AIDS among medical, nursing, and paramedical students. *Psychological Reports,* 61, 867–870.

Royse, D., Dhooper, S., and Hatch, L.R. (1987). Undergraduate and graduate students' attitudes towards AIDS. *Psychological Reports,* 60, 1185–1186.

Schulman, J.L., Kupst, M.J., and Suran, B.G. (1976). The worship of "p": Significant yet meaningless research results. *Bulletin of the Menninger Clinic,* 40(2), 134–143.

Weed, P. and Greenwald, S.R. (1973). Brief notes: The Mystics of statistics. *Social Work,* 18, 113–115.

Weinbach, R. (1989). When is statistical significance meaningful? A practical perspective. *Journal of Sociology and Social Welfare,* 16(1), 31–37.

Weinbach, R.W. and Grinnell. (1987). *Statistics for Social Workers.* New York: Longman.

Witkin, S.L., Edleson, J.L., and Lindsey, D. (1980). Social workers and statistics: Preparation, attitudes, and knowledge. *Journal of Social Service Research,* 3(3), 313–322.

10
Program Evaluation

The mission of program evaluation is to provide information that can be used to improve social programs (Tripodi, 1987). Unlike strictly theoretical research, program evaluation is synonymous with applied research. Most often, program evaluation starts with a specific problem or question to be answered, such as: "Is our outpatient treatment program as effective as inpatient treatment?" Or, "Are we as successful with our group counseling program as with our individual counseling?" Administrators, board members, and others may want to know if the program is a "good" program. If they decide that the program is not "good," then corrective action may be taken or funding may be cut off. Program evaluation, then, is an aid to program managers. It can improve program effectiveness and aid in decision-making.

Program evaluation attempts to answer such general questions as:

1. Are clients being helped?
2. Is there a better (cheaper, faster) way of doing this?
3. How does this effort or level of activity compare with what was produced or accomplished last year? (Did we achieve our objectives?)
4. How does our success rate compare with those of other agencies?
5. Should this program be continued?
6. How can we improve our program?

Why do we need to conduct program evaluation? The best argument for evaluating social service programs comes from an analogy suggested by Martin Bloom: conducting a program without evaluating it is like driving a car blindfolded. You certainly are going places, but you don't know where you are or who you've endangered along the way. Program evaluation provides accountability. It can be used to assure the public, funders of programs, and even the clients themselves that a particular program works and that it deserves further financial support. Program evaluation can be used to ensure that certain expectations are met, that efforts are appropriately applied to the identified needs, and that the community is better off because the program is having a positive effect. There are many other reasons for conducting program evaluation. In addition to accountability, Posavac and Carey (1985) list: fulfillment of accreditation requirements; answering requests for information; making administrative decisions; assisting staff in program development; and learning about unintended effects of programs. Ultimately, program evaluation benefits clients. It tells us whether clients are being helped or not, and it can indicate how we can better assist clients.

Program evaluation fits into the program development cycle outlined by Lewis and Lewis (1983) and others. Briefly (and perhaps ideally), the program development process starts with a needs assessment being conducted before a program is funded. The documentation of unmet needs in the community results in funds being allocated for a new program. As the new program is planned, attention is given to ways the program can be evaluated. After the program has been implemented, conscientious managers ask: Is there a better way to provide this program? What have we accomplished? Are we having an impact on the community's needs? And, is this a good program? Funding sources may ask, "Should we continue this program next year?"

Starting to Think about Conducting a Program Evaluation

Think about a social service program with which you have been associated. Perhaps it was in an agency where you were employed or where you had a field practicum. Suppose the agency director asked to see you one day and said, "I've got to convince our principal funding source that we run a good program. And I don't have the slightest idea how to go about it. They aren't interested in our opinions about the program. I get the impression that they want some objective data. Since you are taking classes at the university, I'm sure that planning a program evaluation won't be difficult for you. After all, we know we

TABLE 10.1   The Reasonably Healthy Minds Agency: Annual Report of Client Data

	Program A	Program B	Program C
Number of clients served this fiscal year	523	750	297
Female clients	45%	69%	57%
Minority admissions	5%	9%	10%
Clients under 21	98%	5%	0%
Clients 21–55	2%	91%	8%
Clients 56 and older	0%	4%	92%
Clients on public assistance	13%	94%	24%
Prior mental health service	20%	40%	50%
Self-referrals	60%	25%	15%

have a good program, we just have to demonstrate it. Take a couple of days to sketch out an evaluation plan, and let's go over it at our administrative team meeting on Friday. We'll want to have the evaluation completed in about sixty days."

What would you do if you found yourself in this situation? What information would you need to have? How would you demonstrate that any program was "good"?

Beginning a Program Evaluation

Once you understand (1) the purpose of the evaluation (including important questions to be answered or hypotheses to be tested), (2) the audience (those who will be reading the evaluation report), (3) the time frame, and (4) the funds that can be expended, you are in a position to start thinking about designing an evaluation process.

On the most basic level, you can begin to gather some descriptive data (e.g., the number of clients who used the program in the past six or twelve months). And you can obtain information on the proportion of these clients who are minorities, elderly, children, and low income, or who are referred by specific sources. However, this **client utilization** or **patterns of use data** can tell you something about only those clients who have expressed a need for the program (by their appearing on your agency's doorstep). It will tell you nothing about those who *could* have benefited from your program but who did not request services. Table 10.1 displays some client utilization data from a fictitious agency.

As demonstrated in table 10.1, descriptive data do not allow us to conclude that programs are "good," effective, or efficient. While the data inform us about the number of clients served and allow us to establish who the recipients of our services were, they tell us nothing about the quality of care clients were provided. We can reach no conclusion about whether the clients were better off as a result of being served by one of the agency's three programs. Even though many social service agencies report descriptive client utilization data in their annual reports, such information by itself does not constitute an evaluation of the agencies' activities or programs.

Patterns of use data are best used for indicating pockets of clients who are within the agency's target group for services but who are not being served. Once we start thinking about this problem, it is apparent that table 10.1 would be much more meaningful if census data were included so that we could determine which groups were not being served in proportion to their representation in the population. For instance, if you knew that 15 percent of the community's residents were minorities, then it would be easy to determine that all three of the programs presented in table 10.1 are underserving minorities. Data presented in this way are useful for **program monitoring**.

Program monitoring is described by Rossi and Freeman (1985) as measuring the extent to which a program reaches its intended target population and whether the service being provided matches what was intended to be delivered. Despite the best intentions, programs sometimes slowly change or drift away from their original mission.

I once observed this firsthand with an agency that had drifted away from its primary mission of serving the whole community. At the time I encountered the agency, the vast majority of its clientele were white middle-class persons who were young, fairly articulate, and motivated to work on their problems. This public agency had chosen to serve a select group of clients, the bulk of whom could have obtained assistance from private practitioners. Since there were no other agencies in that area to serve low income families, these families simply were not being served. This situation came about because there was no program monitoring being done. Program managers ought to monitor who is being served and who is not. When done regularly and routinely, program monitoring can be considered a basic form of program evaluation. While it may not answer many questions, it does provide a foundation upon which to start a program evaluation.

Types of Program Evaluation

If your principal funding sources are impressed with the kind of data presented in table 10.1, then your program evaluation need go no further. If their expectations are greater (for the reasons we've already discussed), then it may be necessary to consider another type of program evaluation.

Because social workers are employed in so many diverse fields of practice (e.g., health, aging, schools, mental health, substance abuse), choosing an evaluation design or model is sometimes problematic. No one model fits all situations and circumstances. Lipsey (1988) observed, "We can now distinguish quantitative and qualitative evaluation, experimental and naturalistic evaluation, outcome and process evaluation, summative and formative evaluation, and a host of other such variants" (p. 5). Dush and Cassileth (1985) have noted, "There are as many evaluative strategies as evaluation questions" (p. 61). While this may be an exaggeration, there are quite a few evaluation models or strategies. Patton listed one hundred different types of evaluation in his 1981 book and thirty-three others in 1982. Let's take his word for it and not double-check his arithmetic. With so many different evaluation designs to choose from, it is not as important that you memorize every possible variation of a design as it is that you be able to *conceptualize* ways to evaluate programs.

In addition to program monitoring, another type of program evaluation is **formative evaluation**. Formation evaluation is not specifically concerned with the "worth" of a program. Instead, it focuses on improving programs.

Formative evaluations are used to modify or shape programs that are still in development (i.e., model programs). Formative evaluations vary with regard to sophistication. On some occasions they may involve an "evaluator" who is an "expert" employed by another agency that operates a program similar to the model program. This evaluator may visit clients and staff, tour the facility, and perhaps observe some of the programming. Ultimately, he or she produces a report that contains some constructive information about how the program could be improved. These evaluations are sometimes referred to as **process evaluations** and tend to be more qualitative in approach than quantitative. Process evaluations look at how a product or outcome was produced rather than at the product itself.

Process evaluations explain what worked and what didn't and can be useful to other organizations that are considering implementing similar programs. From process evaluations others can learn how long it took the program to start up, unexpected problems that arose, and how these problems were handled. Process evaluations tend to be popular with federally funded research and demonstration projects.

Formative evaluations usually rely upon participant observation and informal interviews. They tend to be descriptive and don't rely upon statistics or analysis of numerical data. However, one can use qualitative methods to evaluate any program. Like formative evaluations, qualitative evaluations usually do not produce conclusions about whether the program is successful or not; rather, they describe how participants (staff and clients) experience the program (Schuerman, 1983). Such qualitative evaluations are sometimes called goal-free evaluations. The qualitative description of a program at a particular point in time may be useful in helping to explain later findings of outcome evaluations that determine the degree of success of the program.

Another type of program evaluation could be called **outcome, effectiveness**, or **impact evaluation**. This program evaluation effort involves quantitative-comparative techniques and has the best chance of providing information about treatment effectiveness. It may use experimental or quasi-experimental designs and aims to gather "hard" evidence that could be used to demonstrate the worth of a program.

In the remainder of this chapter we will be primarily concerned with evaluating program outcome. We will examine several general purpose evaluation designs that can be used in a variety of settings. These designs are not experimental nor could they always be considered quasi-experimental. Each has its own name and perspective on program evaluation.

Think of evaluation designs as blueprints or guides for the evaluative process. They do not in themselves provide any guarantee that the results will be noteworthy or that every expectation of the evaluation will be met. They describe the key features and procedures to be followed in conducting an evaluation. A design is a plan that "dictates when and from whom measurements will be gathered during the course of an evaluation" (Fitz-Gibbon and Morris, 1987, p. 9). Your evaluation is valuable to the audience reading your evaluation report because it provides answers to the questions they asked. Your choice of a particular design needs to follow from the questions or concerns about a program.

Experimental and Quasi-Experimental Designs

If, in thinking about how you might plan an agency evaluation, you consider the experimental and quasi-experimental designs of chapter 5, you are on the right track. The classical experimental design would certainly be the traditional scholarly approach to determining if a program were effective. And it would be a good choice if you could randomly assign clients to a control group and if pretesting, posttesting, and intervention could be accomplished within the sixty days allocated for the program evaluation in our hypothetical example. In situations where randomization and the use of control groups are not possible, you need to be able to conceptualize other ways of evaluating programs.

The Discrepancy Model

The Discrepancy Model can be attributed to Malcolm Provus (1971), although it has been discussed and refined by others in the field of educational evaluation. In its simplest form, a discrepancy approach to evaluating a program entails a comparison of a program's performance against some standard(s). Variances are identified according to where the program "ought to be" and where it actually "is."

Three different types of sources provide these standards. First, an evaluator could turn to accrediting bodies or national organizations and examine the standards they have produced. For instance, some of the standards published by the Child Welfare League of America include: *Standards for Organizations and Administration for All Child Welfare Services; Standards for Child Protective Service; Standards for Day Care Service; Standards for Foster Family Service;* and *Standards for Residential Centers for Children.* The American Correctional Association has published standards for: *Juvenile Community Residential Facilities; Juvenile Probation and Aftercare Services;* and *Juvenile Detention Facilities and Juvenile Training Schools.* Among the many standards prepared by the Joint Commission on the Accreditation of Healthcare Organizations are the *Hospice Standards Manual* and the *Ambulatory Health Care Standards.* The National League for Nursing has prepared standards for home health care in *Accreditation Criteria, Standards and Substantiating Evidences.*

This is just a small sampling of a wide range of standards that already exist for certain programs. Within your area, various state departments may have developed standards for certain programs. Standards contained in these documents may provide guidelines for directing a local program. Sometimes, however, these standards are vague, minimal, or so general that much is left open for interpretation. Some standards may specify that the program have a written policy and procedures manual, but they do not specify what should be in it. Other standards may be very specific about limitations on staff caseload or the amount of time within which certain types of services must be provided. If you are attempting to provide a formative evaluation, you may find such standards helpful. They will not be as helpful for evaluations when outcomes or impact data are needed.

A second source of standards is journal articles or studies that have been conducted on programs similar to the one you are interested in evaluating. Carter (1983) located information on client outcomes in a number of different program areas; he reported that with regard to a delinquency program, between 27 percent and 52 percent of all males will be rearrested within twelve months after release, but between 16 percent and 30 percent of the females will be rearrested within twelve months. Between 24 percent and 49 percent of foster care cases achieved a permanent placement within six months; and in child protective services, between 17 percent and 33 percent of substantiated abuse or neglect cases will reabuse or reneglect. In marital counseling, about two-thirds of clients and counselors reported improvement in the presenting problem.

Clearly, if your agency has a delinquency program (or foster care, protective services, or marital counseling program) and experiences higher rates of recidivism or dissatisfaction than those cited in the literature, then there is a discrepancy between what was expected and actual performance. On the other hand, your program may perform better than these rates, and you would have some basis for concluding that your program is a "good" program.

These first two sources of standards of evaluation rely on finding *available* literature or standards. Formal standards that have been prepared by an accreditating body or professional organization may be readily available or already known to the evaluator. It may be more difficult for the evaluator to identify relevant studies in the literature that would provide standards against which his or her program can be measured.

Because of differences in the way programs evolve, the availability of resources, and the mix of clients and staff, there is great variability in the way even similar programs are structured. One divorce support group may meet twice a week for six weeks with both male and female co-leaders, while another may run for twelve weeks, meeting only once a week and utilizing only a female therapist. Are these programs similar? Probably not. You are likely to be disappointed if you expect to find useful comparative data for a program exactly like yours. While there may be programs similar to yours that have conducted evaluations, the reports of these evaluations may not have made it into the professional literature. An alternative is to approach agencies that you know have similar programs and request client outcome data for comparison with your program.

A third way to find standards for your program's performance is to look within your agency. Most programs have concrete, measurable objectives that were developed earlier (perhaps prior to the start of the program or at the beginning of the program year). These objectives may be stated as:

OBJECTIVES

1. To place 225 new job trainees in full-time paid positions by January 1, 1998.
2. To increase admissions from minority clients by 20 percent over the number served last year.
3. To reduce the number of clients who recidivate by 25 percent during the first six months of the calendar year 1997.
4. To have 75 percent of the program participants attain a G.E.D. prior to release by June 30, 1999.

Notice that these objectives have in common several characteristics: (1) they are specific—they state a desired result; (2) they are measurable (easily verified); and (3) they indicate when the result can be expected. Contrast these objectives with the following goals:

GOALS

1. To eliminate poverty.
2. To reduce the incidence of child abuse.
3. To promote happier, healthier families.

Goals provide direction; they help us recognize if some activity may not be appropriate given a chosen goal. However, note that there is a certain ambiguousness associated with goals. At an agency or program level, goals may never be achieved. While all hunger may never be eliminated from the state of Texas, the goal can still be a most worthwhile one to work toward. The problem comes when agencies confuse goals with objectives. Often, the first actions of the evaluator are to help the program administrator and staff to develop measurable program objectives.

Once you establish program objectives, you can use the discrepancy model to determine whether the objectives were met. This approach could also be described simply as program monitoring. That is, the evaluator is trying to determine if the program is going to meet the objectives that it set for itself. If the objectives are met, the evaluator could conclude that the program is doing what it ought to do. If the objectives are not being met, then perhaps they were unrealistic or unmeasurable, or there may have been mitigating circumstances that could explain the discrepancy.

The problem with reliance upon the program's own objectives to determine how the program is doing is that whoever developed the objectives may have made them so easy to accomplish that they are essentially worthless. For instance, if a program objective stated that 2,200 new clients would be served within the year, but for the past two years the agency has been serving almost 2,500 new clients, the objective will have been met—there was no discrepancy—but we would still have no idea about how "good" or effective the program was. Ideally, a program should have to stretch a bit in order to meet its objectives. Objectives should be attainable, but not be so easy to reach that no special effort is required.

The Hammond Model

A completely different evaluation model has been proposed by Robert Hammond (1975). The Hammond Model (table 10.2) is a systematic approach that is useful for conceptualizing alternatives for program evaluation. For instance, a population (those individuals involved in or influenced by the program) can be conceptualized as consisting of three elements: clients, staff, and administration. A program operates in an environment defined by its intents (the purposes, goals, or objectives established for it), its methods (whatever intervention is employed), and its resources (the people, money, space, materials, and equipment used to implement the methods).

Once these program elements have been identified, the evaluator can organize questions into two groups: those that relate to areas of opinion (judgments and beliefs) and those that relate to behavioral performance.

With this model the evaluator has a number of choices. He or she can decide to be very comprehensive and cover all of the population and environmental elements with regard to opinions and perfor-

TABLE 10.2   The Hammond Model

Population	Environment	Behavior
Clients	Intents	Performance
Staff	Methods	Opinion
Administration	Resources	

mance. Or, the evaluator may select some of the elements under each heading. In our initial example, in which we have only sixty days to conduct a program evaluation, we might choose to interview *staff* (a population element) concerning their *opinions* of *clients' perfor-mance* after a certain intervention (environment element).

We might also choose to survey clients from a particular pro-gram about their opinions of staff performance (were they satisfied with the services they received?). We could ask clients if they were satisfied with the program objectives or the resources available to the program. We might examine clients' outcomes (performance) as a result of receiving a specific intervention. The strength of the Ham-mond Model is that it suggests a variety of elements for evaluators to consider in planning an evaluation.

The Judicial Model

Another evaluation model has been described by Wolf (1975), Levine et al. (1978), Smith (1985), and others. The Judicial or Adversa-rial Model relies upon testimony and a judge or jury to weigh the evi-dence. Being a litigious society, we understand the judicial process. We derive a certain amount of satisfaction from being able to present our best arguments and evidence as to why a program is "good" and worthy of being continued. (Where there is no natural adversary to argue against a program, staff can be given the assignment to serve as the adversary.)

Several strengths are associated with the use of a Judicial Model. The jury or hearing panel can be formed with experts, consumers of services, board members, representatives from the funding source, ordinary citizens, or some combination of these. If, in the presenta-tion of data, a particular point is not understood, the hearing officer or the jury panel can request additional information and clarification on the spot. Perhaps the greatest strength of this approach is that it en-courages a wide variety of perspectives and alternative interpreta-tions of evidence, allowing program administrators to get a better (more balanced) view of their programs.

Wolf (1975) indicates that this approach is dependent upon hav-ing clearly communicated hearing rules and procedures dealing with such items as cross-examination, criteria for determining the admis-sibility of evidence, instructions for the hearing panel, and so forth. While he reports that six months of planning took place before a two-day hearing, I believe this process could be simplified and utilized with much less planning. Many United Ways across the country ap-pear to use a much less formal version of this approach when they have citizen committees make recommendations regarding continued funding for new programs.

Client Satisfaction Approaches

When asked to plan a program evaluation, many students have a tendency to think only of client feedback or client satisfaction surveys. While clients' input should certainly not be denigrated or excluded from a comprehensive program evaluation, client feedback data alone will not necessarily provide information about the worth or benefit of a program. The vast majority of published consumer satisfaction studies show that clients almost invariably report high levels of satisfaction (Royse, 1985).

What constitutes high levels of satisfaction? Lebow (1982) reviewed twenty-six studies examining satisfaction with mental health treatment and found half of the studies reported satisfaction in the range of 80–100 percent. More than three-quarters of the studies had satisfaction rates higher than 70 percent in spite of the surveys being conducted of totally different programs in dissimilar settings and using various counseling approaches and assessment methods. As Lebow (1982) has noted, these high satisfaction rates come from clients who "have little choice of facility, type of treatment, or practitioner" (p. 250).

Positive client evaluations are not proof of a "good" program. In fact, Rocheleau and Mackesey (1980) suggest that a problem may be indicated if a program receives satisfaction rates *less* than 70–75 percent. If only two-thirds of your clients are pleased with your services, then your program may warrant closer inspection.

There can be many reasons why consumer satisfaction studies tend to reveal positive findings. First of all, client feedback instruments are often "homemade," and nothing is known about their reliability or validity. Your program could receive very high marks on an instrument of your making, which could later be found to be lacking reliability or validity. (Remember our discussion of these topics in chapter 5.) Another reason is that persons who are dissatisfied with services tend to drop out early. If you are conducting a study of those who have completed services, you may not be capturing a representational sample of all the clients who came into your agency for assistance.

Third, the methodology for distributing the survey instrument may present some difficulties. Clients may move frequently and not leave forwarding addresses. If a high percentage of clients have low educational levels, they will not be as responsive to mailed questionnaires as those with higher levels of education. Finally, since you can estimate that only about 30 percent will respond to a mailed questionnaire, what do you conclude about the 70 percent who chose not to respond? Did they tend to be satisfied or dissatisfied? The results of a survey with only a 30 percent response rate are virtually meaningless.

On the other hand, clients receiving their consumer satisfaction questionnaires in the social worker's office may be more likely to respond, but these clients may feel that their anonymity is threatened. Clients may also have concerns about receiving future services if they report any dissatisfaction.

There are several reasons for conducting client satisfaction studies: (1) they tend to be relatively inexpensive; (2) they can be implemented with a minimal amount of prior planning; and (3) they require very little research or statistical expertise (the results tend to be obvious). Sometimes because of time constraints, cost, or inadequate planning for other types of program evaluation, a client satisfaction approach is the only type of program evaluation that can be implemented. Here are a few recommendations for getting data:

1. Use a scale that has good reliability and has been used successfully in other studies. An example of this would be the Client Satisfaction Questionnaire developed by Larsen and his colleagues (1979). The use of a standard scale will eliminate many of the problems found in hastily designed questionnaires.

2. This instrument should be used to monitor satisfaction over time so that there is a baseline from which to observe departures. If client satisfaction studies are conducted regularly and routinely, then data can be compared periodically with results from prior efforts. One way to get data regularly that is not as biased as mailing to those who completed services is the "ballot box" approach. For one week every quarter, each client coming into the agency is given a brief questionnaire and asked to complete it. (If a significant proportion of the agency's clients are illiterate, procedures have to be developed for those who cannot read.)

3. At least one or two open-ended questions should be employed—given the opportunity, consumers may inform you about problems you didn't suspect and couldn't anticipate (e.g., the receptionist is extremely rude to consumers but not to staff). Ask, "How could our program be improved?" or, "Can you think of any ways the agency's services can be improved?"

Other Models

A good many models have originated from the field of education, for instance, Stufflebeam's CIPP Model. CIPP is an acronym made up of the first letters of Context, Input, Process, and Product. According to Stufflebeam, these represent four types of evaluation. Context evaluation is similar to needs assessment. Input evaluation is a means of identifying and assessing competing plans. Process evaluation assesses and guides the implementation of plans. Product evaluation assesses outcomes (Stufflebeam, 1983). The CIPP Model is seen as presenting a system view and does not so much guide a specific evaluation as provide an outline for ongoing evaluation of a program. The CIPP Model can be used with either a formative evaluation or a **summative evaluation** (where a conclusive statement is rendered regarding the worth of a program).

No discussion about evaluation models would be complete without at least a mention of cost-analytic models. These models are sometimes discussed in terms of benefit-cost analysis, cost-benefit analysis, or cost-effectiveness studies. A number of misconceptions are often associated with them (Roid, 1982). First, cost-benefit analysis and cost-effectiveness studies are not the same thing. Cost-benefit analysis involves estimating the monetary value of benefits. When the benefits are intangible, such as the value stemming from the creation of a new park or recreational area, the findings should be cautiously viewed until the methodology and assumptions can be accepted. For an example of a cost-benefit study of social work services in a hospital emergency room, see Ponto and Berg (1992). Lewis, Johnson, Chen, and Erickson (1992) have described the use of benefit-cost analyses by state vocational rehabilitation agencies.

Cost-effectiveness studies examine the cost of an intervention in terms of the outcomes actually obtained. Perhaps for this reason, I find them more appealing. For example, a cost-effectiveness study might show that implementing an employee assistance program in a factory saves thousands of dollars in reduced absenteeism and medical expenses.

Greene, Lovely, and Ondrich (1993) have examined the cost-effectiveness of community services in a frail elderly population. Winegar, Bistline, and Sheridan (1992) have discussed the cost-effectiveness of implementing a group therapy program in a managed-care setting.

Although much more could be said about cost-analytic models than space allows, social workers should not leave this type of evaluation for economists to do. In my opinion, the profession of social work will be enhanced to the extent to which we can show a skeptical public that costs to society are far greater when social services are inadequately funded than when sufficient funds are provided for prevention and remediation programs.

This chapter has presented an overview aimed at simplifying what can be a complex subject. I have not discussed in any depth the topic of needs assessment (an evaluation conducted to identify the need for the program before a new program is begun) or evaluability assessment (an effort directed toward assessing the feasibility of various evaluation methods that might be used), although both of these can be considered types of evaluation. Nor have I discussed a type of evaluation known as meta-evaluation (which can be thought of as an evaluation of previous evaluations). Meta-evaluations aggregate pertinent research findings across prior studies in order to obtain a better understanding of developments in an area of interest. Gibbs (1989), for instance, constructed an instrument to help practitioners "synthesize" or make practical sense out of multiple evaluations—as when trying to determine what is the most effective treatment when there are numerous competing approaches. Fischer (1990), Videka-Sherman (1990, 1988), Wilner, Freeman, Surber, and Goldstein (1985) also contain informative discussions regarding meta-evaluation.

I have tried to remove some of the complexity associated with program evaluation without limiting the focus to the topics of effort, effectiveness, or efficiency. What should be apparent to you by now is that there is probably an infinite number of approaches available to the program evaluator. The designs presented in this chapter are illustrative of the variety available for your use. You are free to take any one of these or to combine elements from several designs to fit the requirements of an actual situation.

Practical Considerations

When you have finished reading this chapter you will have some ideas about how you might go about conducting a program evaluation. While the conceptualization of the evaluation design may be the most difficult part of a program evaluation, any number of factors can influence the choice of a design, such as political considerations within the agency as well as pragmatic considerations.

All evaluation is inherently threatening. Most of us feel a little uncomfortable when we know we are being evaluated—especially when the evaluator is unknown to us. We are even more threatened when that person is not perceived as being our advocate. Therefore, you need to be sensitive to the feelings of those who may be affected

273

by the findings of your program evaluation. Try not to create anxiety within the staff. Communicate frequently with involved personnel about what will be happening. Avoid surprises. If at all possible, involve staff in the planning of the evaluation. Remember that evaluations take place within an agency's political arena. Someone may have a vested interest in making one program look good at the expense of another program. Some managers may hope to use the program evaluation to justify firing staff or to justify past expenditures.

Second, obstacles to program evaluation may arise from unexpected quarters. Staff members may have strongly held opinions that what they do is too complex or too intangible to measure. Or, they may feel that any problems they have could be eliminated if only the program had a larger budget. Other professionals who make referrals to a program may not be completely candid if asked to evaluate a program. They may feel that criticism will jeopardize acceptance of future referrals or that the program could be cut out altogether—a serious problem if there are no other similar services for their clients. Additional issues and obstacles to conducting program evaluation are addressed in Palumbo (1987).

Third, develop a contract with the organization you are doing the evaluation for (even if you are a staff member there) that clearly sets down their expectations about the evaluation. This agreement should cover such items as:

1. The *purpose* of the evaluation (alternatively, list questions to be answered or hypotheses to be tested).
2. The *audience* for whom you will be writing the evaluation report. (Will this report go only to the program director, the whole staff, the board of directors, the agency administrator? Will it be made available to the public?)
3. The *amount of time* you have to conduct the evaluation. (When is the final report expected?)
4. The terms of your *reimbursement* or statement regarding your release from other duties in order to allow you to conduct the evaluation. Also, specify any funds that you may require for the conduct of the evaluation (e.g., postage, or the purchase of standardized instruments or computer processing).

Program evaluations often require a lot of negotiation, and you should feel free to negotiate any areas that may present a problem. For instance, will you be free to utilize the evaluation design of your choosing? Is a certain methodology specified by the agency? To what extent will you have (or do you need) cooperation of the staff? Who will "own" the data, and can it be used for publication? Finally, don't take on too much at one time. When you conduct your first program evaluation, don't attempt to evaluate a comprehensive service delivery agency—start with one program.

Reading Program Evaluation Reports

Even if you don't think you will ever be interested in conducting a program evaluation, at some point in your social work career you will come across a program evaluation report. It may be an evaluation of your program that has been conducted by some "outsider" or consultant. You may be asked to read an evaluation of a program in order to determine if that program should be adopted by your agency. As a board member, administrator, or policymaker, you may attend a program evaluation presentation so that decisions can be made about whether a program should be continued, curtailed, or expanded. Some evaluations will be poorly done and have little merit; others will be thoughtfully conceptualized and well executed, providing substantive evaluative information for decisionmaking. What are some of the criteria to help you distinguish the better from the poorer evaluations?

Blythe (1983), in analyzing outcome evaluations of child abuse treatment programs, found that these studies tended to have problems in several areas. We can draw from her findings to discuss elements that are essential to good evaluation reports. Whether you are reading an evaluation report or preparing one yourself, the report should contain enough information on the topics listed below so that others can fully comprehend what was done and to whom.

1. *Target populations*. The population should be clearly described. Even if all the sample cases involve child abuse, it is important to know such details as whether the perpetrators were first offenders or repeat offenders, if the abuse was physical or sexual, and the severity of the abuse. Is the intervention group homogeneous with regard to these traits? It is conceivable that an intervention designed for parents who had abused their children could have worked differently with a sample of college graduates, persons on welfare, or persons who were severely abused themselves as children. How was the sample selected? Was random sampling used? Before you compare the results from your intervention with results from another intervention program, you need to know if the populations are similar. To what extent do the clients in the intervention group resemble those with whom you are familiar?

2. *Evaluation design*. Random assignment to a control or intervention group is a very strong evaluation design. If no control group is used, how do

you know that the intervention was responsible for the changes in clients' behavior? (Remember the discussion of threats to internal validity in chapter 4). It is also important to look at the posttest or follow-up data. Ideally, evaluators should allow enough time to pass after intervention for problem behavior to recur. Two or three weeks after an intervention for child abuse is an inadequate period of time to allow for a follow-up if one wants to conclude that the intervention is instrumental in reducing child abuse. Six, nine, or even better, twelve months after the intervention is a more creditable length of time. (Guidance on the choice of the time frame should follow from the review of the literature.)

3. *Measurement of variables.* When reading an evaluation of an intervention, we must fully understand what was provided in the treatment. Did the treatment result from interventions described in the literature, or was it totally new—a locally designed intervention? The evaluation report should give the length, duration, and frequency of interventive sessions. It should describe the staff (e.g., their professional training) and tell whether the same staff provided all the treatment or if some responsibilities were shared (e.g., with volunteers). Enough detail to permit replication should be provided.

More credibility will be given to those studies that use scales for which there is information about reliability and validity. If an instrument has no reliability, then even "conclusive" or "definitive" differences between the control and intervention groups should be viewed with skepticism.

When you study social problems such as child abuse, official reports of abuse and behavioral measures may be the preferred dependent variable, instead of "change of attitude" or "increase of knowledge about parenting." As a rule, dependent variables should be clearly defined, objective, and verifiable. Do not rely upon abusive parents to inform you of the number of incidents of emotional or physical child abuse in their home during past six months. They may fail to remember or have an unequivocal interest in minimizing the incidents, and the number of incidents is not easily verified. While there is no rule requiring more than one dependent variable, two or more nonredundant estimates of a treatment's effectiveness provide greater confidence in the results (LeCroy, 1985).

4. *Results and interpretation of the data.* Do the authors present their data so that it can be understood? Are there analyses involving the dependent variable(s)? Are all of the hypotheses or research questions addressed? Is there baseline data? Are the sample sizes adequate? Do the authors attempt to overgeneralize? Can the results be generalized across time, geography, and environment? Are differences between groups statistically significant? Are limitations of the evaluation discussed? Finally, based upon the presented data, would any intelligent, rational person come to the same conclusions as the author of the evaluation report?

Students who are preparing to evaluate a program or who need to critique the report of an evaluation may also want to read Thyer's (1991) guidelines for outcome studies in social work practice.

Final Comments

How important is it for social workers to know about program evaluation? Miller and Hester (1986) informally polled two dozen local alcoholism treatment programs about their cost and effectiveness. Slightly fewer than half of the programs were able to quote percentages of treatment success. Upon further inquiry, none of these programs were able to provide data to substantiate their claims of success. When you make referrals to treatment programs, aren't you interested in how successful their interventions are? Don't clients have a right to know this information?

While sometimes we perform program evaluations because they are mandated, the best reason for conducting them is to demonstrate that we are helping our clients. How do we know that we aren't in fact hurting them? How do we improve our programs without some kind of evaluative feedback?

The editors-in-chief of *Social Work* and *Social Work Research and Abstracts* have contributed another reason why social workers should engage in program evaluation.

> When social work fails to use research effectively, other professionals gain more public credibility in what we have considered "our" traditional areas (such as psychologists' and nurses' work in the area of child abuse). These professionals are able to show funding agencies evaluative research that demonstrates the effectiveness of their interventions. (Hopps and Gambrill, 1988, p. 387)

Given the increasing research prowess of other human service professionals, social workers cannot shy away from those areas where research is required. We cannot continue to rely upon others to demonstrate that our clients benefit from our services.

Questions for Class Discussion

1. The following could be called "Exemplars of Poor Evaluation Designs." What is wrong with each of the following plans for evaluating programs?
   a. The agency is a halfway house run by the Department of Corrections. Residents are all young men (under thirty) who have been in prison for the first time and are now on parole in a prerelease program. In this program evaluation, three new residents who have outward signs of depression will be selected and compared with two other residents who are not depressed. The Zung Self-Rating Depression Inventory will

be the instrument used to determine if a caring attitude by the program staff and conjugal visits can help with adjustment from prison to the larger community. A pretest-posttest design will be employed.

b. A school is planning to develop a latchkey program for students in kindergarten through the sixth grade. This program will be open to parents who can pay $45 per week per child for enrollment. A quasi-experimental design (nonequivalent control group) will be used to compare students enrolled in the latchkey program with students not enrolled in the program but whom teachers suspect are in need of a latchkey program. Comparisons between the two groups of students will be made at the beginning and end of the school year in terms of their academic achievement levels and the number of incidents with the police.

c. A special intensive services unit was devised by a social service agency for families who had been referred because of child abuse. With this demonstration program, each social worker had no more than five families at a time. Each worker in this program selected the families to be initially involved with intensive services. After the first wave of families completed the intervention, random assignment of additional families was then employed. The control group consisted of families who were also referred for child abuse but who received only a regular caseworker. Each family received intensive services for no more than eight weeks. Fourteen months after the opening of each case a graduate assistant called the family to learn if the victim of the abuse was still in the home. It is hypothesized that those families that received the intensive services will have a higher proportion of children still in the home.

d. After phone calls were made to the families described in number 3 above, it was found that only twenty-four of the thirty families that were served by the intensive services staff could be located by phone. However, three-quarters of these families still had their children at home with them. In contrast thirty-five of the fifty families in the control group could be located by phone, but only 66 percent of these families retained their children. Can the graduate assistant conclude that the program is a success because 75 percent of the families receiving intensive services retained their children compared with 66 percent of those families that received regular casework services?

2. What is wrong with the following objectives? How could they be reworded to make them better?
   a. Maintain and improve community forensic services.
   b. Expand the hospital volunteer services program.
   c. Develop needed community residential facilities.
   d. Provide psychiatric services to inmates of the county jail.
   e. Increase the openness in communications between adolescents and their parents.
3. A social work student working in her practicum was asked to evaluate a program designed to prevent adolescent pregnancies among high school students. The developers of the program had four expectations for the students participating in the ten-week education program: (a) students will become more knowledgeable about reproduction; (b) students will become more knowledgeable about contraception; (c) parent/adolescent communications about sexuality will become less strained and more open; (d) there will be fewer pregnancies among females who complete the program than among those who were not able to participate because of the scheduling of required classes. Which of these expectations will be the easiest to measure? What would be the best evidence for success of this program?
4. Look back at table 10.1. What additional information would you need in order to determine whether any of those three programs were "good," effective, or efficient?
5. What political and pragmatic considerations could influence program evaluations to be conducted in the social service agencies with which you are familiar?

Mini-Projects for Experiencing Research Firsthand

1. Locate an example of client utilization data from a social service agency. (Sometimes this information is printed in annual reports.) Examine this data to see if you can determine what groups the agency is primarily serving. Then, obtain census data for the same geographic region. Compare rates of key variables. For instance, if the percentage of older adults in the larger population is 10 percent, what percentage of older adults is the agency serving? How do the rates of minorities in the community and those being served compare? What other comparisons would be important to make?
2. Design a program evaluation to demonstrate that the Reasonably Healthy Minds Agency runs a "good" outpatient counseling program for families with children. Address the following:

   a. What questions do you want to investigate?

   b. Define your dependent and independent variables.

   c. Which design or methodological approach will you use?

   d. How will you collect your data?

   e. How will you analyze your data?

   f. What limitations will your study have?

3. Think of a social service program. Briefly describe it. How would you go about showing that this program ultimately had a favorable impact within the community? Could you design a program evaluation to show taxpayers that the program saved more money than it cost to operate it? Describe the approach you would use.

4. Choose a human service program with which you are familiar, and then do the following:

   a. Briefly describe it.

   b. Write at least one program goal.

   c. Write three specific program objectives.

Resources and References

Austin, M. and Associates. (1982). *Evaluating Your Agency's Programs.* Beverly Hills, CA: Sage.

Blythe, B.J. (1983). A critique of outcome evaluation in child abuse treatment. *Child Welfare*, 62(4), 325–335.

Carter, R.K. (1983). *The Accountable Agency.* Beverly Hills, CA: Sage.

Decker, J.T., Starrett, R., and Redhorse, J. (1986). Evaluating the cost-effectiveness of employee assistance programs. *Social Work*, 31(5), 391–393.

Dush, D.M., and Cassileth, B.R. (1985). Program evaluation in terminal care. *Hospice Journal*, 1(1), 55–72.

Fischer, J. (1990). Problems and issues in meta-analysis. In Lynn Videka-Sherman and William J. Reid (Eds.). *Advances in Clinical Social Work Research.* Silver Spring, MD: NASW Press.

Fitz-Gibbon, C.T. and Morris, L.L. (1987). *How to Design a Program Evaluation.* Beverly Hills, CA: Sage.

Gibbs, L.E. (1989). Quality of study rating form: An instrument for synthesizing evaluation studies. *Journal of Social Work Education*, 25(1), 55–67.

Greene, V.L., Lovely, M.E., and Ondrich, J.I. (1993). The cost-effectiveness of community services in a frail elderly population. *The Gerontologist*, 33(2): 177–189.

Hammond, R.L. (1975). Establishing priorities for information and design specifications for evaluating community education programs. *Community Education Journal*, March/April, 1975.

Hogarty, G.E. (1989). Meta-analysis of the effects of practice with the chronically mentally ill: A critique and reappraisal of the literature. *Social Work*, 34(4), 363–373.

Hopps, J.G. and Gambrill, E. (1988). Who's Losing? *Social Work*, 33(5), 387–388.

Hornick, J.P. and Burrows, B. (1988). Program evaluation. In R. M. Grinnell, Jr. (Ed.), *Social Work Research and Evaluation*. Itasca, IL: Peacock.

Kushler, M.G. and Davidson, W.S. (1979). Using experimental designs to evaluate social programs. *Social Work Research and Abstracts*, 15(1), 27–32.

Larsen, D.L., Attkisson, C.C., Hargreaves, W.A., and Nguyen, T.D. (1979). Assessment of client/patient satisfaction: development of a general scale. *Evaluation and Program Planning*, 2, 197–207.

Lebow, J. (1982). Consumer satisfaction with mental health treatment. *Psychological Bulletin*, 91(2), 244–259.

LeCroy, C.W. (1985). Methodological issues in the evaluation of social work practice. *Social Service Review*, 59(3), 345–357.

Levin, H.M. (1983). *Cost-effectiveness: A Primer*. Beverly Hills, CA: Sage.

Levine, M., Brown, E., Fitzgerald, C., Goplerud, E., Gordon, M.E., Jayne-Lazarus, C., Rosenberg, N., and Slater, J. (1978). Adapting the jury trial for program evaluation: A report of an experience. *Evaluation and Program Planning*, 1, 177–186.

Lewis, D.R., Johnson, D.R., Chen, and Erickson, R.N. (1992). The use and reporting of benefit-cost analyses by state vocational rehabilitation agencies. *Evaluation Review*, 16(3), 266–287.

Lewis, J.A. and Lewis, M.D. (1983). *Management of Human Service Programs*. Monterey, CA: Brooks/Cole.

Lipsey, M.W. (1988). Practice and malpractice in evaluation research. *Evaluation Practice*, 9(4), 5–24.

McMahon, P.M. (1987). Shifts in intervention procedures: A problem in evaluating human service interventions. *Social Work Research and Abstracts*, 23(4), 13–16.

Miller, W.R. and Hestor, R.K. (1986). Inpatient alcoholism treatment: Who benefits? *American Psychologist*, 41(7), 794–805.

Morris, M. and Cohn, R. (1993). Program evaluators and ethical challenges. *Evaluation Review*, 17(6), 621–642.

Nurius, P.S. (1984). Utility of data synthesis for social work. *Social Work Research and Abstracts*, 20(3), 23–32.

Palumbo, D.J. (1987). *The Politics of Program Evaluation*. Beverly Hills, CA: Sage.

Patton, M.Q. (1990). *Qualitative Evaluation and Research Methods*. Newbury Park, CA: Sage.

Ponto, J.M. and Berg, W. (1992). Social work services in the emergency department: A cost-benefit analysis of an extended coverage program. *Health in Social Work*, 17(1): 66–73.

Posavac, E.J. and Carey, R.G. (1985). *Program Evaluation: Methods and Case Studies*. Englewood Cliffs, NJ: Prentice-Hall.

Provus, M. (1971). *Discrepancy Evaluation for Educational Program Improvement and Assessment*. Berkeley, CA: McCutchan.

Roberts, A.R. (1988). A strategy for making decisions and evaluating alternative juvenile offender treatment programs. *Evaluation and Program Planning*, 11, 115–122.

Roberts, A.R. (1988). Wilderness programs for juvenile offenders: A challenging alternative. *Juvenile and Family Court Journal*, 39(1), 1–12.

Rocheleau, B. and Mackesey, T. (1980). What, consumer feedback surveys again? *Evaluation and the Health Professions*, 3(4), 405–419.

Roid, G.H. (1982). Cost-effectiveness analysis in mental health policy research. *American Psychologist*, 37(1), 94–95.

Rossi, P.H. and Freeman, H.E. (1985). *Evaluation: A Systematic Approach*. Beverly Hills, CA: Sage.

Royse, D. (1985). Client satisfaction with the helping process: A review for the pastoral counselor. *Journal of Pastoral Care*, 39(1), 3–11.

Rubin, A. (1985). Practice effectiveness: More grounds for optimism. *Social Work*, 30(6), 469–476.

Schuerman, J.R. (1983). *Research and Evaluation in the Human Services*. New York: Free Press.

Smith. N. (1985). Adversary and committee hearings as evaluation methods. *Evaluation Review*, 9(6), 735–750.

Stufflebeam, D. (1983). In George F. Madaus, Michael S. Scriven, and Daniel L. Stufflebeam (Eds.), *Evaluation Models: Viewpoints on Educational and Human Services Evaluation*. Boston: Kluwer-Nijhoff.

Thyer, B. (1991). Guidelines for evaluating outcome studies on social work practice. *Research on Social Work Practice*, 1(1), 76–91.

Tripodi, T. (1987). Program evaluation. In Sumner M. Rosen, David Fanshel and Marey E. Lutz, (Eds.), *Encyclopedia of Social Work*. Silver Spring, MD: National Association of Social Workers.

Videka-Sherman, L. (1988). Meta-analysis of research on social work practice in mental health. *Social Work*, 33(4), 325–338.

Videka-Sherman, L. (1990). Meta-analysis: A user's perspective. In Lynn Videka-Sherman and William J. Reid (Eds.). *Advances in Clinical Social Work Research*. Silver Spring, MD: NASW Press.

Wilner, D.M., Freeman, H.E., Surber, M., and Goldstein, M.S. (1985). Success in mental health treatment interventions: A review of 211 random assignment studies. *Journal of Social Service Review*, 8(4), 1–21.

Winegar, N., Bistline, J.L., and Sheridan, S. (1992). Implementing a group therapy program in a managed-care setting: Combining cost-effectiveness and quality care. *Families in Society*, 73(1): 56–58.

Wolf, R.L. (1975). Trial by jury: A new evaluation method. *Phi Delta Kappan*, 57, 185–187.

11
Qualitative Research

Have you ever wondered what it would be like to be an older adult? Do you know what it feels like to be eighty-five years old and frail? If you were eighty-five, do you think people would look out for you, or would they tend to ignore and overlook you? What is it like to reside in a nursing home or a mental hospital? What is it like to have to use food stamps or to be physically handicapped? How do you think drug addicts and prostitutes experience the world? These questions illustrate the kinds of topics that cannot be measured with standardized instruments and scales and for which randomization, sample sizes, and control groups are not relevant. Such questions as these beg to be investigated by qualitative research methods.

Qualitative researchers seek to understand lifestyles and social phenomena firsthand. They try to describe subgroups or cultures (e.g., the world of drug addicts, the chronically mentally ill, illegal immigrants) from the point of view of the persons being studied. A goal of understanding is emphasized rather than prediction regarding some dependent variable.

Social workers often discover that their clients use special terms and vocabularies different from their own. A fine example of this has been provided by Rosenstiel (1980) in his study of black heroin addicts. He discovered that "punks" are men who do not defend themselves and who are used sexually by other men (in institutional settings) with the consequence that they are not respected and have a low status. According to Rosenstiel, one informant was a punk who, in nine months of group and personal therapy, never discussed this problem. While most of his fellow addicts knew of his status, none of the staff at a residential treatment center knew. The informant was "promoted to a therapy group leader, but was powerless in his group. No one from the streets listens to a 'punk' " (p. 230). It is important to understand the language and values of these clients in order to be effective as an agent of change.

Qualitative approaches provide detail and add richness and depth to our understanding of any phenomenon being investigated and are similar to the "case studies" so familiar to social workers. Let's take the question "What is it like to live in a nursing home?" Using a quantitative approach, we would begin by identifying some problem or by stating a testable hypothesis, for example, "The majority of nursing home residents would rather live somewhere else," or, "Nursing home residents are more lonely or depressed than older adults who do not live in nursing homes." Even if we surveyed a large sample of older adults and gathered sufficient data, we still would have only a limited perspective on what life is like in a nursing home; the quality of the day-to-day life in the home would escape us.

In contrast, a qualitative research approach to this problem might involve an investigator living in the nursing home in order to talk informally with the residents, to observe what happens in their social world, and to experience the kinds of interactions that they have with staff and with each other.

A story told to me by a former student provides an illustration of how one incident can tell much about the quality of life in a particular nursing home. In talking with a resident about what it was like living in the home, the student heard the following account: One day, several residents were in the back wing of the building watching television when two fellows, who didn't look like they belonged there, appeared. They announced that they were television repairmen and proceeded to cart away the television, which had been working perfectly. Being somewhat suspicious, one resident slipped away to her room and pressed her call button, which rang at the nurses' station. Meanwhile, the men loaded the television into a truck and left. Twenty minutes later, one of the staff strolled back to the resident's room to see why the call button had been used.

This incident raises several questions. First, why did it take the staff so long to answer the call button? What would have happened if there had been a true emergency, such as a nursing home resident choking on a piece of food or falling out of bed? How good is the security in the facility—do residents fear that they will be robbed or their personal possessions stolen? If we were to informally interview other residents from this nursing home, we might find other equally alarming accounts. Such accounts provide a richer image of the quality of life in the nursing home than any objective scale that quantitatively measures such dimensions as the residents' satisfaction with life, or their loneliness and depression.

Qualitative research is different from the type of research that has been discussed so far. In quantitative research, the investigator relies on counting, measuring, and analyzing numbers. In qualitative research, there is little or no use made of statistics. While counting may be employed, it is not the major emphasis. The qualitative researcher seeks to understand social relationships and patterns of interaction. Anecdotal accounts are used to describe the world of the persons being investigated.

Qualitative researchers are flexible; their research goals or questions may be altered even while data are being collected. While they usually have a methodology in mind prior to starting their project, they do not require that the research design and methodology be rigidly and unalterably stated before they begin to collect data. There is nothing "wrong" with this fluidity, since many researchers feel that the purpose of qualitative research is to generate hypotheses for later testing. In this sense, qualitative research is commonly regarded as being exploratory.

For instance, Olson and Haynes (1993) set out to discover how successful single parents raised their children. Their data came from an exploratory study of twenty-six parents who were obtained by contacting psychologists, clergy, educators, and medical personnel who nominated individuals with positive attitudes toward their parental role and who also appeared competent in that role. From fifty nominations, twenty-six having the most traits associated with healthy families were personally interviewed for approximately two hours each. The transcripts from these interviews were read by the researchers and themes were identified. From these interviews seven themes emerged, such as: acceptance of the responsibility and challenges of being a single parent, prioritization of the parental role, and employment of consistent, nonpunitive discipline that provided structure and logical consequences for behaviors.

Among social scientists, cultural anthropologists are best known for their use of qualitative research methods. Sometimes these approaches are known as **ethnography** (folk description). One prominent ethnographer describes ethnography as follows: "Such work requires an intensive personal involvement, an abandonment of traditional scientific control, an improvisational style to meet situations not of the researcher's making, and an ability to learn from a long series of mistakes" (Agar, 1986, p. 12).

To what extent do subcultures exist all around the culture that we know best? Students may find such ethnographies as those about stealing, Crowell, Olson, and Avary (1990); hookers, Prus and Irini (1988); soup kitchen patrons, Glasser (1988); and illegal immigrants, Conover (1987) very interesting reading.

Methods of Qualitative Research

Qualitative research (also known as field research) uses procedures that produce descriptive data: personal observations and people's spoken or written words. Qualitative research allows investigators to know their subjects personally and to understand their struggles and explanations of their world (Bogdan and Taylor, 1975). It involves participant observation and in-depth interviewing, although analysis of personal documents (such as letters and diaries) is also done.

Participant observation involves immersion in the world of those being investigated. If you are investigating a nursing home, this may require that you live in the home where you are awakened from a sound sleep at 6:30 A.M. so that vital signs can be checked, where you experience the frustration of being ignored by staff, and where twenty-four hours a day you are surrounded with the same sights, sounds, and smells. Eating a meal there once or twice may not be quite the same as eating all of your meals there for an extended period. (Some qualitative researchers feel that at least one year in residence is required in order to fully understand another culture.)

As a participant observer, you experience the world of those who are being observed by living alongside them and sharing their activities. You do what your subjects do (without violating personal or professional ethics, of course).

There are several ways to approach participant observation. You could stress the observer role and place less emphasis on the participant role. For instance, you could go directly to your subjects or to your informant and begin interviewing. Steffensmeier (1986) uses this approach to learn about the world of the fence (a dealer in stolen goods). Steffensmeier was a participant only in the sense that he interviewed, at some length, a fence and observed the fence at work. He did not fence goods himself. He also interviewed thieves, the fence's customers and friends, other fences, and the police. One's degree of involvement as participant or observer depends on the nature of the subjects being studied.

Another approach is to become an active participant in addition to being an observer. Because Estroff (1981) felt it essential to establish her position in the polarized staff-client social system, she informed long-term psychiatric patients in a community treatment program that she was not staff. She says that she did not masquerade as a client, but she admits to looking too much like a staff member on the first day, and subsequently she dressed more inconspicuously. Estroff's approach was to participate as if she were a client. She attended recreational and treatment-related activities, visited clients in their apartments, sought out clients in the street, ate at a lunch counter frequented by clients, sometimes took clients shopping or went bar hopping with them, and so forth. In order to more fully understand the everyday world of the psychiatric patient, Estroff even took a potent antipsychotic medication (Prolixin) for six weeks.

Participant observation can also involve a greater level of masquerade. For example, the book *Disguised* (1985) describes the experiences of a young woman who masquerades as an eighty-five-year-old. It took her up to four hours to apply special latex foam make-up to give her face the folds and wrinkles of an elderly woman. There are numerous examples, some occurring over forty years ago, of investigators using disguised observation in order to learn firsthand about life in institutions. (See, for example, Caudill, Redlich, Gilmore, and Brody, 1952; Deane, 1961; Ishiyama, Batman, and Hewitt, 1967; Goldman, Bohr, and Steinberg, 1970; Rosenhan, 1973.)

Participant observers make use of notes (often called "field notes") to help recall important events, conversations, and persons. Field notes are brief condensations of conversations or observations that are developed later when the investigator is away from the field. Unlike those investigators who are more interested in quantification, qualitative researchers record feelings and interpretations in these field notes.

Sometimes when a criminal subgroup (e.g., drug dealers, prostitutes, gang members) is being studied, the investigator may need to acquire a special vocabulary used by the group. Qualitative researchers ask questions that allow the subjects to talk about themselves and their world so that special experiences, ways of viewing the world, or vocabulary can be learned. In qualitative research, few questions are developed ahead of time. The majority of questions flow from the investigator's interactions with subjects and his or her desire to understand various aspects of their world.

Steps in Doing Qualitative Research

The first step in qualitative research is identifying a topic (or group of people) of interest. Generally, you will have an initial question or set of questions about the topic or group that you want answered.

Let's say that you are interested in poverty and how impoverished people survive and cope under adverse conditions. Since poverty is a broad topic, you may want to narrow the focus and concentrate on impoverished families in Appalachian coal-mining communities or on impoverished tenant farmers in the southern part of the United States.

Generally, it is a good idea to become familiar with any literature relevant to your topic. However, with qualitative research, there is no requirement that the literature review come before data collection. Bogdan and Taylor (1975) have written, "After and perhaps during the intensive observation stage of the research, the observer consults the professional literature" (p. 84). These researchers seem to feel that the purpose of the literature review is to enable the investigator to look for unanswered questions that the present study might address and to compare findings. Agar (1980) sees literature review as "clouding" the researcher's mind with misconceptions and the mistakes of others. Early in his career he found that a thorough literature review "introduced a lot of unnecessary noise into my mind as I tried to learn about being a heroin addict from 'patients' in the institution" (p. 25).

The argument for diminishing the importance of the literature review is based on the belief that the ethnographer's role is "to give some sense of different lifestyles to people who either do not know about them, or who are so bogged down in their own stereotypes that they do not understand them" (Agar, 1980, 26–27). Agar recommends that the investigator become familiar with the topic by talking with people who have worked with the group of interest, by reading novels that produce a "feel" for the lifestyle of the group, and by viewing existing literature with a skeptic's eye.

The third step in conducting qualitative research requires locating one or more informants. These are the insiders or group members who are "native speakers" and teachers for the investigator (Spradley, 1979). Informants are the "insider" experts on the culture or group who relay their information to the researcher (who can be thought of as a student or apprentice). They are willing to share their everyday experiences and serve as translators—helping the ethnographer acquire the necessary vocabulary to maneuver within the culture.

Once informants have been located and rapport established, the qualitative researcher begins to interview them. Interviews may involve predetermined questions or no prior planning. Whyte (1984) and perhaps a majority of qualitative researchers tend to make greater use of the "nondirective" interview. These informal interviews occur in the workplace, in homes, on the street, or wherever the respondents may be. Because the qualitative researcher is a learner, he or she does a lot of listening and spends time establishing rapport. Ethnographers tend to develop long-term relationships; over time, they are able to see the various sides of their respondents as revealed in various situations.

It is much easier to stress the importance of establishing rapport than it is to actually accomplish good rapport. Every culture or subculture is different. Rapport can be difficult to establish if the researcher is insensitive to local practices and patterns of communication. For instance, Thompson (1989), in writing about her experiences in Islamic countries, noted that indirect methods of communication and action are socially preferable to direct methods.

> If a person wants to raise an issue with another, he or she will visit the other, have tea, talk a great deal about generalities, and only at the end of the visit mention his or her real purpose in an offhanded way. . . . They couch negative responses in carefully selected terms so as not to offend or disappoint others. (P. 40)

The way one would go about building rapport with an informant in an Islamic country is very different from the approach one would use on the streets of New York.

Questions about the culture or subgroup arise from observation of informants in different situations as they engage in various activities as well as from the need to confirm or consolidate newly acquired knowledge. Agar (1980) expressed his interest in predetermined questions this way:

> It's not necessarily that ethnographers don't want to test hypotheses. It's just that if they do, the variables and operationalizations and sample specifications must grow from an understanding of the group rather than from being hammered on top of it no matter how poor the fit. (Pp. 69–70)

Recording the data is the next step. When you record (whether on the site or later, when you are at home) and how you record (tape-recorder or written notes) are up to you. Even with guarantees of anonymity, respondents often will not talk freely in the presence of a tape recorder or other such devices. While informants may not be as threatened by note-taking, this will depend upon what they are saying and where they are at the time. In addition to interesting incidents, record the setting, the participants involved, and key words in conversations (if you are unable to record conversations verbatim). It is not crucial to have a perfect reproduction of what was said. Approximate wording and paraphrasing are acceptable. However, it is important to capture the meaning of any remarks. If you make sketchy notes in the field, expand them as soon afterwards as possible so that the details of important observations and incidents are not forgotten.

The last step in qualitative research is analyzing the data and writing a report. As with quantitative methods, the investigator is looking for patterns. In order to find these patterns, transcriptions of interviews may be sorted or catalogued. Computer software exists to assist the researcher in finding selected key words from pages of text (Uriarte-Gaston, 1987). Gilgun and Connor (1989), in studying how perpetrators view child sexual abuse, analyzed life history interviews of fourteen male perpetrators using the computer program *Ethnograph.*

Lofland and Lofland (1984) suggest that at least half of the final report should be devoted to accounts of incidents, events, exchanges, remarks, conversations, actions, and so forth. From this data, the investigator should discuss commonly held meanings and norms of behavior in that setting and implications of the findings. From insights garnered, field investigators are then in a position to make recommendations about how social workers can better direct their efforts to the special population that was observed.

Qualitative researchers sometimes employ standardized scales or instruments; they may sample from available respondents or attempt in other ways to provide some confirmation that their findings are reliable. Agar (1980) discusses the use of a small survey as well as simulated and hypothetical situations to confirm his understanding of the heroin addict's world. He feels that the qualitative researcher's findings have good reliability because "something learned in a conversation becomes a hypothesis to check in further conversations or observations" (p. 171). In this way, the meaning of a new term or the significance of some observation can be verified on various occasions and with different respondents within the same culture.

Qualitative researchers seek to establish reliability in other ways. Sometimes they have those who were being studied read the report in order to ferret out inaccuracies or misrepresentations. Information can also be confirmed through public records or by officials (police and legal officials read and commented on parts of Steffensmeier's manuscript).

How strong are the findings produced by qualitative research? To paraphrase Van Maanen (1983), the strength of qualitative research derives from its reliance upon multiple sources of data—it is not committed to one source alone. Babbie (1986) refers to the "superior validity" of field research as compared with surveys and experiments. This stems from the qualitative researcher "being there" and, as a result of those experiences, being able to furnish detailed and extensive illustrations of the phenomenon being studied. This contrasts markedly with the more objective social survey approach of learning about something by asking a series of prepared (sometimes abstract and hypothetical) questions in a standard Likert-type format.

The Great Debate

Because of the enormous differences in the way that the research is conducted, quantitatively minded researchers are often suspicious of the findings of qualitative researchers. In the 1950s and 1960s, a debate began in professional journals regarding the relative virtues of quantitative and qualitative methodology (Bryman, 1984). A continuation of this debate over appropriate research methods for social work has vigorously reappeared in recent social work journals. Peile (1988) has provided a brief overview of some of the major protagonists and their arguments. The debate appears to have surfaced once again because social work researchers are making greater use of the quantitative, empirical, scientific (sometimes known as the logical positivist) approach. Advocates for the use of quantitative methods believe that qualitative methods will not produce the knowledge needed to document effectiveness and to guide practice.

On the other hand, those who advocate for greater use of qualitative approaches argue that the trend toward empiricism results in research that is too restrictive and superficial, because of the tendency to investigate only those aspects that can be operationally defined and measured and for which data can be collected. Instead of looking at the whole situation, empiricists fragment a situation and focus on what they can easily count. In the empiricists' quest for "objectivity," important interactions between participants or other details are often overlooked.

Which viewpoint is right? What is the most appropriate research method for social work? Actually, both sides are right. There are limitations associated with both quantitative and qualitative approaches to learning about a phenomenon. As researchers-in-training, you should learn how to use both approaches. Both methodologies can be used profitably by social workers in their practice. Each approach can be used to enrich the findings of the other.

Madey (1982) has addressed the benefits of integrating qualitative and quantitative methods in program evaluation. Some of the ways each approach enriches the other are as follows: Qualitative approaches can assist with the selection of survey items to be used in instrument construction. They can provide external validation of empirically generated constructs. From the field notes of qualitative researchers come real-life examples that can be used to help illustrate the findings of a quantitative study. Quantitative procedures benefit the qualitative researcher by: identifying representative and unrepresentative (overlooked) informants/cases; providing leads for later interviews and observations; correcting "elite bias" (the tendency to interview primarily the elite or gatekeepers in a social system) in the collection of data; and verifying the findings of a qualitative study by systematically collecting data on a larger scale.

A number of other writers have called for qualitative and quantitative approaches to be used together. Kidder and Judd (1986), for instance, note that participant observation can involve quantitative measures. They cite a qualitative study of parole officers in which the investigator used a quantitative approach to investigate a hypothesis dealing with the amount of paperwork performed by each parole officer. The investigator analyzed the number of copies made by each parole officer on the office's photocopying machine as a quantitative (and unobtrusive) measure of parole violations.

Patton (1990) discusses a methodological mix of both quantitative and qualitative strategies in an effort called "triangulation." The name is a reference to navigation and surveying, which use multiple reference points to locate an exact position. Thus, multiple methods (methodological triangulation) could be used to study a single problem or phenomenon.

Finally, a noted qualitative researcher, William Foote Whyte (1984), said this about the integration of qualitative and quantitative methods:

> Reliance upon a single research method is bound to impede the progress of science. If we use the survey alone, we may gather highly quantitative data measuring the subjective states of respondents, in relation to certain demographic characteristics. . . . Some apparently objective questions may yield answers of doubtful validity. . . . In any case, the survey yields a snapshot of responses at a particular time. We can fill in this dimension partially with a resurvey, but this by itself only provides evidence of the direction and magnitude of change. Without the use of other methods, we can only speculate on the dynamics of change. (P. 149)

Final Thoughts on the Quantitative-Qualitative Controversy

Sometimes it seems easy to divide all the world into two parts. Under such a schema, we may identify those who think like we do and those who are "wrong" or "out of it." For example, you may be sympathetic to the qualitative perspective, while your best friend may recognize only research that uses quantitative procedures. Like disagreements over politics and religion, you may become frustrated if you try to convert your friend to your viewpoint. In my opinion, it is more important to recognize the strengths and advantages that each perspective brings to the understanding of a problem or phenomenon than it is to insist upon the superiority of one approach over another.

The findings of qualitative research can be rich and comprehensive, providing insight into poorly understood behaviors or cultures through the use of accounts of actual dialogue and graphic descriptions. Qualitative research vividly brings out perspectives that may be quite different from those with which we started. Ruckdeschel (1985) noted, "The researcher thus discovers no single, universal truth, but rather, different perspectives that reflect how different groups with different interests view the same situation" (p. 19).

Some will feel attracted to qualitative approaches because of the flexibility in determining research designs (and ease of modifying them once data collection has begun) and data collection techniques. This "freedom" becomes abundantly clear in the following humorous account of graduate student folklore from Agar (1980):

> A graduate student, at the end of her first year, was given a few hundred dollars by the department and told to go and study an Indian group during the summer. Not only had no one told her how to do ethnography; neither had anyone bothered to describe the location of the tribe. With trembling heart and sweaty palms, she approached the door of Kroeber himself [one of the founding fathers of American anthropology] for some advice. After several passes by the open door, she entered and nervously cleared her throat. Kroeber was typing (naturally) and did not look up for a minute or so. When he did, the student explained her dilemma and asked for advice. "Well," said Kroeber, returning to his typing, "I suggest you buy a notebook and pencil." (P. 2)

While this account may or may not be true, it serves to illustrate the point that qualitative researchers do not need extensive planning, nor do they need to be too concerned about instruments, sampling, computers, or statistical procedures. You want to know something about a group that is poorly understood. An informant is found. Questions are asked. More questions are asked. The focus might even shift from the original one. Qualitative research can be relatively inexpensive to do if you choose subjects or a culture close by. But, if you must travel quite a distance and have no means to support yourself in that setting, the research could be quite expensive.

It could be said that a qualitative researcher is always prepared when an interesting topic comes across his or her path. No scrambling to find a control group or representative sample is necessary, and there is no need to spend hours in the library trying to find the most psychometrically sound instrument(s) to measure the dependent variables. Most quantitatively oriented researchers could not begin their work so easily.

One criticism of qualitative research is that the results are not objective—that they reflect the perspective of one investigator whose view is colored by his or her biases. A related problem is that there is potential for biased sampling of respondents and perhaps even a tendency to overgeneralize. However, qualitative researchers are interested in objectivity—if this means that others would be likely to obtain the same results providing that they were able to follow the same procedures with the same group (Kirk and Miller, 1986).

Qualitative approaches can use procedures to minimize the likelihood that findings are the product of a single misguided observer. A large number of informants and a variety of sources can be used to confirm observations. Since researchers devote an extended period of time to observing and studying the group, there are multiple occasions to "check out" new insights. Open-ended questions may be asked in order to understand other points of view without predetermining them through prior selection of questionnaire items. Then, other participant observers can be brought in to verify findings. The qualitative researcher can even use small-group or informal surveys to test hypotheses.

For these and other reasons, I believe that it is short-sighted to dismiss qualitative research or to insist that it is less valuable than quantitative research. The contributions of both the quantitative and qualitative approaches have been highlighted by Madey (1982) in a quote from Willems and Raush (1969):

> The methods are analogous to zooming in and zooming out with a lens. To the extent that they are reproduced objectively, wide-angle, tele-photo, and microscopic views must be simultaneously valid, and zooming from different directions merely focuses attention on different facets of the same phenomenon. . . . There are no grounds, logical or otherwise, for calling any view simple. We can start anywhere and zoom in to infinite detail or zoom out to indefinite scope. (Pp. 82–83).

Both approaches attempt to explain the world around us. There are times when one approach will have an advantage over the other or will provide information that the other cannot. Choosing a qualitative or quantitative approach might be likened to interviewing clients. There are times when social workers ask open-ended questions and times when they need to probe for specific detail and obtain precise responses. Seldom would they find that they could conduct their interventions using just open-ended questions or closed-ended ones.

As social workers, we are trained in the use of ethnographic techniques (although they are not usually presented under that label). We acquire these techniques in the process of becoming social workers, and they remain a part of us. Rompf (1989) made this point in her ethnographic case study of large-scale economic change in a rural community:

> My social work background provided a solid foundation for using ethnographic techniques. I was taught how to be a good listener and a keen observer, especially of nonverbal communication. I learned how to interview people and analyze the dynamics of group work. I was taught how to record interviews and group meetings. I was encouraged to be self-aware, to recognize my biases, and to strive to overcome them. (Pp. 47–48)

Qualitative research methods are valuable tools to use in trying to better understand our clients and the world in which they live.

Irving Yalom unintentionally made this point in his book *Love's Executioner*. A psychiatrist, Yalom scheduled one-year follow-up sessions with his clients after completion of therapy to judge the success of his intervention. Playing back a tape recording made of an initial interview, one of Yalom's clients made a humorous remark indicating his progress since that time. Yalom notes:

> Having heard the same reaction from many patients, I have come to regard it as a valid marker of change. Marvin, in effect, was saying, "I'm a different person now. I hardly recognize that Marvin of a year ago. Those things I used to do—refusing to look at my life; trying to control or intimidate others; trying to impress others with my intelligence, my charts, my thoroughness—they're gone. I don't do that any more."

Yalom then remarks:

> These are no minor adjustments: they represent basic modifications in personhood. Yet they are so subtle in character that they generally elude most research outcome questionnaires. (P. 269)

Many, perhaps most, topics can be explored either qualitatively or quantitatively; the researcher makes the decision. Take the question "What is life like for those on death row?" If you could get permission to do so, being locked away in a penitentiary for several months would give you experiences and insights that you might not otherwise obtain. Even if you didn't want the firsthand experience, the question might be pursued qualitatively because of time constraints or sampling problems (e.g., the warden won't allow you to interview all of those on death row, but only a few).

Interviewing ten or twelve inmates could give you a reasonable idea of what their life was like. On the other hand, if you wanted your findings to be more generalizable, then you would likely have to think more quantitatively—and about such issues as how to obtain a random sample, sample size, how to collect the data, types of questions to use, hypotheses, how you wanted to analyze the data, and so forth.

A qualitative researcher interviewing in depth ten or twelve inmates might even use procedures generally favored by those who are more quantitatively-minded (like administering standardized instruments to verify diagnostic impressions). There are plenty of opportunities for social work researchers to do research that can be either quantitative or qualitative, or more accurately, research that is *mostly* one or the other.

Questions for Class Discussion

1. Suppose you want to know what it is like to live in poverty, so you interview an impoverished person in-depth one Saturday afternoon. Compare and contrast a lengthy interview with an ethnographic study of impoverished persons. In what ways would they be similar? How would they differ?
2. Which research approach has the greatest potential for advancing social work practice? (List arguments for and against qualitative and quantitative approaches.)
3. What are the pros and cons associated with not doing a thorough literature search before beginning an ethnographic study?
4. Discuss any books, movies, or plays that recently may have helped you better understand the life of a unique group of persons.
5. Share your life experiences that have given you insight into other cultures. What special world views or vocabularies were discovered?

6. Into what situations or settings would you like to go in disguise? What would you learn that you couldn't learn without disguise?
7. Discuss how qualitative research is different from research employing a single system design.

Mini-Projects for Experiencing Research Firsthand

1. Spend no less that eight hours observing (it can be on separate occasions) one of the following persons. Try to discover what problems they encounter, their coping or survival strategies, and any special terms or vocabulary that they use. Write a report summarizing what you learned.
   a. An impoverished person
   b. An elderly person
   c. A person with physical handicaps
   d. A social worker with a child-abuse protection team
2. Arrange to spend the night in a shelter for homeless persons. Keep a notebook with you and record your impressions and significant events. Share your observations with the class. If more than one person in your class engages in this activity, what patterns or themes emerge from the observations?
3. Consider a problem common to many persons who receive some form of welfare payment or food stamps. Since the amount of support is inadequate to their needs, they run out of food toward the end of the month. How do they survive? Do they borrow money to buy groceries? Do they go without food? Do they pool their supplies with neighbors or other family members? Do they go to soup kitchens? Draft a design for an ethnographic study of impoverished families that could provide some answers to these questions. Assume that you have received a grant that will allow you to take up to six months to live with or observe these families. Where would you go to begin your study? How would you find informants? What kinds of questions would you start with? How would you ensure that your findings weren't fabrications of your observed family or a product of your own presuppositions about poverty?
4. Interview in-depth a recent immigrant to this country. Obtain a life history or autobiography. Try to capture the experiences that would assist your fellow classmates in understanding both the quality of life in the home culture and the experiences the immigrant has had in adjusting to the new culture.

5. To understand a little more the kinds of problems experienced by certain individuals in our society, spend at least 12 hours with one of the following simulated disabilities:
   a. paraplegia (borrow or rent a wheel chair and spend a day in it)
   b. cataracts (smear Vaseline on a pair of eyeglasses)
   c. hearing impairment (wear ear plugs)
   d. birth defect or stroke (immobilize your right hand or arm with a splint, bandage, or sling)
   e. aphasia (try to go the whole day without speech)

Resources and References

Agar, M. (1980). *The Professional Stranger: An Informal Introduction to Ethnography.* New York: Academic Press.

Agar, M. (1986). *Speaking of Ethnography.* Beverly Hills, CA: Sage.

Babbie, E. (1986). *The Practice of Social Research.* Belmont, CA: Wadsworth.

Becker, D.G., Blumenfield, S., and Gordon, N. (1984). Voices from the eighties and beyond: Reminiscences of nursing home residents. *Journal of Gerontological Social Work,* 8(1,2), 83–100.

Bogdan, R. (1974). *Being Different: The Autobiography of Jane Fry.* New York: Wiley.

Bogdan, R. (1992). *Qualitative Research for Education: An Introduction to Theory and Methods.* Boston: Allyn & Bacon.

Bogdan, R. and Taylor, S.J. (1975). *Introduction to Qualitative Research Methods.* New York: Wiley.

Bryman, A. (1984). The debate about quantitative and qualitative research: A question of method or epistemology? *British Journal of Sociology,* 35(1), 75–92.

Caudill, W., Redlich, F.C., Gilmore, H.R., and Brody, E.B. (1952). Social structure and interaction processes on a psychiatric ward. *American Journal of Orthopsychiatry,* 22, 314–334.

Conover, T. (1987). *Coyotes: A Journey Through the Secret World of America's Illegal Aliens.* New York: Random House.

Cromwell, P.F., Olson, J.N., and Avary, D.W. (1990). *Breaking and Entering: An Ethnographic Analysis of Burglary.* Newbury Park, CA: Sage.

Deane, W.N. (1961). The reactions of a nonpatient to a stay on a mental hospital ward. *Psychiatry,* 24, 61–68.

Estroff, S. (1981). *Making It Crazy: An Ethnography of Psychiatric Clients in an American Community.* Berkeley, CA: University of California Press.

Fetterman, D. M. (1989). *Ethnography: Step by Step.* Beverly Hills, CA: Sage.

Fielding, N.G. (1991). *Using Computers in Qualitative Research.* Newbury Park, CA: Sage.

Gilgun, J.F. and Connor, T.M. (1989). How perpetrators view child sexual abuse. *Social Work,* 34(3), 249–251.

Glasser, I. (1988). *More Than Bread: Ethnography of a Soup Kitchen.* Tuscaloosa: University of Alabama Press.

Goldman, A.R., Bohr, R.H., and Steinberg, T.A. (1970). On posing as mental patients: Reminiscences and recommendations. *Professional Psychology,* 1(5), 427–434.

Goldstein, H. (1991). Qualitative research and social work practice: Partners in discovery. *Journal of Sociology and Social Welfare,* 18(4), 101–119.

Ishiyama, T., Batman, R., and Hewitt, E. (1967). Let's be patients. *American Journal of Nursing,* 67, 569–571.

Jacobsen, G.M. (1988). Rural social work: A case for qualitative methods. *Human Services in the Rural Environment,* 11(3), 22–28.

Johnson, J.C. (1990). *Selecting Ethnographic Informants.* Newbury Park, CA: Sage.

Keigher, S.M. (1992). Rediscovering the asylum. *Journal of Sociology and Social Welfare,* 19(4), 177–197.

Kidder, L.H. and Judd, C.M. (1986). *Research Methods in Social Relations.* New York: Holt, Rinehart and Winston.

Kirk, J. and Miller, M.L. (1986). *Reliability and Validity in Qualitative Research.* Beverly Hills, CA: Sage.

Lofland, J. and Lofland, L.H. (1984). *Analyzing Social Settings.* Belmont, CA: Wadsworth.

Madey, D.L. (1982). Some benefits of integrating qualitative and quantitative methods in program evaluation, with illustrations. *Educational Evaluation,* 4(2), 223–236.

Marshall, C. and Rossman, G.B. (1989). *Designing Qualitative Research.* Beverly Hills, CA: Sage.

Miles, M.B. and Huberman, A.M. (1984). *Qualitative Data Analysis.* Newbury Park, CA: Sage.

Moore, P. and Conn, P. (1985). *Disguised.* Waco, TX: Word Books.

Morse, J.M. (1993). *Critical Issues in Qualitative Research Methods.* Newbury Park, CA: Sage.

Olson, M.R. and Haynes, J.A. (1993). Successful single parents. *Families in Society,* 74(5), 259–267.

Patton, M.Q. (1990). *Qualitative Evaluation Methods.* Newbury Park, CA: Sage.

Peile, C. (1988). Research paradigms in social work: From stalemate to creative synthesis. *Social Service Review,* 62, 1–18.

Prus, R., and Irini, S. (1988). *Hookers, Rounders, & Desk Clerks.* Salem, WI: Sheffield Publishing Co.

Riessman, C.K. (1993). *Qualitative Studies in Social Work Research.* Newbury Park, CA: Sage.

Rosenhan, D.L. (1973). Being sane in insane places. *Science,* 179 (Jan.), 250–258.

Rosenstiel, C.R. (1980). That fast life: An emic ethnography of the black heroin addict hustler. Doctoral dissertation, University of Kentucky.

Rousseau, A.M. (1981). *Shopping Bag Ladies: Homeless Women Speak about Their Lives.* New York: Pilgrim Press.

Ruckdeschel, R.A. (1985). Qualitative research as a perspective. *Social Work Research and Abstracts*, 21(2), 17–21.

Ruckdeschel, R.A. and Farris, B.E. (1982). Science: Critical faith or dogmatic ritual: A rebuttal. *Social Casework*, 63, 272–275.

Sander, J. (1991). *Before Their Time: Four Generations of Teenage Mothers*. New York: Harcourt Brace Jovanovich.

Shaffir, W.B. and Stebbins, R.A. (1991). *Experiencing Fieldwork: An Inside View of Qualitative Research*. Newbury Park, CA: Sage.

Silverman, D. (1993). *Interpreting Qualitative Data*. Newbury Park, CA: Sage.

Skoll, G.R. (1992). *Walk the Walk and Talk the Talk: An Ethnography of a Drug Abuse Treatment Facility*. Philadelphia: Temple University Press.

Spradley, J.P. (1979). *The Ethnographic Interview*. New York: Holt, Rinehart and Winston.

Steffensmeier, D.J. (1986). *The Fence: In the Shadow of Two Worlds*. Totowa, NJ: Rowman & Littlefield.

Strauss, A. and Corbin, J. (1990). *Basics of Qualitative Research*. Newbury Park, CA: Sage.

Thompson, R.J. (1989). Evaluator as power broker: Issues in the Maghreb. International Innovations in Evaluation Methodology. *New Directions for Program Evaluation*, 42 (Summer), 39–48.

Uriarte-Gaston, M. (1987). Computer analysis of qualitative data. *Social Work Research and Abstracts*, 23(4), 9–12.

Van Maanen, J. (1983). Epilogue: Qualitative methods reclaimed. In John Van Maanen (Ed.), *Qualitative Methodology*. Beverly Hills, CA: Sage.

Whyte, W.F. (1984). *Learning from the Field: A Guide from Experience*. Beverly Hills, CA: Sage.

Willems, E.P. and Raush, H.L. (1969). *Naturalistic Viewpoints in Psychological Research*. New York: Holt, Rinehart and Winston.

Wolcott, H.F. (1990). *Writing Up Qualitative Research*. Newbury Park, CA: Sage.

Yalom, I. (1989). *Love's Executioner and Other Tales of Psychotherapy*. New York: Basic Books.

12
Ethical Thinking and Research

Would it ever be right to intentionally deceive in the interest of research? Was Moore wrong to disguise herself as an eighty-five-year-old woman in order to learn firsthand the way society interacts with older adults? If no harm came to anyone she observed, did she do anything unethical as a researcher? (The only risk, it seems, was to her. Once, while in disguise, she was mugged.) Would she have gathered useful information if she informed those around her that she wasn't really eighty-five years old but that they should act as if she were?

In his book, Conover (1987) describes how his participant observation almost got him into trouble with governmental authorities because he drove a car containing (and therefore assisted) illegal immigrants traveling in America. Do you think that driving in a car with illegal immigrants in order to learn about their problems and experiences is unethical? What is the difference between illegal and unethical behaviors?

As social workers, we learn about the powerful "expectancy" effects that labeling can have. Persons who are expected to act in a certain way ("mentally retarded," "behavioral problem," "delinquent") often find it difficult to perform outside of expectations. Is this a legitimate area for social workers to study? If you agree, then one way to study expectancy effects might be to give false information to a group (e.g., workshop supervisors of persons with mental retardation) and to indicate that some of the trainees could be expected to "blossom" in intelligence and workshop performance as shown by their scores on a fictitious "Latent Capabilities Scale." Unlike studies that focus on negative expectations and labels, Wellons (1973) created positive expectations. At the end of one month he found that the experimental group of adult trainees not only had a higher level of productivity, but also showed gains in intelligence tests. There were no changes of this sort for the control group. The subjects were not harmed; instead, they benefited from the experiment. Was this research unethical?

Almost all of the social workers I have known have struck me as being ethical individuals. They (for the most part) seem to be concerned with such issues as protecting clients' confidentiality and privacy. This being the case, why do we need a chapter on ethics? Simply because ethical behavior involves much more than protecting anonymity and confidentiality. Even social workers who know the National Association of Social Work's Code of Ethics can become involved in unethical research practices.

Because the Code of Ethics is based on values that are difficult to operationalize, it may also be difficult to determine if a specific situation is a violation of the Code. For example, try to operationalize "integrity" or the following principle from the Code of Ethics: "The social worker should maintain high standards of personal conduct in the capacity or identity as social worker." It is hard to anticipate every way in which a social worker might violate "high standards of personal conduct" or fail to demonstrate integrity. Codes of ethics provide guidelines that, because they are so general, are often open to individual interpretation. We see this in the next example.

I once was asked to evaluate a counseling agency and its director. While this agency had its own board of directors, it was also accountable to a funding agency with another board of directors. The directors of the funding agency had reason to believe that the counseling agency could do a better job. They believed that the director of the counseling agency spent an excessive amount of time playing tennis during business hours and was generally not conscientious as an agency manager.

I went about the evaluation by contacting key professionals in the community who either had been or who should have been making referrals to the agency. I obtained a mixed bag of comments. While it was evident that the agency could have done better in some areas, it also did some things reasonably well. I knew that the way the results were presented could affect whether or not the director continued in that position. Since the instructions to me had been vague, I chose to present the findings in a formative manner rather than in a summative style. I attempted to make a balanced presentation, and in so far as possible, to let the data speak for itself. I did not feel comfortable concluding what the policymakers should do in this situation. Had they been kindly disposed toward the agency director, some of the findings from the evaluation would have been seen as providing constructive suggestions for change. Other statements would have provided positive strokes for the agency and its staff. However, there were political shenanigans going on.

The director of the counseling agency felt that the evaluation of the agency was an undeserved and unwarranted affront and soon resigned. At the funding agency, the individual who had been the strongest critic of the outgoing director, the one who pushed the hardest for an evaluation of the agency, applied for the director's position and was subsequently hired.

I came away with a firm sense of having been used to oust the former agency director. The new agency director (the individual who had advocated for an evaluation of the outgoing director) had a master's degree in social work and would have been incensed if anyone suggested that something "unethical" had been done. What do you think? Is the act of causing an evaluation to be conducted unethical? At what point was something unethical done?

Heated controversies occasionally arise because of disagreements over what constitutes an unethical act. My final example involves a researcher who submitted a fabricated study of the benefits of temporarily separating asthmatic children from their parents to 146 journals in social work and related fields (Coughlin, 1988). One version of the article claimed that social work intervention benefited the children. A second version indicated that the intervention had no effect. Upon acceptance or rejection of the manuscript, the study's investigator notified the journal of the real purpose of his study—to collect data on whether there was a tendency among journals to accept articles that confirm the value of social work intervention.

The controversy arose when an editor of the *Social Service Review* lodged a formal complaint against the author with the National Association of Social Workers. The author's position is that the review procedures of journals ought to be investigated because of their potential influence in determining what will be printed in professional journals. Some argue that the author should not have initiated such a large-scale deception of journals, but how does one investigate the hypothesis that professional journals have a bias that constitutes "prior censorship" without using a little deception? In many instances of unethical research, some harm results. Who was harmed in this example?

Historical Context

Guidelines to protect the subjects of research originated with the Nuremberg trials after World War II, which, among other areas of concern, examined the Nazis' medical experiments upon involuntary prisoners. Nazi physicians conducted cruel and harmful experiments on human subjects. Some of their experiments, for example, were designed to determine how long it was possible for human subjects to live in ice water. Prisoners were subjected to conditions that literally froze them. Female prisoners were ordered to warm the frozen subjects with their naked bodies in order to determine if more subjects lived with slow thawing than with quick thawing.

Other prisoners (including children) were injected with diseases such as typhus, malaria, and epidemic jaundice in order to test vaccines. To test antibiotics, human beings were wounded and had limbs amputated. Grass, dirt, gangrene cultures, and other debris were rubbed into the wounds so that the injuries would simulate those received on the battlefield. To simulate the problems of high altitude flying, test chambers were created where oxygen was removed and the effect of oxygen starvation on humans studied. Other prisoners of the Nazis were given intravenous injections of gasoline or various forms of poison to study how long it would take them to die. These involuntary subjects experienced extreme pain, and of those few who lived, most suffered permanent injury or mutilation (Conot, 1983; Faden and Beauchamp, 1986; Grundner, 1986).

These and other atrocities resulted in what became known as the Nuremberg Code—a set of ethical standards by which research with human subjects can be judged. Organizations such as the World Medical Association subsequently developed their own guidelines (The Declaration of Helsinki) for distinguishing ethical from unethical clinical research. The American Medical Association and other groups endorsed the Declaration or developed similar guidelines.

Despite awareness of the Nazi atrocities and the development of ethical guidelines for research by a number of organizations and professional associations, there have been unfortunate incidents in this country in which subjects were experimented upon without their permission. In the 1960s in New York, a physician injected cancer cells into twenty-two geriatric patients. Some were informed orally that they were involved in an experiment, but were not told that they were being given injections of cancer cells. No written consent was acquired, and some patients were incompetent to give informed consent. Later it was learned that the study had not been presented to the hospital's research committee and that several physicians directly responsible for the care of the patients involved in the study had not been consulted (Faden and Beauchamp, 1986).

Another notorious case involved a sample of men with syphilis. In 1932 four hundred mostly poor and illiterate black males with tertiary stage syphilis were informed that they would receive free treatment for their "bad blood." In actuality, these men received no treatment for syphilis. They received free physical exams, periodic blood testing, hot meals on examination days, free treatment for minor disorders, and a modest burial fee for cooperating with the investigators. The researchers (supported by the Public Health Service) were interested only in tracing the pathological evolution of syphilis. Although the study was reviewed several times by Public Health Service officials and was reported in thirteen articles in prestigious medical and public health journals, it continued uninterrupted until 1972, when a reporter exposed the study in the *New York Times*. The survivors were given treatment for their disease only after this publicity. After the story broke, the Department of Health, Education and Welfare appointed an advisory panel to review the study. Not until 1975 did the government extend treatment to subjects' wives who had contracted syphilis and their children born with congenital syphilis (Jones, 1981).

These and other abuses led Congress in 1974 to pass the National Research Act (Public Law 93–348), which requires any organization involved in the conduct of biomedical or behavioral research involving human subjects to establish an Institutional Review Board (IRB) to review the research to be conducted or sponsored. This act also created the National Commission for the Protection of Human Subjects of Biomedical and Behavioral Research. In October 1978, this commission produced recommendations for public comment. The Department of Health, Education and Welfare (HEW) refined the recommendations and, in 1981, issued them as regulations for research being conducted with its funds. In 1983, specific regulations protecting children were incorporated.

The impact of these standards was that colleges, universities, hospitals, and other organizations engaging in research and receiving federal funds from HEW (now the Department of Health and Human Services) and selected other departments established institutional review boards (sometimes called human subjects committees) to review and oversee research conducted by investigators affiliated with their organizations. Under some circumstances, the IRBs review students' proposed research as well. These review boards have the authority to approve, disapprove, or modify research activities covered by the regulations, to conduct a continuing review of research involving human subjects, to ensure that there is an informed consent process, and to suspend or terminate the approval of any research.

Institutional Review Boards

Institutional review boards are now firmly established as our society's "watchdogs" protecting human subjects from risky or harmful research. This does not mean that IRBs prevent all unethical research practices. They cannot monitor research that is covert or not brought to their attention. However, there is much greater monitoring of research today than there was twenty or so years ago. Currently, federal agencies are adopting a common set of regulations that will apply to all research involving human subjects conducted, supported, or subject to regulation by twenty-two federal departments or agencies. This uniform policy will provide even greater protection of the rights and welfare of human subjects involved in research. Most universities and medical settings have required for some years that all proposed human subject research be approved by the local institutional review board regardless of whether federal or outside funding is supporting it.

Under the new federal regulations, each institutional review board must provide written assurance that it complies with the regulations supported by the federal department funding the research. In addition to these regulations, universities and other institutions where research is commonly done often have their own policies and procedures. Generally speaking, any investigator proposing research involving human subjects must prepare a description of the proposed research and submit this to the IRB. These descriptions vary in length and format depending upon the planned research and the procedures established by the local IRB. There are several levels of review, from the most cursory (the exempt status) to full review. Federal regulations allow for some kinds of research to be exempted from a full review by the IRB. Those activities most applicable to social work are:

1. Research conducted in established or commonly accepted educational settings, such as research on normal educational practices involving instructional strategies or research on the effectiveness of instructional techniques, curricula, or classroom management methods.
2. Research involving the use of educational tests (cognitive, diagnostic, aptitude, achievement) if information taken from these sources is recorded in such a manner that subjects cannot be identified, directly or through identifiers linked to the subjects,

and if any disclosure of the human subjects' responses outside the research would not place the subjects at risk of criminal or civil liability or be damaging to the subjects' financial standing, employability, or reputation.

3. Research involving survey or interview procedures and observation of public behavior is exempted when meeting the conditions specified in (2) above.

4. Research involving the collection or study of existing data, documents, or records if these sources are publicly available or if the information is recorded by the investigator in such a manner that subjects cannot be identified directly or through identifiers linked to the subjects.

5. Research and demonstration projects conducted by or subject to the approval of federal department or agency heads that examine or evaluate public benefit or service programs or procedures for obtaining benefits or services under those programs, including possible changes in programs or procedures.

6. Research involving survey or interview procedures and educational tests when the respondents are elected or appointed public officials or candidates for public office or when federal statutes require, without exception, the confidentiality of the personally identifiable information will be maintained through the research and thereafter.

Exemptions may not always be available from IRBs. In such an instance, the researcher may complete a lengthier application and may be required to appear before the IRB to make a presentation or to respond to questions. Presently, most IRBs will not grant exemptions to research involving certain vulnerable populations (children, prisoners, the mentally disabled, and economically or educationally disadvantaged persons), or when there is deception of subjects or use of techniques that expose the subject to discomfort or harassment beyond levels normally encountered in daily life. Further, exemption is not usually available when the information obtained from medical records is recorded in such a way that subjects can be identified directly or through identifiers linked to the subjects. However, some local IRBs may be more lenient than others in exemptions granted.

Under the exemption certificate, the researcher provides such information as the title of the project, the research objectives, the subject population, plans for the recruitment of the subjects, the research procedures to be followed, and potential psychological, physical, social, or legal risks.

Generally speaking, students are not required to seek approval from institutional review boards when their research projects are primarily for educational purposes (e.g., an assignment to interview a small sample of people in order to learn about interviewing, recording data, or other aspects of the research). However, if the project involves living human subjects and is likely to contribute to generalizable knowledge (that is, research that is likely to be of publishable quality), students ought to seek IRB approval. Normally, student projects with the greatest potential for generating generalizable knowledge are doctoral dissertations and some master's theses.

General Guidelines for Ethical Research

Social workers do not, as a rule, get involved in biomedical or other research where physical harm to subjects is likely to occur. Research conducted by social workers involves surveys and interviews that require a certain amount of cooperation from the participants in the study. The risks to the subjects of social work research derive from the possibility that a third party will use the research data and cause the subject physical, psychological, social, or economic harm. The risk of identification is particularly acute for those subjects engaged in or with past histories of illegal acts (Murray, Donovan, Kail, and Medvene, 1980).

When questionnaires are used or interviews are conducted with adults who are not in a vulnerable population, the principle of "implied consent" is applied. The act of participation is seen as giving informed consent. In these instances, IRBs do not require written documentation that subjects gave their consent. A problem arises when potential subjects feel that they cannot refuse to participate. If potential subjects are clients (e.g., persons on probation or parole, or recipients of some form of public assistance), they may not feel free to refuse without putting themselves in some jeopardy. This is when consultation with an institutional review board can come in handy. They may suggest alternative ways to collect data or to reduce any implied coercion by informing potential subjects of their rights in writing. (A written consent form is often required that specifies clearly that the potential subject has the right to refuse participation without any penalty or loss of service.) Social workers must be alert to the possibility that encouraging their clients to participate in research could be perceived as coercion. Since social workers are often "gatekeepers" of services, clients could feel pressured into participating in order to gain access to or continue receiving services.

Not every social worker is employed by an organization or university that has an institutional review board to consult about problems associated with conducting applied research. With this in mind, the following set of guidelines has been developed. However, guidelines and codes of ethics are limited—they will not fit every situation. This is why so many are written in very general language—they must be written in such a manner to cover various types of research and situations, from large-scale program evaluations to participant observation studies. Finally, these guidelines are based on the assumption that the proposed research is worth doing—that it is not trivial. Good research in the social sciences should improve the quality of life by increasing our understanding of social problems or by providing information about how to make our interventions more effective.

Guideline 1: Research Subjects Must Be Volunteers

Social work research is not something imposed upon involuntary subjects. All of those participating in a research effort should freely decide to participate. No coercion of any kind should be used to secure participants for a study.

All subjects must be competent enough to understand their choice. If they are not able to fully comprehend (e.g., individuals under the age of majority), then their legal caretakers must give permission, and the subjects also must assent. Even if parents give permission for their children to participate in a research project, the children may still refuse to participate. The subject's right to self-determination is respected, and any research subject is free to withdraw from a study at any time.

The use of written consent forms helps assure that research subjects know that they are volunteers. These forms provide brief, general information about the nature of the research, the procedures to be followed, and any foreseeable risks, discomforts, or benefits, and they indicate that the research subject is free to withdraw consent and to discontinue participation in the project at any time without penalty or loss of benefits. Consent forms generally contain the name of someone to contact should there be questions about the research or the subject's rights.

Guideline 2: Potential Research Subjects Should Be Given Sufficient Information about the Study to Determine Any Possible Risks or Discomforts as Well as Benefits

"Sufficient information" includes an explanation of the purpose of the research, the expected duration of the subject's participation, the procedures to be followed, and the identification of those procedures that might be experimental. The exact hypothesis does not have to be given away; it can be stated generally. However, the researcher must be specific about procedures that will involve the research subjects. If there are potential risks, these must be identified. Subjects should be given the opportunity to raise and have answered any questions about the study or procedures that will be used. Subjects must also be allowed to inquire at any time about procedures and have their questions answered.

Benefits expected from participation in a study can be described in a general fashion. For example, Maloney (1984), in a study of former residents of Boys Town, used the following in a consent form: "I understand the potential benefits of the studies are that they will help future boys experience programs that are most likely to help them after they leave Boys Town. It also will permit distribution of Boys Town methods around the world" (p. 135). If a consent form is used, it should be written at a level of readability that the potential subjects can understand. Several methods can be used to estimate the grade level equivalence of the consent form. Flesch (1948) has devised a formula that counts the number of syllables in 100-word samples. Fry's (1968) method also allows one to estimate grade level equivalences.

Guideline 3: No Harm Shall Result as a Consequence of Participation in the Research

Social work researchers are not likely to propose research that would result in evident harm to their subjects. But one's perspective on harmful effects should not be limited to the active participants in a study. Punch (1986) related a dilemma that he faced. A group of female students wanted to study the reactions of policemen to reports of rape. In order to conduct this study they would have had to fabricate stories. While policemen might have been quite insensitive in their dealings with rape victims, Punch objected to the study on several grounds. First, there could have been legal repercussions for filing false police reports. Second, subsequent disclosure might have made the police distrustful of researchers. But most important, it might have led police to be skeptical of legitimate claims of sexually assaulted women. The benefits did not seem to outweigh the risks and the potential harm to others that could result.

Researchers have a responsibility to identify and to minimize harm or risk of harm that might befall the research subjects. And researchers should constantly monitor the subjects for harmful effects of the research. Subjects should not go away from a study with a feeling of lowered self-esteem or sense of self-worth, or that they possess undesirable traits. Often, "debriefings" are used to inform subjects and to neutralize negative feelings once participation in a project has concluded.

Guideline 4: Sensitive Information Shall Be Protected

This guideline suggests that no harm to research subjects should result from improper handling of information. The privacy of research subjects may be protected in several ways: (1) Allow the subject to respond anonymously. (2) If the research design cannot accommodate anonymity, provide protection by separating identifying information from the research data through the use of numeric or other special codes. Where complete anonymity is not possible (e.g., because pretest and posttest scores have to be matched for each subject), it may be necessary to use special codes (such as the first four letters of a subject's mother's maiden name and the last four digits of his or her social security number) to help guard against unauthorized persons accidentally recognizing or identifying your research subject.

The confidentiality of research subjects can be maintained by not reporting personal information (such as names, addresses, phone numbers, and personal descriptors like "Mayor, Lexington, Ky.") that would result in subjects being identified by persons other than the study's investigators. Another technique is to keep sensitive data (including master lists of codes, completed questionnaires, and transcripts of interviews) in locked cabinets or files until they are no longer needed and then destroying the raw data.

As a rule, research findings are reported in the aggregate; that is, you report a group's average score or amount of improvement. It would be unethical to report the results in this fashion: "In our study the mayor and head of the personnel department showed the least improvement, while the police chief improved the most." Under no circumstances should data be reported in any fashion that would result in the identification of persons who agreed to participate on the condition that their responses would be confidential. When it is necessary to report on a "typical" research subject or to use vignettes or anecdotes, pseudonyms should be used.

A problem may arise when an "outside" researcher makes a request of a social service agency to interview clients or to collect information beyond what may be available from agency files. When former or present clients must be contacted to supply additional information for research purposes, their right to privacy must be safeguarded. Clients' privacy is protected when the agency obtains permission from clients to share personally identifying information (e.g., names, addresses, and phone numbers) with the researcher, who could then contact clients interested in assisting with the research.

Potential Ethical Problems in Research

Deception

One of the thorniest ethical problems facing researchers in the social sciences has to do with deception. Our guidelines suggest that deception ought not be employed, because the research participants would not be in a position to be fully informed about the intent of the research. But, some research could not be conducted if deception were not allowed. The *IRB Guidebook* (1982) seems to acknowledge this:

> Deception or incomplete disclosure may be the only valid approach for certain research. An example of such research would be a study designed to determine the effect of group pressure (responses of others) on a subject's estimate of the length of a series of lines. In some groups, pseudo-subjects would be told in advance to give incorrect answers to questions about the length of lines in order to determine the effect of misinformation on the real subjects' responses. Obviously, if the subjects were told all about the research design and its purpose in advance, it would not be possible to do the research. (P. 4–A3)

When Moore (1985) disguised herself as an eighty-five-year-old woman, there was very little, if any, risk of harm to those around her. People who came in contact with her were unlikely to act other than normally. It could be argued that there was no harm associated with their being unwitting participants. Certainly no one was degraded, and there was no emotional or psychological harm. This is quite a different situation from falsely reporting a criminal act in order to study police reactions.

Conover's (1987) observation of illegal immigrants seemed to result in no harm and may have been of help when a group of immigrants were being interrogated by the Mexican police. However, Conover's project could have resulted in his being arrested for assisting the illegal immigrants. Since Conover's level of masquerade was much less than that used by Moore, it seems less likely that anyone would be concerned about potential unethical behavior associated with his use of deception. In this instance, Conover was more at risk for engaging in *illegal* than in unethical behavior. Although there was some deception in both of these examples, in neither case did harm to the research subjects/participants seem to result.

We should also consider Haywood's (1977) contention that we could be guilty of unethical conduct if we fail to conduct important and needed research. If we reflect upon the Conover and Moore examples as well as those mentioned in chapter 11 (e.g., the qualitative researchers who admitted themselves to mental institutions to learn about the treatment of patients), we realize that we probably have a better understanding of the problems of old age, migrant workers, and the institutional treatment of mentally ill persons as a result of these studies. Other studies that have involved deception in order to investigate discrimination or racism have helped bring about needed institutional and social change.

Although there has been little evidence of direct physical or mental harm to participants in deception experiments (Korchin and Cowan, 1982), the social work researcher must weigh the potential harmful effects of deception against the possible benefits. When deception is employed, subjects should not come away with a feeling of having been degraded or exploited. Debriefing the subjects after an experiment is often required by IRBs as a mechanism to counter potentially adverse effects caused by the use of deception.

The decision to use deception should not be made without consultation with friends and co-workers. As part of this process, alternative methodologies for studying the problem of interest should be examined. Since it is likely that an institutional review board would not approve of blatant deception (excluding research in controlled laboratory settings), social workers engaging in such deception without IRB approval run a risk of being labeled "unethical." Possible adverse effects on the researcher's professional and private life must be considered against the possible benefits of engaging in the study.

Denial of Treatment

Another problem for social workers who contemplate research is that use of a control group may be unethical because some clients would be denied services. It would indeed be unethical to deliberately deny beneficial services to a client for the purposes of research.

But there are ways to obtain control groups without being unethical. For instance, if we wanted to evaluate a new program or intervention, we could compare clients receiving the new or experimental intervention with those who receive the typical set of services. In this scenario, there would be no denial of services. Some clients would get a slightly different intervention or set of services from those clients normally receive. This could be to their advantage.

In those agencies or programs where there is a long waiting list, researchers might consider as a control group those clients who are at the end of the list. For instance, if a wait of six weeks or longer is inevitable before those on the waiting list could begin receiving services, there is no denial of benefits. In fact, clients on a waiting list might appreciate a periodic contact with an agency representative (even if it is limited to the administration of a pretest and posttest), because it would constitute evidence that they have not been forgotten by the agency and that they are still actively queued for services. If these clients had similar problems (e.g., alcoholism), it might be possible to distribute educational pamphlets or materials to them while they were waiting for service. This group of clients could be considered to be receiving an educational intervention. While it may be a weaker or milder intervention than they would later receive, it would be better than nothing at all and may help the researcher feel better about gathering data from them. Comparisons could be made to the waiting-list clients (the control group) and those who received the new intervention (the experimental group).

Another way to obtain a control group would be to compare your program participants with the clientele of a similar program or agency. While the groups would not be equivalent (since random assignment wasn't possible), at least you would have beginning evaluative data. Still another "natural" control group could be found in that group of clients who keep one or two appointments, then drop out of treatment. This group could be compared with those individuals who complete the intervention.

These are only some of the ways in which control groups can be identified without denying treatment.

Should Some Research Questions Not Be Investigated?

Living in an open society as we do, the suggestion that we should not investigate some research questions sounds strange indeed. However, remember that research results can be used for purposes other than those for which they were intended. Research could be conducted to support stereotypes or prejudices. For example, one research question that should not be investigated is: "Are there racial differences in intelligence?" (Sieber and Stanley, 1988). While it is conceivable that some interest groups could make funds or grants available for the conduct of such research, the ethical social work researcher has a responsibility to not engage in research that could be used to denigrate or harm a group of individuals.

Compensation ✓

Is paying respondents or research subjects unethical? While reimbursing subjects for costs incurred (e.g., baby-sitting, time away from work, transportation) seems reasonable and is not offensive to most, questions are raised when there is a large financial incentive for participation. Yelaja (1982) suggests that researchers are ethically required to ensure that the incentive is not so great that it is excessive or constitutes "undue inducement." When large financial rewards are offered for research subjects, there is a risk that some individuals may fabricate information in order to become eligible for the money.

Research Without Clients' Consent

Although many community mental health centers and other such agencies routinely request clients to sign consent forms in the event that a researcher or program evaluator will need to look at their records some day, many agencies do not use consent forms unless their clients are involved in a specific study.

Suppose you wanted to do research within a state psychiatric hospital to determine if more multiple personalities were being diagnosed in a recent year than ten years ago. In such a situation, would you be prevented from conducting your research because clients did not give their permission for you to perform archival research involving their records? Probably not—if you are a legitimate researcher and have the approval of one or more institutional review boards.

As an official student or faculty member, you would go first to your own university's institutional review board, stating your research objectives, how you would collect the data, and so forth. Once you received their approval, you'd be in a stronger position with the state hospital's human subjects committee. Your study has a greater likelihood of being approved if it has the potential for making a contribution to our knowledge base or if it would be useful to the hospital.

Archival research of this type is not generally viewed as having any real potential for harming subjects. Further, in some localities the information you want might even be a matter of public record. Even so, some agencies may have you sign an agreement of confidentiality before allowing you access to their records.

Final Thoughts

It might be argued that going through an institutional review board is a waste of time for the knowledgeable and ethical researcher who will not be doing any harm with a simple survey. However, to bypass review boards entails a certain risk—even if no harm is done to the participants. A recent article noted the case of a university-based investigator who did not get approval for a controversial questionnaire administered within a school district. To avoid hostile parental reaction and a possible lawsuit, a school official shredded several hundred already completed questionnaires (Schilling, Schinke, Kirkham, Meltzer, and Norelius, 1988). You can imagine how much time was lost—to say nothing about the likely fate of that research project. Consulting with a review board and having a general demeanor of openness about research is better than going it alone. Ultimately, however, it is the researcher who is responsible for the ethics of the research effort. Even with the approval of an institutional review board or other advisory group, the researcher must constantly be vigilant and stop any research project in which harmful effects may be occurring.

In order to help clarify the ethical and unethical dimensions of research, some of the unfortunate consequences of unbridled research have been presented. What "should" or "ought" to be done has been emphasized. However, I do not want to leave you with a sense of burden or responsibility so great that you would never consider doing research because of fear of doing something unethical. Most researchers have little fear of doing any real "harm" to their subjects, because their interviews, surveys, or questionnaires are so innocuous. When their research proposal has been reviewed by an institutional review board or other advisory group and proper safeguards are taken to protect access to confidential information, most researchers can relax and focus their energies on their project with little fear of being "unethical."

Being a research subject can have positive effects. In clinical interventions, subjects may gain from new therapeutic procedures. Even if that doesn't occur, subjects may feel that the research is important and that they have made a contribution that will be of help to others. Participants may experience an increase in self-worth because they feel honored to have been selected to participate in "research." Sometimes participants receive some form of remuneration, and they appreciate it—even if it is inconsequential. Another consideration is that some research projects are interesting. Participants don't mind giving their opinions or sharing their insights. These are just some of the benefits to research participants noted by Korchin and Cowan (1982).

Finally, as social work students, you should be familiar with (or at least know where you can find a copy of) the National Association of Social Work's Code of Ethics. A portion of the Code directly pertains to the profession's concern for ethical research. It is reproduced here for your use:

E. Scholarship and Research. The social worker engaged in study and research should be guided by the conventions of scholarly inquiry.

1. The social worker engaged in research should consider carefully its possible consequences for human beings.
2. The social worker engaged in research should ascertain that the consent of participants in the research is voluntary and informed, without any implied deprivation or penalty for refusal to participate, and with due regard for participants' privacy and dignity.
3. The social worker engaged in research should protect participants from unwarranted physical or mental discomfort, distress, harm, danger, or deprivation.
4. The social worker who engages in the evaluation of services or cases should discuss them only for professional purposes and only with persons directly and professionally concerned with them.
5. Information obtained about participants in research should be treated as confidential.
6. The social worker should take credit only for work actually done in connection with scholarly and research endeavors and credit contributions made by others.

Questions for Class Discussion

1. Make lists of situations in which it would be acceptable and not acceptable to involve people in research without their knowledge.
2. A researcher wants to interview children in families where there has been a hospitalization for mental illness within the past three years. Discuss the potential ethical issues that will have to be addressed.
3. A researcher is interested in observing family functioning in families that have experienced a recent suicide. What precautions would the researcher need to take to ensure that no psychological or emotional harm resulted from the interviews?
4. A doctoral student studying the terminally ill participating in a hospice program finds that 15 percent of the subjects are contemplating suicide. Discuss what you would do with this information?

5. A researcher wants to investigate the emotional consequences associated with abortion. Because of the difficulty in getting access to the names and addresses of women who have had abortions, the researcher proposes a snowball sampling design. What are the ethical issues involved in the use of this design?

Mini-Projects for Experiencing Research Firsthand

1. In the late 1950s, a series of experiments were conducted to confirm the usefulness of gamma globulin to immunize against hepatitis. The researchers went to a residential school, the Willowbrook State School, where a hepatitis epidemic was in progress. Researchers obtained the consent of the parents and divided the children into experimental and control groups that received hepatitis virus at various levels of infectiousness and gamma globulin inoculations at various strengths. Some of the gamma globulin was given below the strength known to be effective. When the results were published in the professional literature, they produced a storm of controversy (Harris, 1986). Why? Because all of the children in the Willowbrook State School were children with mental retardation. Even though all the children who contracted the disease recovered, and the researchers argued that valuable medical knowledge was gained from the experiments, do you believe that this research should have been allowed? Try to find some of the arguments for and against this research and write a paper defending your position. The original articles reporting the experiment were: Ward, R., Krugman, S., Giles, J.P., Jacobs, A.M., and Bodansky, O. (1958), "Infectious hepatitis: Studies of its natural history and prevention," *New England Journal of Medicine,* 258(9) (Feb. 27), 407–416; and Krugman, S., Ward, R., Giles, J.P., Bodansky, O., and Jacobs, A.M. (1959), "Infectious hepatitis: Detection of the virus during the incubation period and clinically inapparent infection," *New England Journal of Medicine,* 261(15) (Oct. 8), 729–734.

2. In the late 1960s, a sociologist, Laud Humphreys, reported his study of homosexual activity occurring in "tearooms" or public restrooms. He volunteered to be a "watchqueen"—that is, to serve as a lookout for the individuals engaged in this form of sexual activity. In order to obtain additional demographic information about homosexual men, Humphreys recorded the license numbers of their cars and traced the men to their homes. A year later, he posed as a health service interviewer and collected personal information from them. It could be argued that his re-

search was important for its contributions to our understanding of this type of behavior. He found, for instance, that only a small percentage of his subjects were members of the gay community. Many were married men. Humphreys certainly was guilty of deception and invading the private lives of the subjects. Do you feel that the benefits of such research outweigh the methods that he used? Read Laud Humphreys' *Tearoom Trade* (1970) and other commentaries on his book, and write a paper defending your position.

3. Stanley Milgram, a social psychologist at Yale University, began a series of studies on obedience in the 1960s. His experiments involved an elaborate deception. He led subjects to believe that they were giving a dangerous level of electrical shocks to other subjects who had not learned a list of words. Those who thought they were administering the shocks believed that the study was of the effects of punishment on learning (therefore justifying the electrical shock). The "learner" did not actually receive any electrical shock, but was instructed to feign discomfort upon receipt of the shock. In actuality, Milgram was interested in the extent to which subjects obeyed authority and would administer apparently dangerous levels of electricity to other participants in the research. It could be argued that Milgram's experiments constitute important findings on how ordinary people can be led to engage in the inhuman treatment of others. Milgram's report of his findings was met with much controversy. Do you feel that the benefits of such research outweigh any potentially unethical practices involved in the use of deception? He did, after all, debrief his subjects so that they knew no electrical shock had really been administered. Read Stanley Milgram's *Obedience to Authority* (New York: Harper & Row, 1974) in order to write a paper defending your position.

4. Obtain a copy of the exemption certification form used by the institutional review board at your college or university. Think of some research that you would like to conduct. Develop this idea, sketch out a research design, and then complete the exemption form. Bring these to class, and exchange forms with a fellow student. Critique each other's effort.

Resources and References

Annas, G.J. and Grodin, M.A. (1992). *The Nazi Doctors and the Nuremberg Code: Human Rights in Human Experimentation.* New York: Oxford University Press.

Baumrind, D. (1985). Research using intentional deception: Ethical issues revisited. *American Psychologist*, 40(2), 165–174.

Caplan, A.L. (1992). Twenty years after, the legacy of the Tuskegee syphilis study: When evil intrudes. *Hastings Center Report*, 22(6), 29–32.

Conot, R.E. (1983). *Justice at Nuremberg*. New York: Harper & Row.

Conover, T. (1987). *Coyotes: A Journey Through the Secret World of America's Illegal Aliens*. New York: Random House.

Coughlin, E.K. (1988). Scholar who submitted bogus article to journals may be disciplined. *Chronicle of Higher Education*, Nov. 2, p. A7.

Edgar, H. (1992). Twenty years after, the legacy of the Tuskegee syphilis study: Outside the community. *Hastings Center Report*, 22(6), 32–35.

Faden, R.R. and Beauchamp, T.L. (1986). *A History and Theory of Informed Consent*. New York: Oxford Unversity Press.

Flesch, R. (1948). A new readability yardstick. *Journal of Applied Psychology*, 32(3), 221–233.

Fry, E. (1968). A readability formula that saves time. *Journal of Reading*, 11, 513–516, 575–578.

Gray, B.H. (1975). *Human Subjects in Medical Experimentations*. New York: Wiley.

Grundner, T.M. (1986). *Informed Consent: A Tutorial*. Owings Mill, MD: Rynd Communications.

Harris, E.E., Jr. (1986). *Applying Moral Theories*. Belmont, CA: Wadsworth.

Haywood, H.C. (1977). The ethics of doing research . . . and of not doing it. *American Journal of Mental Deficiency*, 81(4), 311–317.

IRB Guidebook. (1982). Bethesda, MD: President's Commission for the Study of Ethical Problems in Medicine and Biomedical and Behavioral Research.

Jones, J.H. (1981). *Bad Blood: The Tuskegee Syphilis Experiment*. New York: Free Press.

Kimmel, A.J. (1988). *Ethics and Values in Applied Social Research*. Beverly Hills, CA: Sage.

King, P.A. (1992). Twenty years after, the legacy of the Tuskegee syphilis study: The dangers of difference. *Hastings Center Report*, 22(6), 35–38.

Korchin, S.J. and Cowan, P.A. (1982). Ethical perspectives in clinical research. In P.C. Kendall and J.N. Butcher (Eds.), *Handbook of Research Methods in Clinical Psychology*. New York: Wiley.

La Pierre, R.T. (1935). Attitudes vs. actions. *Social Forces*, 13, 230–37.

Lifton, R.J. (1986). *The Nazi Doctors: Medical Killing and the Psychology of Genocide*. New York: Basic Books.

Maloney, D.M. (1984). *Protection of Human Research Subjects: A Practical Guide to Federal Laws and Regulations*. New York: Plenum Press.

Marshall, G.D. and Zimbardo, P.G. (1979). Affective consequences of inadequately explained physiological arousal. *Journal of Personality and Social Psychology*, 37, 970–988.

Milgram, S. (1977). Ethical issues in the study of obedience. In S. Milgram (Ed.), *The Individual in a Social World*. Reading, MA: Addison-Wesley.

Mitscherlich, A. and Mielke, F. (1949). *Doctors of Infamy: The Story of the Nazi Medical Crimes.* New York: Henry Schuman.

Moore, P. and Conn, P. (1985). *Disguised.* Waco, TX: Word Books.

Morris, M. and Cohn, R. (1993). Program evaluators and ethical challenges. *Evaluation Review*, 17(6), 621–642.

Murray, L., Donovan, R., Kail, B.L., and Medvene, L.J. (1980). Protecting human subjects during social work research: Researchers' opinions. *Social Work Research and Abstracts*, 16(2), 25–30.

Punch, M. (1986). *The Politics and Ethics of Fieldwork.* Beverly Hills, CA: Sage.

Reamer, F.G. (1990). *Ethical Dilemmas in Social Service* (2d ed.). New York: Columbia University Press.

Schilling, R.F., Schinke, S.P., Kirkham, M.A., Meltzer, N.J., and Norelius, K.L. (1988). Social work research in social service agencies: Issues and guidelines. *Journal of Social Service Research*, 11(4), 75–87.

Sieber, J.E. (1992). *Planning Ethically Responsible Research: A Guide for Students and Internal Review Boards.* Newbury Park, CA: Sage.

Sieber, J.E. and Stanley, B. (1988). Ethical and professional dimensions of socially sensitive research. *American Psychologist*, 43(1), 49–55.

Wellons, K. (1973). The expectancy component in mental retardation. Doctoral dissertation, University of California, Berkeley.

Yelaja, S.A. (1982). *Ethical Issues in Social Work.* Springfield, IL: C.C. Thomas.

Zimbardo, P.G., Andersen, S.M., and Kabat, L.G. (1981). Induced hearing deficit generates experimental paranoia. *Science*, 212 (June), 1529–1531.

13
Writing Research Reports and Journal Articles

You have conducted some exciting research and now you want to (or have been asked to) communicate your findings in writing. You might be prompted to write about your research because it was funded through a grant and you are obligated to report your findings to the sponsoring organization. If the research was conducted for your thesis or dissertation, the findings must be "packaged" in a certain way for your professors. The same research results might also be used to prepare an article for a professional journal. Similarities occur in all research reports. The purpose of this chapter is to help you prepare a report of your research findings for a sponsoring organization, university faculty, or reviewers for a professional journal.

Publication as a Practice Goal

Williams and Hopps (1987) note that while few social workers "achieve comfort or familiarity with publishing," one of the hallmarks of a mature profession is that verifiable knowledge derived from practice is used to increase the quality, effectiveness, and efficiency of all practice. Where does verifiable knowledge come from? It does not flow automatically from the conduct of research, but is dependent upon reporting or communication of the research. All too often, good applied social work research is never "written up," but remains in file folders or on someone's desk until it becomes outdated or is thrown away. For the results of research to guide practice, the findings must be disseminated to colleagues and other professionals.

Meyer (1983) notes that "a profession is known by what it does. The chief way in which professional colleagues and the public get to know what social work does is through publication of its efforts" (p. 3). Writing about the successes and failures of interventions and about the problems of clients is clearly a responsibility of professional social workers. Indeed, the following passage is found in the National Association of Social Workers' Code of Ethics under "Development of Knowledge":

> The social worker should contribute to the knowledge base of social work and share research knowledge and practice wisdom with colleagues.

Writing for professional audiences can also provide a great deal of personal satisfaction as well as recognition.

The basic structure and key elements needed to report research findings are the same whether one is writing a thesis, an evaluation report, or a journal article. Of course, there are some observable differences when we compare these three types of reports. For one thing, academic committees expect the literature review section of a thesis or dissertation to be longer than that of most journal articles.

Regardless of the purpose for which the final research report is intended, its basic components are the same (Bausell, 1986). Further, the elements of the research report (the Introduction, Literature Review, Methodology, Findings, Discussion, References, and Appendices) are required for writing most research proposals—whether you are applying to a funding source to secure a grant to enable you to conduct the research or whether you are writing a prospectus for a proposed thesis or dissertation. (Of course, if you are proposing research, you will not be able to fully develop the Results and Discussion section. The bulk of the proposal will be the first three sections. However, it is possible to briefly address what findings you expect and any known limitations of the study.) An outline of the major elements in research reporting is as follows:

Components of a Research Report

1. Introduction
   a. Description of Problem
   b. Statement of research question or hypothesis
   c. Significance of problem and rationale for studying it

2. Literature Review
   a. Theoretical and historical perspectives
   b. Identified gaps in literature
   c. Reiteration of purpose of study
3. Methodology
   a. Research design and data collection procedures
   b. Characteristics of subjects
   c. Sampling design
   d. Description of instrumentation
   e. Data analysis procedures
4. Findings (Results)
   a. Factual information presented
   b. Tables, charts
   c. Statistical and practical significance discussed
5. Discussion
   a. Brief summary of findings
   b. Explanation of unexpected findings
   c. Applications to practice
   d. Weaknesses or limitations of research
   e. Suggestions for future research
6. References
7. Appendices

Introduction

The purpose of the Introduction is to present the research question or problem and to place it within some context or frame of reference. This generally entails describing the problem and its extent. For instance, in an article entitled "To Parent or Relinquish: Consequences for Adolescent Mothers," the authors note that of the more than one million teenaged girls who become pregnant each year, about half give birth and 7 percent place the child for adoption (McLaughlin, Pearce, Manninen, and Winges, 1988). The authors discuss the assumptions held by some researchers and pregnancy counselors that mothers who relinquish their children suffer few negative psychological effects. The authors then summarize studies where these mothers were found to have negative psychological effects. The problem of psychological effects becomes important because of the apparent contradiction between what may be believed by some pregnancy counselors and the studies that found negative consequences. It is obvious that the problem introduced early in the article is worthy of further study. Introductions help the reader understand why the research is important and was conducted.

Sometimes the Introduction distinguishes the research being reported from similar research. Your research may be unlike other studies because you have approached the problem with a different theoretical perspective and have used innovative methods or found new ways to measure outcome variables. The Introduction gives you an opportunity to briefly present the unique features of your study. By the end of the Introduction the reader should be aware of the focus of your research, its significance, and why the study was needed.

The Introduction should also be viewed as an opportunity to awaken the reader's interest in your topic. Skillful writers are often able to do this by catching our interest with their first paragraph. Take, for instance, the first line of a recent article by Walter and Greif (1988): "Should we educate students for private practice?" This line alone is successful in posing an interesting problem to consider. Consequently, many social workers would want to read more of the article.

Consider a second example of a thought-provoking opening to an article (Johnson, 1988):

> For the past two decades, the hyperactive child has generated controversy. Debates have centered around whether a hyperactive syndrome exists[1]; whether its etiology is physiological or psychogenic[2]; and whether medication, diet, behavior modification, cognitive therapy, family systems therapy, or psychodynamic psychotherapy is the treatment of choice.[3] (P. 349)

If the problem of hyperactivity interests you, this paragraph should whet your appetite for the rest of Johnson's article. After reading this paragraph you probably want to know more about the controversy. Perhaps you want to discover whether the approach you would take is the one chosen by the author of the article. While examples of dry, uninteresting introductions could also be provided here, I suspect you have read enough of these and do not want to imitate them.

The easiest research reports to read are those that engage your interest. Williams and Hopps (1988) have noted, "Getting off to a good start truly is three-quarters of the battle" (p. 456). One way to do this is to present the problem early in the Introduction instead of burying it toward the end. Material discussed in your Introduction makes more sense when the reader has a clear understanding of the problem prompting your investigation.

Review of the Literature

The literature review section of a report or journal article is where the notable and relevant theoretical explanations of the social problem or phenomenon of interest are summarized. You need not describe every study that has ever been conducted on your topic. Cite only those pertinent to the issues with which you are dealing (Kidder and Judd, 1986). For example, consider the following fictitious excerpt:

> While little has been written in the literature of criminology about shoplifting, it is an area of interest to practitioners and social scientists because of the seemingly complex dynamics involved. Financial need does not appear to be a significant motivating factor. Almost all of the studies have shown that poverty is not a major explanation for shoplifting.[1] Shoplifters tend to come from all economic classes,[2] and the overwhelming majority of persons caught shoplifting do not intend to resell the item.[3,4] It has also been noted that in only a minority of cases is shoplifting associated with mental illness, and the majority of arrested shoplifters do not have any psychotic features.[5] Recent studies have shown that shoplifters are not apprehended differentially by race, sex, or age when control variables are employed.[6,7]

From this brief example we can learn that theories based upon economic deprivation or mental illness have not been found to explain shoplifting. Further, explanations involving a greater level of absent-mindedness among the elderly do not seem to be viable. Since these theories have been tested and then discarded, the way is open for a new theoretical explanation—perhaps that shoplifting is a help-seeking activity unconsciously motivated by high levels of stress.

This excerpt also demonstrates that quite a few studies can be succinctly summarized in a short amount of space. This is necessary when writing for journals as most do not want long manuscripts. Many times students provide too much irrelevant information in the literature review. It is, for example, usually inconsequential whether the studies were conducted in Idaho or Missouri, or whether very large or medium-sized survey samples were used. It is more important that the literature review show trends in the major findings of these studies. The location, methodology, sample size, and other facets of the earlier research take on more importance only when you describe your study as being different from or similar to that research. In this instance, you may want to go into more detail in describing the study you are departing from or replicating. Why is it important to replicate or depart from another study? There may be legitimate reasons. You may want to correct for problems the previous study had with internal validity. Otherwise, it is not important to go into great detail regarding the methodology and each finding in all of the prior studies mentioned in your review of the literature.

Another common mistake authors make is to cite lengthy passages of background material. This is done either because the writer does not know how to paraphrase or summarize or because these passages provide "proof" that the writer actually read the background material. About this, Leedy (1989) gives some good advice: "Review the literature; don't reproduce it" (p. 71).

After you have thoroughly reviewed the material available on your topic, this information must be organized in some fashion. Generally, the reviews can be organized in one of two schemes: by chronological order or by theoretical orientation. A chronological organization involves an overview of the problem—mention the classic or pioneering studies, then move on to more recent studies that are most like the research you have conducted.

The other approach, organizing by major theoretical orientation, is illustrated by the following example: In reviewing the literature on child sexual abuse, you have found a sizable number of articles written from a psychoanalytic perspective. Even though you may not subscribe to that set of theoretical explanations, you still owe it to your readers to acknowledge rival theories or explanations. This provides some of the controversy or interest that can make reading your article or report enjoyable. The rival theories, however, do not need to receive an equal amount of space or coverage.

Since new research is usually conducted on those topics about which there is not much literature, the review of the literature section helps justify your research by pointing out gaps in the knowledge base. Unless you are replicating someone's study, you are likely to be conducting research in an area where not much is known. This gap in knowledge provides a major impetus for research.

After you have reviewed the relevant literature and noted the gaps in knowledge on a particular problem or topic, it is helpful to restate the purpose of your study. The reader may not be as familiar with the problem area as you are, and restating your hypothesis or research question will assist the reader in assimilating the potpourri of literature to which he or she has just been exposed.

The Method

The Method section of the report describes in detail how the study was done. In this section, the reader learns the procedures for and things you did when collecting the data. Typically, the following are described:

328

1. The research design. (Was it a single system design with multiple baselines, a survey research project, or some other design?)
2. Data collection procedures. (Did you use mailed questionnaires or personally interview the respondents? How was the informed consent obtained?)
3. The subjects. (How were they selected? What were their characteristics?)
4. The instrumentation. (What is known about the instrument's reliability and validity? How has the instrument been used?)
5. The statistical tests and measures to be used to analyze the data.

Following is a hypothetical example of a Method section.

METHOD

Subjects

The subjects were 350 first-offender shoplifters referred by the Municipal Court to the Downtown Mental Health Center during the calendar year 1990 for post-sentencing assessment. Their average age was 29 years. Seventy-five percent of the subjects were under the age of 45; 10 percent were 60 years of age or older. Eighty-six percent of the shoplifters were Caucasian. Slightly more than half (53%) were male; 57 percent were employed. Forty percent of all shoplifters were married. Divorced, separated, and widowed persons made up 20 percent of the sample.

Procedure

Upon referral from the Court and contact with the Downtown Mental Health Center for a scheduled psychosocial assessment, each subject was asked to complete the Symptom Checklist 90-Revised (Derogatis, 1983). This instrument is a 90-item self-report of psychological functioning with nine symptom scales and three global indices. The reliability and validity of the SCL-90-R are excellent and well-documented. Test-retest and internal consistency coefficients have been reported to range from .77 to .90 on the nine dimensions. The SCL-90-R has been used in a broad variety of clinical and medical contexts and has received positive independent evaluations (Edwards, 1978; Dies and MacKenzie, 1983).

After completing the SCL-90-R, each subject met with one of the Mental Health Center's social workers for a psychosocial assessment. These assessments were later typed and after any personally identifying information had been removed, were presented to a panel of three mental health program directors from an adjoining county. This panel independently read the assessments and reviewed the scores from the

SCL-90-Revised in order to check for appropriateness and agreement with the initial recommendations made to the Municipal Court. The panel rated each assessment using a scoring scheme where 10 indicated complete agreement with the assessment and recommendations and 0 indicated their complete lack of agreement concerning the reports made to the Court. The panel's ratings were summed to produce an overall rating. Each assessment could then receive a rating ranging between 0 and 30. Pearson Correlations were used to determine the association between the two dependent variables: overall assessment ratings and the SCL-90-R scores. A t-test was used to test for differences in the dependent variables when the first-time offenders were grouped by whether or not they received mental health counseling within the year following their arrest.

Enough information should be provided in the Method section to permit replication by any other interested researcher. In this section, operational definitions are reported along with procedures that were followed in collecting the data. Setting or location of the study can be important to mention, as well as the specifics of the data collection. For instance, Behling (1984) suggests that in field interviews, using white interviewers in a black community may lead to a distortion of the gathered information. In other words, rather than just stating that four interviewers were used, the researcher ought to specify the sex, age, and race of the interviewers.

The Results

This section of the report or article contains what you actually discovered from conducting your research. The Results section summarizes the data. It does not present the raw data; it reports aggregate or average scores. Up to this point, you have not revealed your findings. Now it is time to exhibit your findings. Your task in this section is to present the results factually, without opinion. The facts must stand by themselves.

You can organize your findings in many ways. The most common practice is to present the major findings first. If you have used several hypotheses, report your findings relative to the first hypothesis, then move to the second hypothesis, and so on.

Many researchers and would-be authors often feel overwhelmed because there appears to be too much information for a single research report. This can happen when they have lots of hypotheses or as a result of doing data analysis to the point that their shelves sag from the weight of computer printouts. Thinking that findings are all equally important contributes to a feeling of drowning in data. It might be helpful to realize that you do not have to present any more data than is needed to test your hypotheses (Mullins, 1977). Becker (1986) notes, "We know we cannot describe everything. In fact, one aim of science and scholarship is exactly to reduce what has to be described to manageable proportions" (p. 133).

I find it helpful to get a blank sheet of paper and write down what I would report if I were limited to one major point. I then ask myself, "What is the second most important finding coming from this study?" This process continues until all of the important points have been identified. Once the important findings have been noted, I begin thinking about how I will present them. Tables and charts are helpful in that they visually break up the narrative while providing precise information that makes pretty dry reading if it is incorporated into the text.

Most research reports contain tables as a way of summarizing data or reducing verbiage. You should develop at least one or two tables for your research report, particularly if you have gone beyond univariate analysis. However, having too many tables is almost as bad as not having enough. Because of space limitations and the expense required to reproduce tables, you will seldom see journal articles with more than four or five. When too many tables are employed, it is hard for a reader or reviewer to keep all of the main points in mind; the information tends to run together.

In the Results section you will also report the outcomes of the statistical tests you have conducted. For example, if your studies found that BSW social workers received higher quality assurance ratings than MSW social workers, it will be important to determine if the difference in ratings is statistically significant. Do not allow your readers to conclude that a difference of three points, for example, makes BSW social workers superior to MSW social workers if a t-test or other appropriate statistical test reveals no statistically significant difference in their scores. Report the average scores, the results of statistical tests, and the associated probability. (Refer to chapter 9 if you need to see examples of tables or ways to express statistical information.) Further elaboration and explanation of the data are usually presented in the Discussion section.

The Discussion

The Discussion section often begins with a brief summary of your findings. It is not necessary to go into a lot of detail—this information was just exhibited in the Results. Just address the major findings or the highlights of your study. Once that is done, you can begin to expound on the findings. Perhaps you were surprised to find that the BSWs in your study performed better than the MSW employees; here is the place to elaborate the reasons for your surprise. You can reveal any unexpected findings—as well as what didn't go as planned.

Most importantly, the Discussion section should interpret the findings for the reader and address the relevance of these findings for practice. What do the findings mean or suggest to you? Are you recommending that social service agencies hire BSWs rather than persons with other undergraduate degrees? Does additional training seem to be indicated for the type of employee covered in your study? Do social work educators need to re-examine and possibly revise the curricula at their institutions? What implications does your study have for practice or policy? Discuss findings that have practical significance—even if there was no statistical significance. As Reid (1988) has indicated, our findings do not always "prove," "establish," or make a point so strongly that there can be no other interpretation. Usually, Discussion sections contain what he calls "appropriately qualified language"— phrases that indicate that the findings "provide evidence for," "suggest the possibility that," or "raise questions about."

The part of the Discussion section that many researchers do not like to write is the description of what did not go according to the research design. Sometimes secretaries forget to administer questionnaires. Clients drop out of studies or forget to bring needed documentation. Questionnaires may not be mailed on time. These glitches are normal in applied social science research. Social workers don't have the same degree of control that laboratory scientists have. So, admit any major departures from planned research procedures. The problems you encountered in collecting your data may well explain why you got the results that you did. For instance, someone forgetting to mail reminder postcards could have caused you to have a lower response rate for one group than for another. A change in agency policies during the middle of your study could have changed staff morale or increased the proportion of employees who felt "burned out"— which in turn could have affected the quality of their work. Also, recognize biases that may have crept into your study or that you discovered too late to do anything about.

Your study may have significant limitations. While you had hoped for a representative sampling of social workers from all educational backgrounds, and you heard from 75 percent of all the BSWs, perhaps only 8 percent of the MSWs responded. Eight percent certainly would not represent the majority of the MSW sample. Your subjects may not be representative because the sample was not random, or the study may not be generalizable because other agencies do not organize their services in the same way. You cannot survey adults in one locality (e.g., Moorhead, Minnesota) and generalize those findings to adults in another completely different location (e.g., the Everglades) unless you sample from both locations. In this section you can discuss the extent to which it is possible to generalize your research.

Almost every study has some limitations—perhaps the most common one is some sort of selection bias. If it is hard for you to think of limitations, you may want to review the section on internal and external threats to the validity of a study.

Many authors conclude their research reports and journal articles by indicating areas for future research. As a result of their experiences, they may have suggestions for other researchers about procedures, instruments, the operationalization of variables, sampling techniques, and so on. This is done for altruistic reasons—a researcher may not plan on further work in that area and wishes others to benefit from what has been learned in the process of conducting the present research.

References, Appendices, and Abstracts

Whenever other written documents have been cited in your research reporting, they need to be listed in the **Reference** section at the end of the report or manuscript. References are usually listed alphabetically by authors' names, and there are various styles or ways in which the titles can appear. The reference style that you use is likely to be more important to academic committees and journals than it will be to funding sources. Some journals have their own style. When preparing your Reference section, look for examples or ask a person in authority which style you should use. (This is discussed a little more in the next section.)

The **Appendix** is where you place a copy of instruments, written instructions given to subjects, or important materials that may have been used during the course of your study. Research reports (especially those prepared for academic committees) are not complete without a copy of your instrument. However, most journals do not require or expect you to submit a manuscript with an appendix. Journals seldom have the space to publish instruments used in research reports.

Abstracts are brief summaries of reports or manuscripts. Generally, they average 100 to 150 words, (although some journals may want a 25 to 50 word abstract). Abstracts are prepared to help readers decide whether they want to read a journal article, to help those who are attending national or regional conferences decide which presentations they will go to, and to help those who are categorizing research know which subject headings to use. Abstracts are almost always difficult to write because of the need to compress a voluminous report into one paragraph or less. When you write an abstract, limit yourself to two or three sentences to introduce the study and two or three sentences to present your major finding. If you get stumped, look at several abstracts in a recent issue of *Social Work Abstracts* for ideas on how to be succinct.

Writing for Professional Journals

You must remember a few additional things if you decide to prepare your research report for submission to a professional journal. First of all, journals vary considerably in the way they want manuscripts structured. Some journals use a combined Results and Discussion section. Some want a separate Conclusion and others don't. When you prepare a manuscript, have a specific journal in mind. Become familiar with that journal. Are its articles written for the practitioner or for the scholar? Journals have different audiences. Journals that want articles for the practitioner may expect case examples, vignettes, or suggestions for working with a particular type of client. Other journals expect sophisticated analytical procedures. Some journals want a very detailed literature review, while others don't. You will have more success placing articles in a journal when you become well acquainted with it (e.g., know the style, format, and type of article that the journal tends to publish).

Practically all journals carry a statement informing readers and prospective authors of the type of content with which they are concerned. By reading such statements, prospective authors determine if their manuscripts would be appropriate for the journals. For instance, this statement is found in *Social Work*:

> Social Work is a professional journal committed to improving practice and extending knowledge in social work and social welfare. The Editorial Board welcomes manuscripts that yield new insights into established practices, evaluate new techniques and research, examine current social problems, or bring serious critical analysis to bear on the problems of the profession itself.

When writing for a journal, keep in mind that the entire manuscript (including references) should not exceed sixteen or seventeen double-spaced pages. Since it is not unusual for research reports and theses to contain a hundred or more pages, probably the biggest chore before you will be trying to find a way to condense the literature review to two or three typed pages.

Journals want original manuscripts that are clearly written, of timely interest, appropriate to the journal, of the right length, and in the correct style. Journal reviewers look for an adequate literature review, reasonable research design, and the correct use of statistical techniques. But beyond those considerations, reviewers must decide whether or not your manuscript makes a "contribution" to the knowledge base. Reviewers may decide that your manuscript makes no contribution because of severe limitations in its generalizability, or because a more thorough literature review would have revealed the existence of studies similar to the one being reported. A manuscript might even be judged "interesting" but not relevant to social work practice.

You will probably increase your chances of publication if you find a journal that, in the last six years or so, has published similar (or somewhat related) articles to the one you are preparing. While this is no guarantee that the journal will publish your article, at least it indicates that the reviewers have had an interest in your topic. Study the articles that have recently appeared in the journal. Observe the reference style, the use of tables, the length of the literature review, and the general level at which the article is written.

When you have narrowed down your choice of journals to one or two, obtain their "Information for Authors." You can write, for instance, to the publications office of the National Association of Social Work (NASW), and they will send you a brochure covering the NASW journals. Other journals print instructions for authors once or twice a year within an issue of their journal.

In recent years there has been a movement toward the use of the reference style of the American Psychological Association (APA). This reference style is a good one to learn even if you don't use it to write journal manuscripts. The APA style is widely accepted and convenient to use. A professional appearance, the correct reference style, a catchy title, and a thought-provoking introduction will undoubtedly improve the odds of your manuscript getting a favorable response from reviewers.

After you revise and polish your manuscript to the point where you think it is finished, set it aside. After several days, reread it. Make necessary revisions, and prepare a clean copy. Share that with two or three persons whose opinions you respect. Find someone who can give you constructive criticism without battering your ego. If you know that you are weak in the grammar department, seek a reviewer who knows that area.

One thing that you should *not* do is send your manuscript to more than one journal at a time. Most journals will not review your manuscript if it is being reviewed by another journal. If your manuscript is rejected by the first journal you choose, do not be discouraged. A rejection does not necessarily mean that your manuscript is poorly conceptualized or written. It could be that the journal just accepted a similar article on the same topic last week. Or, it may mean that the journal is planning special issues, and your manuscript does not fit their needs. You may have submitted your article to an inappropriate journal. Sometimes, reviewers may not completely understand your approach. Reviews are conducted "blind"—that is, you will not know who read your manuscript and will have no way of knowing whether the reviewer knew as much about your topic or your methodology as you do. So, even good articles can be rejected. If your first effort is rejected, dust off your pride and try to objectively read your manuscript again. Revise it if necessary, and submit it to the second journal of your choice.

Journal reviewers usually make one of four decisions: they accept, accept on condition, reject, or reject but encourage resubmission. Most journals send the reviewers' comments when revisions are needed and when a manuscript has been rejected. I have run into only one journal that did not send back the reviewers' comments when a manuscript was rejected. Generally, but not always, when the requested revisions have been made, your article will be accepted.

Even if your manuscript is rejected twice, it still may have a chance at publication. You may want to get Mendelsohn's (1993) *Author's Guide to Social Work Journals* for suggestions of additional journals that might be interested in your manuscript. This guide also gives the acceptance rate of over sixty journals. Some journals accept proportionately a much larger percentage of manuscripts than others.

If your manuscript has been rejected three times, should you continue trying to get it published? This is the point at which I become frustrated and tired of working with one manuscript and I quit. However, if you feel that yours is basically a good manuscript, and some of the reviewers have encouraged revision, then you should try it again.

Getting a manuscript published is like most other things in life that require practice. The more you practice, the better you will become at this activity. Carlton (1988) says that it is like learning to ride a bicycle. The way to learn is by getting back up and trying again! Along the way, there are some very helpful resources available to you in learning how to write more professionally. I recommend Strunk and White's (1979) *The Elements of Style*, Mullins' (1977) *A Guide to Writing and Publishing in the Social and Behavioral Sciences*, and Becker's (1986) *Writing for Social Scientists: How to Start and Finish Your Thesis, Book, or Article*. And, of course, there are many other books that librarians can recommend to assist you with your writing.

Reading and Critiquing Research Manuscripts

Students have a tendency to believe that any research that manages to appear in print is "good" research. I wish that this were so. Unfortunately, some pretty shoddy research can be found in journals without too much difficulty. As I stated in the beginning of this book, one reason you are required to enroll in a research methods course is to help you recognize poor or inadequate research. Flawed research (if unrecognized) could lead you to conclusions that are not warranted and could be dangerous to your clients.

Using the major content areas of research reports, we can construct a set of criteria to use in evaluating research reports, journal articles, or manuscripts. (These criteria can also be used to double-check your manuscripts.) I'm indebted to Garfield (1984) for his observations and guidelines on this topic.

CRITERIA FOR EVALUATING RESEARCH REPORTS

1. Does the Introduction provide a clear notion of (a) the problem, (b) the purpose of the research, and (c) its significance?
2. Are the stated hypotheses reasonable? Do they appear to logically follow from the review of the literature?
3. Is the literature review (a) relevant to the study, (b) thorough, and (c) current?
4. Is a research design stated? Do the subjects appear to have been selected without overt bias? If there is a control group, does it seem to be an appropriate group for comparison? Is the number of subjects sufficient?
5. Is there a discussion of the reliability and validity of the instruments that are used?
6. Is there enough information on (a) the procedures and (b) the instruments and the operational definitions of the variables to allow you to replicate this study?
7. Are statistical tests present when needed? If statistical tests are used, are they the appropriate tests?

8. Are the findings discussed in terms of their implications and practical significance? Are the conclusions supported by and do they logically follow from the data that have been presented? Is the author guilty of overgeneralizing? Has actual or potential bias been recognized?

When evaluating a research report, you should find yourself answering "yes" to most of the criteria questions. Strong research articles will elicit a greater number of affirmative responses. Weak articles will receive a larger number of negative responses. You can use these criteria not only to evaluate the research reports prepared by others, but also to check your own report or manuscript to ensure that you have included all of the crucial elements.

This chapter has attempted to provide you with instruction in the key components in research report writing. Three points cannot be emphasized enough: (1) the importance of studying examples of other research reports and literature; (2) the importance of social workers' publishing their research results; and (3) the need to have perseverance when first efforts are rejected by journal reviewers.

When you publish your research, you contribute to the knowledge base of social work and allow others to build upon your research. Knowledge is an incremental process; it moves forward in small steps rather than large leaps. Any movement toward the goal of advancing social work knowledge starts with understanding the research process. Knowledge tends to become obsolete with the passage of time, so it is necessary that social workers not only read research as a way of keeping up with new developments in the field but also engage in research and seek professional outlets for the dissemination of research efforts. Otherwise, as Williams and Hopps (1987) have noted, "the profession does not advance, clients cannot thrive, and practice does not improve" (p. 376).

Questions for Class Discussion

1. Discuss the ways in which a research report is similar to and different from the customary term paper.
2. Discuss what it is about a "good" journal article that makes it interesting or fun to read and what it is about some journal articles that make them dull and uninteresting.
3. How is writing for professional audiences different from writing to relatives or friends?
4. Think about the various sections of the research report. Tell the class what you think would be the most difficult section to write and your reasons for thinking this.

Mini-Projects for Experiencing Research Firsthand

1. Select a term paper you have recently written. Prepare it as you would if you were going to submit it to a social work journal. If you do not have real data, use fictitious data for the Results section and for the purpose of preparing a table or two. If you are feeling especially brave, exchange this effort with a classmate for friendly criticism concerning your writing style and understanding of this chapter.

2. Go to the library and locate several dissertations on topics of interest to you. Select one and summarize the important points made under each of the major sections of the dissertation. Briefly discuss what you learned from this project.

3. Interview one or more faculty members about their experiences with professional writing. What have been their joys and frustrations? What advice do they have for you?

4. Find an evaluation report or some research reported in a journal article. Using the criteria suggested in this chapter, evaluate the research. What did you learn in the process?

Resources and References

American Psychological Association. (1983). *Publication Manual of the American Psychological Association.* 3rd ed. Washington, DC.

Bausell, R.B. (1986). *A Practical Guide to Conducting Empirical Research.* New York: Harper & Row.

Beaver, M., Gottlieb, N., and Rosenblatt, A. (1983). Dilemmas in manuscript evaluations. *Social Work,* 28(4), 326.

Becker, H.S. (1986). *Writing for Social Scientists: How to Start and Finish Your Thesis, Book, or Article.* Chicago, IL: University of Chicago Press.

Beebe, L. (1993). *Professional Writing for the Human Services.* Washington, DC: NASW Press.

Behling, J.H. (1984). *Guidelines for Preparing the Research Proposal.* New York: University Press of America.

Carlton, T.O. (1987). Who are our authors? *Health and Social Work,* 12(Spring), 82–84.

Carlton, T.O. (1988). Publishing as a professional activity. *Health and Social Work,* 13(Spring), 85–89.

Garfield, S.L. (1984). The evaluation of research: An editorial perspective. In A.S. Bellack and M. Hersen (Eds.), *Research Methods in Clinical Psychology.* New York: Pergamon Press.

Johnson, H.C. (1988). Drugs, dialogue, or diet: Diagnosing and treating the hyperactive child. *Social Work,* 33(4), 349–355.

Kidder, L.H. and Judd, C.M. (1986). *Research Methods in Social Relations.* New York: Holt, Rinehart and Winston.

Leedy, P.D. (1989). *Practical Research: Planning and Design.* New York: Macmillan.

Leukefeld, C.G. and Ries, J.B. (1993). Strategies to compete for federal grant funding for research on social work practice. *Research on Social Work Practice,* 3(2), 208–218.

McLaughlin, S.D., Pearce, S.E., Manninen, D.L., and Winges, L.D. (1988). To parent or relinquish: Consequences for adolescent mothers. *Social Work,* 33(4), 320–324.

Mendelsohn, H. (1993). *An Author's Guide to Social Work Journals.* Silver Spring, MD: National Association of Social Workers.

Meyer, C.H. (1983). Responsibility in publishing. *Social Work,* 28(1), 3.

Mullins, C.J. (1977). *A Guide to Writing and Publishing in the Social and Behavioral Sciences.* New York: Wiley.

Reid, W.J. (1988). Writing research reports. In R.M. Grinnell (Ed.), *Social Work Research and Evaluation.* Itasca, IL: Peacock.

Ross-Larson, B. (1982). *Edit Yourself: A Manual for Everyone Who Works with Words.* New York: Norton.

Strunk, W. and White, E.B. (1979). *The Elements of Style.* New York: Macmillan.

Walter, C.A. and Greif, G.L. (1988). To do or not to do: Social work education for private practice. *Journal of Independent Social Work,* 2(3), 17–24.

Williams, L.F. and Hopps, J.G. (1987). Publication as a practice goal: Enhancing opportunities for social workers. *Social Work,* 32(5), 373–376.

Williams, L.F. and Hopps, J.G. (1988). On the nature of professional communications: Publication for practitioners. *Social Work,* 33(5), 453–459.

Appendices

A. Attitudes about Research Courses
B. How to Use a Table of Random Numbers
   Table of Random Numbers
C. Drug Attitude Questionnaire

A
Attitudes about Research Courses

1. Check the following courses that you successfully completed in *high school*:

   Algebra I _____   Geometry _____

   Algebra II _____   Calculus _____

2. What is your age? _____

3. What is your gender? Male _____   Female _____

4. Consider for a moment the extent (if any) of your fear of research courses. Indicate your fear on the scale below:

No fear				*Some fear*				*Lots of fear*	
1	2	3	4	5	6	7	8	9	10

5. On the following scale, rate your perception of how useful you think research courses will be to you.

Not very useful				*Some use*				*Very useful*	
1	2	3	4	5	6	7	8	9	10

6. On the following scale, rate your interest in taking research courses.

No interest				*Some interest*				*Lots of interest*	
1	2	3	4	5	6	7	8	9	10

In order to better understand your feelings about research, indicate whether the following statements are true or false.

7. T or F   I dread speaking before a large group of people more than taking a research course.

8. T or F I would rather take a research course than ask a waitress to return an improperly cooked meal to the chef.

9. T or F My fear of snakes is greater than my fear of taking a research course.

10. T or F My fear of spiders is less than my fear of taking a research course.

11. T or F I would rather take a research course than ask a total stranger to do a favor for me.

12. T or F My fear of research is such that I would rather the university require an additional two courses of my choosing than take one research course.

13. T or F I dread going to the dentist more than taking a research course.

14. T or F I fear a statistics course more than a research methodology course.

15. T or F I have always "hated math."

The following symbols frequently appear in research studies that utilize statistical analyses. To the best of your ability, identify the statistical symbols. If unknown, write "unknown." (Example: the symbol + means addition.)

16. F

17. df

18. t

19. r

20. X^2

21. $p < .05$

22. $\overline{X}$, M

23. SD, S

B

How to Use a Table of Random Numbers

Assume that you have 500 clients and you need to select a random sample of 25 from that population. You have already made a list of these persons and accurately counted or numbered them from 1 to 500. In order to draw a random sample, you will need to get a random starting place on the Table of Random Numbers. Before you do this, you need to think about a way to encompass every numerical possibility that will occur within your population. If you choose a single digit number—for example, 9—as the starting place, any number larger than one digit (the numbers 10 through 99, and 100 through 500) would be excluded. There is no possibility of their being chosen. If you choose a two-digit number, you would still exclude the three-digit numbers. Therefore, you have to look at the numbers in the Random Number Table in groups of three—numbers such as 009, 147, 935, and so on. This will allow the lowest possible number (001) and the highest possible number (500) in your population (as well as all the numbers in between) to have an equal chance of being chosen.

Now you are ready to draw a sample from the Random Number Table. Since the values on the table are arranged in no particular order, it makes no difference where or how you start. You could, for instance, roll a pair of dice. The number of dots on one could direct you to a particular column and the value on the other would direct you to a particular row of random numbers. You can start from the top or bottom of the table and from the left or right side. You could also shuffle a deck of cards and select two cards—again letting the value of the first indicate a specific column and the value of the second, a particular row.

A third way to find a random starting place would be to shut your eyes and, holding a pencil or pen, let your hand come down somewhere on the page. Start from that point and take the next twenty-five three-digit numbers. Of course, if you select a number like 947 or 515, you will have to discard them as they fall outside of the range (1–500).

As you look at the Table of Random Numbers, you will notice that they are grouped in sets of six. It makes no difference if you ignore the first three digits and use the last three of each set or vice versa. When you have selected twenty-five three-digit numbers falling between 1 and 500, you have your random sample! For your convenience, six-digit random numbers have been provided, as well as two-digit numbers. All of the random numbers appearing in these tables were created using StatPac (Walonick Associates, Minneapolis, MN), a computer software program for IBM personal computers.

Table of Random Numbers

```
360062 190148 438921 828610 137813 597216 745136 848373 980702 292403
934762 289048 055252 239359 049231 215708 828323 995602 968653 358123
316630 308216 845177 333584 306213 537904 849376 571680 527394 587341
827749 459314 277743 328793 589905 452433 234203 534213 474746 301166
103359 918057 943330 745098 125601 036980 264454 594793 641501 882535
375215 397377 256691 478121 756814 210058 534319 441724 852186 016678
711032 882621 934206 136008 254288 288709 678536 919749 453691 818526
804845 256068 781681 476628 926897 721293 885133 841857 170057 958707
597462 768354 455724 262587 204958 059064 129034 774120 391834 283950
383424 363439 565399 148896 123675 712072 996343 282454 249228 733297
845446 785274 471471 718267 294703 952780 751216 614147 457324 357589
171037 236626 116308 872015 117031 393199 195654 417915 018433 885064
663704 963322 005562 992787 948421 510794 503441 139789 965668 766346
523120 499512 649587 503120 800718 621563 607424 665129 444721 989526
943685 339626 172547 475197 315309 814281 493565 095760 286835 187233
558632 445148 561021 599971 695121 839266 279515 263519 094626 630463
688812 481716 366194 887525 382441 049265 372731 024735 983979 595913
432063 938512 127163 196425 190817 044621 282333 700128 923578 279450
616425 385590 995664 296416 700414 148695 772517 274528 450435 312249
177081 382698 762128 096542 471251 085339 773561 531650 371110 232144
530653 007347 034621 130744 819405 044061 723251 190820 948230 420664
859438 714944 839905 399521 403420 389841 865691 925150 534086 261256
478363 028813 179916 334684 484782 273687 169375 159339 855149 501638
179879 858717 458259 662477 496169 146879 054723 012672 049258 883983
197394 745101 457920 776831 870531 729547 653602 451897 126884 288820
864168 863472 759723 713886 954710 314435 427718 136254 608664 820371
289783 139474 443702 674947 482657 948359 675381 826215 567342 320576
453771 612352 964705 584665 576308 021767 131857 121105 116437 586709
771929 432675 678846 540545 261755 722765 349004 558358 061999 470437
438957 456465 462582 436340 439747 995892 780771 086956 331691 334670
423067 313598 952164 288314 368104 215367 758617 797918 015908 268229
635581 071294 187198 997320 028534 678312 990718 802314 896228 742233
469967 251190 422673 372251 056526 859375 364695 542428 278938 354415
229743 588774 943979 332417 965270 655637 884089 696910 950841 324693
191392 506200 244620 456768 704170 114582 215714 082047 211036 557119
```

694263 645228 571122 404316 476840 552599 105398 446706 612208 069318
351932 442182 850948 841429 173236 187547 552477 131697 916519 029457
558148 431434 478713 007287 886565 575708 286567 724930 298812 943466
038521 199608 271446 416385 236335 462221 229815 538351 988086 718374
864765 228339 185429 574355 140673 021209 909292 244733 669420 291568
974542 569344 959914 700605 782962 169014 973246 671660 192281 661616
264162 109862 867096 687032 598209 665463 066929 722172 590366 238613
445488 309098 421077 946418 127374 286528 764465 273529 294707 920736
467002 286904 132511 993433 649861 827461 222143 556678 432181 456489
986860 978646 111117 024382 603227 377658 573793 128952 716583 775441
169511 226369 780706 930881 685925 294012 262731 544159 377025 570185
308173 625996 969762 979549 664350 012532 512684 588049 318207 564618
878811 783706 910275 112341 218124 652945 171602 527991 229607 815838
278763 297234 048362 308910 187519 185283 364950 433522 704987 059778
530363 171119 888942 167106 088337 519772 911971 607160 913710 779405
866869 688575 126713 737843 574003 216753 721812 813626 255670 771795
891861 442215 376581 850219 389477 925962 585869 161312 936721 760627
322786 491593 429552 836224 607442 327051 112775 664766 725967 795476
076249 431363 462194 445651 805690 228695 133676 011440 587539 484783
874146 718672 417301 913406 186209 028230 580430 488330 156319 472929
104513 534446 071772 923958 277696 438183 363891 736907 792323 033881
272359 342335 479491 752199 439043 135940 177676 489942 823149 389964
837251 449346 990749 232106 849040 246120 915151 046574 086474 951102
300239 526082 275425 864644 255618 586659 586779 634811 760206 651101
326919 522280 135116 633716 242288 394810 469045 913214 872541 623147
286540 344675 688627 747112 218430 889465 713441 164061 743321 129213
562576 417784 123878 615964 731064 206033 649060 029306 462497 898382
147167 122636 428552 479679 677090 334296 418436 971886 821828 209413
315649 417693 433447 275273 904126 206837 305433 749136 239819 340865
648650 778748 858718 907534 373539 203721 640184 172232 611261 695838
834730 325729 777355 126053 304084 159225 329256 882337 370627 413617
987275 175087 613310 441852 625687 662889 133838 518255 276538 821307
251799 323724 543163 013816 700677 155137 326035 491384 273298 032312
753162 993738 040435 680578 852692 539350 267744 294590 782261 034416
784092 496125 541474 182310 976291 621721 230184 471211 841234 930067
841844 938184 109491 957664 477333 847088 913504 515006 077653 126463
545078 063366 627602 995358 264044 544670 882557 476983 389775 456239
164724 120527 179080 309514 047799 061393 645651 769262 163020 459569
761433 081901 050561 360229 561105 175595 713613 669764 123888 087305
902684 551644 837068 171911 627997 674947 239108 661286 731266 497194
261632 555061 730594 275155 828748 240707 615985 267413 621999 374517
958988 356182 869666 864566 413596 101896 333437 354502 938975 863428
748569 455584 418153 160238 095463 330085 258035 676887 492603 251398
995430 641294 427426 455163 943985 384488 136526 964447 746515 708724
956215 830348 525163 609376 455178 737630 152265 501178 703582 295828
511139 546370 855892 789137 746091 842430 607468 087634 739539 400568
189068 404796 138075 639059 919469 252411 707994 210365 141856 495632
589571 313497 071962 517638 720857 612681 382192 322761 077542 828422
984835 822396 659712 589836 271442 033396 303404 613157 532634 037025
845293 981683 615881 219591 527250 452723 708748 830794 564915 434747
124531 129637 652386 578694 131967 450529 117483 486800 816065 227018

384639 949459 093621 295163 276654 473410 491026 594617 795927 569888
243543 695889 922952 881611 877041 352198 915765 396644 081382 975151
622302 483201 644443 967914 390779 151218 644301 899950 062328 025854
857471 031119 165942 167312 924395 321514 366357 392558 956718 249373
178286 684356 809681 131210 176870 448290 609916 973228 379069 791758
443008 158904 779758 189283 350316 979783 587586 374269 589338 968024
598940 868212 983014 378833 826406 891028 734779 456553 288100 592301
370939 841968 182186 454701 230046 045351 844519 428438 950725 112235
398881 185248 365169 472322 751988 275591 454914 904038 886313 776566
156138 853547 912549 723498 325563 964226 493813 063187 617240 290437
408062 150806 152468 739663 981826 202206 698117 590745 814507 112806
721228 112073 056712 264597 451561 147033 100817 535994 326176 614676
721190 399214 293671 353228 931598 325218 335996 935316 867382 373235
154787 240715 535107 689927 762804 321127 775267 792724 467721 155978
532643 369843 798877 608447 172582 429622 143483 417422 287601 057343
154144 691289 519238 863037 622625 197219 371853 899947 595789 309547
746845 478417 342906 350916 514353 088278 507124 685727 594705 656146
001035 537965 927346 685597 076802 730995 592412 870556 090309 634497
377141 615820 622926 964942 143322 550171 325874 362046 561667 626383
135918 415509 545895 146601 144155 929658 071321 203839 814732 952532
670012 611934 878476 206920 071128 566623 775407 723438 125868 362163
735642 074829 697719 112493 206493 228157 680488 816144 307254 101267
694556 165996 438329 225530 689537 928896 492600 869972 615567 786554
484205 333404 735725 462430 474932 391296 794264 192903 849922 147401
862537 675645 905221 283924 694956 264651 187131 111245 153893 168577
610323 954314 499918 203838 622421 964812 658753 258581 440881 827922
824517 677577 142000 853789 327631 005242 575257 611859 586983 997421
425936 475266 965271 630342 811155 290622 282301 529180 961431 071887
249194 821913 226211 214979 142871 323025 866573 239377 196238 124983
624517 718822 914510 807246 287277 222788 972259 101272 368951 145111
588724 622573 651468 149139 210402 561132 473894 713883 034079 333652
444542 120017 512157 242871 815654 472193 531818 303038 159597 463842

24 05 35 72 53 97 56 04 97 75 15 12 35 23 94 96 95 70 37 44
65 94 98 51 65 60 65 87 05 91 71 54 45 83 31 42 41 93 89 98
83 38 35 06 01 82 53 67 24 04 43 39 20 47 70 46 28 65 09 56
98 38 94 52 86 06 90 94 11 88 31 37 29 51 15 54 71 70 10 66
97 21 59 36 07 87 22 45 01 22 90 50 20 11 74 44 71 55 31 40
63 27 69 38 17 77 35 69 83 43 67 07 50 17 65 45 75 88 27 20
84 45 52 45 65 70 82 89 91 24 94 47 59 75 14 78 87 24 27 09
52 23 62 72 26 36 55 79 77 76 85 28 52 04 51 82 32 40 52 64
32 96 64 53 63 97 30 99 35 21 78 89 22 35 90 08 93 32 72 44
50 78 88 85 42 88 20 86 38 63 76 09 37 83 74 74 24 37 09 51
06 19 39 97 91 28 94 16 65 94 62 25 61 63 86 87 38 13 53 80
12 03 03 27 74 80 60 68 06 51 94 73 80 15 76 04 09 07 43 00
82 24 80 04 12 00 91 52 55 96 50 25 18 54 03 47 40 84 32 98
30 94 19 05 63 21 06 51 42 51 80 24 19 92 90 59 87 75 25 69
83 37 12 32 42 20 55 14 01 38 74 51 13 37 89 32 63 88 28 46
85 66 88 13 37 09 77 11 40 09 15 03 85 35 04 75 79 86 51 62
92 00 87 93 88 04 36 59 69 14 51 75 83 78 39 12 10 22 82 41
60 51 55 79 56 39 49 59 96 62 75 76 84 09 93 15 48 90 14 13
48 32 19 35 57 26 79 52 53 26 18 00 58 38 18 64 68 14 38 24

94	67	67	56	46	12	99	94	97	08	77	25	34	85	91	49	54	80	78	92
45	76	36	57	05	45	64	95	21	54	34	97	64	43	44	19	23	95	54	33
65	31	88	44	29	07	58	43	93	20	74	61	73	97	23	43	96	73	18	55
88	87	40	47	88	35	29	50	32	16	13	81	68	64	83	53	10	57	31	51
67	71	02	31	99	68	34	88	92	86	18	38	91	11	80	97	39	88	13	14
68	93	02	45	95	71	99	11	54	26	27	33	18	09	66	80	45	55	42	81
58	49	16	33	18	97	53	97	11	55	74	94	65	66	39	74	82	65	42	09
15	72	97	85	77	39	64	67	87	66	28	92	82	07	34	38	57	81	48	64
44	94	80	90	78	45	83	34	45	18	60	71	73	51	27	76	85	51	29	94
32	83	21	38	47	87	23	97	38	89	83	72	44	66	18	67	72	46	97	38
07	69	16	09	94	51	35	18	69	27	96	15	54	47	81	69	73	12	37	64
54	40	07	75	21	35	68	94	75	85	46	90	68	97	87	91	03	16	00	53
86	95	66	28	20	22	16	18	98	93	83	43	25	58	10	80	99	90	94	15
35	64	89	69	82	87	46	12	25	59	29	48	46	88	01	67	64	13	31	13
94	80	15	98	90	06	66	91	95	64	17	81	69	47	80	93	67	71	38	11
66	08	77	92	77	01	06	18	28	63	98	78	18	84	14	73	11	53	93	40
28	73	84	96	78	21	86	12	99	57	90	51	51	74	19	25	30	54	83	34
46	15	42	79	55	04	53	08	36	64	62	04	09	37	99	23	56	76	79	99
79	56	67	84	28	57	81	39	71	08	38	23	26	59	41	74	68	15	57	58
95	24	40	38	32	39	25	63	96	49	04	20	29	04	93	98	83	47	90	30
25	53	02	01	38	07	87	04	86	93	38	78	85	31	22	42	37	56	44	86
82	95	94	98	92	95	41	35	45	12	51	41	72	99	90	20	22	63	85	37
22	91	86	32	55	63	36	67	77	72	91	00	56	07	51	45	62	39	75	43
63	23	41	94	82	83	83	78	40	71	15	09	70	63	88	23	00	18	03	52
01	86	03	55	74	15	86	21	88	03	36	81	39	09	83	95	83	57	50	57
64	85	26	07	27	50	94	09	43	31	06	77	38	59	17	33	60	24	87	71
20	37	72	07	32	82	94	44	77	74	38	96	35	71	27	09	49	94	86	36
71	32	19	72	38	69	35	49	56	45	59	96	66	87	53	79	69	43	46	96
47	92	32	73	45	59	45	94	43	05	66	98	53	25	35	35	21	62	92	95
36	98	50	11	94	50	52	41	11	64	26	48	68	90	26	54	84	24	81	36
50	61	17	98	18	35	64	71	31	53	03	41	30	96	55	51	28	04	07	48
49	38	52	47	68	02	89	66	49	88	25	65	66	34	83	89	73	84	30	04
63	10	89	95	52	26	86	28	76	07	66	70	19	51	88	11	99	20	56	41
94	52	53	53	73	91	76	55	54	77	54	83	08	70	32	01	22	96	99	38
63	64	04	59	43	30	66	98	46	97	51	61	73	34	16	45	24	20	76	86
89	21	74	95	68	47	07	01	17	52	81	37	19	24	24	26	38	89	87	79
45	60	17	16	09	78	76	45	89	01	98	55	28	52	09	95	62	43	89	47
45	49	53	33	11	95	34	17	96	60	67	99	13	42	21	04	27	63	54	90

C
Drug Attitude Questionnaire

Please read each of the following items carefully and rate your agreement or disagreement by checking the appropriate blank to the right of the question.

	Strongly Agree	Agree	Undecided	Disagree	Strongly Disagree
1. Using marijuana or beer often leads to becoming addicted to more harmful drugs	____	____	____	____	____
2. Drugs are basically an "unnatural" way to enjoy life	____	____	____	____	____
3. I see nothing wrong with getting drunk occasionally	____	____	____	____	____
4. Too many of society's problems are blamed on kids who use alcohol or drugs regularly	____	____	____	____	____
5. Even if my best friend gave me some drugs, I probably wouldn't use them	____	____	____	____	____
6. If I become a parent, I don't intend to hassle my kids about their use of drugs or alcohol	____	____	____	____	____
7. Certain drugs like marijuana are all right to use because you can't become addicted	____	____	____	____	____
8. It is not difficult for me to turn down an opportunity to get high	____	____	____	____	____
9. Marijuana should not be legalized	____	____	____	____	____

	Strongly Agree	Agree	Undecided	Disagree	Strongly Disagree
10. It is not O.K. with me if my friends get high or drunk	___	___	___	___	___
11. I would rather occasionally use drugs or alcohol with my friends than lose this set of friends	___	___	___	___	___
12. Someone who regularly uses drugs or alcohol may be considered a sick person	___	___	___	___	___
13. Most of my friends have experimented with drugs	___	___	___	___	___
14. Personally, use of alcohol is more acceptable than use of drugs	___	___	___	___	___
15. Any addict with willpower should be able to give up drugs on his/her own	___	___	___	___	___
16. Either drug addiction or alcoholism leads to family problems	___	___	___	___	___
17. Most Americans do not heavily rely on drugs	___	___	___	___	___
18. Some experience with drugs or alcohol is important for a teenager in today's society	___	___	___	___	___
19. Kids who use drugs are less popular than kids who do not	___	___	___	___	___
20. Drugs or alcohol provide a good way to "get away from it all"	___	___	___	___	___
21. I think the legal drinking age should be lowered	___	___	___	___	___
22. Teachers should place more emphasis on teaching American ideals and values	___	___	___	___	___
23. It is all right to get around the law if you don't actually break it	___	___	___	___	___

Index

Abstracts, 23–24, 333–334
Accidental samples, 172
Accountability, 8, 9, 260
Acquiescence, 194–195
All-inclusive terms, 194
Alternative explanations, 85, 87, 92
Analysis of data. *See* data analysis
Anonymity, 157, 311
ANOVA. *See* one-way analysis of variance
Appendices (in research reports), 333
Archival data, 96, 206, 209, 315
Attitude Toward the Provision of Long-Term Care Scale, 129–132
Available samples, 172
Axioms of treatment, 33

Baseline, 54, 58–59, 61, 67, 70
Bias, 36–39, 153, 162, 170, 172, 208, 294, 337
Bivariate analysis, 244–252

Case studies, 50–51, 60–61
Causal inference, 67, 98
Celeration line, 67–68
Census, U.S., 215

Central tendency, 41, 241
CES-D Scale, 52–53
Child Abuse Potential Inventory, 35
Chi-square, 246, 247
CIPP model, 272
Client satisfaction, 270–271
Client utilization data, 261–262
Clinical anxiety scale, 85
Closed-ended questions, 184–186, 235, 238
Cluster sampling designs, 163–164
Codebook, 237–238
Code of ethics, 302, 317, 324
Coding, 235–239
Cohort surveys, 171
Community Living Skills Scale, 117–120
Compensation. *See* Incentives
Computerized data bases, 25, 214–217
Computer processing of data, 69, 107, 214, 221, 225, 234–235, 290
Concurrent validity, 110, 122
Confidence level, 165–167
Confidentiality, 311
Consent forms, 309, 310, 315

Construct validity, 111
Content analysis, 217, 220–227
Content validity, 109–110
Contingency questions, 189
Control group, 84–86, 89, 95, 100,
  313–314, 337
Convenience sample, 155,
  168–169, 172
Correlation coefficient, 41,
  106–108, 110, 249–252
Correlation matrix, 252
Cost analysis, 272
Cost-benefit, 272
Cost-effectiveness, 272
Council on Social Work Educa-
  tion, 10–11
Criterion validity, 110, 130, 198
Cross-sectional survey design, 170
Crosstabulation, 244–245, 247

Data analysis, 40–41, 185–186,
  233–254
Data collection, 36–40
Deception, 303, 312–313
Deduction, 18
Dependent variables, 21, 31–32,
  52, 242–243, 247, 252, 253,
  276
Descriptive research design, 28–29
Descriptive surveys, 147, 261
Designs, research, 27–30, 329
Discrepancy model, 265–268
Discussion section (in research re-
  port), 331–333
Double-barreled questions, 187,
  188
Drug Attitude Questionnaire,
  110–111, 351–352

Effectiveness, 259, 264
Empirically based practice, 13
Ethical considerations, 301–317
Ethical dilemmas, 99–100
Ethical guidelines. *See* guidelines
  for ethical research
Ethnography, 285
Evaluation designs, 264, 275–276

Expectancy effects, 301
Experimental designs, 82–87,
  264–265
Explanatory research design,
  28–29
Explanatory surveys, 147
Exploratory research, 28–29, 169,
  285
Exploratory surveys, 147
External validity, 67, 89–91
Extraneous variables, 92–93, 99

Face validity, 110
Field notes, 287
Formative evaluation, 263, 272
Frequency distribution, 240–241,
  243, 244

Gallup organization, 154,
  160–161, 216
Generalizability, 28, 38, 67, 70,
  89, 91, 198–199, 332, 335
General Social Survey, 214,
  217–219
Goals, 267–268
Graphs, 53, 57–59, 62, 65, 66, 68
Guidelines for ethical research,
  309–317
Guidelines for questionnaire de-
  sign, 187–197

Hammond model, 268–269
Harmful effects, 209, 310
Hawthorne effect, 206
Helping Behavior Checklist,
  134–137
Historical data. *See* archival data
History (effect of), 88, 92, 98
Hypotheses, 18–20, 28–29, 40, 42,
  69, 86, 98, 207, 213, 214, 215,
  223, 244, 246, 249, 261, 276,
  284, 294, 310, 331, 337

Impact evaluation, 264
Implied consent, 308
Incentives, 151, 315

Incidence, 209, 212
Independent variables, 32, 252
Index of Marital Satisfaction, 34
Induction, 18
Inflammatory language, 190
Informants, 283, 288–289, 294
Insensitive language, 190
Institutional Review Board, 82,
     306–308, 315, 316
Instrumentation (effect), 88, 92, 99
Instruments, 32–35, 52, 55–56,
     105–141, 290, 296
Interaction effects, 88, 90, 92, 95
Intercept surveys, 155, 158
Internal consistency, 107–108,
     118, 130, 132, 140, 329
Internal validity, 87–89, 91, 92,
     95, 97–99, 276
Interrupted Time Series, 96–98
Interval level data, 242–243, 247
Interviewing, 149, 152, 154–158,
     170, 173, 185, 288–289, 330
Introduction (in writing research
     report), 325–326, 337

Jargon, 190
Job Satisfaction Scale, 139–141
Journals, social work, 26
Judicial model, 269–270

Law of the hammer, 79
Leading questions, 188
Levels of measurement, 241–243
Likert scales, 34, 236
Limitations, 70, 332–333
Literature review, 20–27, 114,
     183, 192, 288, 326–328, 337
Longitudinal surveys, 170–171

Mail surveys, 148–151, 157, 158,
     183, 196
Margin of error, 165–167
Matching, 95
Maternal Characteristics Scale,
     132–134
Math anxiety, 22–23
Maturation, 88, 92, 98

Mean (average), 242, 248
Measurement, 33
Median, 241
Meta-evaluations, 273
Methodology (in research report),
     42, 328–330
Mode, 241
Mortality, 88, 99
Multiple baseline designs, 64–67
Multiple time series design, 97–98
Multiple treatment interaction, 90
Multistage cluster sampling, 164
Multivariate analysis, 252–253
Mutually exclusive response
     choices, 191–192

National Opinion Research Cen-
     ter, 156, 216
Needs Assessment, 146, 200, 260,
     273
Negatively constructed items, 194
Nominal data, 241, 243, 246
Nonequivalent control group de-
     sign, 94–96
Nonprobability samples, 155–156,
     168–170, 171
Null hypotheses, 20, 248, 249
Nuremberg trials, 304

Objectives, 267–268
One-group posttest only design, 92
One-group pretest-posttest design,
     92
One-stage cluster sampling, 164
One-way analysis of variance, 249
Open-ended questions, 184–187,
     235, 238–239, 271, 294–295
Operational definitions, 30–36,
     105–106, 337
Ordinal data, 214–215
Outcome evaluations, 264
Overgeneralization, 38, 276, 338

Panel Surveys, 171
Participant observation, 286–287,
     301
Patterns of use data, 261–262

Personal interviews. *See* interviewing
Pie chart, 244
Pilot test, 172, 186, 199
Posttest, 85
Posttest only control group design, 86
Posttest only design with nonequivalent groups, 93
Practitioner-Scientist training model, 7
Predictive validity, 110–111, 141
Pre-experimental designs, 91–94, 100
Pretest, 85, 86, 193, 205
Pretest-posttest control group design, 84–85
Probability sampling, 159–168, 171
Process evaluation, 263, 272
Program evaluation, 259–277
Program monitoring, 262
Prosocial Tendencies Scale for Children, 122–129
Purposive sampling, 169

Qualitative research, 1–2, 283–296
Quasi-experimental designs, 94–98, 264–265
Questionnaire design, 148–151, 181–200
Quota sampling, 170

Random assignment, 85, 89, 93, 94, 95, 100, 275
Random number table, 160, 162, 345–349
Random samples, 151, 155, 160
Rapid assessment instruments, 33
Ratio level data, 243, 247
Raw data, 233–234, 239, 244
Reactive effects, 89–90
References (in research reports), 333, 335
Reliability, 34, 106–109, 111, 115–117, 193, 196–198, 210, 222, 271, 276, 290, 337

Replication, 30, 224, 337
Representativeness, 28, 38–39, 89, 153, 155, 160, 162–163, 168, 170, 332
Research designs, 27–30, 79–100, 337
Research process, 14, 17–43
Response choices, 34–35, 114, 184–185
Response rate, 149, 151, 153–154, 169, 172–173
Results (in research reports), 330–331
Review of the literature. *See* literature review
Role Strain Index, 137–139
Roper Center, 216–217

Sampling, 157–175
Sampling frame, 160
Sampling ratio, 162
Scales, 33–36, 56, 71, 105–141, 183, 236, 271, 276, 290
Scientific method, 17
Scientist-Professional training model, 7
Secondary data, 206–217
Selection bias, 88, 90
Self-anchored scales, 197–198
Sequence of questions, 194–195
Simple random sampling design, 160, 162
Single-item scales, 197–198
Single system designs, 49–72, 80
Snowball sampling, 169
Social desirability, 190–191
Social distance scale, 114
Social indicators, 211, 213
Social Work Abstracts, 19, 24
Social Work Empowerment Scale, 120–122
Social work journals, 26
Software, 69, 71, 107, 221, 225, 234, 235, 248, 290
Solomon Four-Group Design, 87–88
Standards for programs, 265–266

Statistical regression, 88, 99
Statistical significance, 246–248, 251, 252, 331
Statistical symbols, 254–255, 344
Stratified random sampling, 163
Suicide rates, 209
Summative evaluation, 272
Survey Research Center, 156
Surveys, 12, 145–175, 214–217, 290
Symptom Checklist 90-R, 35, 329
Systematic sampling, 162–163

Target behavior, 52, 53, 54, 55–58
Task-centered process, 43
Telephone surveys, 152–154, 157, 158, 183
Testing effects, 88–89, 92, 99
Theory, theoretical models, 11, 14, 21–23, 327, 328

Time Series Design, 96–98
Total Design Method, 150–151
Trend surveys, 171
Triangulation, 292
T-tests, 248, 249
Two-stage cluster sampling, 164

Units of analysis, 223–224, 225
Univariate Analysis, 239–244
Unlisted phones, 153
Unobtrusive approaches, 205–227
Unrepresentative samples, 162–163

Vague questionnaire items, 192–193
Validity, 34, 109–111, 115, 276, 291–292, 337

Writing the report, 41–42